For John McClecuny

with good wishes.

Griffin Bell

UNCOMMON SENSE

UNCOMMON SENSE

The Achievement of Griffin Bell

REG MURPHY

LONGSTREET
Atlanta, Georgia

Published by
LONGSTREET, INC.
A subsidiary of Cox Newspapers
A subsidiary of Cox Enterprises, Inc.
2140 Newmarket Parkway
Suite 122
Marietta, GA 30067

Printed in the United States of America

1st printing 1999

Library of Congress Catalog Card Number: 99-61755

ISBN: 1-56352-582-8

Cover photograph by Flo Fitzgerald

Jacket and book design by Burtch Hunter

Visit Longstreet on the World Wide Web
www.lspress.com

For Diana
Who always helps

CONTENTS

UNCOMMON SENSE

INTRODUCTION

A spry figure clad in a bright orange jacket trampled the underbrush as he rushed toward a liver-and-white pointer rigidly holding his position. "Look at Griffin run," marveled a friend. "Eager as a boy." The figure moved closer to the dog, and suddenly a lone quail flailed into flight. Shotgun rose to left shoulder, one shot rang through the piney woods, and then another. "Dead bird," the spry man said. "Hunt!" The dog picked up the bird and brought him to the hunter, who climbed back into the rubber-tired wagon, which wobbled toward more quarry in the rough fields along the Georgia-Florida line.

The hunter is Griffin Bell, home again. Or, rather, at home in one of the many places where an eighty-year-old has found he can function with ease and effectiveness. This hunt happens to be in the South, near the place of his birth. But the following day could find him on the forty-third floor of a building that symbolizes the New South. Or in the power corridors in Washington, where he redefined the job of the Justice Department. Or in a tense New York corporate boardroom, where fortunes are made or destroyed with a single vote. Or most anywhere that important people gather to act on the advice of a most uncommon lawyer.

Most truly significant people are remembered for remarkable efforts over a limited amount of time. Only rarely does the eight-decade lifespan of a man track the life of a region or of a country. More frequently, history looks back to a stunningly brief period where the efforts of a few people wrought great change.

One can think of the Founding Fathers—Washington, Jefferson, Madison—and say that their activities coincided with the birth of the United States, a monumental achievement in a compressed period. In business, John D. Rockefeller came from obscurity to transform northeastern capitalist power near the close of the nineteenth century. In regional politics, Gov. Huey Long of Louisiana became the very symbol of the South, giving dramatic life to the hell-raising Populist movement, before being gunned down. And others were at the epicenter of the times in their home areas. Generally, however, great deeds were done within short time spans.

Public lives that spread-eagle across eras of great change have not necessarily been confined to politics or the amassing of great wealth. Martin Luther King Jr. was an elemental force for human change who made an eternal mark on history. Indeed, history may look back on his achievements as the most significant of the century. Alas, he was not given a long life with which to work. Inventors, politicians, writers, and academics sometimes have been able to produce great changes. But most of the time those lives are remembered for one overarching achievement, not the span of a life's work.

At the beginning of my research for this book, it had not occurred to me that Griffin Boyette Bell's career was so much like the history of the modern South. I had known, of course, that his pursuits had been at the juncture of some important events. A book chronicling his time would have presented an interesting person who had lived a special kind of life.

But what the research led to was a revelation. The Judge's life fit the history of the twentieth-century South like an acetate overlay on a basic document. Or, perhaps, like a seersucker suit fits one's image of a Southern lawyer in summertime. Or, maybe, like a young Southerner's expectations of Atlanta.

Consider: Griffin Bell was born in the midst of a uniquely Southern cotton-field depression. His family was part of the painful migration from rural to semiurban living. His introduction to politics came in the midst of the New Deal when the South was changing its mind about the responsibility of government to its people. His timing was appropriate for gaining an education through the GI Bill. His selection of the law as a career came as the region became much more litigious. His move to Atlanta coincided with the beginning of the growth of one of America's great cities. He comanaged the last Democratic presidential triumph in Georgia for almost a generation. When the toughest of the school desegregation cases were before the courts, he was wearing judicial robes and issuing injunctions to obey the law. When the first Deep South president of modern times was sworn in, he was clearing the Senate confirmation process to become the nation's principal lawyer. And when Dixie became the New South and was ready to participate fully in the economic growth of the nation, he became the most prolific rainmaker the region had known. Through it all, he retained his deep skepticism about government and its ability to solve all of the world's problems in the courtroom, a view shared by a majority of his fellow Southerners.

Were those merely coincidences? Hardly. Were they luck? Only if one believes that luck means being prepared to be fortunate. What seemed to be happening here, the further one reaches into the history of the South, was a confluence of man and moment. It was an extraordinary discovery for a writer who had set out to chronicle a successful life at the bar, on the bench, at the Justice Department and along the spine of the South.

When he went to Washington to become attorney general, Griffin Bell followed a line of Georgians who had been great

powers there—and who had established a tradition of achievement over a lifetime. Sen. Walter F. George had chaired the
Foreign Relations Committee with great distinction. Bell remembered the white-maned senator coming to Mercer University to
sit around with two dozen law students "just talking." Sen.
Richard B. Russell headed the Armed Services Committee at the
height of the Cold War and was a confidant of presidents. Rep.
Carl Vinson, who headed the House Armed Services Committee,
became the first House member to serve for fifty years. These
men left behind a legacy of service that was well known to those
who applauded when Bell went to the Justice Department.

Those who expect to find a liberal here will find one—if they
accept his definition: "I was reared to think a liberal was somebody
who would fight the government on behalf of the individual."
Those who expect to find a conservative will find a man who
believes, "We are regulating ourselves to death. There is too much
law abroad in the land." And those who don't quite know what to
expect will find a mind that seeks good, commonsense solutions to
complex problems, as when he gave a segregation-minded Southern
school board a "civics lesson" that defused a highly dangerous community argument, when he could have handed down a hard-edged
judicial decision.

He has left sociological jargon to others. His speech is blunt, plain,
clear, authoritative. When new statistics showed that crime was high
and on the rise in the United States, a television reporter asked how to
account for it. Bell said, "We've got a lot of bad people in this country."

The South has always been categorized and haunted by its dif-
ferentness. Frequently it has fought with an inferiority complex.
Sometimes it has chafed under the burden of being treated differently from the rest of the nation. And all too often it has caused its
own problems. For an energetic refugee from the boll-weevil-
infested cotton fields of the South, this has been a golden period
of opportunity to participate fully in changing the national outlook
toward the region. In this journey through the life of a Southerner,

one sees clearly the conflict between the heartfelt desire to be part of worldwide movements and the tug toward regional pride.

BORN TO BE A LAWYER

On Halloween Day in 1918, two significant events were happening in Sumter County, Georgia. A tiny little insect, the boll weevil, was gnawing away at the staple of the Cotton South. In a very few years, the cash crop of the region would be gone, throwing white farmers into insolvency and black farm workers into jobless hopelessness. This would become the Southern economic crash that preceded the Great Depression of a decade later.

Inside a country house on one of those cotton farms seven miles from Americus, the county seat, Thelma Leola Pilcher Bell was giving birth to Griffin Bell. That baby would come someday to guide the destiny of hundreds of Southern schools, become what some called the best attorney general of the United States in modern history, and finally be recognized as the most accomplished rainmaker ever to manage a Southern law firm.

Those events were intertwined in ways that nobody could have guessed on October 31, 1918. But it is the Southern way for things to converge and separate and come together again in trends that differentiate the region from the rest of the United States. Like a great river parting to accommodate an island and rejoining downstream, Southern events flow from family and custom into the mainstream of daily life. As we shall see, the death of the cotton farm and the birth of a very bright child came to have tremendous impact on the life of the South. But first there was some growing to do.

Griffin Bell would grow up listening to his father, Adlai Cleveland Bell, and his grandparents talk farming and politics, as well as Civil War history, Baptist religion, and family. A. C. Bell was a cotton farmer, as were his father and his recent ancestors, in the great crescent of fertile farmland left when the Atlantic Ocean and the Gulf of Mexico receded millennia before. A. C.'s mother, Virginia King, who grew up in adjoining Webster County, had three brothers who served in the Confederate Army. Two of the brothers were killed, and the third wounded.

These forebears had grown up listening to tales of those Civil War skirmishes. One could scarcely have avoided the memories of that conflict; the prison for Union soldiers just down the road at Andersonville existed for a brief but horrible fourteen months during the war. It was the largest Confederate prison, holding more than forty-five thousand Union troops within a twenty-six-acre complex. It became infamous because thirteen thousand of the prisoners died there.

Thelma Pilcher Bell's grandfather was a wounded Confederate veteran who fought in the Army of Northern Virginia. He was respectful enough of "The Cause" to name his son Robert Lee Pilcher, who in turn named his daughter Leola Thelma. Robert Lee married the daughter of a Baptist preacher, William Alamo Griffin.

So . . . with the Union prison on one hand and a wounded farmer on the other, black farm workers slowly being worn out by tilling cotton fields, and politicians railing at the federal government, politics, religion and the Civil War—this was the emotional cauldron where the boy grew to manhood.

(As fate would have it, Griffin Bell was asked to go back to Andersonville eight decades later to dedicate the National Prisoner of War Museum. He agreed and made the speech.)

The Bells and Pilchers were modestly successful, in the

Southern way. They grew cotton in the broad, sun-washed, tree-bordered fields, and Grandfather Bell ran a country store on the property, seven miles out the Buena Vista Highway from Americus, in the Concord community. But that world of long burlap bags slowly filling with cotton picked by two or three generations of black workers—and mules pulling farm wagons along dusty roads to cotton gins—was in serious jeopardy as the 1920s began, for the boll weevil had begun its unseen invasion. Farmers had no chemicals to combat it, much less any genetically treated seed to resist it. It would spread across the South until impoverished farmers like A. C. Bell would abandon cotton crops and move to town.

Young Griffin's family was part of the migration. And it was no easy transition. His family started him in the little country schoolhouse in the Shiloh community near Concord at age five. He knew how to read before he got there: "My mother's sister taught me to read before I went to school," Bell recalls. There were five or six grades being taught in one room. "So you listened to what the teacher was saying to every class."

One day the Sumter County school superintendent came to the little school. "For some reason he singled me out and said, 'You're a smart boy. You ought to study hard.'" It made an impression on the seven-year-old, one that would stay with him. Was it the inspiration that led to his later successes? Perhaps. "Education wasn't a big thing in my family," he remembered. Yet, "one of my early memories is of winning the spelling bee."

By the time Griffin was winning the spelling bee, the economic outlook on the farm had grown considerably worse. Cotton bolls would not come to maturity because their insides had been eaten away by boll weevils. No other cash crop was in sight. "People who couldn't think up something else to do for themselves were in bad shape," the boy understood. Anyone could see that life would not be the same because the cash crop was damaged and would not regain its health until the 1990s.

The boll weevil was mystery and misery from 1910 through the 1920s. A typical snout beetle, it came creeping across the Southern states beginning in 1894. Early in the new century Dr. Seaman A. Knapp, a scientist at the U.S. Department of Agriculture, was trying to control the bug. He knew that it would devastate the Cotton South if it spread, and so he demonstrated that a combination of using selective seed and intensively cultivating the crop could contain the weevil. He enlisted the richest man in the world, John D. Rockefeller, as a private contributor to fund some of his experiments. If he could halt the creeping spread of the weevil, the depopulation of the rural South would be stopped. But there were not enough weevil-resistant seeds, and not nearly enough farm education, to change the ancient ways of dealing with the plague.

By 1907 the bug bumbled its way across the Mississippi River, and by 1917 "it had infested cotton in most of Georgia," wrote R. L. Ridgway and E. P. Lloyd in a report for the Department of Agriculture. Farmers like A. C. Bell had no idea how to combat the weevils. "They overwinter as adults in forests and hedgerow litter. They return to cotton fields in the spring where they feed on the terminals of spring plants and then feed on and reproduce in squares [flower buds]. They later attack the fruit [bolls of cotton]," Ridgway and Lloyd continued.

Ironically, this dumb pest could not recognize cotton from a distance "greater than a few inches. . . . The first boll weevils seeking cotton in the early season apparently find it only through random movement," the government later found. But that was no help to the Sumter County farmers sweating literally from heat and financially from depleted funds, for the boll weevil increased at a tenfold rate per generation, and several generations were propagated in a growing season. All the Bells' neighbor farmers knew, without the affirmation of scientists, was that the weevils completed "multiple matings," for there seemed no way to eradicate them. The farmers tried everything. They plowed up infested plants. They prayed in the Baptist churches. Heartbreakingly, they stooped to collect the fallen infested squares one at a time, to no avail. Finally they applied poison (calcium arsenate). The weevils continued to breed and multiply.

A way of life was slipping away. The farmers sold their cotton for a top price of twenty-five cents a pound in 1915, and there was relative prosperity. It shot up to thirty-five cents in the year of Griffin's birth, because of the shortage created by World War I. But then it slumped to sixteen cents by 1920, even as the boll weevil cut production in the Georgia fields to roughly one-fourth of its previous yield. In the first year the weevil was found, but before it had much impact, the state produced 2,122,000 bales of cotton. Five years later, only 588,000 bales were produced, a decrease of 72 percent. Life could not be sustained on such meager financial returns when the land was already almost exhausted from hard usage. An Agriculture Department official wrote that he found "depleted soil, shoddy livestock, inadequate farm equipment, crude agricultural practices, crippled institutions, a defeated and impoverished people."

Indeed, the boll weevil had changed the way all America would live in the future. The loss of the cotton crops meant there was no work for hundreds of thousands of black field hands. Men, women, and children who had lived on these farms for generations dating back to slavery had nothing at all to do to earn their livings. So a great wave of immigration began—to Detroit to make the cars, to Chicago to pack beef, to New York for odd jobs. It was the African-American diaspora. Writers chronicled the migration of blacks riding trains and buses north, meager possessions carried in boxes bound with string or rope.

Many of those who left the farms sent back a big proportion of their earnings to support relatives left behind, but rarely was there a sufficiency to sustain quality life. White landowners also suffered in the boll weevil depression, but in sheer numbers of displaced people, it was black Southerners who suffered worst.

"We had a maid when I was a boy," Griffin remembered. "She just left and went to Hartford, Connecticut. We never heard from her again." He said it with sadness.

Like most Southerners, he never went to school with black children but played with them after school. It didn't seem incongruous at the time, although most would look back on it with disbelief. The individual stories then were the ones that touched people's souls, but it was the magnitude of the migration that would come to amaze people like Griffin years later, when he was on the federal bench. "I saw the statistics that maybe a million black people left Mississippi between 1930 and 1950. That really compounded the race problem, because it divided families and because it took so many smart black people out of the South."

Fortunately, A. C. was a resourceful husband, father, and breadwinner. He moved his family seven miles into Americus, then a town of several thousand people. Here he would find limited success while allowing Griffin to make progress in a school better than the one-room schoolhouse out in the country. A visitor who arrived in Americus just prior to the young boy's move there wrote, "The streets are paved with wood blocks and there are forty miles of paved sidewalks." The blocks had disappeared by the time Griffin got there.

Although Griffin was not a freckle-faced-boy-with-fishing-pole stereotype, he did live in a good environment. The town was pointed toward agriculture, as were its counterparts in South Georgia. W. J. Cash wrote (in *The Mind of the South*) about just such a place: "The mind of the section . . . is continuous with the past. And its primary form is determined not nearly so much by industry as by the purely agricultural conditions of that past." Memories of a better farm life than actually existed sustained many a family that had been forced to town. But they also carried with them the leave-the-door-unlocked traditions of earlier life.

Griffin was only four when the Georgia Populist senator Tom Watson died in 1922, and with him the Populist movement that would leave Georgia again as a one-party Democratic state. He would not have seen the very earliest Eugene Talmadge campaigns for governor, in which that rural hero proclaimed that he would never campaign in a town big enough to have trolley cars.

He would have been just six years old when Clarence Darrow stripped off his dark suit coat, stood in his white shirt and galluses, and demanded that his defendant in the Scopes evolution trial in Dayton, Tennessee, be allowed to teach something other than Divine Creation. (Darrow asked a witness, "But you do believe he made them—that he made such a fish and that it was big enough to swallow Jonah?" To which the witness replied, "No, the Bible doesn't say.")

The Bible and ol' Gene Talmadge, that was the ambiance in which A. C. Bell brought his family to Americus to recover from the calamity of the boll weevil. First he invested in a gas station, joined a partner in a Frigidaire distributorship, got involved in the distribution of Shell gasoline, and then started representing the Firestone Tire Company. It was a living all through the Great Depression, but it was not a wealth-making professional career. A. C. had his ideas and so he had income, unlike all too many of his contemporaries.

What may have been more important to young Griffin was his father's political activity. A. C. was elected to the Americus City Council. "He was the first person I ever heard talk about term limits," Griffin recalled. "He said if they stayed in office too long they would ruin the country." In the '20s and '30s, that was not a radical idea. Most Southern governors were limited to one or two terms. Distrust of political alliances ran high, and agrarian or populist reformers were abroad in the land. Power was particularly suspect after the fiercely independent Southern cotton farmers were forced to seek jobs in the towns and cities.

A. C.'s success as a political leader grew. He became chairman of the Sumter County Democratic Party. There was, of course, no Republican Party to speak of in the county. Reconstruction may have been a thing of the past, but the children and grandchildren of Confederate veterans would not think kindly of the Republicans until Sen. Barry Goldwater tapped into an ideological vein of conservatism in the 1960s.

To be aligned with the Democratic Party of Georgia in those days was to be associated with some of the most influential Southerners, surefire winners just beginning their great careers. Senators Richard B. Russell and Walter F. George were about ready to begin their decades-long domination of defense and foreign affairs. Gov. Gene Talmadge was ready to make the three-dollar auto tag his rallying cry for the self-styled Crackers in Georgia politics. Rep. Carl Vinson would dominate the House Armed Services Committee for almost half a century. These were luminaries whose presence would gladden the heart of any county party chairman intent on winning—and looking toward better times.

Powerful as they would become, they singly were not so important as the County Unit System in Georgia. As we shall see, the Unit System would figure significantly in Griffin's career. What it did for A. C. was to give him a voice in Georgia politics, since a vote in his county was worth many times a vote in one of the state's more populous counties.

So young Griffin grew up in a home where business was the order of the day but politics was the talk of the household. During one of Senator George's early campaigns, Griffin's father came home and said, "We must go to a rally over in Webster County," another South Georgia entity. A rally was a major event and considered entertainment in South Georgia. Thousands would descend on the courthouse square. The candidate's supporters would have worked through the night preparing a gigantic barbecue of beef or pork. There would be a band, playing popular and/or country music. The candidate would speak on a statewide radio network. County chairmen frequently would be recognized and applauded. Senator George was a rather dignified candidate, interested in the law and

in world affairs. His rallies were not the raucous affairs that dominated and lent great color to many Southern campaigns.
Nevertheless, Griffin would remember George's courthouse
speeches as significant events in his political upbringing.

In sharp contrast were the Saturday afternoon gatherings for
Gene Talmadge, the governor wearing red galluses and shouting
populist slogans ("They say I stole money, and I did; I stole it for
you"). Griffin Bell was taken to a Talmadge rally on a county courthouse square. "It was right in the middle of the Depression," he
recalled, still amazed, "but there were poor farmers pressing money
into his hands when they hardly had enough to feed their families."
It was an experience that the youngster would not forget for its
excess in a time of poverty.

(And it was significantly at variance with Bell's experience in
1960, when he became President John F. Kennedy's Georgia campaign co-chairman. He went home to tell his mother he would be
leading the campaign. "Saw it in the paper," she said. "You know he's
a Roman Catholic," Bell told his mother, a Baptist preacher's grand-
daughter. "Better to support a Roman Catholic than a Republican,"
she replied, still remembering tales of Reconstruction.)

Childhood was not, however, all about politics. It was a time
when communications was beginning to change. No radios doing
live sports broadcasting, and no television, of course. Bell remembered going down to the local newspaper office with his father and
standing outside with several hundred townsfolk. The *Americus
Times-Recorder* was receiving a round-by-round account of the Jack
Dempsey–Gene Tunney heavyweight boxing championship bout.
After each round, a representative of the newspaper would come to
the door and read the running account of the fight. As he recalls it
now, Griffin and his father were pleased that Dempsey won. He was
learning to value successful people.

This was a youngster who achieved mightily in school. The
principal, Charles Hale, told him that he had a "very high IQ." It
put additional pressure on young Griffin, who already had enough

pressure. He had started school at age five, had been "advanced" from the second to the third grade in the middle of the term, and therefore was at least two years younger than his classmates. Not large even for his own age, he was considerably smaller than the older children in his classes. But he persevered and made the high school varsity football team as a fifteen-year-old senior.

His social life was like that of many other young Southerners. He went to the Baptist church on Sunday mornings, and sometimes again that same evening. He grew to know other young people in Sumter County through church outings. One of his earliest acquaintances outside the immediate circle was Don Carter, through the Baptist Young People's Union (BYPU to many young Southerners). Carter was a first cousin of future president Jimmy Carter, but Griffin could not recall meeting Jimmy during those years. What all of them could remember was summed up later by Don Carter: "We were real country boys and we came along at a time when money was really scarce."

He was growing up in what the agrarian writer Alan Tate called "Uncle Sam's Other Province." The South certainly was different from the glittery world where Dempsey fought Tunney. Or the pompous one in which the Senate was called "the great debating society." Perhaps nobody has described Southern towns like these better than Harper Lee did in *To Kill a Mockingbird:* "People moved slowly then. They ambled across the square, shuffled in and out of the stores around it, took their time about everything. A day was twenty-four hours long but seemed longer. There was no hurry, for there was nowhere to go, nothing to buy and no money to buy it with, nothing to see outside the boundaries of Maycomb County. But it was a time of vague optimism for some of the people: Maycomb County had recently been told that it had nothing to fear but fear itself."

If A. C. was struggling to find the right enterprise for himself, he already knew what he wanted for his son—the law. "My father took it in his head that he wanted me to be a lawyer," Griffin recalled. And so the father would take the son to the courthouse to watch the trials on blistering summer days when other children were playing in the shade. The Sumter County courthouse he visited was the third erected on the grounds. Long torn down now to make way for a bank, it was a handsome two-story brick structure. To get into the building visitors had to walk past a large cast-iron bell installed on the courthouse grounds.

Like all courthouses, it was more than just a big room with a judge on a pedestal. Here was where a young couple came for a marriage license, where a father excitedly applied for his first-born's birth certificate, where an elderly couple recorded the homestead deed when the mortgage was paid off, where people came to grumble about high taxes, where lawyers fought their civil cases, where the innocent hoped to find mercy, where the accused were manacled, where the water fountains were labeled "white only" (and "colored" if one was supplied). This is where people came to receive justice—or justice gone awry. The boy had heard of all these human transactions before and after he listened to the arguments in the courts, but here they were crystallized in formal presentations.

A second cousin of A. C.'s was Judge Reason C. Bell, later chief justice of the Georgia Supreme Court. Judge Reason Bell's reputation and affluence probably influenced both father and son in thinking that the legal profession would be an appropriate challenge for a bright young man. It certainly held more promise than the sales activities that A. C. found for himself in the trough of the Great Depression. And in the South, before the proliferation of lawyers and racial upheaval in the middle of the century, the law was an exalted place for a young man to use his intellect. Later it might become the object of thousands of wry jokes, but that was not true in the '30s, when father and son were puzzling out the future.

One of the keys to the future was in the family's heritage. Griffin would recall later in his book *Taking Care of the Law* (with Ronald J. Ostrow), "In the old days, Americans would go to the justice of the peace for relief. My grandfather, William Sampson Bell, was a justice of the peace for Sumter County, Georgia, and people came to him—not the high court, which is what the trial court was called—unless they had a problem of considerable weight. Unfortunately, the justices of the peace didn't join the migration to the cities, so the people lost an effective means of resolving disputes." The JPs, as they were called, practiced rough justice instead of nuanced legal argumentation. The grandfather's use of common sense foreshadowed the style that the grandson would use for most of his legal career.

Given all of the stress on the law, in normal circumstances young Griffin probably would have graduated from Americus High School and headed directly for college and law school. But the nation was in the midst of the Great Depression when he walked across the stage to receive his diploma. A. C. did not have unlimited funds. After a short stint as a commuting student to Georgia Southwestern College in his hometown, Griffin found that he needed to make money. The question that snagged him was what every young Southerner had to resolve in the middle of the Depression: How to start a lifetime career when there were neither resources nor opportunities?

His answer was to turn to his father's business. A. C. was a Firestone dealer by then, and it was a living. Young Griffin made his way to Atlanta for three weeks of education on how to sell new tires to people whose old tires had gone bald and who certainly had no money to buy new cars. Firestone promised a job for a year if he would go through the training program. After he accepted the offer, he first was assigned to Bristol, Virginia, for a few months, and then he returned to Americus to work for his father. As a salesman, he had a future—in the law.

By 1940 the United States had turned from worrying about jobs to worrying about the war. Adolf Hitler was marching through Eastern Europe, bullying the world, trying to exterminate Jews, leveling his guns on little nations, and preparing to cross the

English Channel. It was a time when Americans had their noses to the grindstone to earn their daily bread, but also a time when it was particularly hard to concentrate on the merits of one tire tread over another, for they knew that they could not stay out of the war indefinitely.

YOU'RE IN THE ARMY NOW

Ayear after he began to work for Firestone in 1942, the notice from the Sumter County draft board arrived, instructing Griffin and his friend Don Carter to report for their physicals. Both boarded a bus in Americus, traveled to the Army Reception Center in Atlanta, and were accepted as privates. They reported initially to Fort McPherson in Atlanta. Griffin was assigned to the Quartermaster Corps first and later to the Transportation Corps, while Carter went into the infantry. (Carter later would transfer into military intelligence, return to private life, and become a highly successful newspaper executive.)

"I remember those days when we were drafted into the army," Bell said many years later. "I went back to Fort McPherson to make a speech on Law Day, and I told them that the week I spent there as a private draftee was no longer than they were anywhere else, it just seemed longer."

By now the youngest boy in his high school class had grown into a tall, thin, handsome young man. He wore glasses that others said made him look owlish. His voice began to acquire the timbre that demanded attention when he spoke. He started to acquire a taste for management. "If you can manage in the army, you can manage anywhere," he said. "There is a chain of command to follow, and it works."

Like many another young man, the army experience would shape much more than his ability to shoot. He recalled, "I went to Officer Candidate School, then I became a company commander. I had troops to look after. I ended up with about five hundred people under me. I had all the transportation responsibilities at the Fort Lewis [Washington] staging area. And I was about twenty-three or twenty-four years old when all that was going on. You don't get that kind of experience except in a war setting. The war had a big impact on me, like it did on other people."

His talent for management was soon noticed by his superiors. "It was like running a huge truck line." And it ran well. He declared it was the most valuable management experience he could have received for his later career. He had developed a sense that a command tree was valuable to other organizations, and he would refer to it over and over again throughout his working career. Whenever people asked him in later life whether so-and-so could manage, he would refer to their military experiences, frequently recruiting those who had leadership roles in the services.

While he was learning to be a soldier, he was also fretting. His friends had been shipped overseas to fight. Not one to be left out, he had applied for the air force because he thought that would get him into the shooting war. Alas, he was color-blind, and that stopped his chances of becoming a flyboy. Once in the army, he never could get himself assigned overseas, at one point even offering to take a reduction in rank from captain to lieutenant so as to transfer to combat service. That fell through; the army said he was essential as a commander of transportation troops.

During his service at Fort Lee in Virginia, he was invited to a reception at a private home in Richmond with a group of fellow soldiers. The hosts also had invited some young ladies to the occasion, a custom many followed during the war. As young people will, they all decided to go on to dinner. A vivacious young lady, Mary Powell, was in the group, and Griffin thought her most attractive. So attractive, in fact, that he invited her for "a late date." No, Mary said, she was not allowed to have late dates. And they went their separate ways. Out of sight but not out of mind; Griffin learned that night that Mary's mother had relatives living in Plains and Americus. Practically homefolks!

Weeks later, Mary was returning to Virginia from North Carolina and passed through the Richmond railroad station. One of the handsome young second lieutenants in the station was Griffin. "He offered to drive me home, and I accepted. We just hit it off," she enthused.

And so the country boy from Americus started seeing an outgoing young woman who had been born in Atlanta, where she lived for twelve years, and had attended boarding schools in Atlanta and Raleigh, North Carolina, before moving with her family to Virginia. "That was in the Great Depression, but we survived," she said. Her life was certainly more sophisticated than Griffin's had been.

Her parents were taken with the soldier. "My father said, 'That boy sits up straight and looks you in the eye when he talks to you.' They got along very well. My father didn't say that about any other boys," she said.

With the war expanding and military orders in constant flux, a wedding was hard to plan. But they persevered. Griffin was transferred to Camp Blanding near Jacksonville, and they decided that would be the right place for the ceremony. Mary rounded up her bridesmaids and took them to Jacksonville with her. Griffin invited his family and some of his buddies from the military to the wedding and reception.

The newlyweds could not make major plans. Gasoline was rationed. Military orders were changing almost daily. Like young people all over the nation, they had to be adaptable and understanding of each other. But this was to be a very special relationship, and it would weather the first of many uncertainties with panache.

Two other new brides joined Mary in an automobile trek across the country to San Diego, where they had been advised the soldiers were likely to be transferred.

During the trip, Mary discovered that she was pregnant. Once they arrived, they learned that the men would go to Fort Mason in San Francisco, not San Diego. And so they drove north to rejoin their husbands.

Housing was difficult. The wives went in search of lodging. Mary found an apartment—"above a dry cleaner, if you can imagine it"—and they moved in. San Franciscans were accustomed to stringing clotheslines between buildings and hanging the wash out in that chilly, windy city. Griffin took a look out the window and exclaimed, "My God, if that's what he has to look out on, we'll have the saddest child on earth." So they went just south of the city and located a nice little apartment in Burlingame, moving immediately.

As they settled in, Griffin became a truck company commander at Camp Blanding in 1942 as part of a regiment. His assignments would take him to Fort Mason, California; Fort Lawton, Washington; and Fort Lewis, Washington, where he was in charge of all motor transportation. All the while he was learning to manage, a skill he would treasure.

CHAPTER 3

"HE DIDN'T USE BAD LANGUAGE"

Mary Bell would not remain in San Francisco for many months. She would return to Richmond because she "wanted the baby to be a Virginian if at all possible." In San Francisco, the father was anxious as he awaited both the birth and the assignment that would send him into World War II. Mary was anxious, too, while she spent time with her parents in Virginia.

Griffin Bell Jr. came into the world on February 16, 1944, on the first anniversary of his parents' wedding, like so many others of his generation—as a war baby. The mother and father were overjoyed, but the celebration had to be constrained. The baby's father was still running his transportation unit, and his mother, after returning to California with her newborn son, was learning to be what she had not been before—a homemaker. "I was spoiled," she said. "My mother would have died if she had known what I was doing," such as scrubbing diapers without a washing machine and doing housework that had been done for her.

But this couple knew that they would not be content simply to get along. They wanted to participate in the great expansion they felt would come after the war. They wrote a check to a savings account every month Griffin was in the army, no matter how much it pinched,

to make later professional training a possibility. "We were penni-
less," Mary said. "But Griffin always had it worked out as to what
he wanted to do." Ambition might grow even stronger in the future,
but the young couple had determined that they would succeed both
financially and as a family.

From San Francisco, the young officer was transferred to Fort
Lawton in Seattle. Those were turbulent military days, and people
didn't stay put very long. Soon he was transferred out past the big
Boeing Aircraft factories to Tacoma, Washington. And finally, in
January 1946 came the orders that both Griffin and Mary were
waiting for: his discharge from the army. The little family was free
to go back to Georgia.

Hold on, the military said. It hadn't let him transfer to the
infantry and get to the shooting war. But if he would stay in the
regular army now, instead of returning to civilian life, he would be
sent to the Command and General Staff school. That would assure
him of a career in the military service. "I was ready to leave the
army, and I declined," he said.

Griffin bought a secondhand car, and the family began driving
home. Down the West Coast all the way to southern California,
across Arizona, across New Mexico, across Texas, nearer and nearer to the future. By the time they got to Americus in late January,
they were bubbling over with energy, ready to get on with making
a civilian life.

Shucking the military lifestyle, they celebrated the return to
Georgia, visited with friends and made new ones for a couple of
months. And then it was time to leave Americus and begin the
search for a more promising future. Like so many others, the Bells
could rely on the GI Bill for sustenance. They were headed for the
University of Georgia, driving up from South Georgia. Passing
through Macon, Griffin recalled that he had been admitted to
Mercer University's law school before the war, but had not attended because of both the draft and money.

"I said to Mary, 'You know, I'll bet I could go to Mercer and get

In Griffin's army days, elective politics almost faded from consciousness. In the Mercer University law school, students discussed the campaigns but in an intermittent and desultory way. Starting a family, studying for the bar exams, making decisions about which law firms to join—all those took priority. But once Griffin had moved to Savannah and begun to make some real money, his latent interest in public affairs reemerged. He began to attend state bar association meetings, the hot-stove league of Georgia politics.

Gradually an informal network began to build. Robert Jordan, a classmate at Georgia Southwestern who later would become chief justice of the Georgia Supreme Court, was a member of the group. James Dunlap, a Gainesville lawyer who was chosen chairman of the University System Board of Regents, joined in, as did John Langdale of Valdosta, later chairman of the Georgia Ports Authority. The geographic spread extended to Columbus to include Howell Hollis, a state senator, and Bob Norman of Augusta, a lawyer. In all, perhaps a dozen people began to find themselves on common ground at the bar association meetings. And all would become interested in Georgia politics.

Griffin did not see himself as a practicing politician, and neither did the others. Rather, they thought of him as a manager with quality ideas. "They never thought I knew anything about politics, any of them. I hadn't been in the legislature. I was more like the lawyer. I would have to get up position papers and advise them on the law and then do what I could do politically."

Perhaps there is too much self-deprecation in that thought. They didn't think of him as a *candidate* out shaking hands and ladling Brunswick stew to the multitudes. Articulate though he was, the mind's eye did not see him standing on the back of a flatbed truck, a country music band in the background, shucking off his coat to reveal red galluses, launching a speech about the glories of the Old South.

✦

By 1958, Georgia politics were in turmoil. Marvin Griffin was coming to the close of his term as governor. His administration was riddled with corruption; thirty-two state employees had been indicted
of everything from bribery to conspiracy to defraud the state, and
more than a dozen had been convicted. To counteract the accusa-
tions, Governor Griffin and his associates were attacking "the lyin'
Atlanta newspapers" and proposing a series of evasions to stop the
desegregation of the public schools. In the sarcastic words of respected *Atlanta Journal* political writer Charles Pou, "If you ain't for
cheatin', you ain't for segregation."

More than anything else, Governor Griffin wanted to stop the
investigations that were moving closer and closer to the governor's
office itself. He cast about for a successor and finally settled on a
South Georgia legislator and Baptist preacher, the Reverend
William T. Bodenhamer. Goodness only knows why he chose such
a misfit. Bodenhamer may have represented churchly respectability
to the governor, or perhaps it was a desperation choice.
Nonetheless, there were some knowledgable prognosticators who
thought the reverend could pull the South Georgia rural vote
together and win the governorship.

His principal opposition would be S. Ernest Vandiver, who had
won the lieutenant governor's office four years previously. Vandiver
had presided over the state Senate with decorum and skill. Moreover,
he had drawn a clear distinction between himself and Governor
Griffin. By the lights of the Georgia electorate, he would appear to
be the reform candidate.

Handsome, deep-voiced, schooled in politics, Vandiver also
brought impeccable connections to the campaign. He had built strong
ties to influential politicians ever since his undergraduate days at the
University of Georgia. In the coming campaign, he would use all of
those bonds to great advantage.

A Bodenhamer-Vandiver campaign was about as incongruous as

one could imagine. One based his appeal on his Baptist preaching; the other ran on a reform platform that hooked into the business and professional classes.

Griffin was not unaware of the coming campaign, of course, but he had settled in King & Spalding in the 1950s and gradually assumed a larger leadership role in the community. The law practice was expanding every month, and he didn't see the future as being consumed by political and government office. He was busy managing the firm and pursuing his own practice.

Because he was associated with a high-profile law firm and had many acquaintances in politics, he met with leading national politicians who came to Atlanta. Among them was the young Massachusetts senator who almost won the 1956 Democratic vice presidential nomination, Jack Kennedy. As the 1960 primaries began to take shape, Bobby Kennedy also came calling. Bell's partner Robert Troutman Jr. was a roommate of older brother Joe Kennedy, and so the King & Spalding connections were made. Bell did not get involved in the early part of that campaign.

In his spare time, though, Bell continued to associate frequently with the group of lawyers who did participate heavily in Georgia politics. Among them was his friend Robert Jordan, a combination scholar and political operative who was close to Vandiver.

Jordan introduced Griffin to Vandiver and asked that he help with the campaign. Griffin understood that there were strong similarities in their backgrounds. Vandiver came from Lavonia, a town even smaller than Americus. He was a lawyer. He was a straight shooter. He had a reputation for honesty. And he had leadership qualities. All those were important to Griffin, who shared them. What they also had in common was even more important; Betty Vandiver was as lively, vivacious, and attractive as Mary Bell. They could share social times as well as political events, and they did.

When the group of lawyers supporting Vandiver asked Griffin to join the inner circle, it seemed like both an opportunity and an interesting challenge. The campaign manager would be one of the wiliest politicians in the state's history, Jim L. Gillis of Soperton. The campaign would be waged under the county unit system—the same one that Bell and his group had kept out of the state Constitution while he lived in Savannah. Like the rest of them, Gillis had his origins in a rural county. Unlike the rest of them, he was a veteran of political campaigns. Before the race was over, Griffin Bell had learned a great deal about politics.

In the latter stages of the campaign, Vandiver did "something that was entirely unnecessary," Bell said. Fearing that Bodenhamer was gaining through his support for segregated schools, Vandiver sat down with two of his advisers, his brother-in-law Robert Russell Jr. and Peter Zack Geer, who later would be elected lieutenant governor. They decided on a three-word phrase that echoed some of the words from hymns they and the voters had heard since childhood.

Vandiver declared in campaign speeches, "No, not one" black child would enter a white school. It was a phrase that would haunt Vandiver and Griffin Bell for years to come. Whether it had any real bearing on the Georgia governor's race was doubtful; Vandiver won in a landslide in the urban areas as well as the rural counties. It undoubtedly had great negative impact on Vandiver's political future. He showed great courage in dealing with desegregation issues, but black voters never forgave him for the phrase.

As he took office after the years of corruption, Vandiver asked Bell to become his chief of staff. Imposing though the title sounded, it was honorary; there was no pay. The only duties were as an adviser. With unintended irony and with no hint of what was to come, the local newspaper reported, "He will continue to devote his full time to the practice of law."

The Vandiver years began with widely accepted reform programs. Increasingly, Griffin and Mary Bell found themselves entertained at the old, fusty, crumbling governor's mansion in Ansley Park, a section of Atlanta with winding streets, magnolia-scented lawns, and fading memories of another South. Griffin, the man who said he was valued for his legal advice and not his political acumen, was in fact very much involved in political decisions. His law practice grew and grew.

But the era of goodwill and easy times would last only a few months. In 1959 the federal courts ordered the desegregation of Atlanta schools. When Vandiver asked Bell to become his chief of staff, Bell said, "That threw me into the middle of the race business." And they had to find some solution to the question of whether to keep the schools open and how they should operate. Vandiver formed a five-member committee of lawyers with Bell as chairman. He asked the group to advise him on desegregation. As they began to organize, the Supreme Court handed down a second ruling on the Little Rock schools, saying that the threat of violence was not a valid excuse for continuing segregated schools. Vandiver asked the committee to visit other Southern states to see how they were coping with the orders. In Virginia, Gov. Lindsey Almond shook his head. In Alabama, Gov. John Patterson extended his arms upward. "Nobody had any idea what to do," Bell reported.

So he went home and wrote in longhand his own plan. The state would form a commission to listen to Georgians on their feelings. It would travel about the state seeking advice. And it would take some of the heat off the politicians at the state capitol. Another of Vandiver's close advisers, Holcombe Perry, agreed it was a good idea. Two others, Charles Bloch and B. D. (Buck) Murphy, weren't much in favor. But Vandiver thought it a good plan, if only they could find the right chairman.

Casting about, they chose several committee members, all of whom represented such organized groups as the Parent-Teacher Association, the unions and business groups. But Vandiver really wanted John Sibley, the chairman of the Trust Company of Georgia, to head the group. Sibley was formerly a lawyer at King & Spalding and was a respected Atlanta leader. With the help of Hughes Spalding, Bell and Vandiver prevailed upon Sibley to take the demanding and unpopular job. But wait; everybody else was the head of some organization. What about Sibley? "We finally figured out it would be all right because he was the president of the University of Georgia Alumni Society," Bell said.

The Georgia Legislature ordered the Sibley Commission to study what to do about public school desegregation and come back to the 1961 session with a recommendation. It toured all ten congressional districts, took testimony from about eighteen hundred witnesses, and prepared its report. Voting eleven to ten to allow all systems a local option, the commission came down on the side of keeping public schools.

Before the commission could report back to the legislature, however, a federal court ordered two black Atlanta students, Hamilton Holmes and Charlayne Hunter, admitted to the University of Georgia, Vandiver's alma mater.

As a reporter for the *Atlanta Constitution,* I spoke by telephone with Vandiver the night before the two were to attend classes. He was an anguished man who neither wanted to close his alma mater nor risk the possibility that students could get hurt the way they had at the University of Mississippi. He said he intended to close the university to avoid violence. I could hear the pain in his voice, but I could not know that he was still considering another course.

The *Constitution* therefore carried a lead story that declared the school was being closed, because that was what Vandiver said publicly. The television stations showed demonstrations in the streets. Politicians made their loud predictions—and parents were desperately worried about what would happen to their sons and daughters in Athens. Federal Judge William Augustus Bootle in Macon issued orders that the school remain open and that the state use its powers to maintain order. In the swirl of events, nobody knew what the morrow would bring.

What I also did not know as I prepared that newspaper article was that a dramatic meeting was underway at the governor's mansion.

Vandiver had assembled his kitchen cabinet, perhaps twenty people in all. The dean of the Georgia political kingmakers, Jim Gillis; the governor's House floor leader, Frank Twitty; a rising state

Senate star, Carl Sanders; and other advisers. Somber probably is not a strong enough description of the mood. Bell, who was both chief of staff and the best-informed lawyer in the group, described the meeting later:

> Most of the top officials of the state were present when the governor announced to them that he could not bring himself to close the University (his alma mater) as he was being urged to do. Therefore, the court order would be carried out. Whether he could have legally closed the University was not debated; he simply said he would not do so.
>
> Then he bade all of his top officials farewell—thinking that they would not wish to serve with him because he was giving in to the law. In one of the most remarkable turnabouts in political history, none of the officials would leave. All agreed to back the governor as he called a special session of the legislature to remove the Georgia laws requiring segregation. Thus, a big shift came in the history of Georgia, carried out by elected officials.

As he frequently did, Bell then pointed to the court order, which came from Federal District Court Judge Bootle in Macon, a man he credited with great courage. It was Bell who insisted that the order must be obeyed.

The university remained open; Holmes and Hunter became students and graduated. Both became great successes: Holmes as a physician and professor at Emory University, Hunter as a television news correspondent and analyst for the Public Broadcasting System and currently with the Cable News Network.

RUNNING THE KENNEDY-JOHNSON CAMPAIGN

Organizing the Sibley Commission and assembling its membership was a singular success in Georgia, and much of the credit went to the governor's chief of staff. Other political challenges would follow.

The 1960 presidential campaign pitted two powerful and fundamentally different candidates against each other. Jack Kennedy and Lyndon Johnson sought the nomination. Kennedy, the charismatic star, and Johnson, the consummate insider, would present the Democrats with diametrically opposite campaigns. In that year, the delegate counting had not become so sophisticated that everyone knew weeks in advance who would be chosen. Southern politicians naturally found affinity with Johnson. A growing band of moderates would find themselves attracted to Kennedy's more modern politics.

Because Kennedy's brother had roomed at Harvard with King & Spalding partner Bobby Troutman Jr., Troutman had an Atlanta reception for Jack Kennedy. Though there was no Georgia primary to choose delegates representing one candidate or another, Kennedy was assiduous in his search for delegates. One of the people he saw at the reception was Griffin Bell. "I was a Kennedy supporter," Bell recalled. But Georgia senator Richard B. Russell and Johnson were friends and colleagues for many years. Russell asked Vandiver to get the Georgia delegation to support Johnson. The Georgia senator's request had special weight; Betty Vandiver was the senator's niece. It thus was foreordained that Johnson would get the Georgia votes on the first ballot.

Kennedy came to meet with the Georgia delegation in a crowded, noisy room at the Los Angeles hotel, even though it was clearly committed to Johnson. As the candidate came sweeping into the caucus, Kennedy asked, "Where's Taxi?" Taxi Smith was at that time the mayor of Albany, Georgia, and a power in southwest Georgia politics. The delegation was mightily impressed that a harried, pressured candidate could inquire about one of their own even in the last stages of the nomination fight.

Nevertheless, the Georgians maintained their support for Johnson on the first ballot, then happily fell in line when Kennedy was chosen. It had been a cantankerous convention, and the grumbling became louder when it came time for Kennedy to choose his vice presidential running mate. John Connally, who had been in the Nixon cabinet before his election as governor of Texas, came to see Bell and said there were a lot of hard feelings. The Johnson supporters felt they were being treated badly.

Connally asked Bell to help line up delegates for Johnson. He did work at the project, but Kennedy chose the Texan before it came to a vote. Then the Georgia delegation went with all the other Democrats to the Los Angeles Coliseum, a huge open-air stadium, to watch the "Boston to Austin" team begin their quest for the presidency.

Georgia tradition held that the two senators and the governor should stay out of national elections. Breaking from that tradition, Governor Vandiver joined senators Russell and Talmadge in choosing Bell and George L. Smith, the portly and popular speaker of the Georgia House of Representatives, to co-chair the Kennedy-Johnson campaign in Georgia.

But several other factions in the state wanted to head the

campaign. Some had been loyal to either Kennedy or Johnson for years and felt they should be accorded the honor of being campaign chairmen.

Bell was dispatched to Washington to meet with Kennedy. Meeting in the Senate's sergeant-at-arms office, the two faced up to the need for a single entity to run the campaign. They agreed that Vandiver, Russell, Talmadge and the co-chairs would be responsible for and speak for the campaign in Georgia.

A photograph from that time shows Griffin and Kennedy smiling and shaking hands. What the picture does not convey is a poignant moment when Kennedy spoke of his Roman Catholic religion.

What about Griffin? he asked. "I'm a Baptist," Griffin said.

Well, would he be embarrassed to represent a Catholic? "Not at all. But I am embarrassed for our country that you would think to ask me that question."

Then Bell and Smith went to work organizing the state, county by county. Each congressional district had its own organizing committee. The larger towns had their own headquarters, sometimes matched by offices for the Nixon campaign.

The political reporters who wrote about Georgia politics were startled at the choices for co-chairmen. Bell professed to know about the law but disclaimed knowledge of the broadscale effort to woo voters. Smith was a keen student of Georgia politics who had been a legislator for sixteen years, several of them as House speaker pro tem during the time of Gov. Herman Talmadge. He was known to be much more conservative than any Kennedy-Johnson campaign could be and still entertain hopes of winning the national election.

Smith dealt with the obvious problems in his first statement about the campaign: "We are vehemently opposed to the 'civil rights' section of the Democratic platform, and some other sections of the document, but let us remind Georgians that the Congress enacts the laws of this country and the South has able and staunch defenders of our principles."

Despite their misgivings, they went to work, or at least Bell went to work. Bell declared in September that Kennedy had forged ahead of former vice president Richard Nixon in the state. He insisted that the absence of senators Talmadge and Russell, who traveled to avoid having to campaign for the Democratic ticket, would not damage the campaign. They "have certainly not come out for Nixon," he added gamely.

A few days later, Republicans were arguing that a vote for Nixon would promote a two-party state to supplant the Democratic primaries as the place where Georgians chose their elected officials. "Talking about a two-party system is certainly not going to bring one to the state. I think the best way to get a two-party system in the state would be for some of these Democrats who are switching over to the Republican side to run for office," Bell said.

Kennedy then came to Warm Springs, the quiet little place where Franklin D. Roosevelt had spent recuperative time during his presidency and where he had died. In Democratic politics, Warm Springs was almost a sacred place, and there was nothing to compare with the enthusiasm Kennedy found there. It was the year of the "jumpers," women who literally bounced on the balls of their feet from the exuberance of the campaign. Several thousand of them appeared at Warm Springs to give the Democrat one of his most rousing rallies.

The inspiration for the visit to such a hallowed place? "The idea was wholly that of Governor Vandiver and his speechwriter, Ed Bridges," Bell said.

Johnson also made it to Georgia, campaigning from the back of a train whistlestopping its way through the South. Though the turnout for Johnson in Atlanta was restrained compared to Kennedy's visit, it continued the momentum that Bell had spoken of weeks before.

The campaign proceeded without great trouble until Wednesday, October 19, just about two weeks prior to the election.

On that day a group of young blacks went to the Magnolia Room in the downtown Rich's department store. They sat down at a lunch counter to order sandwiches. Dr. Martin Luther King Jr. joined them. All were arrested for violating the Georgia trespass law.

Within five days the others were released from jail, but King received different treatment. It helps at this late date to see the rest of the event through the reportage of Theodore H. White:

> What does one say when a Martin Luther King is arrested for sitting down at a lunch counter, quietly insisting on his rights? Is this a civil right, a human right or a legal right? What does one say or do when all other protesters but Martin Luther King are released within five days yet he, on a technicality, is carted off in handcuffs to a jail in deep cracker country, where his life may be in danger? When his six-month-pregnant wife, who has always feared that white men will eventually kill King, believes he will be lynched now—how does one comfort her? . . . This is one man's life, a black man, held in a state prison.

King was held on the technical charge of violating the terms of a twelve-month suspended sentence for driving with an expired license. He was initially taken to DeKalb County before Judge Oscar Mitchell. And it was Mitchell who ordered him transported to the Reidsville jail.

The question that presented itself to both the Kennedy and Nixon campaigns was how to respond to the incarceration. Neither knew how many votes were at stake; that is to say, neither knew whether action would cause white defections in sufficient numbers to offset black gains. As vice president, Nixon could have gotten the Justice Department involved but did not. Kennedy quietly called Coretta Scott King to say he would do everything he could to make sure King remained safe. According to Kennedy biographer Thomas C. Reeves, Bobby Kennedy "flew into a rage on learning of the call, predicting that it might cost three Southern states and the election." Bobby Kennedy ordered the campaign workers not to let anyone know of the call. But Mrs. King already had alerted the *New York Times*, which reported the conversation.

Bell, speaking for the Georgia campaign organization and the governor's chief of staff, said only, "We know that Senator Kennedy would never interfere with the affairs of a sovereign state." There wasn't a whole lot else he could have said, given that Governor Vandiver believed it would be political suicide for him to get into a public discussion of King's situation. Furthermore, Bell had no indication that the state leadership was getting involved in a clandestine way.

What went on behind the scenes was more intriguing. Years later, Vandiver related it to Jim Minter, formerly the managing editor of the *Atlanta Constitution*:

> I called Bob Russell, my brother-in-law and confidant, and we talked about it. We agreed it would be political suicide for me to be publicly identified with the effort. We decided to ask George Stewart, executive secretary of the Georgia Democratic Party, to approach Judge Oscar Mitchell in DeKalb County. George did, and Judge Mitchell said he would release Dr. King if he got a call from either John Kennedy or Robert Kennedy.
>
> Senator Kennedy was out campaigning in New York, but I got in touch with Robert Kennedy and told him what Judge Mitchell had said. Bobby called Judge Mitchell and Dr. King was released.

After prison, Dr. King declined to endorse anyone. But his father, a respected Baptist minister, said, "I had expected to vote against Senator Kennedy because of his religion. But now he can be my president, Catholic or whatever he is. It took courage to call my daughter-in-law at a time like this. He has the moral courage to stand up for what he knows is right."

A day or two after the release, Bobby Kennedy called Bell and asked what the impact might be. "We had no scientific polling at the time, and I told him that as near as I could tell, the reaction was mixed and that it was too early to tell what would happen."

One thing that did happen immediately: George L. Smith went home to Emanuel County. He was finished with the campaign. Fearing that his constituents in southeast Georgia would believe he was involved in obtaining King's release, he withdrew from the national race and concentrated on getting reelected to the Georgia House of Representatives.

Senator Kennedy said later he believed his call, the endorsement by the elder King, and the enthusiasm it generated in the black community was enough to assure him of victory.

On election night, the figures showed that Georgia had given the Kennedy-Johnson ticket a larger margin than any other state. And it was the last time Georgia would vote for a Democratic candidate for president until one of their own, Jimmy Carter, was elected.

A CHOICE OF APPOINTMENTS

With the election over, Bell felt gratified—and perhaps a little curious—as to how the Kennedy crowd would respond. During the campaign, Bobby had asked several times what sort of job Bell would like. Bell's answer was that he didn't want a federal job. But the pressure of the campaign was over now; would the workers be forgotten?

Bobby Kennedy called again to inquire what, if any, appointment would interest him. Could that mean a cabinet appointment? Getting in line for the Supreme Court? An ambassadorship to an important country? Bell was, after all, one of those who had been significantly important in the election and he presumably could have been a successful candidate for any number of prestigious appointments.

"I understand two circuit court judgeships might open up," Bell said. "I would be interested in being considered for one of them." He had "always thought of being a judge at some point in my career."

That might be possible, Bobby Kennedy said, but several senators were seeking appointments for friends in their own states. The Alabama senators Hill and Sparkman had been promised one of the judgeships. Texas and Florida senators were angling for the other.

While Kennedy carried that idea to the president-elect, other forces were moving that could cause trouble. A Macon lawyer, Ellsworth Hall, wanted a court seat. And he had a very powerful ally, Congressman Carl Vinson, who was on his way to fifty years in the House. Jack Kennedy had served on Vinson's committee in the House. Vinson's feelings were understandable; Hall lived only thirty miles from Vinson's hometown and had been a supporter of the congressman for many years. Still, it was an awkward time. Georgia clearly would not get two judgeships; either Bell or Hall would have to prevail.

Normally, the Democratic senators from Georgia (Russell and Talmadge) would have been granted the patronage decision. They both supported Bell. But Vinson was such a power that he could block the nomination for a time. When it became clear that he was the holdup, the Justice Department decreed that a vote should be held, one of the few judicial appointments ever decided by a vote of the state's congressmen.

No contest. Griffin Bell won nine to one. Vinson became even more determined that Bell would not become the circuit judge. Enter John Sibley, the same powerhouse who had headed the committee that held the public school hearings. Sibley had grown up with Vinson, and he took the train to Washington to reason with his boyhood friend. Ultimately, Vinson relented and Bell was confirmed.

Victory would not be a cause for uncontrolled joy, however. The South in the early '60s had to face up to what it had avoided for so long—obeying the desegregation rulings of the Supreme Court. Federal judges spent an enormous amount of their time, talents, and patience requiring local communities to fashion their own plans for sending children to schools that were truly equal instead of *separate but equal.*

Like all ideas that profoundly alter human existence, this one would move in little jumps. White Southerners (and many in the rest of the nation) adopted a more benign viewpoint when the issue moved into their consciousness. Then many took a step back when the idea proved too painful. They hopped sideways when President Harry Truman introduced ideas like fair employment practices in the late 1940s. Some skipped ahead of the majority when they began to form biracial farm communes such as Koinonia Farm in Griffin Bell's and Jimmy Carter's home county. Some retreated in horror when Georgia governor Marvin Griffin talked about "cutting down some blackjack saplings" with which to deter blacks who wanted to use desegregated facilities, including churches. Some elected Lester Maddox governor in 1966 after he chased demonstrators from his Atlanta restaurant with ax handles. Many were appalled when Sen. Herman Talmadge said "blood would run in the streets" if the Supreme Court attempted to enforce its school desegregation decisions; many more approved and continued to elect him to high public office.

The turmoil was both mental and verbal for most white Southerners; they thought and talked about the issue all the time in the '50s. What had been in the backs of their minds had been forced to the highest level of consciousness, and many hated having to think about it.

Black Southerners for the most part had known these days were coming; they just didn't know when or how. Martin Luther King Jr. graduated from Morehouse College in Atlanta and entered the ministry knowing the great injustices, but not knowing how he could become the force to correct them. The Reverend Andrew Young would become Dr. King's alter ego, but that was in the future. Jesse Jackson would emerge from a hardscrabble South Carolina existence to lead marches and become a firebrand for the cause after a slow start. Julian Bond would try radicalism, then switch to elective politics to try to change the system.

One July Fourth in Atlanta, a heroic John Lewis would lead a small group of demonstrators into Lakewood Park, where Mississippi governor Ross Barnett was spewing his racist venom to an all-white audience. As Lewis and his tiny group of black demonstrators moved toward the speaker's stand in protest, members of the white audience picked up their metal folding chairs and beat the group almost senseless.

What once had been an emotional struggle to deal with the inequality of racial lives had grown into murderous rhetoric and hateful violence way beyond the Ku Klux Klan and the Citizens Councils and the redneck fringe. Parents of both races dreaded sending their young off to school. Ministers lost their pastorates for simply suggesting that blacks should be admitted to worship services. Moderate to liberal newspapers faced economic boycotts from advertisers. State governments financed the snooping of disreputable racists on the activities of people who were believed to be in favor of "mixing." State legislatures enacted foolish laws that pretended that a state could "interpose" its power and prevent the federal government from enforcing the orders of the highest court.

It was against this backdrop of anger and anguish, violence and penance, defiance and acquiescence, that the federal judges had to fashion a workable plan. It was perhaps the most thankless task American citizens had been asked to undertake in peacetime. Griffin Bell would become one of those whose time and energy would be consumed by the issue.

◎

The ornate high-ceilinged courtroom in Atlanta was familiar to the attorney who had spent some of his professional life trying cases in that very room. The man administering the oath of office, Judge Elbert P. Tuttle, was not an old acquaintance. But the occasion was an especially meaningful one for Griffin B. Bell. His immediate family was there, together with virtually every partner of King & Spalding. Many of his friends had shown up. Judge John R. Brown joined Judge Tuttle in their black robes. What he would remember most, however, was that "my mother and father were still living, so they came. It was wonderful to have them there."

Tuttle would serve for many years as chief judge of the Fifth

Circuit. Brown would become known as one of the most liberal judges of the circuit. But this day their thoughts ran mostly to where people had been and where they were going. Tuttle had started his professional life as a newspaper reporter in Hawaii. He was cognizant of what his written opinions would mean to people in the streets—and in the streets of the Southern towns then in the throes of court-ordered desegregation.

Brown's thoughts ran more to limits on the powers of the judges. "I'll never forget one thing that Judge Brown said at the ceremony," Griffin Bell recalled. "He said, 'Now that you are a federal judge, you probably think that you have a lot of power. You *would* if you were on the District Court, where you act alone. But on this court, you have to get one more vote to have a majority of two out of three. You'll find that will hold you down.'"

About one month shy of his forty-third birthday, then, in October 1961, Griffin Bell assumed the title his friends would use ever after in addressing him: Judge. With the applause of the crowd in the courtroom still in his memory, he embarked on a tumultuous journey.

Together with judges Brown and John Minor Wisdom, he traveled to Hattiesburg, Mississippi, to try the clerk of the state court. Theron Lynd, the clerk, was charged with disobeying a federal court order to allow blacks to register to vote. "They were turning down every black, including a high-school math professor who was a Cornell graduate. Even he couldn't pass the test. It turned out that none of the blacks could ever answer the question 'What militia district do you live in?' The reason they couldn't answer was that the only map of the county was hidden in the clerk's office at the courthouse. Whites knew their militia district by reason of having previously registered or by word of mouth. We found the clerk guilty of contempt in spite of the fact that he had the entire Hattiesburg bar defending him. We stayed there for five full days and found him guilty from the bench. We made the clerk pay several thousand dollars in court costs and he carried out the order. Sadly, we were told that there was a public collection taken to pay the court costs."

The Judge would not forget what that courtroom looked like. "The blacks sat on one side and the whites on the other side. After five full days of trial and the decision, we shook hands with people in the audience—both black and white—with our robes still on." Did the clerk go to jail? "No. We were mainly interested in getting the order carried out so that black people could register to vote. This was before the Voting Rights Act came to be [1961; the act was passed in 1964]. Once we found out what militia districts people lived in, I guess it all worked out."

Even while they were trying to sort out the militia district question, the three judges were being asked to hand down orders in one of the most famous civil rights cases of the '60s.

James Howard Meredith was a Mississippi native and an African American who had served his country by enlisting in the air force in the early '50s. He said later that he had been inspired by President Theodore Roosevelt's now familiar credo: "The credit belongs to the man who is actually in the arena; whose face is marred by dust and sweat and blood; who strives valiantly; who errs and comes short again and again; who knows the great enthusiasm, the great devotion, and spends himself in a worthy cause."

But it was another president, John F. Kennedy, who convinced Meredith the time had come for him to strive valiantly. He decided he would like to attend Ole Miss, the justly famous school in Oxford. So, less than nine months before Griffin Bell became Judge Bell, Meredith, twenty-eight, mailed his application for admission to the university. "I sincerely hope," he wrote in the application, "that your attitude toward me as a potential member of your student body reflects the attitude of the school and that it will not change on learning that I am not a White applicant." Of course, the attitude did change because he was black. And of course the case would wind its tortuous way through the courts until Judge Bell and his colleagues were sitting on panels that were engaged in trying to decide historic constitutional questions.

Meredith was denied admission by the university, and he went to the federal district court asking for help. Judge Sidney Mize, with tortured logic, found that "the overwhelming weight of the testimony is that the plaintiff [Meredith] was not denied admission because of his color or race." Gov. Ross Barnett aroused the local passions with speeches, and the White Citizens Council further stirred racial attitudes. The state began to fund groups that investigated the political views of newspaper editors and college professors who expressed any support for the Supreme Court's school desegregation decisions. Ultimately the appeals court instructed Judge Mize to issue an injunction and order the university officials to admit Meredith, holding that his race most certainly was the reason he had been excluded.

But one of the Fifth Circuit judges, Benjamin Franklin Cameron, issued four separate stays in direct opposition to the orders of his fellow judges.

While this unprecedented wrangling was going on, Judge Bell joined judges Brown and Wisdom in trying to bring order out of chaos. They had to move quickly into the constitutional crisis, because after midnight of the day Meredith was to enroll, the Mississippi state legislature and Governor Barnett again got into the argument, defying the court injunction declaring that Meredith must be admitted.

The legislature passed a law prohibiting the university from enrolling any applicant who faced a criminal charge of moral turpitude. Meredith's criminal charge? He had said that his home county was his legal residence, but he had attempted to register to vote in Hinds County, where he was attending Jackson State College. Therefore, in the view of the state of Mississippi, he had misrepresented the place where he was entitled to register to vote. The governor declared himself the university's registrar, and he refused to admit Meredith. Moreover, there was talk of arresting Meredith. Hold it a minute, said judges Bell, Brown, and Wisdom. They enjoined the state officials from making the arrest or from barring Meredith.

Barnett then said he was interposing his state's sovereignty. He directed state officials to arrest any federal officers who tried to keep state officials from carrying out their official duties, including the arrest of Meredith. The governor had thus directly defied the orders of the court, and the case moved on to contempt when he blocked the doors and refused to enroll the young black man.

Eight of the Fifth Circuit judges met *en banc* and found the governor of Mississippi guilty of civil contempt and came close to ordering his arrest. They also considered whether to fine him ten thousand dollars per day for his defiance of the court orders. Judge Bell was in the minority when the court voted five to three to impose the fine. But even the judges who thought the fine should be collected admitted that Barnett was likely to "interpose" the state treasury not to pay the fine.

Tragically, violence broke out at Ole Miss while the federal judges wrestled with the problem of how to make the governor obey the law. Two persons were killed and more than seventy wounded in the riots around the college campus. Meredith began to attend classes, but he was harassed and roughed up continually.

Barnett sent his lawyer, Charles Clark, back to the Fifth Circuit to say the governor *would not interfere further unless it conflicted with his duties as the governor of the sovereign state of Mississippi.* Some of the judges wondered aloud how the nation would work if officials were to be allowed to choose which laws they would obey, claiming their jobs as governors superseded federal law. Clark, who later would join those same judges on the Fifth Circuit bench, had no answers that satisfied them that day.

The ever-practical Judge Bell finally got to the heart of the problem: "I thought we were going to get this straightened out today. I came all the way from Jacksonville [where he was attending to court business]. We are just tilting at windmills. I have great sympathy for you, Mr. Clark, but you may agree to something here today and when you get back to Jackson may write a letter that you didn't have the authority to go that far. I don't see that we are getting anywhere." In other words: Don't just come here and tell us Governor Barnett has chosen to disobey the court; that won't get us anywhere. In his decision, Judge Bell wrote:

> Prior to becoming president, Abraham Lincoln, when told with reference to slavery that the law was wrong in taking a man's liberty without trial by jury, responded that slavery was ungodly.
> "But it is the law of the land, and we must obey it."
> New legal precedents of recent years, with resultant changes in the existing order, have brought this maxim of another day, expressing an American tradition, into sharp focus. The necessary accommodation has differed in degree and manner; running the scale from prompt compliance, on through the middle ground of painful but responsible and dignified adjustment, down to extreme recalcitrance or out-right refusal even to obey court orders entered, as they must be, pursuant to these precedents.

Federal judges then needed all the help they could get. Beleaguered by racists who pasted the roadsides with demands that judges be impeached, savagely attacked for their "race-mixing" rulings, they heard scant applause. They did, however, hear from a very impor-tant supporter—President Kennedy. He made a national broadcast from the Oval Office in which he appealed for calm and called the roll of heroes in the Mississippi situation, citing Judge Bell by name as one of the heroes.

And there were some Southerners who spoke up. Ralph McGill wrote a column in the *Atlanta Constitution* that began,

> In the wake of the wholly unnecessary and brutal riots at the University of Mississippi, history and civilization focus a bright and revealing spotlight on Alabama and South Carolina. In these states the leadership in the capital, the

congressional delegations, the press, the pulpit and business
community must soon give answer. The question is whether
it is determined to follow the Ross Barnett blueprint of
forcing federal authority to act to preserve the national
integrity, or if it will provide the people with compliance
with laws to meet the inevitable decisions of the future. The
eloquent and conciliatory words of President Kennedy on
Sunday evening before the riots deserve to be heard again
and again. . . . The issue of segregation has, therefore,
become a secondary and relatively minor one. . . . The primary issue has become the authority of the United States
government to govern by laws. . . . Let it be said again, we
cannot escape history.

Meredith continued in school, federal marshals and army personnel
continued to try to protect him, and the courts ground on with one
of the toughest questions it would face: Could the federal courts
hold the governor and lieutenant governor of a state in criminal contempt? Could they be arrested? And were they entitled to a trial by
jury? The Mississippians argued that the governor and lieutenant
governor were obeying the law of the state, and that it was the federal court that had violated the law.

The lawyers were all agreed on one point: this was a very great
constitutional crisis. Verbal clashes between the federal courts and
state officials had many precedents; governors arguing that state law
superseded federal court orders was a graver matter. Asking for a
trial by jury in a criminal contempt case was at the heart of the
argument. If Barnett could obtain a jury trial in Mississippi, and
even one of the jurors opposed the federal court orders, he could not
be convicted.

The Supreme Court had held frequently that the right to trial
by jury did not extend to criminal contempt. But it was a subject
constantly being revisited. Moreover, the federal appeals courts did
not normally hold jury trials; they listened to oral arguments, read

briefs from lower courts, and entered opinions. No machinery existed for them to impanel jurors. The eight Fifth Circuit judges hearing the arguments voted to certify the case to the Supreme Court for a decision, and they split four to four among themselves on whether a jury trial was appropriate. Bell was one of the four voting for a jury trial. He reasoned that the appeals court had heard the case, and therefore had acted like a district court. District courts speak to the litigants, whereas the appeals court hears appeals of district court rulings. Thus, a jury trial was appropriate.

Ultimately, the question of the jury trial became a footnote to history. Bell's side, if there was such a thing, won in the Supreme Court. Justice Tom Clark wrote the decision, saying, "I conclude that defendants' [governor and lieutenant governor] trial should be by a jury. . . . I reject the government's 'necessity' argument, that 'the independence of the federal courts . . . would be seriously undermined if their orders could be nullified by an unsympathetic jury.'" That merely extended the age-old argument that some guilty persons might be set free after a jury trial, the Supreme Court held.

By the time the decision came down, more than a year after the question had arisen, the outcome was moot. Ole Miss was integrated and James Meredith was an Ole Miss student. The federal courts had moved on to other civil rights questions. Soon the nation would be consumed by an even more difficult question: Was desegregation enough, or was integration required? The continuing challenge confronting judges was to find appropriate answers amid a swirl of emotions and practical problems.

Judge Bell found himself then in hearings all over the South. The Fifth Circuit would meet in New Orleans or Houston regularly. But there were the counties that defied the courts, and those where it was necessary for the Judge to hold court to begin the process of desegregation.

Those cases came before him at the very beginning of his time as a judge. Following them were years of angry, dangerous, fundamentally divisive arguments before an appeals court split almost

WHAT A JUDGE SHOULD BE

The dusty, quiet words of Article II, Section 2 of the United States Constitution say: *"The President . . . shall nominate and with the advice and consent of the Senate shall appoint . . . judges of the Supreme Court."*

From the formation of the Union until today, attorneys have pursued their profession while thinking somewhere in the backs of their minds about the Supreme Court bench. Judge Robert Bork, one of those nominated but rejected for the post, gave it the proper description: "an intellectual feast." The nation sometimes has damned the nine justices, but more frequently held them in higher esteem than other government officials. In the South, they were seen in such diverse ways as to fit no neat category.

Sitting as a Fifth Circuit judge, thinking about the momentous decisions that were being made in the late 1960s, Judge Bell could not have been deaf to the rumors that President Richard Nixon was thinking of naming a Democrat to the high court. Nor could he ignore the fact that some of the barristers around him thought he would make an excellent choice, given his seasoning and his comparative youth (middle fifties). So it was no surprise when he learned that Mississippi senator John Stennis, a Democrat and a conservative, favored him for the bench, as did one of his colleagues on the Fifth Circuit, Judge J. P. Coleman, who would later become chief judge of the circuit.

Rumor had it that Stennis and Coleman had gone to Attorney General John Mitchell and asked him to present Bell's credentials to President Nixon. At the time, it was widely believed that Nixon looked favorably on the idea. Newspaper reporters heard the further rumor that Nixon finally asked Mitchell to call Bell and report that he could not justify the appointment. Those rumors were inaccurate, as was much of the information that swirled around the Nixon administration in the turbulence of the Vietnam era.

What apparently happened says much about Southern politics. Some of the Southern Republicans who wanted one of their own to reach the Supreme Court sought an audience with Sen. Strom Thurmond of South Carolina. "They told Senator Thurmond that I was a big liberal, and that just wouldn't do on the Supreme Court. That really made me mad," the Judge said. "That was the last time I really thought about the Supreme Court." Thurmond made it clear to the White House staff that he would block Bell's nomination, and the issue was dead.

(The fact that the Judge dropped any aspirations to the Court at that time will come as a surprise to those who thought Bell later accepted President Carter's request that he come to Washington so as to position himself for a Supreme Court appointment. "I couldn't have been appointed then. It would have been a terrible conflict of interest. I was supposed to be representing the president, and I had compiled a list of people he could appoint." As it turned out, no vacancies occurred during the Carter administration.)

Why was he not chosen for the high court? Justice Felix Frankfurter said that all such appointments were "an odd lottery."

Moreover, being a good (or even great) judge was no guarantee of ascension to the Supreme Court. Judge Learned Hand was a federal judge for more than fifty years beginning in 1909; he never achieved the title of Justice despite being called the greatest living judge for many of those years. Hand lightly called his place an "inferior court." But he gladly continued to scratch out his decisions in longhand, revising them three or four times, accepting the fact he couldn't pick and choose only major cases that engaged his intellect. If he could not sit on a court made honorable by such men as Louis D. Brandeis, Benjamin N. Cardozo, Oliver Wendell Holmes, John Marshall, and others, he could still establish an enviable place in judicial history.

Many other judges, both the great ones and the mediocre, chose to serve in the lower courts. Most probably thought wistfully of the job—Judge Hand was quoted as saying to a law clerk, "Every time I went to Washington, for about twenty years or so, I said, 'Oh, wouldn't it be wonderful if I got on the Supreme Court.'" Then he added, "I don't have any regret now."

In the aftermath of considering Judge Bell, President Nixon chose two other nominees who would not be confirmed by the Senate. Clement F. Haynsworth, a South Carolinian who served on the Federal Appeals Court, was nominated in the summer of 1969 to replace Justice Abe Fortas, who resigned. Three months later the Senate refused to give its consent by a vote of 55–45. Haynsworth said the nomination had been "a great honor" but that he felt tarnished by the Senate vote.

Nixon pondered a new list for a couple of months and, in January 1970, nominated Irwinton, Georgia, native G. Harrold Carswell to the bench. With Haynsworth rejected and his own chances of going to the Court down to nothing, Bell sent a letter supporting Carswell's nomination. The Bells and Carswells were friends, and the men served in the same circuit. They frequently sat on three-judge panels together. Because it became so controversial in Bell's own confirmation hearings in the Senate, the letter is reproduced here in full:

Dear Sirs:
This statement is in support of Hon. G. Harrold Carswell whom you are now considering for confirmation as an

Associate Justice of the Supreme Court.

I have known Judge Carswell for 24 years and have frequently visited in his home as he has in mine. I am familiar with his career as a lawyer and a judge, and with his personal life. His character and integrity, including intellectual honesty, is of the highest order. His intellect and ability are also of the highest order.

Judge Carswell will take a standard of excellence to the Supreme Court, based on many years of experience as a trial judge and the equivalent of two years as a circuit judge (considering sittings with the Fifth Circuit as a district judge), which will substantially contribute from the inception to that court. His particular experience cannot be matched by anyone presently on the court and will fill a need now existing on that court.

I recommend Judge Carswell for confirmation without any hesitation or reservation whatever.

Yours sincerely,
Griffin B. Bell

As we shall see, it was a letter that in retrospect was overly complimentary to a judge who in his early days had made a racist speech (though Bell did not know of the speech). Two days after the announcement, reporters dug up the ugly remarks Carswell had made back in 1948 when he ran for the Georgia House of Representatives. His opponent, Joe Boone, accused the young Carswell of being too soft on segregation. In response, Carswell made a speech in which he said: "Segregation of the races is proper and the only practical and correct way of life in our states. I have always so believed and I shall always so act."

Carswell immediately went on television to disown that twenty-two-year-old speech: "Specifically and categorically, I renounce and reject the words themselves and the thought they represent; they are abhorrent." But it was too late. He could not be confirmed, losing by a vote of 51–45. Nixon called the rejections of Haynsworth and Carswell an "act of regional discrimination."

Newsweek magazine may have summed it up best: "Haynsworth fell because the Senate thought him not quite fastidious enough about his shareholdings. And Carswell's doom was sealed by the widespread notion that he has been a mediocre judge for his twelve years on the Federal bench—a supposition that in the end moved thirteen Republicans and four Southerners to vote with the liberal Democrats against him."

❖

As if the Judge were not busy enough with his Fifth Circuit duties, his adopted hometown called on him in the middle '60s to help with another problem: crime. Ralph McGill had written that "the fleas come with the dog; the bigger the dog, the more the fleas." Atlanta was growing ever more rapidly, and size begat crime. Ivan Allen was the mayor, universally recognized as a Southerner who had become an enlightened leader. He was greatly concerned about the increase in crime, juvenile delinquency, and related issues.

Would the Judge consider heading the Atlanta Commission on Crime and Juvenile Delinquency? He would. Bell and Mayor Allen together chose a twenty-one-member group that would look into the problems. "The idea is visionary in that it combines imagination and hope, but withal a sense of the possible," the Judge said. He told his fellow commission members, "We . . . are privileged to be the first group in the nation to make the unique comprehensive approach which we today begin." The commission would not study murder or robbery in isolation; it would consider health, poverty, and organized crime as contributing to the rising rates in Atlanta.

One of its first recommendations was to create an Atlanta Youth Council. It proposed an expanded program of job training, saying that was a "badly neglected aspect" of the school system. It called for improved school programs for culturally deprived and academically retarded children. As for the twenty-seven different programs that were supposed to be dealing with delinquency prevention, "There has been very little communication among these agencies." To lend gravity to the report, the Judge had it delivered in his chambers at the federal courthouse.

Digging deeper into the crime issue, the Judge said, "The 75 percent of the people who are doing all right in this city had better remember that 25 percent are not." His thinking echoed a national address by President Kennedy, who said, "If a free society cannot help the many who are poor, it cannot save the few who are rich."

The report stirred the city. An editorial in the *Atlanta Constitution* said:

> Federal Judge Griffin Bell's Crime Commission has described a child Atlanta must get to know. He has no legitimate father. His day is unsupervised. Affection for his family fails. He is not disciplined, nor is he stimulated intellectually. He learns no self-control. He has never dealt with authority so he doesn't even recognize it. He is a slum child.
>
> When he starts school it is probably on double session. . . . The child shows up for first grade without knowing discipline. No one has taught him how to behave or even how to talk. He may not know how to use a fork and spoon. His unstimulated mind is dull. He resents control. He performs poorly, falls behind, drops out, roams the streets, and breaks the law. He is a juvenile delinquent.

The report found that forty-five hundred children under seventeen were arrested in 1965. Of those, 80 percent were three or more years behind in school. Though it did not eradicate the problems, the report stung a city that had called itself "too busy to hate" and had spent millions on a national advertising campaign.

Delving into the relationships of minorities to the governing authorities, the commission found great suspicion. "They distrust everybody but the public health nurse because everybody but the public health nurse can do something to them," the Judge reported. To build bridges, the Commission said the city should establish police counselors to improve communication. Speaking as usual without pretense, the Judge put it in perspective: "The policeman must be more than a man who arrests you. He must also protect you."

Trying to effect change was like digging in hard rock. The commission wanted to make more pretrial investigation possible through the state courts. It tried to get the Georgia Legislature to pass a first-offender law, being lenient with those who were caught the first time but bearing down on repeat offenders. And it wanted the judge to pass sentence after having studied the defendant's record, instead of a jury meting out justice without knowing about the convicted person's past. Under the gold dome of the Georgia capital, things did not move swiftly: "We didn't get much cooperation from the legislature" in the beginning, the Judge said.

Eventually, however, most of the reforms recommended by the commission worked their way through the legal system. They did not stop lawlessness in Atlanta; the crime rate grew in the 1960s and 1970s, and it soared in the 1980s, with violent crime almost tripling.

But the question had to be posed properly: Would crime have been worse without the changes the group recommended? There was a consensus that the commission's work kept the crime rates lower than they would have been otherwise.

Fighting crime became one of the principal promises of incoming president Ronald Reagan in 1981, who asserted that lawlessness had become "an American epidemic." He asserted that "the jungle is always there . . . ready to take us over." His new attorney general, William French Smith, appointed Bell to co-chair a new federal commission, along with Illinois governor James Thompson. The task force was given sixty days to make its recommendations for changes in federal law-enforcement efforts without new legislation and another sixty days to recommend changes that would require either additional funding or new legislation. In other words, what to do immediately to deal with escalating violent crime?

In the plain language that people had come to expect, Bell said, "We're constantly wringing our hands about what we can do to rehabilitate people and place them on probation, and worry very little about the victims of crime. . . . The truth is, there are a lot of bad people who ought to be locked up to protect the rest of us. And unless we're willing to face that, then we don't really deserve to have a safe society."

Ultimately, that commission developed sixty-four recommendations to deal with violent crime. Bell thought the single most significant goal was to spend $2 billion in federal funds to build new prisons. Cell shortages were so acute that prisoners were being held in county jails; many never even went to state or federal prisons. No deterrent there, the Judge said. "It's not the length of the sentence always. It's the fact that you've got to *serve* the sentence." Over time, new prisons were build or expanded. But overcrowding continued to be a problem, with accused murderers being released without ever being tried. In some cases, they stayed in city and county jails for three years but never saw judge or jury.

Pushed constantly by Reagan, Congress finally began to enact some of the commission's recommendations.

Beyond the prison need, the commission declared that the nation needed a uniform sentencing code that would specify punishment for specific crimes. That code was adopted, although in time it became controversial and was amended.

Attorney General Smith said, "The result of their efforts was the best and most useful government report I have ever seen. . . . Not only was it exactly what we wanted, but it was done within the time allotted! Perceptive, innovative, imaginative, aggressive, and practical, the report contained fifteen recommendations for Phase One [no new legislation] and forty-nine for Phase Two [new laws or funding]. Of that total number, we were able to begin implementing 80 percent of them right away. . . . "

❁

Sitting in courtroom or chambers day after day, Bell inevitably gave much thought to what a judge should be. But he has been more forthcoming than others about the traits that make for a good person on the bench. Just to underscore it, he went to the Federal Courthouse in Macon, Georgia, in June 1998, to dedicate the naming of the courthouse for retired Judge William Augustus Bootle, who was then ninety-six. Bootle had been appointed to the district court in 1954, just after the *Brown* v. *Board of Education* school desegregation decision. "As much as any federal judge of the South, Judge Bootle was at the vortex of the civil rights revolution," Bell told the assembled crowd, which contained more than a dozen other federal judges.

His words about Bootle speak to how he saw much of the judiciary: "In the highest tradition of service as a federal judge, he [Bootle] served with understanding, compassion and courage. His was a difficult service. He endured criticism but never flinched from his duty. The decisions of the Supreme Court had to be carried out by the lower courts; indeed, it was the duty of the lower courts to do so. But it was the lower courts and particularly the district courts which bore the brunt of the dissatisfaction of the parents of children with respect to integrating the public schools."

One could almost hear Judge Bell saying, *That was all of us. We had to do the job that nobody else would do.* "Section 5 of the 14th Amendment had provided, from its adoption shortly after the Civil War, that it was to be enforced by the Congress, but Congress never acted. In the end, it was enforced by the court system at the behest of the Supreme Court decisions."

Bootle, a scholarly former Walter F. George Law School dean, and Bell agreed that freedom of choice would be the best way of desegregating the schools. Their thought was to let the kids go where they wanted—probably to the school nearest home.

Bootle wrote in one of his decisions: "Freedom of choice, when fully free and unfettered, comports so much more beautifully with the American dream and with the concept of the worth and dignity of the individual than does the suggestion of lifting pupils from their schools and moving them to new schools, regardless of their wishes and regardless of the wishes of their parents." Bell quoted the opinion with discernible relish.

"Alas," Bell continued, "His plan was not to be. The Fifth Circuit Court of Appeals ordered more integration in the Macon system, and Judge Bootle promptly implemented the order of that court. This caused great consternation in Macon, including a march by white citizens on Judge Bootle's home. He stood his ground, entered another order making clear that the law had to be upheld regardless of threats of violence. He was eloquent but forceful in applying the law as perceived by the Supreme Court notwithstanding his own personal concept of freedom of choice to end discrimination." By then Judge Bell was saying to the naysayers, *See, that's what would have been the wise course:*

"This lucid observation by a wise and seasoned judge and leader is now, almost thirty years later, becoming the norm. Neighborhood assignment initially with freedom of choice is more and more the norm in student assignment today. . . . We must leave to history how and when the prayer of the plaintiff children in *Brown* to be allowed to attend the schools nearest their homes was ratcheted up by the Supreme Court—and some lower courts—to forced integration and mandatory busing. History also must provide the answer to whether good or harm resulted from this loss of freedom suffered at the behest of the federal government by two generations of children."

The tone was civil, as befitted the occasion. It was Judge Bootle's day, when the downtown courthouse was named in his honor, not to be torn apart with ugly rhetoric. But it also was a day to point out that there were other answers to the desegregation question. Bell, Bootle, and many others believed that the schools had been damaged almost beyond repair because the justices of the Supreme Court kept overturning plans that would have allowed children to go to the schools nearest their homes.

Judge Bell recalled the fateful days in January 1961, when Judge Bootle held that the state of Georgia could not cut off funding and thereby close the University of Georgia because African-Americans Charlayne Hunter and Hamilton Holmes were enrolling. At the same time, a demonstration at the Athens campus got out of hand and became violent. The state said it would suspend the two students, and they were taken off the campus. Judge Bootle issued an order that reinstated Hunter and Holmes. He wrote that "the constitutional rights of plaintiffs were not to be sacrificed or yielded to violence and disorder . . . nor can the lawful orders of this court be frustrated by violence and disorder."

His summation declared that Judge Bootle had been "a caring and reasonable public official."

❂

The more the Judge got into the question of quality in schools, the more frustrated he became. The imbalances in rural educational opportunities gnawed at him but so did some of the changes that seemed to threaten the best of the old system. Making a speech to a white male audience many years after he had taken off the long black judge's robe for the last time, he said,

> I remember once when I was a judge I was invited to Americus by Gene Wise, who was chairman of the Americus school board to make a speech at the high school. He said I would have to make two speeches—one at the black high school and one at the white high school. I went to the black school first. Every young man there had on a

coat and tie, and they started the service—that's what it was, almost like a church service—by having a prayer followed by a reading of the Scriptures. Then someone introduced me and I made my speech. The audience was very impressive.

I left there and went over to the white Americus High School where I had been a student. Every boy there had on blue jeans and his shirttail out—slovenly looking characters. And this was just at the beginning of the time we were going to integrate the schools. So I said to my friend Gene Wise, "If the blacks take the habits of the whites, we're sunk." The blacks seemed to have better manners and be better dressed than the whites were. Well, that was another era because those black teachers had strict discipline, and they ran their schools really well in Americus.

That was far from his only judgment on the school issue. Indeed, he had been concerned with the poor quality of education of black children for years before the Supreme Court ruling. "In the rural areas the schools were a disgrace; they were an embarrassment. I remember the first time I was conscious of a black school in the country. I was going to law school. I was down in South Georgia somewhere and passed a school with a lot of children in front, and it looked like a shack out in the country, but it was a school building. And I said, 'You know, this is really bad to treat the black children in any such way.'"

❂

As a young man, Griffin Bell had driven past that tumble-down shack and thought, "This is really bad." As a middle-aged federal judge, he had to create workable solutions. Like some of his colleagues on the bench, he agonized over how to reconcile such conflicting views without destroying the entire school system in the Fifth Circuit, covering the southeast.

Years later, a group of thoughtful men who met regularly at Sea

Island asked the Judge to talk about his experiences, and he chose to recall the great struggle over how to bring equality to Southern schools. "What I really want to talk about is the 'dumbing down' of public education in our country," he began.

That has happened over two generations, starting with the *Brown* decision of the Supreme Court in 1954. To better understand where we were then and where we are now, you have to remember that we had no public education when the country was young. The first public education in America was in the cities. . . . But the counties—the rural areas—had no public schools.

Things went along on a segregated basis because no one had ever thought that you had to integrate the schools. . . . Now, in the rural areas the schools were a disgrace; they were an embarrassment. (They would have to be changed.) Well, that idea spread—people all over the country had the same idea, almost simultaneously. A big agitation started over whether you could have separate schools, the idea being that no matter how well the concept of separate but equal was being carried out, it was inherently discriminatory to have black schools and white schools. Well, no one could imagine that we could do away with the dual school system because we had always had dual schools. After all, in the District of Columbia, which of course is owned by the government, they had separate schools. So people really didn't worry much that there was a lot of talk about doing away with segregated schools. . . .

Then, in 1953, the Supreme Court in a unanimous opinion held that separate schools were inherently discriminatory. Well, that set off alarms all over the South and really many other parts of the country as to what was going to happen. *They didn't decide what to do*—they just made that conclusion. . . . In 1954, the Supreme Court had another hearing in *Brown* v. *Board of Education* to decide on the remedy. Here is what the black plaintiffs wanted: They wanted to be able to go to school *nearest their home*. They said having to walk by a white school to get to a black school was not fair. They simply wanted to be able to go to school nearest their home. Think what public education would be today if that's all we had ever done.

The Supreme Court did not define what was to be done—what was meant by desegregation. They just gave an indefinite time to desegregate the schools. That was in 1955, and the methods were left to the lower federal courts.

It was that leeway, and the various ideas that were advanced as to how the decision should be implemented, that caused turmoil in the lower courts, he declared. And it was the cause for so much anguish among the judges, for they became de facto county school administrators for years while they tried to fashion remedies. The Judge pointed out that some school systems decided to integrate one grade per year, and he questioned whether the courts were the right place to find the appropriate response to the multitude of cases building up in the courts. He continued:

Senator [Richard] Russell [Georgia Democrat] made a statement that it would take twenty-five years to desegregate the schools. Well, it turned out to take longer than that, but it was a prophetic statement. Senator Russell opposed many of the civil rights movements, but he said that if we were going to desegregate, it ought to be done by the Congress—there should be a law, not something made up by the courts. When the Public Accommodations Law passed a few years later and the Supreme Court upheld it, he issued a statement saying, "Now that the Congress has acted and the courts have upheld the law as made by the Congress, it is our duty to obey it." We never had any trouble after that with public accommodations.

"But we never had anything but trouble with the school cases," his voice growing graver and deeper now, *"because the judges had gone into the social planning business, as it turned out, and in their own minds didn't exactly know how you desegregated schools."* Most of the judges had neither experience with school administration or with black schools, he added. "Things were being said like, 'Desegregation is easy; just schools is all we want.' Well, what did that mean?"

Like many others, he drew a distinction between *desegregate* and *integrate.* Desegregate meant to many that students would have freedom of choice to go to schools, primarily in their own neighborhoods. Integrate meant to many others that each school in the local system would have to achieve a racial ratio that reflected the total school population in the geographic entity. That, in the Judge's view, was the crucial point. The Fourth Circuit judges in Richmond came down for desegregation. The Fifth Circuit meeting in New Orleans divided, with the majority deciding for integration. Bell was one of the dissenters, believing that desegregation was the desired path. The dispute would consume politicians and activists for years. But the courts had to come to some conclusion relatively quickly. Bell related the story as follows:

> Well, finally, a district judge in Charlotte, Judge McMillan, came up with what is known as a balancing plan. He put a race balance in every school in the Charlotte/Mecklenburg County School District. His order was set aside by the Fourth Circuit Court of Appeals. Meanwhile, in our Fifth Circuit Court, I wrote an opinion involving Orange County, Orlando, which is a county larger than the state of Rhode Island, with more than one hundred school buildings. The ruling we made was that you would be assigned to a school nearest your home. That put blacks and whites together in all the school buildings in the county except three. We [said] that

> if somebody who was in an all-black school or in an all-white school wanted to go to another school where their race was in the minority, they would have the right to what we called the majority to minority transfer.

His white male audience sat quietly as he explained the intricacies of the court procedures. The fateful choice was made by the NAACP Legal Defense Fund lawyers. Those lawyers would have to go to the Supreme Court for adjudication of either the Charlotte plan, with busing of many children, or the Orange County plan, which mostly sent children to the nearest school regardless of race. The Legal Defense Fund lawyers decided to ask the Supreme Court to uphold the Charlotte plan, including busing. That plan was declared constitutional, and, he went on, "so we had to decide whether we would have forced busing." That caused "warfare" among the Fifth Circuit judges, some of whom, like Bell, were very much opposed to busing students. "I never did make a ruling that you had to bus to get a racial balance. I was able to escape that somehow, although our court was divided on the subject."

He recalled talking to two judicial colleagues from that time and saying, "I have been thinking all these years about what a gross violation of the due process of the children it was to order them bused far away from their homes. Their mothers had to get up at least an hour earlier in the morning to get them on the bus, which would haul them for one hour in the morning and one hour in the afternoon, just for the sake of racial integration."

One of the retired judges answered, "You know, that is an interesting argument—I never heard anyone make that argument." To which Bell responded, "Well, if I had thought of it when I was on the court, I would have made that argument myself, but it just came to me later in life."

Bell went on to say, "Right now the public education system is not good, and I hold the court system and Congress responsible for it—Congress because of its inaction and the courts went further than they ought to go in social engineering. For judges, I have always said, the best use of power is not to use it, or to use it as sparingly as possible. That's what we should have done for the schools.

"I must say it was tough not to join in with the idea of total integration for racial balances—the whole country was just wrapped up in that and people overlooked any idea of where it was taking us."

Most of his audience had known him for a long time. None had ever heard a federal judge speak more candidly about what went on in the chambers after the lawyers finished arguing in open court. Nor had they heard enough. Some were young enough to recall their own experiences in those tumultuous days. "I was school-age in 1970, entering the seventh grade," recalled a pillar of the South Georgia community, one whose parents could have chosen to send him to the most expensive private school in the nation, but didn't. "They just took every seventh-grade student in the county and bused us all to what had been the black junior high school. So they didn't worry about racial quotas or anything else, because every single one of us was in one school. They did the same with teachers and staff. I can tell you it was a completely wasted year; it was just terrible."

The way out? Vouchers to pay for education, with a choice as to which school the child would attend. Bell said, "You could get a voucher and go to another public school. You wouldn't have to go to a private school. It would build up competition in the public schools. You [teachers and administrators] would be very embarrassed if all your children left your school to go to another one."

As for his own grandchildren, they "have never been in a public school. I don't think that's really good for the country. They need to learn to deal with people who are products of the public schools. So the voucher is the only thing I know to put competition in, and we know competition makes everything run better."

Answering another question, he held out hope that neighborhood schools "are going to come back." His experience in getting the black and white school board members in Columbus, Georgia, to agree to the concept might prove to be a pilot. "They will end up with one of the better school systems in Georgia," he predicted.

Those hard times dealing with the public schools always remained with him. As a man who thought change should be gradual, he had been depicted as a conservative. And as a Southerner who thought the wrongs ought to be righted in a constructive way, he was attacked as a flaming liberal. His fellow judges had some second thoughts about how they had dealt with him and his opinions.

Judge Wisdom was one of the great liberals on the court, and it was he who argued strongly for the busing of students to achieve integration. Several years later, Wisdom and Bell were having a conversation about their decisions. Bell remembers Wisdom saying, "Now, you know that I didn't set out to ruin the public schools."

To which the Judge rejoined, "But you'll have to admit they are ruined."

His solace, if there is such, was wrapped up in a phrase that came out of the poem "John Brown's Body": "Say not of this time that it is blessed or that it is cursed; only that it is here." The time had come for change, and when it was here, something had to happen.

"The people cared about their schools. But they never heard the judges debate whether the schools would be worse—it was just taken for granted that they would be. We thought so little of the schools that we used them for an experiment. Anybody with one eye and half sense should have known that busing would ruin them. The neighborhood strengths were lost."

❖

Crawfordville is like many other small Georgia towns. A square surrounded by turn-of-the-century buildings. A courthouse in the center of the square. Some run-down houses alongside better dwellings. A relatively large African-American population. With one distinguishing feature: Crawfordville was the hometown of

Alexander H. Stephens, orator, congressman, and ultimately vice president of the Confederate States of America. Stephens is remembered at a National Historic Landmark site that includes his library, many of his furnishings, and some outbuildings.

In the spring of 1965, the nation was beginning the long convulsion over the war in Vietnam. But in Crawfordville and Taliaferro County, the war be damned. They were worried about schools, their segregated schools, their boys and girls going to school together.

Whites wanted segregation to last, and they filed a plan in Washington. The federal government threw it out. Blacks wanted integration to come, with the elimination of Murden High School, their old segregated school. They had lawyers and Dr. Martin Luther King Jr. on their side.

This story exemplifies the confrontations that occurred all over the South in those times: It involved a tiny farm community where violence could erupt at any time. But it also had quirks of its own, including untested maneuvers by white parents to move their children to schools in nearby communities.

With back-to-school time approaching, white parents spirited their children across the county lines to Greene and Warren Counties to register for the new year. All 165 white kids abandoned Murden High School. Blacks knew nothing about those transfers. And so, on the opening day of school, white kids boarded the buses and the black kids found the white school closed; they were without white classmates.

Anybody with even a little intelligence knew this spelled trouble, and it didn't take long to arrive. And everybody knew it would have to be resolved in the federal courts, that is, in the lap of Judge Griffin Bell.

Late in September, the black kids blocked school buses carrying the white kids to nearby Greensboro and Warrenton. State troopers moved the black demonstrators out of the way, but they were adamant that they would not attend a segregated school.

Firebrand civil rights activist Hosea Williams came down from Atlanta to begin organizing the protest. Gov. Carl Sanders told the students the state's compulsory school attendance laws would be enforced, that they must enroll now.

But the black kids came back the next day and tried to board the buses carrying the white students. The troopers kept them off the buses. People talked about "tackle football," meaning policemen tackling black students as they tried to board. Then the black students just lay down in front of the buses. Troopers dragged them out of the wet street, for it had rained that morning, and nobody was hurt.

And then, on October 4, the black demonstrators tried to run past the troopers again. Several were pulled to the ground. A trooper pulled one of the youths back to his feet, and he was grabbed by Calvin Craig, the Georgia Grand Dragon of the Ku Klux Klan. "Kill him, kill him!" John L. Brock Jr. shouted, as witnesses later told the House Un-American Activities Committee. Craig released the youngster and fortunately nobody was hurt.

As events swirled dangerously close to violence, national news crews began to show up. They wanted footage of this drama. And they also wanted to tell a dramatic story that illustrated how the frenzy over the desegregation efforts reached new heights. It was an event that no respectable news organization could ignore. But they would have to endure some hardships with the rest of us. There was one restaurant on the square in Crawfordville, Bonner's. It quickly declared itself a "private club" to keep both reporters and demonstrators out; we would have to eat in Greensboro, fifteen miles away, or go hungry.

Arthur Bolton was the state's attorney general, a cautious man. He petitioned the federal court to enjoin blacks from demonstrating and interfering with the operation of the school system. That was met with derision at the red-brick Friendship Baptist Church, where singing and praying black people met nightly to discuss the situation. After the meetings, they were sometimes led down a blacktop road to the courthouse by Andrew Young, the brilliant strategist who was then Dr. King's principal assistant.

On one of those nights, lit by a clear, full moon, the marchers headed for the courthouse, singing through their fears. Spreading trees cast long shadows in the moonlight. And there lurked danger. State troopers found two white men carrying firearms and took them away. How close were they to firing on the marchers? We never knew.

Another day a white man calling himself Reverend Ward gathered eighteen people on the courthouse lawn and started preaching to them. Black demonstrators chanted and broke up the meeting. Georgia law forbade anyone to interrupt "divine worship." Judge Bell was trying to sort out the mess, and he didn't have a whole lot of faith that this was a serious service. In court, he said, "We may have to bring the Reverend Ward and his congregation here to find out if this was divine worship."

By October 12, dangerous cross-currents threatened the community. Donald L. Hollowell, the handsome and forceful black man who argued so many civil rights cases before accepting a federal government appointment, asked not only that the federal court act, but that the three-judge panel meeting in Augusta be dissolved. In addition to Judge Bell, Judges Frank Scarlett and Lewis R. Morgan comprised the panel. The real motivation was to get Judge Scarlett out of the case. It bears pointing out here that not all federal judges saw these cases the same way; Judge Scarlett once told a new judge the most important thing was to find a big, strong black man (he didn't say "black man") who could take care of his personal needs.

Even while that hearing was underway, all hell was breaking loose in Crawfordville. Brig Cabe, age twenty-three, the black Southern Christian Leadership Conference photographer, was making pictures at the courthouse. A picture that appeared on the front page of many American newspapers the next morning told the story: Cabe fleeing, chased by a white man, Cecil Myers, with fist held high. The *New York Times* headline read, "Klansman Arrested After Attack on Negro Cameraman in Georgia."

Myers and another Klansman were held briefly and released on a hundred dollars' bond. Cabe was arrested and accused of violating a safety ordinance because he had some small firecrackers in his pocket. He was held on five hundred dollars' bond. The discrepancy in treatment of the Klansmen and the black man further inflamed the black community.

A few days later, black Taliaferro County farmer George Turner was forced to drive his car off U.S. Highway 78 by seven white men in three cars. They pointed sawed-off shotguns and pistols at him and tried to make him leave the car, but his brother arrived and the assailants left. The county sheriff came to Turner's defense by saying, "He's just a good ol' darky. He's never caused anybody any trouble."

Law enforcement officers didn't have any trouble finding the wanted men; they were arrested in the café that had become a private club to avoid having to serve reporters and civil rights activists. All seven were identified as Black Shirts, a splinter of the Ku Klux Klan. They were released six hours later on $250 bond each.

Griffin Bell was looking for a solution in a hurry, and he found one. The Georgia Department of Education was granting the county $180,000 in operating funds and $35,000 in transportation funds annually. Without them, the county could not operate its buses, much less its schools. So, the Judge took a page from bankruptcy courts with the concurrence of the other judges. He placed the schools in receivership, with State School Superintendent Claude Purcell as receiver. Work it out so that eighty-seven black students could either attend a desegregated school in Crawfordville or transport them to adjoining counties with the white students who were already being bused there.

On November 17, United Press International told the end of the tale: "Forty-two Negroes boarded white school buses without incident today in [Crawfordville] where repeated demonstrations have been staged over the busing of white students to out-of-county schools. . . . There were no white spectators at the three schools when the Negroes arrived."

LEAVING THE BENCH

After fourteen years, the Judge had tired of listening to arguments that he considered routine, wearied of writing opinions on questions that no longer challenged him intellectually, fretted about the larger world outside his courtroom, thought wistfully of some of the freedoms of becoming a lawyer in private practice, recalled going to Sunday school without the fear of someone saying something inappropriate about court decisions.

The Fifth Circuit was not an especially happy place, either. The judges had worked together for a long time, and inevitably, hard decisions left a residue of distasteful disagreement. This was the hard reality, juxtaposed against another truth: Federal courts of appeals judges simply did not leave their lifetime appointments with guaranteed income and vast powers. What to do?

The Judge was in his Atlanta office one winter's day in 1975 when an attorney from a local firm made an appointment to meet with him. In lawyerly fashion, they chatted amiably for a while and then the visitor came to the point: Would the Judge consider leaving the bench and joining his firm? The Judge said politely "no." The lawyer thanked the Judge for his time and said if he should reconsider, the lawyer would be happy to resume the conversation. "But it got me to thinking," the Judge said.

Management and Budget to general approbation. When Lance told the country, "If it ain't broke, don't fix it," they applauded him. Others were being confirmed with little or no vexation from the Senate.

Just one casualty, former Kennedy speechwriter Ted Sorenson, had to withdraw. Bell and his fellow lawyer Charles Kirbo were influential in that decision. Somehow the vetting process had failed to record Sorenson's background as a conscientious objector in World War II. The Senate simply could not accept that record in a new CIA director, given all the turmoil in the spy agency in recent years. But for the most part the choices for all the major posts were sailing through with little opposition, especially those who had been favored by the liberal wing of the Democratic Party.

To be sure, the Judge was making some headway. The Georgia senators, Herman Talmadge and Sam Nunn, were introducing him, setting up meetings, preparing their own endorsement speeches. Both Talmadge and Nunn were respected figures in the Senate, and they could cash in a few chips. Eugene Patterson, formerly the editor of the *Atlanta Constitution*, had known the Judge when he worked in Atlanta. Now Patterson wrote a long piece for the *Washington Post*, which said, "When the dust settles, Bell is likely to be seen for what he is: an able and incorruptible lawyer of the highest character and integrity and a principled man, who on the balance of his actions over the last two decades, can be depended upon to demand that civil rights laws be obeyed." In his home state, premier political columnist Bill Shipp of the *Constitution*, wrote, "Griffin Bell not only witnessed his Southland in torment, he played a significant role insuring equal rights for all in restoring a measure of tranquillity and order to the seething region."

Now the showdown approached. It was time for Bell to go to the big room where the Judiciary Committee met. He would insist on sitting alone at the witness table, fearless, no bulging briefing books in front of him and no aides with whom to whisper before answering. A somber man, a man ready to answer, a man wounded by attacks that he considered both unfounded and underhanded. In a deep bass voice that was unaccustomed to rushing, that demanded attention, he would supply quick responses to the charges people were making. The Public Broadcasting System would carry the hearings to the nation. A ring of photographers would capture almost every hand movement or change of expression. Star newspaper reporters would sit behind him carefully noting slips of the tongue as well as eloquent answers.

The preliminaries over, liberal Republican senator Charles Mathias of Maryland, an erudite and thoughtful public servant, began the tough questioning. Mathias was no demagogue; he had opposed much of what the Nixon administration stood for, and he said so with eloquence. As a lawyer, he had a reputation for knowing much about the Constitution. A seasoned campaigner with a sense of what his constituents wanted, particularly those in Baltimore, he was as tough as any Democrat in looking for disagreements with the Supreme Court and the Constitution in the Judge's opinions. He would prove to be one of the most difficult interrogators.

What about the Julian Bond decision? Mathias read verbatim from Bell's opinion, "Mr. Bond's right to speak and dissent as a private citizen is subject to the limitation that he sought to assume membership in the house." The crux of the Bell opinion was that the Georgia Legislature could decide whether to seat a member because of his own actions. Mathias said, "I find that somewhat disturbing. I am wondering whether you adhere to that rule today."

After reviewing the case and pointing out that the Supreme Court had reversed his decision, the Judge said, "It is quite obvious that we were wrong and that the Supreme Court was right about it. . . . I think that everyone who has studied my record picks out opinions that are against me and they say nothing about 490 opinions that might favor me. But if you will study my record, you will find that I am very strong on freedom of speech, freedom to assemble, freedom to petition the government for grievances." The answer would not silence his critics.

When Bond came to the committee, he pointed out that President-elect Carter's slogan was, "Why not the best?" And he went on, "Judge Bell is not the best." Outside the hearing room, Bond talked to reporters who asked whether the Judge was a racist. "I don't think he's a bigot. I think he's a turkey."

Senator Mathias had more on his mind than the Bond case. He was concerned that the Judge had been a principal adviser to former Georgia governor Vandiver, who had won the office on the famous campaign promise that "no, not one" black student would be integrated into a white school. It was called the "massive resistance" strategy. And the question was whether the Judge had been the principal architect of that plan, since he was the chief of staff in the Vandiver administration.

Mathias also questioned how the Judge could have been in favor of G. Harrold Carswell as a Justice of the Supreme Court. That dragged up one of the celebrated fights in Senate history. The senators were beginning to ask about other court decisions, about his leisure time, about his affiliations. The questions were coming in jagged shards, with none being fully explored before the next subject was introduced. And they left a confused picture.

Summing up what he was hearing in the early committee testimony, Ted Kennedy said,

Much of the legislation which was initiated during your service as one of Governor Vandiver's principal legal advisers was overruled by the Supreme Court. If one were to take your work during that period, your membership in the various private clubs, your recommendation on the Carswell nomination, and Julian Bond case, and others, I think a fair conclusion would be that you are not identified as being in the forefront of civil rights. . . . I am interested in your response as to why the people of this country—particularly

the poor, the black, the Indians, and the women . . . should
have confidence in you as a protector of their rights?

The Judge gave an answer that was tepid in national politics but
straightforward in terms of Southern attitudes. "It is only fair to say
that I have never professed to be an activist. I have never professed
to be an extreme liberal. I have always thought that it is only moderates that should be on the bench, that you ought not to be to the
right or to the left if you are trying to judge matters."

The result of that testimony drew a four-column headline on
page one of the *Washington Post* that read: "Bell, at Hearing, Calls
Self a Moderate." In the South, that was the working description of
someone who was willing to follow the law of the land. To the rest
of the nation, it probably sounded like a cop-out.

But the committee wanted to go further into the question of
how he had chosen to write a letter of support for Carswell. For that
discussion, he was well prepared. Former clerk Neal Batson had
compiled a background report that recalled that Carswell ran for
the Georgia Legislature in 1948 (well before the Supreme Court
school desegregation decisions). Carswell had said, "I am a
Southerner by ancestry, birth, training, inclination, belief and practice. I believe that segregation of the races is proper and the only
practical and correct way of life in our states. I have always so
believed, and I shall always so act." That was the speech that
blocked his confirmation to the Court seventeen years later.

Exasperation could be heard in the Judge's voice when he
answered, "When I die, I am sure they will have on my tombstone:
'He wrote a letter for Judge Harrold Carswell.' I will have to keep
answering it. I want to answer it." Bell explained that he and
Carswell had been classmates at the Mercer University law school.
He said they had visited in each other's homes. When Carswell was
appointed a district judge, Bell wrote a letter in support. The same
was true when he joined the appellate court. "It is just a part of my
record that I will have to stand on," he said wearily.

For once, the Senate helped his answer. Bayh said instead of his tombstone saying he wrote the letter, "I would hope that they would put on it: 'Here lies a good attorney general.'"

"That would suit me a lot better," a smiling Judge replied.

But would the Judge be willing to bring black people into the Justice Department? That had been a refrain from the moment the nomination was announced. He had, in fact, already chosen Judge Wade H. McCree, a black Sixth Circuit judge who lived in Detroit, as the solicitor general. But Bell and McCree had agreed that they would not make a public announcement because, Bell said, "I would rather not be the attorney general than to go in on somebody else's record. I do not think a nation needs a weak attorney general."

The senators were persistent, asking, "Can you tell us what color he [the solicitor general] is?" The Judge told them his choice was Judge McCree without ever saying the word "black." It was as if he had willed himself to select the person rather than allowing him to represent a segment of the population. Although he didn't disclose the fact to the committee, he had also already chosen Drew S. Days III, a young black lawyer for the NAACP Legal Defense Fund, as the first of his race to head the civil rights division. He had seen Days in action arguing cases before the Fifth Circuit and had been impressed. Days would go on to serve as solicitor general in the first Clinton administration, but his name was not pried from Bell during the confirmation hearings.

Now it was time to return to the question of whether it was appropriate for the Judge to be a member of private clubs that had no minority members. Sen. Donald Riegle of Michigan, one of the outspoken foes, asked the status. The Judge gave a detailed answer: He had joined the Capital City Club in 1955 while he was in the private practice of law. The club had a downtown facility "where you have lunch and dinner." It also had "a golf course. I play golf." A year later, "I joined a club called Piedmont Driving Club, which is probably the oldest club in Atlanta." He had maintained membership as a judge, although he was now an honorary member "like nonmember judges, ministers, a few other groups, and the governor."

Private clubs had not been at the forefront of his thinking recently. "When I was asked to be attorney general, I had a lot of things to decide, including things like conflict of interest, or whether I wanted to do it, or could afford to do it, or not. I had really not got around to thinking about the clubs." Then the newspapers disclosed that he was a member, and controversy inevitably followed. After a day or two of "tossing over in my mind what I ought to do," Mary entered the discussion. She remembered that "during the Kennedy administration there was some complaint raised about Robert Kennedy for being a member of a club here in Washington. She remembers that. Whether it's true or not, I do not know."

At which point Ted Kennedy interjected, "He resigned."

"That's what she remembered," the Judge said. "We decided that inasmuch as the attorney general is so symbolic of equal justice under the law, then I ought to resign from the clubs, and I intend to do that. Let me add one other thing, because there has been a lot said about this and a lot written about it. I don't judge other people about this. When I went on the court—I grew up in a segregated society—when I went on the court, I was a member of a segregated church. I was a member of a segregated state bar association. I was a member of a segregated Atlanta Bar Association and the Lawyers' Club. They all integrated. . . . I thought it was wrong for the Lawyers' Club not to be integrated. I never went to a meeting for three years there. I helped some lawyers propose a person who is now a black judge in Atlanta. . . . I drew a difference, though, between the social club and the Lawyers' Club. . . . As for social clubs, I thought that you had a right under the freedom of association to be a member of a social club if I ever did think about it very much."

In Atlanta, Bell's fellow club members were asking, "Why us?" With thousands of clubs throughout the nation containing restrictive language in their by-laws or exclusionary votes when minorities were proposed, the Atlantans felt put upon. They had removed the language. Blacks were brought to the clubs as guests of members. Atlanta had advertised itself as "the city too busy to hate." It had desegregated its buses, then its schools. Minorities were being elected to public office.

A black middle class was emerging. The historically black colleges—Morehouse, Spelman, Morris Brown, and others—were producing quality graduates. The city had, in fact, made remarkable progress. Now its reputation was being sullied because a member of the clubs was being proposed for high federal office. If some critics from the rest of the country could just see what progress had been made, they told themselves, this fault-finding would stop. But of course it would not, because all of America was having to reevaluate what it thought about these issues, and it was less painful to point fingers than to deal with one's own situation.

As the committee moved from Bell's club memberships to his political positions, it confronted a much more difficult question. What had the Judge done in 1958 to help Ernest Vandiver get elected governor? And why had Vandiver chosen him to become chief of staff? Was the Judge implicated in the strategy of massive resistance? Did he try to create circumstances to deny equal education to black children? These were questions that the committee had to wrestle to a conclusion. And they were being advised by people of all persuasions.

The Judge said, "I think I more than any other person kept the schools open." He described himself as "a moderating force." He talked about Georgia parents whose feelings were so bitter that closing the schools was more desirable than desegregating them. He had been an architect of the Sibley Commission "to let the people speak to their elected representatives. We were trying to change the customs of centuries, and I thought if the people could somehow make their voices heard, it would save the schools."

The commission, which had held statewide hearings and

which had recommended that local school systems be given the right to operate desegregated schools, had been seen in Georgia as a moderating force. More than eighteen hundred citizens had spoken their minds in eleven different hearings, spread throughout all of the state's congressional districts. Approximately 55 percent of those testifying thought it would be better to abandon the public schools than to have black and white children attend together; 45 percent said the public schools should remain open. The final report had much of the language of the 1950s, saying that no child should be forced to attend an integrated school against the will of his parents. But it went on to talk about the desirability of public schools, and it ventilated public feelings when no other forum existed. It was the Judge's creation, and more than anything else it caused segregationists to stop and consider what the loss of the public schools might mean to the state and its young people.

By 1977, witnesses before the Senate could read the record of the proceedings entirely differently. Nearly two decades of constant debate had changed not only minds, but also the language, of the great debate. Disbelievers felt the Sibley Commission was "a more sophisticated attempt to evade the court's decision." Clarence Mitchell, the distinguished director of the Washington bureau of the NAACP, was one. The Judge, Mitchell said, was "among those who were fashioning programs of resistance for the purpose of trying to see that the Supreme Court's decision was not carried out."

The *Washington Post* by now was reporting that "liberal members of the committee put particular emphasis on questioning Bell about his role as a legal adviser to former Governor Ernest Vandiver's 'massive resistance' to school desegregation during the 1950s and to his 1970 recommendation of G. Harrold Carswell for the Supreme Court."

In response to that and other criticism, the Judge said, "I do not have any regrets about participating in the Vandiver administration.

I think I made a valuable contribution to the times I was in. But that doesn't mean my views haven't changed. I hope I've grown some."

Witnesses were beginning to vie with each other to see who could make the stronger case. Joseph L. Rauh Jr., a celebrated legal activist and former chairman of the Americans for Democratic Action, called the Judge "a man who gave aid and comfort to the segregationists of this country." Rep. Parrin J. Mitchell, the black delegate from Baltimore, called him "the mastermind of Georgia's massive resistance."

But Howard Cochrane, the founder of the Atlanta Negro Voters League and a notable in Georgia politics, came to Bell's aid, saying, "He asked us for help to buy time. He told us he was trying to convince Vandiver to change his position again, that desegregation was the law of the land and would have to be accepted."

Lonnie King, who headed the Atlanta chapter of the NAACP, said he had not intended to testify, but after hearing the testimony of others, "It was clear to me that Judge Bell was going to get a bum rap [on schools]." He recalled going to a meeting where the Judge spoke to both blacks and whites. "His message to that group was unmistakably clear; school desegregation was an established fact of life, the law of the land, and they had best prepare for it because it was here to stay."

Race continued to be the fulcrum for the seesaw in the hearings. Nonetheless, one of the most persistent questions remained his closeness to Carter. The committee believed that they had been very close, and that Bell had raised huge sums for the campaign. Sen. John Heinz of Pennsylvania, in particular, returned frequently to the question of how instrumental the Judge had been. "Are you in position," Heinz asked, "to make available to the committee what individuals or special interest groups or political action committees you might have solicited, either successfully or unsuccessfully, on behalf of Governor Carter?"

"I haven't got my [earlier] testimony," he answered. "I think I said I did not solicit anyone. I gave one thousand dollars." He went on to use some dry humor to try to brighten the dour hearings. "We were very proud of Governor Carter in Georgia during this time. We still are. But this was the first time we ever had a chance to get back into the Union. I might say it's hard to get back all the way." For once, there was laughter in the committee room.

Across the country, sides were being taken. "Hearing Out Griffin Bell" was the headline on the *Post's* editorial:

> There are, as we understand it, two main reasons why Griffin Bell, Jimmy Carter's choice to be Attorney General, has been questioned so closely by the Senate Judiciary Committee this week. One is doubt about his commitment to a society free of institutional racial discrimination. The other is fear that his ties to Mr. Carter are too strong to permit him to run the Justice Department in a properly apolitical way. While both are legitimate concerns, it seems to us that Mr. Bell's testimony over the past couple of days has tended to resolve them in his favor. . . . Even so, the inquiry into Mr. Bell's past record and present commitment on the question of racial justice has been useful. . . . The Senate inquiry has . . . sharpened the public commitment of Mr. Bell *and* the senators to the pursuit of this nation's unfinished racial business. [Italics theirs]

If the principal paper in the nation's capital was leaning toward support, there was less enthusiasm elsewhere. Writing in the review section of the *New York Times* on Sunday, columnist Anthony Lewis assessed the week's hearings:

> Judge Bell answered freely, indeed volubly, seldom ducking behind the usual excuse of delicacy or inadequate information. He appeared eager to please his liberal questioners, sometimes smothering them with helpful answers before

they could get out their specific questions. He said among many other things that he would enforce civil rights and antitrust laws vigorously, press with criminal investigations of intelligence abuses, support the Equal Rights Amendment and order Justice Department lawyers to keep logs on contacts with the White House or other outside influences.

And then, using the columnist's prerogative to close with a stinger, Lewis wrote, "But facile promises may not mean too much in practice."

The public hearings went on for a while. Jesse Jackson, as president of Operation PUSH, came to say that President Carter should withdraw the nomination because it "does not represent moral consistency on the part of Mr. Carter." Failing the president-elect's action, the Judge "should sense that his nomination has already been a divisive factor for the coalition of persons who elected Mr. Carter president, and therefore should of his own volition remove himself from consideration."

Jackson's demand surely was more out of touch with reality than anything else in the hearing. The Judge had been pilloried by too many people, had suffered at the hands of too many witnesses, had stayed up too many nights talking to friend and foe, to simply walk away. A man who had come from an apprenticeship as a Frigidaire salesman to the verge of the highest legal office in the land, he had no patience with such talk and thought it just plain silly.

The *Times* still had not weighed in with its recommendation. Two days before the committee was to vote, it came to a convoluted conclusion:

Some of the reappraisals have been reassuring. Judge Bell now thinks, for example, that his earlier views of the Presidential power to tap telephones were too expansive and that warrants should be required in all such cases. Also, he now says that his view of the First Amendment was too narrow when he voted to affirm the Georgia legislature's right to exclude Julian Bond for antiwar sentiments. And, happily, the nominee changed his mind about taking a leave of absence from discriminating clubs and plans resignations. Nevertheless, the weight and number of positions that had to be changed to square with contemporary standards for an Attorney General are somewhat troubling. . . . Perhaps the best result now will be for senators who still share those doubts to vote "no" to reinforce the debate of recent weeks and to remind Judge Bell and President Carter that their Department of Justice must redeem some weighty promises.

From the rest of the nation, there were mixed reviews. Steve Strasser interviewed many people for a piece in the *Miami Herald* and concluded,

> Bell left the bench . . . after 15 years as an appellate judge. He had helped shape 3,000 decisions, personally wrote more than 500, and streamlined court procedures for handling appeals. . . . A look at his record, and interviews with those who appeared in his court, reveal the portrait of a respected, moderate, and sometimes innovative judge who can claim a share of the court's civil rights accomplishments in a set of decisions that changed the ways of places like Lexington, Miss.; Uvalde, Tex.; Alachua County, Fla.; and Fort Valley, Ga.

In those and a hundred other little communities and bigger towns in the South, lives had changed. The Judge had not liked some of the change. He was convinced that the Supreme Court had made a colossal error in ruling that neighborhood schools did not achieve an acceptable level of integration. Neither did many of the parents like the idea that their children would be transported an hour or more from home to attend school, then face the same hour being transported back home. But when people looked into the record, the fair-minded ones concluded he had followed and applied the law of the land. White Southerners thought he was too liberal; people who made their way to the Senate hearing room generally depicted him as too conservative. Now it was time for the committee to say what it thought.

Chairman Eastland called it to order at five minutes after four on January 19, 1977, just days before a new president would be sworn into office. In his Mississippi drawl, the chairman said, "The question is: Is the nominee to be approved, and has the chairman the right, when the name comes up, to report him forthwith to the Senate with the recommendation that he be approved?" Sen. Strom Thurmond of South Carolina renewed his motion that the Judge be approved. But there was one last piece of business; Senator Mathias had one last statement: "I must say that my opinion has shifted back and forth in weighing the evidence. This afternoon I asked myself if this nomination were made by a Republican President, would I advise him to go forward with it. I have thought of the votes that I have cast against Judge Haynsworth and the votes that I have cast against Judge Carswell. I must say, Mr. Chairman, that I would find it impossible to advise the President to go forward with this nomination."

Senator Kennedy took another tack. He had been disappointed with some of the answers to civil rights questions, but he did not question "the fundamental character and integrity of this nominee." He heard commitments to "programs [that] affect the people of this country." And so, "it is on that basis of his commitment to those areas that I will vote in support of the nomination."

As dusk came to Washington just days before the new administration would take office, Chairman Eastland finally ordered the call of the roll. Ten senators voted aye. Just three Republicans—Mathias, Chafee of Rhode Island, and Heinz of Pennsylvania—voted no. Senator Riegle of Michigan voted present. The nomination went to the Senate, where the result was a foregone conclusion. The government took a few days off to install a new president. And then the Senate prepared to vote.

Indiana Democrat Birch Bayh was the floor manager for the nominee. He spoke forcefully for Bell's nomination and then was questioned sharply by Edward W. Brooke of Massachusetts, the only black Republican senator, about the Judge's commitment to equal rights and his role as chief of staff to Governor Vandiver.

An exasperated Bayh said, "Look, if the senator wants to demagogue this, go ahead . . ."

Brooke broke in sharply, "I've never been a demagogue in my life. I'm not being a demagogue."

"This all took place twenty-five years ago in Atlanta," Bayh countered.

Later Bayh and Brooke agreed that Bayh had spoken "with passion" and that the exchange would be deleted from the record. But it remained a memory with those who had witnessed the long drama of the hearings.

Finally, on January 25, the Senate voted 75–21 to confirm, with five Democrats breaking ranks to vote against the nominee of the new Democratic president.

❂

What had it felt like to undergo such a fierce interrogation about his entire life? "I told people then I would have withdrawn except that it would embarrass the president. I don't believe any American should have to take such abuse. It was so bad, I finally asked Chairman Eastland to be excused from the hearings."

But he didn't withdraw, and he did take away some remembrances of good things that happened. For example, he recalls Billy McKinney, a black state legislator from Georgia (and the father of Cynthia McKinney, who was later elected to Congress), who rode the bus to Washington to testify for him. The Judge recalled that someone said to McKinney that Coretta Scott King was opposed to the nomination, to which McKinney had replied, "What has she been elected to?"

Along with the rancor, there was the partisan politics. Bell said, "A lot of Republicans voted against me. They felt they had to knock out one Carter nominee. Even Bob Dole voted against me. Later he said that was the only vote he cast in the Senate that he wished he could take back."

And he won many converts later. One was Mathias. "He had us out to his farm in Maryland after that. I remember the peacocks wandering into and out of the kitchen while we were cooking hamburgers and hot dogs." Mathias said later on the Senate floor that he had been wrong in his harsh early judgment about Bell.

Bell observed later, "I got started out on the wrong foot with the Senate. It was the clubs. Just a few days after the president made his announcement about me, Bert Lance announced that he was going to resign from the clubs. Then President Carter resigned from the Americus Country Club. Imagine that!"

Years later, he recalled a meeting he had in the Georgia Highway Department in Atlanta. Present were Jim Gillis, the longtime head of the department, and Dixon Oxford, a member of the board that ran the place. They were friends of Governor Vandiver. Bell was his chief of staff. They asked him to come to Gillis's office. "They said, 'You're ruining Vandiver trying to keep the schools open.' I said, 'No, I'm trying to save him. He's in a terrible fix. He's got to follow the law.' They thought I was too liberal. But you can't tell all that in the hearings."

He was just glad to have the hearings behind him so that he could get on with the tumultuous business of running the department. Among the toughest jobs was getting morale up, particularly in the FBI. And so he hit the road whenever he could, visiting outlying areas and promising very little more than a politics-free department that would dispense justice evenhandedly.

On, then, to the ceremony that marks the beginning of a cabinet officer's tenure. The Judge didn't have time for a glorious celebration with champagne (or his favorite, a glass of Scotch and water). He had promised that the front doors of the department would swing wide to symbolize his belief that this was the people's business, to be conducted in public. "We had to have some sort of ceremony," Terry Adamson recalled.

To follow through on the promise, on January 25, 1977, the new president came through the opened doors to administer the oath of office. Accompanying the president into the Great Hall were Chief Justice Warren Burger and Burger's young law clerk, Kenneth Starr.

In the audience were two people who, probably more than any others, understood the significance of the occasion. One was Elbert Tuttle, the chief judge of the Fifth Circuit and one of a handful who had enforced the law of the land in the Southern school cases. The other was John Sibley, by then a little shaky of step and slowed by age. Sibley had led the school commission that enabled Georgia to keep its public schools open. His group's report had been characterized in the hearings as an attempt to circumvent the law. Those who had lived through that time had another view; without the Sibley hearings that vented so much concern and anger, the fate of the Georgia schools could have been much worse. Tuttle had declined an invitation from Senator Mathias to testify against Bell and had come to witness his swearing-in. Sibley had come to the occasion willingly, even though he had been insulted during the hearings. The Judge never forgot to express his appreciation for their presence.

The Great Hall was filled to overflowing. The other cabinet members had already been sworn in. The Carter administration filled out its top ranks when the Judge raised his hand and swore to uphold the Constitution in the presence of the statues of Lady Justice.

To many in the rest of the nation, particularly the moderates and liberals who wanted civil rights to be guaranteed to all, the

If the President were indicted and convicted of a felony, such as perjury or obstruction of justice or witness tampering, before impeachment proceedings began, would anyone argue that he should continue to be President? I don't think so. If the President were subsequently indicted and convicted of a felony, which the Constitution clearly allows, would anyone argue that he should continue to be President? I don't think so. A President cannot faithfully execute the laws if he himself is breaking them. Since this is such a fundamental concept, an impeaching body might well limit itself to inquiring into allegations of conduct that clearly constitutes a high crime. Without this limitation on the inquiry, the process could be viewed as politically driven and arguably outside the bounds of the Constitution. Congress should be at pains to spare the nation a debate over partisanship in assessing the validity of charges involving felonious conduct by the President.

The statutes against perjury, obstruction of justice, and witness tampering rest on vouchsafing the element of truth in judicial proceedings—civil and criminal and particularly in the grand jury. Allegations of this kind are grave indeed.

What he did not express to the House Judiciary Committee was his utter disgust and contempt for a president who he believed had vilified Ken Starr, lied to the grand jury, and dishonored both his office and the Constitution.

❂

In the summer of 1979, the president's popularity was falling. The polls were saying that his ability to fix everything from gasoline shortages to inflation was in doubt. And the president himself was dissatisfied with several of his cabinet officers, as well as with his prospects for reelection. Calling his cabinet and top-level White

House staff to Camp David for a long series of strategy sessions, the president embarked on a new course. He would rebuild the cabinet and staff, eliminating some of the most contentious members. After twelve days of these sessions, the president went to the nation to speak of a "crisis of confidence." He meant the nation as a whole, not his staff. He made the word "malaise" a part of the political lexicon. And his standing in the polls plummeted.

On July 17, 1979, after the Camp David sessions were over, the senior officials were called to a meeting "for principals only" at the White House. That meant the support staffers who usually went to cabinet meetings were not invited. The president spoke for a long time, and cabinet members began to talk about offering their resignations. Which was exactly what the president wanted. Someone said the president had their promises to resign if he wanted them out. Secretary of State Cyrus Vance argued that the oral assurances should be sufficient. Wait a minute, the Judge said. Ever the practical one, he suggested it would be much better if everyone submitted a written resignation and the president chose which ones he wished to accept. He didn't push the point; some chose to write and others gave verbal assurances. In all, thirty-four proud men and women said they would leave if the president desired it.

He did choose. He replaced Joseph A. Califano as secretary of health, education, and welfare. He fired W. Michael Blumenthal, the secretary of the treasury. James R. Schlesinger Jr. resigned as energy secretary, and Brock Adams was forced out as transportation secretary. Also gone was Andrew Young, the ambassador to the United Nations, whose meeting with Palestinian leader Yasir Arafat had created great unrest amongst supporters of Israel.

The Judge was not one of those whose neck was on the block. He had said repeatedly he would not stay for the full four-year term of the president; he wanted to return to Atlanta. But he chose to leave what he called "the greatest job in the world" at the same time the other cabinet officers were dismissed. In fact, he had sent a letter of resignation to the president seven months earlier, but the president had talked him out of resigning at that time.

In the confusion, the public got the impression that Carter had fired him. Protest letters came to the White House. The president asked that he send a second letter of resignation, which he did. The president then responded in such a way that the public knew that Bell had not been dismissed. He promised to stay until his successor had been confirmed by the Senate. Dated August 2, 1979, the second letter reflects both his strong belief that the Justice Department had recovered and his desire to get back to the private practice of law:

> As we have discussed, I hereby formally tender my resignation as Attorney General of the United States, which will be effective upon the appointment and qualification of my successor. . . . As a lawyer and citizen, this has been the highest privilege of my life. For 30 months I have been the lawyer for the people of the United States. The work has been hard; the challenges have been great; and I have given my best effort. . . . When you asked me to undertake this responsibility, I told you I would stay on the job until I could warrant to you that the Department of Justice was strong, running well, and an institution of which you and the American people could be proud. In asking you earlier this year for my release and return to the private sector, I gave you that representation, and I now leave the Department knowing that it is in the hands of good and strong men and women whom you have placed in its top leadership positions and that it is staffed by professionals.
>
> You have been a bulwark of strength to me in leading the Department. I have carried out your direction to develop traditions of excellence and independence in the Department and you, indeed all Americans, can have the satisfaction of knowing that these traditions will be demanded practices for

many years to come. Finally, I simply want to state that serving in your Cabinet has been a great personal honor. I value my friendship with you, and I hope that you will call upon me whenever I can be of service.

To which the president responded with a handwritten note expressing his "genuine regret" that the Judge was resigning to go home and resume his practice, as well as thanking him for serving his country well. That handwritten note would become the focal point in one of the important conference rooms at King & Spalding in Atlanta.

As for a successor, his deputy Benjamin Civiletti was a shoo-in. The cantankerous Senate Judiciary Committee that had given Bell such a tough time before his confirmation was impressed with the shape of the Justice Department now. It had three partial days of hearings and recommended unanimously that Civiletti be confirmed. The *New York Times,* which had wrestled with Bell's confirmation hearings, commented, "In letting Attorney General Griffin Bell have his wish to depart, Mr. Carter also let him pass the Justice Department to his deputy, Benjamin Civiletti. There's no discernible meaning in that switch; the significance will lie in who becomes the new Number Two at Justice."

Civiletti was a striking contrast to Bell. He came from Peekskill, New York, not the South; boasted degrees from Johns Hopkins University and the University of Maryland law school, not small schools. He was a federal prosecutor for a time, then joined the Baltimore firm of Venable, Baetjer & Howard. Brusque where Bell was slow-talking, people began to call him "Uncivil-Civiletti." He had not been a federal judge and was not well known to Carter.

But he had one overwhelming attribute: Bell believed in him. Charlie Kirbo, the president's confidant and the Judge's law partner, had tried a case with him and recommended him. If Kirbo thought somebody was a good man, neither Carter nor Bell was likely to disagree; they had more faith in Kirbo than almost anybody else.

How the Judge worked his initial drafting as his deputy was

typical of his methods of persuasion. Civiletti outlined it years later for the *District of Columbia Bar Report*:

> I was a little ambivalent because I was reasonably successful in the law firm, and I had one child entering high school, one in grammar school and my oldest was preparing to enter college in a year. I had not followed the Department of Justice closely since 1965, [when he resigned as a U.S. attorney] although I was certainly interested in public service. I was encouraged by the Carter administration and Attorney General Griffin Bell's attitude toward the administration of justice, especially after the negative impact of Watergate. . . . Leaving a lucrative private practice, coming to Washington with children in their formative years, and having a lack of experience at the Justice Department made me feel somewhat uncertain.
>
> When I voiced these concerns to Griffin Bell, he said, "Let me worry about whether or not you know enough about the Department of Justice. As to finances, you can always make more money when you leave the government. And you'll be there when your children need you whether you're in government or private practice."

By then, however, Bell was getting very, very good at the patriotic argument as the clincher: "He said, 'There's an overwhelming reason to join the Department of Justice—you will serve your country.' Griffin Bell is very persuasive. I thought about it and then called him back to say I was willing to serve." Maybe Griffin Bell would have made a great Firestone tire salesman, after all.

Bell and Civiletti had worked together, Carter had gotten to know the deputy, some of the senators were impressed, and there was no serious objection to his confirmation. He would move into the big office and unshackle the man who wanted to go home to Atlanta.

And so the Bells moved out of the Watergate, leaving their neighbors Sen. Bob Dole and his wife, Liddy, as well as a host of other notables. In a way, it was a great relief. Mary had never spent much time in Washington, both because of family illnesses and because she just preferred Georgia, and the Judge had commuted to Atlanta many weekends. Never one to take much notice of trappings, he nevertheless carried with him many memories.

"It was sad to be leaving," he remembered. "Being attorney general was the best job I ever had. But I knew I should leave."

Before leaving, however, his enthusiastic supporters in the Justice Department would insist on a gala party in the courtyard. The fountain played, the sun shone, the statue of Bobby Kennedy reminded many of the Judge's early support of President Kennedy, and speakers talked about how he had brought professionalism back to the fore. Bittersweet though it was, the time had come to leave the trappings of Washington, the glare of publicity, the power to command an audience for whatever he said. Many who come to the capital never go home again. They open offices, hire out as lawyers or lobbyists, trade on their connections and live still near the vortex of power. Along K Street, they lunch with the new government officials, talk about policy, and work for (sometimes unseen) clients. Not Griffin Bell. He had come to town, done his work, established himself as an excellent attorney general, and enjoyed one last party before going home. To another party. A great big one. At the Piedmont Driving Club, where his membership had caused so much trouble at his confirmation hearings. The irony was not lost on his Atlanta neighbors, who welcomed him home with Southern backslapping and expressions of distaste for Washington "and all that political crowd."

❁

"I knew I should leave," he said. The pull of his old law partners was important. Two groups came to him from King & Spalding to insist that he return. They cited some internal stresses that were tearing at the collegiality of the firm. They cited individual cases—which the Judge guarded with privacy while talking about the overall problem.

Some senior members of the firm had grown to have great power in Atlanta, representing huge businesses and bringing in huge fees. These seniors believed that they should make the firm's policies and reap the financial benefits of their years of work. "I feared the firm might break up over accountability," the Judge said. "The junior members saw it as a self-protection society."

And so he dug into the toughest of all management jobs in a law firm. "For two years I was the sole judge setting everybody's points [their percentage share of the firm's profits]. I was both the insider and the outsider because I had been away." One of the first things he made clear was that he would not take more money than the other most senior members of the firm, even though he had more responsibility. Another was that he tried to open up ongoing dialogue within the firm. But some of the old-timers didn't much care for giving their compensation powers over to him. "Mary told me if I died, I couldn't get any of the partners to be pallbearers," he laughed.

Aside from his need to return to King & Spalding, there was another reason for him to leave Washington. Some regarded him as an especially close friend of President Carter. That happened not to be the case; although they worked closely together, they were not particularly good friends in either the social or political sense. The Judge was more gregarious; Carter was more likely to avoid a party-like atmosphere. The Judge was more conservative politically. Still, there was the all-important perception of Southern buddies trying to forge another political campaign victory. "I needed to get out of the Justice Department because President Carter was getting ready to run again. His enemies could accuse me of doing things to help the reelection, and I didn't want that. We had worked very hard to get the Justice Department out of politics."

So he left. He didn't take anything back to Atlanta, not even the longhand notes he had left-handedly written in the margins of the memos from his staff. "I didn't want to go through the hassle" of getting clearance to remove his papers from government facilities. "They are in storage somewhere," he said with a shrug.

And back to Atlanta the Bells came, there to resume the Judge's remarkable success as a lawyer, there to allow Mary to return to her circle of Atlanta friends. And there to begin sketching the plans for the second home they would build at Sea Island. They already owned the site. Visiting with lawyer friends at the island off the Georgia coast in 1975, the Judge went walking with his usual abundance of energy. He found a lot on Thirteenth Street that suited his fancy and bought it for thirty-two thousand dollars—an incredible bargain after prices soared on the little barrier island.

Initially Mary had wanted an "old Virginia house." But the Judge and an Atlanta architect sketched out a low tabby structure that picks up the sunrise over the marsh and basks in the glow of sunset across the front. Mary decided she liked the house and furnished it with upholstered rockers, white wicker chairs, country tables, soft carpeting—just the kind of retreat they both wanted. The family room has a cozy fireplace, and "he would build a fire in the summertime if he could stand it," Mary said.

The Judge had acquired some background in world affairs while he remained in office. The Cold War held the world's concern then, and negotiations with the Soviets continued. Along with Terry Adamson and Fred Baron, Bell went to Moscow during his tenure as attorney general to speak with Premier Kosygin. To break the social ice, Bell presented the premier with a coffee-table book about Georgia. The premier flipped to photographs of the Okefenokee Swamp and declared he would not care to live there. In exchange, Bell received a three-volume set of the premier's speeches, autographed with the comment that they would help if he had trouble sleeping.

The serious purpose of the trip was to speak with the Russians about accepting some of the Chinese boat people fleeing their country. Russia and China had tensions of their own, of course, and Kosygin informed Bell, "We have all the Chinese we want." End of serious negotiation.

Late in President Carter's term, Bell was appointed head of the American delegation to the Conference on Security and Cooperation in Europe, meeting in Madrid. For several months he shuttled back and forth between Atlanta and Brussels or Madrid.

After one of his speeches to delegates from the thirty-five nations, the Hungarians approached and shook his hand in a congratulatory manner. That miffed the Czechoslovakians because he had not shaken the hand of their delegate, who also was the ambassador to Washington. While it was no major diplomatic blowup, it did create temporary tensions. Bell's connections again proved to be helpful.

The head of the Czech delegation inquired whether Bell knew of the King and Prince Hotel on St. Simons Island, Georgia. Indeed, he did; his Sea Island home was one causeway and a short highway away. Among his Georgia neighbors were the James Gilberts, whose daughter was married to a Czech minister of the gospel. The preacher had not been allowed to leave the country to visit his in-laws. Bell arranged for a visit on his personal assurance that the minister would return to Czechoslovakia after visiting the Gilbert family.

He must have felt like no good deed goes unpunished; the Czech ambassador then asked if he could use his good offices to have the United States return gold that it had been holding since World War II. "I assured him this was beyond my capacity but that I would certainly let it be known that he had done us a favor."

During these meetings, there was much talk about Afghanistan. The Soviets had placed great military might there, but the war against the guerrillas was not going well. Two top Soviet officials asked for Bell's opinion, and he told them "they would lose just as we had lost in Vietnam and that they should follow the advice that Senator Aiken of Vermont gave in our country: 'Declare victory and get out.'"

Going further, "I told them that we would help them leave and would never let it be known that we were helping. The State Department attachés were quite alarmed over the fact that I was negotiating without help from the State Department. I assured them that I had been making a living negotiating for a long time, and I thought President Carter would be pleased with what I was doing. [But] within a few days, Reagan was elected President. . . . That ended the story."

Not all the post–Justice Department trips overseas had such high serious purpose. The Bells found themselves in London at a meeting of the Law Society Conference. The meeting marked the 350th anniversary of the enactment of the statute of fraud, which meant that contracts must be in writing to be enforceable. The society president proposed a toast: "Here's to the statute of frauds—the statute that has created more legal business than any statute ever enacted." Clicking their glasses, the British and American lawyers responded, "Hear, hear."

In the years to come, the Judge would hark back more than once to that toast, for his business became sorting out which contracts were enforceable.

✪

In the last days before the Judge left Washington, he took time out to play golf at the Burning Tree Club, an exclusive men's retreat in the suburbs. By then, he was thinking of building a law practice one more time, and everybody knew he would be in demand. Not only was he a widely recognized lawyer, and not only was he a well-connected public official, but he also seemed to know *everybody*.

His group was having a post-round drink when Tom Pownall, the president of the Martin Marietta Corporation, entered the Burning Tree bar. The Judge invited Pownall to join the group for a libation. And Pownall in turn invited him to begin thinking about joining the board of directors of the big aerospace and building materials company.

Bell said he couldn't as long as he was on the federal payroll, but the two agreed they would have lunch at the Metropolitan Club in Washington, that red-brick citadel of old capital power, to discuss it. It sounded like the right thing to do, and so he agreed to join. He could not know then that he would become involved in one of the biggest business controversies of the century, one that would redefine how companies were bought and sold. When he found out, he called it a great awakening.

In August 1982, his third year on the board, Martin Marietta received a completely unexpected letter from William M. Agee, the new husband of Mary Cunningham and the chief executive of the Bendix Corporation. Agee already had accumulated 4.5 percent of Martin Marietta's stock—just under the disclosure requirement of 5 percent—without public announcement. Now, the unwelcome letter said, he wanted to pay $43 a share, or a total of about $1.5 billion, to acquire majority control. "It looks like he's trying something big. Martin Marietta's defense business is a very interesting extension of Bendix's product line," an analyst told the press.

The Martin board did not think it was an interesting extension; it thought it was a damned insult. Management and the board knew that forty-three dollars was a low-ball bid, but they didn't know what a full price would be. "If an offer ever gets to be enough, it doesn't stay hostile," the Judge said. "We would be hard-put to resist if this was a good enough offer. What's the tipping point?" The management and board decided there was not enough money on the table, and it resisted.

Additionally, Agee had a very public history. Mary Cunningham had been the vice president for strategic planning until the Bendix board forced her to leave because of her relationship with Agee, who was then married to someone else. When Agee tried to buy RCA, the company stung him, saying, "Mr. Agee has not demonstrated the ability to manage his own affairs, let alone someone else's."

Pownall and Martin CEO J. Donald Rauth summoned the board, including the Judge, to fly company planes for a strategy meeting in Washington. A group of the directors landed at the private plane service center and disembarked just as another company aircraft landed—and the Bendix board members filed out.

For the next month, the two companies would battle in one of the most bizarre takeovers in American corporate history. The Martin board attended seventeen separate meetings. The Bendix board also met at a frenetic pace, but Pownall remembered that Agee was dominant. "If they even had a board we didn't know who they were. . . . We just couldn't tolerate Agee."

Martin countered Bendix's hostile offer with a "Pac-man" defense in which it offered to pay $1.8 billion for Bendix. You threaten to buy us, Martin said, and we'll show you who is the king of this hill. The Bendix stock had sold for approximately fifty dollars a share before the offer, but soared to seventy-five dollars per share when the bid was made. That escalation meant Martin would have to shell out 50 percent more to buy its aggressor. Martin "had smart people, scientists, and engineers. In fact, that was a company of engineers. The employees were irate. They thought Bendix was an *auto parts* company," the Judge recalled.

Both companies began to look around for allies, funding, bank loans, court suits to file, precedents, anything that would help them win. Martin wanted to win more, because it thought of itself differently, but also because it thought it had been sucker-punched. Simultaneously, both wondered whether other companies would come masquerading as white knights but aiming to become buccaneers. Others certainly were interested. Edward L. Hennessy Jr. ran Allied, and he wanted to be involved, particularly with the people who ran Martin. Harry J. Gray, chairman of United Technologies and, like Bell, a Georgian, had his eye on some of the businesses of both.

"This was my baptism, and it was nerve-wracking," Bell said. "Most of the other members of the Martin board were CEOs, and they hadn't seen anything like it either."

Having seen anything like it or not, he was one of those taking a tough line against Bendix. Pownall came to the board one day and said that Agee had requested an opportunity to talk directly with the board members instead of continuing to talk through management. Bell recalled, "I said, 'Have you asked to meet with their board?' He said he hadn't. I said, 'Are you at a point where you feel like you can't handle it?' He said he wasn't. So I said, 'Why are you asking us to meet with him, then?'" In other words, the board needed to trust management and not allow Agee to make an end run.

Agee waited in an anteroom for several hours for an invitation to speak with the board, not knowing that Bell had blocked an appearance with his blunt questions.

The events became so complex that meetings frequently ran into the night. Bendix had not arranged all of its financing in advance and therefore needed time. Bendix also employed the normal strategy of offering to buy 51 percent of the Martin shares at a higher price and the remaining shares at a lower price. The strategy was obvious; most stockholders would tender their holdings early to get the higher price.

For its part, Martin needed to find some chinks in Bendix's armor. One it found was that Martin was chartered in Maryland, while Bendix was a Delaware company. Even if Bendix bought a majority of Martin, it would have to wait ten days under Maryland law to call a shareholder meeting and elect new directors. But if Martin bought a majority of Bendix shares, under Delaware law it could call a shareholder meeting immediately and elect new directors. Thus, Bendix might buy Martin first and then wait to vote those shares. Who knew what might result in those circumstances? That seemed to turn the law on its head, but most of the rest of this extremely complex case was just as wacky.

Martin routinely offered limousine transportation to Agee and his associates when they came to meet with Pownall. After a night meeting, the Bendix entourage was headed from Bethesda back to the airport when Agee asked the cars to stop on the George

Washington Parkway. He had a new idea that he wanted to discuss. His people huddled in the limo, thought they might have a new strategy, and asked the Martin-supplied driver to switch to another vehicle so the strategy talks could continue without a Martin man present while they drove back to Martin headquarters. The driver said something like, "You're not getting this car." And he drove the limo back to Martin headquarters. Drily, the Judge commented, "I think we gave him a commendation later."

Ultimately, Bendix accumulated a majority of Martin stock. Martin bought a majority of Bendix stock. Bendix was in a box. Allan Sloan wrote in *Three Plus One Equals Billions*, "Throughout his business career William Agee had managed to get out of troublesome situations unscathed—he is a very smart, quick, innovative and charming man, exceptionally able in many ways and has the ruthlessness necessary to dispatch adversaries that he has at his mercy. But in the final weeks of the Bendix–Martin Marietta conflict, he came up against two men he could not outwit, charm or overpower": Pownall and Hennessy.

On the very same night that Martin bought Bendix, it sold Bendix to Allied, taking that worry off Martin's mind. Since Bendix had bought many Martin shares, Allied would swap them back to Martin for the shares of Bendix it held. The mind-bending mess left Martin with the company intact but with very large debt. "Our debt to equity ratio was about 80 percent," Pownall said. "We couldn't tolerate that for very long." Sales of some lesser parts of Martin's business over the next couple of years solved the problem.

How about the Martin stockholders? "What the stockholders got was an agreement from the board that we would be more careful with money in the future," Bell said.

Looking back on those days, Pownall said of Bell, "His mind is bigger than the ocean. There's just no way of filling it up. . . . His judgment frequently was the final word on a subject."

15

JUSTICE

The time is coming, if indeed it has not already arrived, when the Southerner will begin to ask himself whether there is really any longer very much point in calling himself a Southerner. Or if he does, he might well wonder occasionally whether it is worth while insisting on the point. So long as he remains at home where everybody knows him the matter hardly becomes an issue. But when he ventures among strangers, particularly up North, how often does he yield to the impulse to suppress the identifying idiom, to avoid the awkward subject, and to blend inconspicuously into the national pattern—to act the role of the standard American?

— C. Vann Woodward
The Burden of Southern History

In December 1998, two decades after Griffin Bell had taken his official leave of the Justice Department and returned to Georgia to resume his private law practice, I asked five of his former assistants who still practiced law in Washington to have dinner and discuss what they remembered of his time as attorney general. The atmosphere in Washington was electric, because in three days the House of Representatives would begin the debate on whether to start the impeachment of President Bill Clinton. And that was all most of Washington had on its mind and its lips. Would Clinton survive? Did he have another escape left? What was the process doing to the nation and its place in the world?

Little did they know that within twenty-four hours, still another crisis would envelop the capital—the bombing raids on Saddam Hussein and his Iraqi strongholds. Had they known, perhaps there would have been even livelier debate about such things as international espionage and Griffin Bell's enduring interest in spy-catching. Surely they would have speculated on how he and the FBI would have assessed the internal danger to the country.

But these dinner guests were all too happy to recall what they remembered from the times they spent with the Judge. In the warmth of a cocktail and a good meal, with the congeniality that comes from good times remembered, they talked so enthusiastically that their words spilled over each other. To the host who had not been part of that era in the Justice Department, it was a stunning tribute to a leader they had not expected and could not forget. What that great historian C. Vann Woodward had asked about the Southerner leaving home was relevant here, for Griffin Bell had ventured onto a national stage, recruited or kept employees who hailed from the rest of the country, and asked them to do the nation's work. What did they think of the man who led them? In the words of Woodward: "Has the Southern heritage become an old hunting jacket that one slips on comfortably while at home but discards when he ventures abroad in favor of some more conventional or modish garb? Or is it perhaps an attic full of ancestral wardrobes useful only in connection with costume balls and play acting—staged primarily in Washington, D.C.?"

Terry Adamson, who perhaps knew him better than any of the others because they had remained close, would lead the discussion. But there were others at the table with their stories to tell: John Dowd, an attorney now at the Akin Gump law firm but then the chief of Strike Force 18, which ran down organized crime; John

Martin, of the OSO Group (a private investigative group), but then leader of the Internal Security Section, who successfully tracked spies; Mark Tuohey III, of Vinson & Elkins, but then a prosecuting attorney who came to the Justice Department to help in public corruption cases; and Phil Jordan of the Swidler & Berlin firm, but then a man who found himself arguing an antitrust case in front of Justice Department lawyers, in a sort of moot court, to see whether it really was a case that should be pursued. They were older, seasoned, thoughtful men not given to false emotions or easy judgments; successful in their own practices now after having given the U.S. government more than it could reasonably ask for.

The words came in a rush. Dowd recalled the prosecution of Dan Flood, the Pennsylvania congressman who had amassed huge influence as chairman of the House Appropriations Committee. House Speaker Thomas P. (Tip) O'Neill had predicted that if the Justice Department indicted and tried Flood, it would be the end of Bell's influence. "There were 384 messages from Congress about Dan Flood which went to Judge Bell," most asking for a return call, most intending to demand that Flood be left alone, Dowd recalled. "I advised him not to return the calls." The Judge paid President Carter the courtesy of advising him of the steamrolling pressure from Congress, but they agreed that they would continue the prosecution.

So the Judge went to the very senior Mississippi senator James O. Eastland and House Judiciary Chairman Peter Rodino of New Jersey, who had proved his mettle in handling the impeachment hearings of President Richard Nixon. The Judge appealed to both for suggestions, and they stood firm in saying that the prosecution should move forward. It was a clear victory for the independence not just of the attorney general, but also for all of the Justice Department prosecutors who had felt themselves restrained in the past. Dowd's voice took on a new enthusiasm when he said, "That was not the way the department had been run."

While he pursued the case, there would be calls from the new attorney general. "Do you have enough agents" to complete the investigation, he would ask. Not a bureaucrat asking for more employees, mind, but an attorney general determined to assemble all the relevant facts. Eventually there would be 150 agents wrapping up all the details, Dowd said. Two weeks before the trial, when Flood's supporters still were bringing pressure, Bell called again to hear about the evidence. "I'm glad to hear it's going all right. . . . Last time we came this far North, we got our a-- whipped at Gettysburg. I don't want that to happen again."

But it almost did happen. The jury came back after a long trial and said it was deadlocked with eleven for conviction and one for acquittal. The case might have been closed had it not been for another juror passing a note to the judge saying that the dissenting juror had brought up information that had not been presented in the trial. Jury tampering became the issue. Eventually Flood entered a guilty plea of conspiracy and left Congress. Dowd would never forget Bell's support during the trial and its aftermath.

Those close to the attorney general had gotten signals early that he would be different. Within a few days after he took office, he got a hurry-up call from Indianapolis. Someone had taken a hostage. The state prosecutor wanted to give the hostage-taker immunity from prosecution; the U.S. attorney wanted no part of immunity. The U.S. attorney called Bell with the startling news that the state prosecutor was talking directly to FBI agents stationed in the White House. Whoa, did he say in the White House? Yep, and they might be leaning toward immunity.

It was the first time Bell had heard that agents were in the White House, but he ordered that the office be closed and the agents removed immediately. He also ordered that all White House communications go through him; law enforcement agents should not be able to go around the boss to political appointees.

Just why the attorney general should communicate with—and have clout in—the White House became clear when Hannafi

Muslims took hostages at three buildings in Washington. The Muslims held their hostages for several days, stacking furniture in a stairwell to block entry or escape. The FBI planned to charge the stairwell, using concussion grenades to stun the Muslims so the hostages could be freed without bloodshed.

But the Defense Department wouldn't release the grenades, holding that it would violate the Posse Comitatus Act, which forbade military men to act as policemen. Bell found out that the secretary of defense was receiving his advice from Jack Watson, the secretary to the cabinet, apparently without consulting the president.

The hostages eventually were released without the grenades, but Bell was told by the president that sometimes it was necessary for the attorney general to deal directly with him.

It was a lesson Bell learned, and one that the Justice Department staff heard about. The staff took it as a good signal that the boss not only would back them, but would go to the highest levels to do so.

John Martin spent thirty-one years at Justice. In the Bell era, his job was to run the Department of Internal Security, reporting directly to Ben Civiletti and through him to the Judge. There were several espionage operations under surveillance, and some cases had been developed. "But spy cases were not being prosecuted," Martin said. "From 1966 to 1975 there was no successful espionage prosecution in the federal court. And that was the time of James Jesus Angleton, the CIA deputy who ruined so many lives with his suspicions but never caught a spy." The relevant agencies said they did not bring the cases to trial, even when they found espionage, because they would have to reveal undercover activities and agents.

Bell's instructions to Martin: "Catch me a spy." Well, there were several to be caught.

One stunning case involved boyhood friends Andrew Daulton Lee and Christopher John Boyce (whose escapades are described in the book *The Falcon and the Snowman* by Robert Lindsey). On

January 6, 1977, at the very moment the Judge was preparing for his confirmation hearings in the Senate, Lee was arrested outside the Soviet Embassy in Mexico City. Initially charged with murder, he claimed he was trying to sell disinformation to the Russians. What the authorities found, instead, were documents stolen from TRW, an American manufacturer of spy satellites. Lee clearly was peddling the details of the satellites to the Soviets.

His accomplice, Boyce, was taken into custody a few days later at a turkey farm in California. He was helping his old pal, Lee, with stealing, photographing, and transporting the secret materials to the Soviet embassy in Mexico City.

Boyce was found guilty of eight counts of espionage and conspiracy to commit espionage. Then the recessed trial of Lee was resumed, and a most unusual procedure followed. For many years the U.S. government had resisted espionage trials, and the CIA most certainly did not want them, fearing their undercover activities would be exposed and their agents identified. But FBI agents, with the backing of the attorney general, did testify in the trial. And Lee then was convicted of espionage and conspiracy to commit espionage, as Boyce had been.

For Martin and his spy-catching colleagues at the FBI, this was gratification long delayed. They had worked diligently to keep up with both internal and external agents who meant the country harm, but repeatedly the government failed to prosecute their catches for fear of revealing sources. Finally, here was an attorney general who would use their information to protect the country. Martin said he was immensely gratified to find a superior who would do something about the undermining of sensitive defense efforts.

Another highly controversial case involved Ronald Humphrey and Truong Dinh Hung, a Vietnamese national whose father had been jailed for running against the incumbent Vietnamese president. The son moved to the United States, changed his name to David Truong, and joined other anti–Vietnam War activists.

Truong began to acquire classified documents from a low-level employee at the United States Information Agency, Ronald L. Humphrey. They concerned political cables about the situation in Vietnam. Truong contacted Yung Krall, another Vietnamese native and the wife of a U.S. naval officer, and got her to agree to carry packages of material to the North Vietnamese officials in Paris. What Truong did not know was that Mrs. Krall was an informant for the American intelligence community.

If Martin was going to catch these spies, he would have to be supported from above in this intriguing, if difficult, case. But it was no place for an attorney general of faint heart. Truong was passing information to the North Vietnamese, they knew, but proving it would be exceptionally difficult in court. So Bell authorized—on his own—both electronic surveillance and the physical opening of packages sent through the mails.

Damning evidence was obtained by these methods, and the suspects were arrested. But once they were arrested, the Justice Department had to defend the use of *warrantless* searches and seizures. In Martin's experience, no other attorney general would have been willing to defend those activities. "Judge Bell volunteered to come to court to defend the propriety of the authorization," the veteran of so much bureaucratic infighting said. "It had all been turf fights. Judge Bell loosened that up."

There still would be no convictions unless the government could use the testimony of Mrs. Krall. And the CIA was adamant in its opposition to her taking the stand. In meetings with her in London, CIA agents argued that she should not agree to expose her cover by testifying in court. Asserting his power to control the intelligence community, Bell ordered the agency to stop meeting with her. The CIA didn't stop; in fact, an agent in London was assigned to continue advising her to decline to testify. Bell told FBI Director William Webster to send one of *his* agents over to counteract the CIA advice.

missed planes before, but this time the rocket found its target. The plane's cockpit exploded in flame.

Hasenfus checked his parachute and his courage. Bail out into the jungle? Try to ride this thing out? Die with the two pilots up front, who were probably being incinerated? He jumped.

When he hit the ground, he didn't speak the language, didn't know which side of the civil war was which, didn't know how to survive in the jungle, didn't know how in hell he was going to get out of there alive. He had a gun and considered shooting one side and ducking, hoping the soldiers would kill each other and he could escape. But that seemed unlikely. So finally he surrendered, and it happened to be to the Sandinista leftist rebels who had staged a coup and come to power after years of dictatorship. The civil war was being waged by conservatives who wanted to throw the Sandinistas back out of power.

Two days later the Managua newspaper (and others) ran a picture of Hasenfus, a rope around his neck. He was being led by José Canales. Canales denied being a hero, but Sandinista sympathizers proclaimed him one. "The most popular man in Nicaragua for the past two weeks has been José Fernando Canales, the quiet teenage soldier who triggered an international incident by shooting American Eugene Hasenfus out of the sky," said a newspaper.

Sally Hasenfus was stunned and scared. She had no money to hire world-class lawyers, and she had small children. Her husband had left Marinette, Wisconsin, to take the flying job because he had lost his job and needed money. She called Ernest Pleger, the family lawyer. He turned her down, saying he didn't have the connections to get Gene out of a rebel jail in a country in the midst of a civil war. "Without a friend in the world," some were saying. But he would try to help.

Sally then composed a short list of people who might have enough connections: Griffin Bell, former vice president Walter Mondale, former secretary of state Cyrus Vance. Bell was her first choice. He first declined, declaring, "We've got five hundred thousand lawyers in the United States. They ought to be able to get one." But then he relented.

Barney Haynes, a King & Spalding partner, walked past the Judge's office and was invited inside. Bell asked if he had been to Nicaragua or spoke Spanish. Haynes said no. Never mind, the Judge said, "You and I are going to Nicaragua next Thursday." When Haynes protested that he was unprepared and could not really help, the Judge said, "Well, we'll just go."

The papers learned that they had been drafted into this sensational case. And then they stumbled on a piece of luck. Lawyer W. Taylor Boone had just celebrated his fortieth birthday and was attending an Atlanta Methodist church. The minister laid it on the congregation: People had to make something more of their lives than just a job. Boone knew that meant him. He called Haynes, said he had read the paper, knew about Haynes and Bell undertaking this mission impossible, and that he spoke both Spanish and Portuguese fluently. Would they like an interpreter? You betcha!

Reporters called, and Bell conceded he personally would represent the downed American at the trial. Hasenfus was accused of violating Nicaraguan security laws by participating in a flight bringing arms and supplies to rebels trying to overthrow the leftist Sandinista government. But he needed a delay. "We can't even get there by Monday. Hopefully, it will be delayed for a few days. I just got into the case."

He hadn't gotten into it soon enough to suit the Sandinistas. The captors paraded Hasenfus before the press. They awakened him in his cell and had him submit to an interview with CBS. He told the cameras he had taken part in ten supply flights coordinated by two CIA agents. If he were convicted—and how could he not be with that admission?—he faced up to thirty years in jail.

Bell said he received a cable from the Sandinistas and "all the cable said was that I did not need a delay or postponement because I was not a member of the Nicaraguan bar. It means he doesn't have any due process."

Flying down to Managua, the lawyers' plane zigzagged because of concern that one of the warring parties might decide to launch another Stinger rocket. But the flight arrived without incident.

In Managua, Bell, Haynes, and Boone were taken to an old ambassador's residence where they found tolerable food, terrible water, and little privacy. Bell met the press, now swollen to 250 members from around the world. The wily lawyer undertook to put the best face on it: "My defense is, he's a grunt. He's a poor man who needed a job, and he does not know anything about the revolution or the counterrevolution. He doesn't know anything about the foreign policy of the Sandinistas or the American government. . . . He's a shover. He shoves things out of a plane. They're trying to have a revolution. I don't care anything about their revolution. . . . This is just one man. I have seen the rules in the Soviet Union, and it doesn't differ too much."

Perhaps no other American lawyer would have referred to his client as just "a shover." But few other lawyers anywhere had the ability to reduce an international fight with ideological ramifications to such simple imagery. By now it was a gift that all Bell's colleagues knew, respected and envied.

Nicaraguan leader Daniel Ortega dismissed the characterization. "We are all clear that the godfather is [President Ronald] Reagan and that Hasenfus and those who died were employees of the godfather."

Bell replied, "I'm not getting into any politics. I'm here as a lawyer. He's an absolute pawn. It's sort of a windfall for Nicaragua . . . and they can put on display the entire foreign policy of the United States." The natives railed against a century of American foreign policy, saying it wiped out lives and aspirations for generations. To which Bell answered, "I have great reason to believe that he was not a terrorist who committed these crimes that happened a hundred years ago."

While the Americans struggled for their client, they fretted that they could not speak to him. And he was doing himself great damage. For television cameras he said, "I'm guilty of everything they've charged. How can I say I wasn't carrying small arms and munitions to their resistance?"

Bad day for his case, that. Bell told Atlanta reporter Bill Shipp, "He's so busy meeting with news people they haven't let him meet with his lawyers. He needs to talk to his lawyers. No one believes he is not being coerced in some way."

A family member who didn't want to be named told reporters, "He said he wished he'd gone down with the plane because dead men don't talk." By all accounts, Hasenfus was "a man's man." A hunter, gun collector, father, former paratrooper—"he was like a retired Green Beret." Apparently he felt his only chance was to own up to his role in ferrying guns to the rebels.

At almost the same moment, Reagan announced he was freeing another $100 million of federal funds to aid the Sandinistas' opponents. Nobody knew then that Reagan's associates were gathering huge amounts of other money in Iran to fund the Contras (rebels) in Nicaragua. The Iran-Contra imbroglio was a few months away.

Sandinista leader Ortega called Bell "a clandestine person." To which he replied, "I do not represent the United States government."

But he was trying everything he could think of, like proposing that nineteen Nicaraguan nationals in American jails, all but one on drug charges, be exchanged for Hasenfus. "If they're interested in it, they'll tell me. I'm just trying to think of something they'll be interested in." The foreign minister said no, emphatically.

Since there were no takers of his offers, it was time to go to the People's Tribunal, a small courthouse in Managua. Standing room only, with armed troops standing against the inside walls, enough to spook any trial. The American lawyers still had not been able to talk to Hasenfus. He would be represented by a local lawyer. The three-judge tribunal consisted of two farmers and a man who turned out to be judge, jury, and prosecutor all in one.

The American lawyers arrived early, and Sally Hasenfus was

there. Her husband came in, and Bell finally met his "client," who looked gaunt and tired.

Bell began, "I am sorry I cannot talk to you. I am not permitted by the court to talk to you. I wish I could. I'm glad to meet you."

"I wish I could talk to you, too, sir," Hasenfus said.

"Keep your spirits up," Bell admonished.

The Sandinistas piled some muddy, bent AK-47s, presumably retrieved from the crashed C-123, in front of their prisoner, and the trial was underway. The prosecutor said, "There are sixteen thousand orphans in Nicaragua because of this war." And the court pronounced him guilty, imposing a sentence of thirty years.

Sally Hasenfus said to the Nicaraguan court, "The hearts of my children as well as my own are locked in your prison. I pray your government will show compassion and let my husband return home."

Bell added grimly, "This is the end of phase one. There will be things done to try to get him released."

Things would be done, indeed. The Judge explored many options. He visited with former secretary of state Henry Kissinger to ask about possibilities. The State Department was wary of getting involved. The CIA found it convenient to let others handle the negotiations. And in Nicaragua, the government turned "very antagonistic" toward Bell's crew. On one of the visits, the Sandinistas picked up his luggage at the airport and didn't return it for several days. He complained to Barney Haynes that he couldn't sleep without pajamas, and the law partner loaned him a pair several sizes too big. The Judge also complained that he was missing thirteen white shirts "and only one of them had frayed cuffs."

Taylor Boone's translation skills scored highly with his colleagues. Both in the law books and in street conversation, he was helpful. But once he frightened even himself. Bell told some reporters that he hoped the government would tell Hasenfus to "go forth and sin no more." Boone made his translation, and then realized he had used the word "pecca," which in some Spanish idioms meant fornicate. He fortunately was in a region where it meant go forth.

Homegrown folks helped more than the government officials. The Judge had once acknowledged the work of the Reverend Joseph Lowery, the leader of the Southern Christian Leadership Conference, the group pulled together originally by Dr. Martin Luther King Jr. Lowery said his work had not been noticed favorably by other white people like the Judge, and he appreciated the Judge's kind words; he called to say he would like to help. Lowery was acquainted with some of the Nicaraguan foreign ministry leadership, and he appealed to them to release Hasenfus for humanitarian reasons.

While Lowery made one kind of appeal, a former Peace Corps worker in Nicaragua, Congressman Christopher Dodd of Connecticut, was thinking of another. Dodd still had friends there and wanted to get involved.

A Nicaraguan official said Hasenfus could be released if President Reagan would meet with a delegation. Reagan declined. How about former president Gerald Ford? Bell arranged for Ford to be a go-between, and Ford came to the Carter Center in Atlanta to meet with the officials. The hitch: Ford wanted Reagan to tell him that he was officially authorized to deal with the problem. Reagan didn't call and for an entire evening Ford dodged the Nicaraguans. "We were in a bad way then," Haynes said.

And then Bell did what he frequently did when there was a momentary lull: He went to Sea Island. To his surprise, he received a call from Chris Dodd offering to do whatever he could and asking permission to talk to the prisoner. "Not only can you talk to him—you can get him out," Bell replied.

A few days later, Bell was hunting birds with Jimmy Blanchard, on whose Synovus Corporation board he served, when he received a call from Dodd. Perhaps Dodd implied to the Sandinistas that it would embarrass Reagan if Hasenfus were released. That certainly would have had weight with the Ortega government, for they

CHAPTER

17

AT HOME ON THE ISLAND

When he reached age seventy-five, Bell concluded that he would like to spend more time at Sea Island in Glynn County. Little wonder. It is a quiet, peaceful little barrier island with few more than five hundred homes and fewer than fifty condominiums. The Bells could look out on a peaceful marsh where the wild grasses change color from green to brown as the sun moves across them. The great Georgia poet Sidney Lanier said in these 1878 lines:

As the marsh-hen secretly builds on the watery sod,
Behold I will build me a nest on the greatness of God . . .
Oh, like to the greatness of God is the greatness within
The range of the marshes, the liberal marshes of Glynn.

They have added an arc of driveway to the front of their coastal house, and have screened it with white picket fencing that is being covered with thick climbing ivy. Mary putters in the kitchen, oversees the work of a part-time maid, and pets the dog, Missy, while the Judge reads history and biography.

In the mornings, he is more than likely at the Ocean Forest Golf Club, a true championship test a mile and a half from his house. Built carefully among the rolling sand dunes and between the marshes along the Atlantic coast, Ocean Forest presents a unique challenge to all golfers. Where the marshes intersect the course, golfers must execute shots that carry for considerable distances. And they play among the delightful distractions of bald eagles and ospreys shrieking their war cries as they fight over a bulky, shaggy twig nest at the top of a dead pine tree between the fourteenth green and sixteenth tee. Fish-eaters both, they need access to the fishy inlets along the course and the ocean beyond.

No snob, the Judge plays with whomever happens to be in residence at the moment. Retired lawyers, former governors, women members, even old newspapermen are on the course with him. But not for a second round if he thinks them too slow; patience is not one of his great virtues.

On a sunny day when he was seventy-eight, he played with three friends, former governor Carl Sanders, lawyer Jim Bishop of Brunswick, and developer Larry Singleton. At the fifth hole, a par three of 140 yards, he struck a six-iron and executed his distinctive low draw. The ball struck the front of the green and began rolling toward the flagstick. His playing companions watched, but the Judge was ready to move, so he walked to the side of the tee. A great whoop went up from the others for his hole-in-one. The Judge didn't see it; he was already moving. "I knew it was going to be close," he said.

A fine young caddie with the group asked, innocently, "Judge Bell, are you the oldest man who ever made a hole-in-one?" It was reliably reported that for once the Judge was momentarily speechless. Because the great occasion had to be preserved for posterity, an emergency call went out for a photographer. The man lugging the camera turned out to be none other that the chief executive officer of the Sea Island Company, Bill Jones III.

Stories about his golf multiplied over the years. David Hudson, a respected Augusta lawyer who was once his law clerk at the Fifth Circuit, mastered the ability to mimic the Judge as well as understand his proclivities. They were at a retreat with family members. The men had planned to play golf, but the weather turned nasty. The conversation was pleasant, but the Judge became restless. "David, let's go play."

"But, Judge, its raining pretty hard, and the wind is really cold."

"Come on, David, let's go. It beats stayin' in the house with the women."

Not that the Judge is opposed to associating with women. Not at all. He laughed for years about how he and I had to rally on the final hole to avoid losing two dollars each to my wife and another Sea Island woman golfer, Charlotte McChesney. At parties, he frequently is surrounded by admiring women while clusters of men stand talking about somber subjects.

But it is not his way to sit when he could be moving. His law partner, Bob Steed, tells of a Saturday morning when they were scheduled to play golf at the stately Peachtree Golf Club in Atlanta, a course Bobby Jones helped design. Awakening to rain, Steed called and asked, "Judge, is it raining as hard out your way as it is here?"

"It's raining, but it'll probably let up. We'll go on out there and have breakfast and it will be gone."

They arrived at Peachtree, where it was indeed raining, but found a cluster of people having breakfast. "Let's just go on out and get ahead of them. They'll be slow," the Judge said.

Steed grumbled a little, mostly because he was hungry, had no umbrella or rain suit, and the rain speckled his glasses. But they played nine holes before giving in to the storm.

Mixing work and play is the pattern of a lifetime. From watching his son play high school football to riding bikes with his grandchildren to hunting with lifelong friends, he has been able to avoid a strict workaholic regimen despite the demands for his legal services. He said in *Taking Care of the Law* that he thought the problems he observed firsthand in Washington had their origins in grind-it-out habits:

Any attempt to diagnose what went wrong and caused the people to vote President Carter out of office must touch on style. The United States—and certainly Jimmy Carter—would have been better off if the president had put his feet up on the railing from time to time, taken a drink and chatted with a few friends of broad experience and mature judgment. Such conversations could have helped the president relax, and perhaps changed his pattern of working so hard on so many matters instead of focusing his energy on the few truly important problems.

Unlike many of his contemporaries, then, he found places to spend half his time, and he wanted to make it right with the other King & Spalding lawyers. He announced that he would get a lawyer to help him negotiate a contract for half-time pay. That astounded the partners. "What do you need a lawyer for?" they asked, meaning he could have whatever terms he chose. But the Judge was resolute; partner Frank Jones would represent him in arriving at a contract.

In truth, there was not much of a negotiation. He and Jones could write the terms and the management committee would approve. Whatever it said. Because he was their partner, their leader, the man who had insisted that there be a cap on the salaries of senior partners so that the younger lawyers could prosper. When it was wrapped up, Jones liked the idea so much that he asked the Judge to represent him in a similar half-time deal.

Walter Driver, who has held all the management positions at the firm following after the Judge, reflected on the settlement. "Every time we meet with him, we ask him to take more money and give us as much time as he can. We want him around all the time." And he probably gave the firm more than half his time, if that includes all the telephone calls to Sea Island and the speeches to judicial conferences and dedicatory addresses for buildings named after his friends.

Occasionally, however, someone would begin to take him for

granted. Driver recalled how a solicitous client had approached him following the decision to work half time: "He was scheduled to argue an appeal. A young staff lawyer for the client's company called him and asked if he wanted to see the briefs in the case, or whether he just wanted a synopsis. Judge took his head off. 'If you think I'm going to risk my reputation by going into that argument unprepared, you're crazy.'"

One firm that learned his worth at a later stage in life was General Motors. Sued in Fulton County Court in a case involving side-mounted fuel tanks on their small trucks, GM pushed aside King & Spalding lawyers and brought in a presumptuous Chicago lawyer to try the case. Bell was matched up against a Columbus, Georgia, plaintiff's lawyer who asked the jury to send GM "a message." They did: A $108 million punitive damages award against GM, a record in such a case.

Ken Starr, who had left the solicitor general's office, was asked to coordinate the appeal to the Georgia Supreme Court. Starr sought out Terry Adamson to coordinate a strategy for obtaining friend-of-the-court briefs. Both thought Bell should be brought into the case, but some GM executives thought him over the hill. Eventually Starr and Adamson obtained a meeting in Detroit between themselves, GM General Counsel Harry Pearce, and Bell, among others.

They discussed the law and the briefs and the strategies for a while. Then Bell asked for an opportunity to drive one of the trucks around the test track. Washed up? Loaded up with ideas, that was more like it. Bell was given the task of arguing the appeal. The Georgia Supreme Court reversed the award. A much smaller sum was paid to settle the case.

And he seemed to have time for everybody. Steed, whose work for King & Spalding is almost as famous as his humor columns in the *Atlanta Constitution*, marveled at how the Judge was fair game. He had, for example, been asked to do a promotion for One Ninety-One, the Peachtree Street building, when it was looking for tenants. The Judge turned it into a video promotion that pointed out that one could find the MARTA mass transportation system less than a block away and stay under shelter all the way to New York and London before going outdoors again.

It was this indefatigable energy that astounded his clients and associates. It seemed to come from a reservoir that was close to inexhaustible.

As the years rolled by and his reputation grew, there came the inevitable complaints from other lawyers and people who thought he demeaned the public offices he had held. He was billing some of the largest corporations in America at $450 an hour after becoming famous in government service. How, the critics wanted to know, could a man working for companies paying him that rate *not* be co-opted? Perhaps the toughest questions came from fellow Atlanta attorney Ralph Knowles, who represented plaintiffs in a class action against Dow Corning. Judge Bell and his King & Spalding associates were hired to look into the company's development of silicone breast implants. The lawyers sorted through three hundred thousand documents, found some alterations in production records, and reported the findings to the Food and Drug Administration, as well as the Judge's recommendations for the future. Dow Corning did not, however, release all of the report.

Knowles said for publication, "Obviously Griffin Bell has a distinguished record and career. Nobody would fault him for his career at all. My concern about Griffin Bell is that in the latter years he has let his reputation be used by corporate America for PR purposes when they've committed fairly atrocious acts."

Unruffled, Bell replied, "I know they say that, but mainly lawyers say it. They'd like to have the same business, I'm sure, some of them. . . . I don't pay any attention to that sort of thing."

If the comments of lawyers didn't raise his dander, that was one thing. But he weighed another consideration that he thought was more important. "People think because I held a public office I ought to be careful who I represent. It's like they have a vested interest in me. I think it's marvelous that the American people would feel that way." What those people could not know was the vast number of unsavory or corrupt potential clients whom the Judge turned away. Some of his critics did not distinguish between the shady characters and the major firms that asked him to conduct investigations. And that led to further misunderstanding. Still, he had to represent people. "That's the kind of business I'm in. I haven't surrendered my law license yet."

When he looked back over his more than half a century of law practice, at the request of the *Georgia Journal of Southern Legal History*, he described how the practice had changed. The firms had grown dramatically. The judges no longer were circuit riders. Lawyers' fees were many times higher. Training was more rigorous; specialists had replaced the generalists of his Savannah days. Recruitment of the best graduating law school students intensified. Management of the larger firms became more professional. In short, the lawyer in this seersucker suit and bow tie was succeeded by a male or female in a dark business suit carrying a soft leather briefcase.

The same interview, conducted by Clifford Kuhn and William Bost and published in 1991, contains vintage Bell views on lawyers and their practicality. Here's how he told a wonderful story about the inane ideas of some lawyers while upholding the worth of the profession: "I went to a bar meeting one time, and a lawyer made a report and said there were going to be twenty-one specialties and no lawyer could have more than three. I said, 'I'd like to ask a question. If you are in a small town and you want to represent people, and you want to cover all the specialties, you would have to get seven lawyers in a firm?' He said, 'That's right.' I said, 'So that would be the minimum number of lawyers in the firm we would have to have to provide adequate services.' He said that was right. I said, 'Well, this idea will never fly.' But they have people studying that, if you can imagine such a thing."

His disdain for complicated rules equaled his delight in spoofing

South Georgia law practice. He once remarked to his aide Frederick Baron that when he was a young Savannah lawyer, "You had to give notice if you were going to look up some law before you went to the courthouse."

Over the course of his remarkable career, the South had changed as much as he had. The mule and plow in the cotton field of his childhood had given way to the multistory office buildings even in the small towns. Farmers in overalls and high-topped shoes watched their sons don loafers and open fast-food franchises. Daughters of the women who had tended the home fires dragged themselves off to sewing plants where the pay was low, but where their husbands could not find even menial jobs. Perhaps nothing had changed more than the practice of law in the last half century.

❁

His own life had been changed as much by Mercer University's Walter F. George School of Law as by any other institution. The little Baptist institution on the western edge of Macon gave him the initial training for his life in the law. He and the school both grew through the twentieth century, and he was influential in its direction.

After his term as attorney general, his connections to the legal profession were world-class and his ability to contribute historical data proved valuable. Almost immediately, he announced that his papers from his time in Washington, as well as other materials, would be donated to the law school.

And he used his acquaintanceship with renowned figures to attract them to the campus. Chief Justice Warren Burger, Sen. John Glenn, Justice Clarence Thomas, Justice William Kennedy, Independent Counsels Lawrence Walsh and Archibald Cox, former White House Counsel Lloyd Cutler, and others came to the campus at his invitation.

The school, in turn, did whatever it could to entice him to have more involvement. In 1983 it made him the first to hold the Mercer

Distinguished Professor title. A few years later the Griffin Bell Chair was established in the law school. He became the chair of a 1983–88 campaign that raised $87 million for the university. Proving that no good deed goes unpunished, he was asked to chair another $130 million campaign that began in 1997.

It was his continuing leadership in the fight to keep the university trustees independent of some in the Georgia Baptist Convention that made headlines. He argued that, although Mercer was church related, it must maintain its academic freedom against inappropriate intrusion from church politics.

For those reasons, and others, he received the Distinguished Service Award in Trusteeship in 1999 from the Association of Governing Boards of Universities and Colleges. Said the fancy calligraphy:

Griffin Boyette Bell. Esteemed trustee of Mercer University Board of Trustees. A courageous advocate for the university's independence and autonomy. An indefatigable contributor and fund-raiser. Distinguished professor of law. A principled and steadfast leader. A model trustee.

CHAPTER
18

TALKING TO THE YOUNG

In the fall of 1998, near his eightieth birthday, the Judge was asked, along with others of legal eminence, to come to Washington to talk about impeachment. "There's enough in here to upset both sides," he said. The essence, however, was that lying to a grand jury could justify the impeachment of President Clinton. Privately, he was dismayed that anyone thought it appropriate for the president to commit perjury. Moreover, he thought the collective spinning of the news from the White House was an outrage that the public should not tolerate.

He was invited to make the graduation speech at the University of Georgia on the very day that the House voted two articles of impeachment against the president. He didn't say that President Clinton had been unpatriotic in choosing to evade the Vietnam War draft; he said instead, "It was during this era that we began to question values that had served us well for generations. Patriotism, for some, meant protest. The idea sprang up that there was no such thing as an absolute truth."

Harking back to the time when politicians studied issues and tried to arrive at sound answers in a representative government, he worried about the uninformed gaining the upper hand over those who knew the issues:

We must ask: Have we lost our capacity to govern in a representative government? Have the pollsters and polls taken over? Is there a need for us to have representatives or are representatives mere rubber stamps to obey the will of the polls? Pure democracy was a form of government rejected by the Founding Fathers. We must remember Jefferson's words that our representatives owe us their best judgment, not their votes. Their judgment is important.

During this period has come an era of bad manners—incivility and rancor in our private and political life, extremism in entertainment and sensationalism in the arts and in the media. How can we improve our discourse? What has happened to old-fashioned courtesy? Nowhere is conduct worse than among the too-clever-by-half lawyers where the smart aleck and ill-mannered so-called advocate is destroying the nobility and high calling of the law, and perhaps the last vestige of good manners as taught us under the English Common Law practice.

As a basketball coliseum full of graduates and parents listened in silence, he said, "We are turning into a sound bite people. . . . Politicians have learned to use the television and radio as a means of spinning the news to suit their purposes. A gullible populace seems to be taken in by the spinners. This is much like the medicine shows that passed through the small towns during my youth."

What really had offended him were Clinton's lies and his inability to admit that he had lied. "I speak of a legal system as being different from justice. Justice is that which is rendered in the legal system. . . . You must take care to see that no fellow citizen is ever denied justice. You must also take care to see that there are no preferred citizens in the sense that the rich and well-to-do can have a different kind of justice. I direct your attention to the latter-day style of trial where the witnesses or prosecutors [read Kenneth Starr] or judges are attacked by packs of lawyers [read White

House] using the media as a way to avoid guilt, although the guilt is never denied. This will not do in a great country."

After the House passed the two articles of impeachment against President Clinton, the Judge's testimony continued to be a rallying point for those who believed that a serious crime had been committed. Stephen E. Buyer, a four-term Indiana Republican and one of the House managers, went to the well of the Senate and said in part:

> We were privileged to have the testimony of Judge Griffin Bell, an individual who has highly distinguished himself in public service. Judge Bell . . . said, "I have thought about this a great deal. This is a serious matter. Trifling with the federal courts is serious, and I guess I am biased because I used to be a federal judge, but I cannot imagine that it wouldn't be a serious crime to lie in a federal grand jury, or to lie before a federal judge, and that is where I come down. . . . And all the civil rights cases that I was in the South depended on the integrity of the federal court, and the federal court orders, and people telling truth, and fairness. Truth and fairness are the two essential elements in a justice system, and of all the statutes I mentioned—perjury, tampering with a witness, obstruction of justice—all deal in the interests of truth. If we don't have truth in the judicial process and in the court system in our country, we don't have anything. We don't have a system."

As you can see, according to Judge Bell, truth and fairness are two cornerstones of our judicial system. President Clinton violated both of those bedrock principles.

Finally, Judge Bell spoke to the issue if a President ever were convicted of a felony. Judge Bell stated, "If the President were indicted and convicted of a felony such as perjury or obstruction of justice or witness tampering before impeachment proceedings began, would anyone argue that he should continue to be President? I don't think so." He continued, "A

President cannot faithfully execute the laws if he himself is breaking them."

Judge Bell hit it right on the head.

On the head or not, the Senate declined to convict Clinton, and the argument moved on to whether the independent counsel law could be modified so that it would expire in 2000. Some thought it could, but not Judge Bell. He was invited to speak to the Senate Governmental Affairs Committee. Sitting at the witness table alongside former senator Howard H. Baker Jr., who called for a cooling-off period before making a decision, Bell was firm in his conviction: "I long ago concluded that this statute is unworkable for a number of reasons and represents very poor governmental policy."

Give the responsibility for investigating suspected wrongdoing at high levels back to the attorney general, he said. That was the system that existed before the Watergate scandal. The attorney general would have the power to appoint outside prosecutors. Those prosecutors would not necessarily have to present evidence to Congress regarding impeachment. Some other witnesses said the necessity of reporting to Congress evidence of "possible impeachable offenses" had altered the dynamics of government.

❂

Birthdays came to be a focus as the Judge extended his lawyering beyond the time when most people turn to doddering. At seventy-five, the firm held an elaborate dinner at which people paid tribute, often with mild digs.

And then came the eightieth birthday, and it took *two* parties at King & Spalding for all the folks to pay their respects. Typically, they had to be held a few days early; he had scheduled a hunting trip to Argentina "where he and other gun-bearing friends would spend the week making the world safe from South American Killer

Doves," as the firm's newsletter put it. His efficient secretary Beth Kroger turned poetic at the first party, authoring an "Ode to an Octogenarian":

> *At the age of six, his parents sent him straight to public school,*
> *Where he gave his teacher quite a fit for breaking cardinal rule;*
> *He persisted writing upside down and using his left hand;*
> *It was only his intelligence that kept down reprimands . . .*
> *As Attorney General he was known as a leader in command.*
> *There was weeping in the nation when in two years he resigned,*
> *But rejoicing in Atlanta as we welcomed back our kind.*
> *It's been almost 20 years he's stayed and aren't we all glad?*
> *If the Judge should ever really leave, the loss would be too sad.*
> *We have gathered here to celebrate his 80 years on earth,*
> *And pay tribute to the man who brings us wisdom, kindness, mirth.*
> *We feel blessed to have him with us and wish for him always*
> *All the best in health and happiness and many more birthdays.*

At the second party, a newsletter reported that the firm's resident wit Bob Steed said he had expressed some concern to partner Byron Attridge that there were too many parties for the Judge's birthday "but was assured by Attridge that the functions were merited because of Judge Bell's legendary 'low self-esteem.'" This provoked Steed into revealing that when Judge Bell left the Justice Department he was asked by a newscaster how he would rate himself on a scale of 1 to 10, to which the Judge replied, "11." Steed said when the puzzled reporter asked what an "11" was, Judge Bell replied, "It's a 10 with no false humility."

Typically, the Judge had the last word. He thanked the firm for the support it had offered him over the years. And then he added one hundred thousand dollars to the King & Spalding Scholarship Fund to honor the firm at his alma mater, the Mercer Law School.

✪

When Griffin Bell talked about the young in 1999, he seemed most to enjoy speaking of Griffin III and Katherine, his grandchildren now grown into adulthood. And they certainly enjoyed talking about him. Katherine had become an accomplished Atlantan. After graduating from Hollins College with a major in art history and a minor in English, she spent part of her time as an artist and part as a real estate agent.

On a Sunday afternoon when Griffin III could have been doing any number of other things, he sat down to talk about his grandfather. He was thinking of leaving his solid technology job and entering law school. Studying his grandfather, he was trying to analyze what made him such a success.

"He leads a simple life—incredibly active but simple," Griffin III says. "He practices law, reads, hunts quail, plays golf. Some lawyers are too frantic to have time with the radio turned off. Not him."

Although Bell has accumulated some wealth, "He always says, 'Don't worry about the dollars. Focus on your job and that'll come. Don't ever chase the last dollar.'"

The grandson also was impressed with what the older man chose not to do. "The last time he did any yard work was May 11, 1959. That was the day he bought the house on Habersham. He said if he could afford the house, he could afford to pay somebody to do the yard work."

Once his friend Charles Kirbo had come to Washington to visit with the attorney general. Kirbo was wearing "half a body cast" because he had been on the roof of his home trying to clean the gutters and had fallen. "That's great. You must have saved thirty-five dollars," Griffin III recalls his grandfather saying.

Another example of conserving time for thinking came to mind. Griffin Junior once was painting the outside of his house. "What in the world are you painting for?" his father asked.

When his son said he was saving money, the Judge asked how

much a professional painter would cost. Eleven dollars an hour. "Can't you make more than that practicing law?" he needled.

What the grandfather has taught Griffin III is to value *thinking* time, not busy time. He refers repeatedly to the Judge's ability to focus on important issues. "He wants the summaries, not the details." This is a trait that has served him well in fashioning settlements in thorny legal cases.

Still, the Judge cannot sit still and wait for others to accomplish the chores. "You go to the gas station and get out to pump gas. He'll be out with a squeegee cleaning the windows," Griffin III says.

The same is true in his office; he frequently can be found in the library reading the research material for himself. He wants to be prepared.

The grandson tells these family anecdotes with easy chuckles and a born storyteller's charm. He doesn't tell them at the expense of others. He simply delights in recounting an unseen part of his doting grandfather's life.

It is a side that a bunch of tough old litigators have never seen.

What the lawyers have seen is a foe relentlessly seeking a solution to whatever problem confronts him. But not just any easy solution; it needs to deal with the problem in a sensible way.

Jim Jardine, one of his principal aides in the Justice Department, recalled one incident that illustrates that well. Federal agents arrested two Russians as spies, and Moscow followed by seizing an International Harvester salesman. The Soviets then proposed a swap. To which the Judge answered: "I'm not trading a tractor salesman for two Russian spies." A more significant exchange was arranged.

Nor did he tolerate imprecise use of language. Bell answered his own phone one day and a voice said, "The White House is calling."

"Buildings don't call. People call," he said, and hung up.

It was that blunt, direct, sometimes caustic way of speaking—and thinking—that won him admirers as well as critics. Near the end of his time in Washington, Bell appeared on NBC's *Today* show. Barbara Walters noted that others in the administration were saying the press was unfair, and she wanted to know if he shared that opinion. "You've treated us all badly but it has been equally bad with other administrations," he answered.

Walters thanked him for his "candor." To which he replied, "Only in Washington would you call that candor."

Former Chief Justice Warren Burger said as the Judge left the Attorney General's office, "No finer man has ever occupied the great office of attorney general of the United States or discharge his duties with greater distinction."

High praise that was for a man whose life began on a boll weevil-infested cotton farm, moved through the scandal-pocket corridors of power and returned to the simple pleasures of shooting quail in the broomsage fields of south Georgia.

Running "eager as a boy" through all of it.

INDEX

respite care facility was located a good six miles out of town, deep in the Worcestershire countryside.

'It doesn't matter, apparently. We're a registered charity, so they're happy to accommodate us. All we have to do is find a day's worth of prizes.'

'We?'

'Simon's helping me.'

'Oh, great.' A stab of irritation provoked by the mention of Jamie's care-worker forced out the response with more sarcasm than he'd intended.

Anna chattered on, oblivious. 'That might look like loads in there, but it'll be nowhere near enough to keep us going for a whole day. This Saturday we're targeting Harborne and Bearwood, asking all the shops if they've got anything to donate.'

'I'm not sure if that's legal.'

'We're only asking them. They're at liberty to say no.' She smiled one of her most persuasive smiles.

'Same as me then; Hobson's choice.' Mariner sat on the edge of the bed to tie his laces.

'You could donate something,' she said suddenly as the thought occurred. 'Granville Lane, I mean.'

'What, like a CS canister signed by the chief superintendent? That would be a coup for an adventurous five-year-old.'

'A weekend for two in the cell block? Or a set of handcuffs. I can think of a few couples who'd go for that.' Her smile was pure mischief. 'There must be something. What about a tour of the nick?'

'I'll give it some thought,' said Mariner. 'In all the spare time I'll have on Saturday.'

'Poor old you. Look, this is the least I can do. Manor Park has been a lifeline for me.'

'I know.' God, she was gorgeous, even with a face like that on her. And she was right. Manor Park had made a huge difference to her life, and his.

'Shall I give you a call when we've finished?' she said.

5

'We could go out somewhere to eat.'

He sighed. 'I suppose it'll have to do.' Fully dressed, he leaned over and gave her a slow parting kiss. 'I'll talk to you soon.'

But driving back to the station Mariner couldn't shake off the creeping sense of dissatisfaction. He hadn't meant to sound so aggrieved. His reaction was especially ironic given that Anna's independence had been, for him, one of the big attractions in the first place. It had been liberating to be with a woman who had more obligations than he did, and who wasn't constantly checking up on him. But somewhere recently the balance had shifted and increasingly the relationship seemed to be only on her terms.

In the beginning her commitment to Jamie had made it inevitable, and Mariner had waited patiently while Anna did what she felt was right by her younger brother. But now with regular respite care Jamie was becoming more independent, and Mariner had always assumed that in consequence they'd get more time together. Instead, she just seemed to find other things to occupy her, such as this round of frenetic fundraising. The fact that she was completely open and honest about her intentions, giving him absolutely no reason to feel threatened, nor casting him as the selfish one, only salted the wound. This was a new experience. Having always been used to being more needed than needy, he found that the reversal wasn't a comfortable one.

The air conditioning had made his car just about tolerable by the time he pulled into the station car park, and he'd have liked to have languished a while in the relative cool. But, glancing up, he caught sight of a familiar figure pacing the pavement outside the main doors, dragging anxiously on a cigarette. He got out and walked over to her.

'Colleen?'

The young woman turned to flick ash on to the pavement. 'You took your time.'

6

'I was out on a call.' Shagging my girlfriend, but we won't go into that. 'What's up?'

'It's my Ricky,' she said. 'He didn't come home last night.'

Here we go again, thought Mariner, but he said nothing and hoped that his face had stayed in neutral. Mariner had known Colleen Skeet for more than ten years, back when he was in uniform and her husband used her as a punch bag on a regular basis. She must be in her mid-thirties now, though she still looked little more than a kid herself, small and painfully thin, her mousy hair pulled back from a pale, freckled face into a tight ponytail. Today, only the dark circles beneath her eyes betrayed her age and the degree of her anxiety.

'Have you reported it in there?' Mariner nodded towards the station.

'They said I could talk to someone. But I wanted to wait for you.'

'Well, here I am. Let's go inside. It's cooler.'

'I can't smoke in there.'

'You can smoke in an interview room.'

'You don't like it though.'

'Christ, Colleen, when did you start considering my sensibilities?' It raised a weak smile and Mariner pushed open the door. 'Come on.'

'So tell me what's happened.' The interview room was eight feet square, with a tiny window, no air and Colleen was putting a flame to her third Marlboro Light. She was right. Mariner didn't like it. But for her sake he put up with it. Doing his public duty.

'Ronnie turned up,' she said, blowing out smoke. She was sitting back in her seat, one hand cupped beneath an elbow. 'He was there Saturday afternoon when I got home from work.'

Mariner shook his head in despair. 'Why do you let him in?'

7

'He's the father of my kids.' Her eye contact was fleeting, defensive. 'Whatever he might have done, he's still their dad. He'd brought Ricky the new Man U shirt, when I'd already said he couldn't have another one.'

'All the options round here and he still supports Man U?' Mariner shook his head sadly. 'That lad's got no sense of loyalty.'

'Ronnie was spinning all sorts of yarns, you know, all the usual crap about how he'd sort things out and one day he'd come home and we could be a real family.'

'I hope you didn't fall for it.'

'What do you think? He'd already had a drink. Ricky knows it's all rubbish too, but underneath it all he really wants to believe him. Ronnie might not have been the best husband but he was good with Ricky; taking him fishing and to the football. Ricky would love to have his dad back and us be a happy family again.'

'Wasn't all that happy as I remember it,' said Mariner.

'You know what I mean. Anyway, Ronnie stayed all day Sunday, took Ricky down the social club with him, stopped the night. On the sofa.' She emphasised those words. 'When we got up Monday morning, Ronnie had done his disappearing act. Ricky was disappointed but I thought he'd get over it. I mean, it's not the first time, is it? When he was little it didn't seem to matter so much; he had me. But now he's growing up. He sees his mates going off to the match or down the pub with their dads and he knows he's missing out.'

'How old is he now?'

'Fifteen, the kind of age where he needs a man about.' She looked up at Mariner, catching him off guard. 'You must remember that.'

Mariner had forgotten how well Colleen knew him. A moment of indiscretion in the dead of night, when she was going through a bad patch; her second beating within a fortnight. 'My dad used to hit me too,' she'd blurted out, through swollen lips, as they'd sat beside each other in A&E. 'I must deserve it.'

8

'That's rubbish,' he said. 'Nobody deserves this.'

She'd laughed, a short bitter laugh. 'Yeah, I don't suppose your old man ever laid a finger on you.'

'No,' he admitted. 'But that's only because I've no idea who or where he is.'

She'd looked at him differently after that.

'It's too long ago,' he lied now. 'I've forgotten.' And in his case there had never been any question of his dad turning up. He wondered if having a dad who comes and goes was worse than having one who's non-existent.

'Anyway,' Colleen went on, 'Ricky went off to school as usual Monday morning, a bit quiet but I never thought anything of it. He wasn't there when I got home from work that night. He must have come in after I'd gone to bed. Then last night, he didn't come in at all. His bed hasn't been slept in.'

'Ricky has done this before,' Mariner reminded her gently. 'Gone off.'

'Not like this. A couple of times he's stayed out all day at the weekend, and sometimes late after school, too.' She leaned in towards Mariner, urgency written all over her features. 'But he's never been out all night. First thing, I got a call from the school asking where he was because he hadn't turned up. When they talked to his friends – and that didn't take long – they hadn't seen him since yesterday afternoon. They got let out early because of the heat. Ricky hasn't stayed out this long since before Ronnie left us.'

'No.' The times Ricky had disappeared before were the occasions when he'd been an unwilling witness to his dad laying into his mum. As gentle as his dad was violent, Ricky hadn't stood a chance. The last time he'd run away it had been in shame because he hadn't been able to protect his mother when she'd needed it. He'd been ten years old. Afterwards, Mariner had spent a lot of time with the boy, trying to reassure him that it wasn't his fault. They'd got to know each other pretty well, too.

9

'When Ricky stays out all day, have you any idea where it is he "goes off" to?' Mariner asked.

Colleen shrugged. 'It's not with his mates. And when I ask him he just says "around". Typical teenager.'

'How's Kelly?' In the past it was Colleen's older daughter who'd been the real headache, disappearing for days at a time.

'Kelly's settled down now. She's got a baby of her own and a nice fella.'

'Are you sure Ricky hasn't taken a leaf out of her book?'

'Ricky's different: he's quiet, sensitive. He's never stayed away all night. And he never misses school. Something's happened to him.'

No, that was another thing: Ricky didn't miss school. The boy's genetic make-up was a mystery. Against the odds, he was a studious kid with big ambitions and the common sense to know what he had to do to achieve them.

'Is everything all right at school? Nobody's giving him a hard time?'

'No.'

'He hasn't fallen out with his mates?'

She snorted. 'He hasn't got many to fall out with. You know Ricky, he keeps himself to himself.'

'Any girlfriends on the scene?'

'No.'

'What about you?' Mariner asked. 'Are you seeing anyone?'

'A guy called Steve. He's a friend.' A touch of defiance crept in. 'A good friend. We've been together nearly a year.'

'Does Steve get on all right with the kids?'

'Yes. No. He finds Ricky hard because he's always got an answer for everything, always coming out with these long words. But he wouldn't be enough to make Ricky stay out all night. I know it.' She stubbed out her cigarette in a final gesture of defiance.

10

'All right, we'll ask around and see what we can dig up,' said Mariner. 'I'm sure Ricky will turn up with a good explanation for all this. I want you to go home. Let me know if you hear anything and we'll keep you posted. And try not to worry, eh?'

She snapped the Zippo and sucked the weak flame into her fifth cigarette. 'Easy for you to say.'

Showing Colleen out, Mariner stood for a few moments breathing deeply, taking advantage of the relatively clean air while he was outside. Ricky Skeet was a puzzle. The disappearing act was out of character, but then he was fifteen: a difficult age even without the unsettled home life. Colleen was right to be worried, but the chances were that seeing his dad again had provoked emotions that he couldn't handle and that in the fullness of time, when he'd got over the turmoil, Ricky would turn up. The kid probably just needed some space. Mariner heard the door behind him swing open. It was Delrose, the civilian receptionist.

'DCI's looking for you,' she called. 'And he seems to be getting a bit impatient.' Well, wasn't this developing into a perfect day? What a shame Anna's pitch at the festival wasn't the wet sponge stall. Suddenly he had in mind a prime target. His mood deteriorating with every pace, Mariner went straight to the DCI's office and knocked on the door.

'Come.' The request was barely audible but Mariner went in anyway. As Acting Detective Chief Inspector Gavin Fiske looked up from his desk, Mariner was reminded of a tortoise emerging from its shell, blinking slowly with a smile that didn't hang around long enough to reach his eyes. His movements were slow and calculated, like those of a reptile conserving energy in the heat. A fly buzzed around the room and it would have been no surprise to Mariner to see the DCI flick out a long tongue to catch it.

11

As smooth as Jack Coleman was rough, Fiske was a good ten years younger than Mariner; all designer suits and Samsonite briefcase, with just the right amount of gel styling his hair and doubtless a bathroom cabinet full of 'male grooming products' at home. His bag for the gym sat conspicuously on the floor of his office, the habit reflected in the toned physique but not the unhealthy, pallid complexion. Mariner could never understand the logic of paying hundreds of pounds for the privilege of walking on a machine in a room full of sweaty bodies when the same effect could be achieved in the fresh air and changing landscape of the countryside. How could MTV ever seriously complete with the stunning view over the vale of Evesham from the top of Breedon?

In the three weeks that Fiske had been in the station covering while Jack Coleman was seconded to Complaints Investigation Bureau on an internal investigation, he'd already acquired a nickname. The first time Mariner had heard him referred to as 'Fido' he didn't get it.

'Thinks he's the big I Am,' a staff sergeant enlightened him. 'Like the dog food.'

'Ah,' Mariner had said. 'And I'd assumed it was because he thinks he's the dog's bollocks.'

'Glad you could find a window,' Fiske said. It took a couple of seconds for Mariner to work out what he meant. The consensus was that Fiske had risen so quickly through the ranks partly due to his snappy vocabulary. He could ring-fence like no other and he was the first man Mariner had come across who regularly diarised, something that sounded to him like a complex medical procedure. What Fiske didn't yet appreciate was that though the buzz words might impress interview panels, in the real world they had the potential to make him a laughing stock. He'd walked into his first briefing at Granville Lane deporting a shield of ignorant self-confidence that had temporarily protected him from the sniggers that greeted his lexical repertoire, but that wouldn't hold for long. Mariner couldn't wait.

'Interesting afternoon, Inspector?' Fiske asked now, his

unfortunate nasal inflection adding value to the patronising tone.

'Yes sir, I've been following up on a missing juvenile.'

'And prior to that? I've been trying to raise you on your mobile.'

'I'm sorry. The battery must be flat, sir.' Mariner hedged, suppressing the slightest twinge of guilt.

'Do I look like a complete prat, Mariner?'

What a question, thought Mariner, wondering if there was any way he could get away with the truth. Luckily the DCI saved him from himself. 'Where were you?' he demanded.

'I was responding to a call sir, PC Grady can conf—'

'Oh yes, from a "Miss Streep". Would that be Meryl by any chance? Fitting you in between filming, was she?' Guilty as charged, Mariner was annoyed to find himself colouring in response. How the hell did Fiske know where he'd been, unless he was checking up on him? Fiske didn't wait for a reply. 'Not exactly the example we want to set for junior officers, is it?' he said mildly. 'If you've ambitions to become Granville Lane's very own Peter Stringfellow, I suggest you wait until the end of the working day like the rest of us.'

'Thanks for the analogy, sir.'

But for all that, Fiske's irritation was carefully controlled. I'm on your side, said the knowing smile. We're all lads in this together. Failing to realise that Mariner wasn't together with anyone nor had he ever been.

The dressing-down complete, Mariner started towards the door. 'I'll take more care in future, sir.' In more ways than one.

But Fiske hadn't finished. 'Talk me through this missing juvenile.'

Stupidly, Mariner mistook the command for interest. 'Ricky Skeet, aged fifteen, went out yesterday morning but didn't come home.'

'Where's home?'

'Nansen Road. It's on the—'

'Oh, I know where that is.'

Mariner wasn't surprised. Long and winding, Nansen Road took its name from the grim council housing estate through which it ran, and whose reputation was notorious. Built in the 60s when housing was cheap and shoddy, the development comprised rows of boxy white stucco houses, interspersed with more space-efficient low-rise flats and maisonettes. During the 70s, the local authority had made it their policy to rehouse 'problem families' on these estates, in the hope that they would learn from their more socially conscientious neighbours. Of course that wasn't the direction in which the osmosis occurred. Instead, what had subsequently developed was a ghetto of problem families living alongside those like Colleen Skeet who couldn't afford to move on. It was also one of the crime hot spots of the locality and it was clear that Fiske had already passed judgement.

'Why wasn't this just reported to the duty sergeant and passed to uniform?' he asked.

'I have a history with this family.'

'Oh? Would that be personal or professional?'

Mariner hardened his voice. 'Colleen Skeet's former partner was violent. Over the years I got called to the house a number of times—' Where he'd spent hours trying to persuade Colleen to go into a refuge. On one occasion he'd succeeded, but she hadn't stayed long.

'Was?'

'Ronnie Skeet did everyone a favour and cleared off a couple of years ago, with another woman.'

'And is that the sole basis for your relationship with this family?' Mariner hesitated. 'I can look up the case notes,' Fiske reminded him.

'The older girl has been in trouble: truanting, shoplifting, that kind of thing. She's run away before, too.'

'So. Not what you'd call a model family.'

'Colleen's had her share of problems over the years,

14

yes, sir. She's a woman on her own trying to raise her kids and keep them from being poisoned by the influences around them. It doesn't make her a bad person. And I thought that was what we were here for, sir. To help people who are in trouble.'

'Don't lecture me, Mariner. Are we sure that this is a genuine disappearance?'

'I'm sorry, sir?'

'Are we sure that this boy wants to be found?'

'His mother wants him found. That's why she came to me.' Mariner made to leave. 'And if there's nothing else, sir, I need to get started on the risk assessment paper-work.'

'Someone else can do that. I need your expertise on something else.' *Expertise.* Good choice of word. Mariner should have been flattered. He wasn't.

'With respect, sir, this mother has approached me directly. I know the family and I think I'm the person best placed to—'

'And as your superior officer I think *I'm* the person best placed to determine your priorities, don't you think, Inspector?'

'And they are?'

'Another missing teenager.' His face said that the irony wasn't lost even on him. Christ. The OCU covered only one small area of the south of the city. What were the chances of two kids disappearing on their patch in the same day? 'In this case it's a seventeen-year-old girl,' said Fiske. 'I want you to handle it.'

Mariner had a premonition of a poisoned chalice heading his way. 'But I'm already—'

'Charlie Glover can take that on.'

'So that I can look for another missing kid? That makes sense.'

'Don't play the smart arse with me, Mariner. It won't do you any favours.' Fiske's voice was icy. 'This case is not the same as Ricky Skeet.'

15

'Oh, really,' said Mariner, unconvinced.

'I want you to follow it up. Consider it an order.' The pulse at his temple throbbed dangerously.

'Yes, sir.' And fuck you, too.

Fiske handed Mariner a picture of a young Asian girl who smiled happily from a standard school portrait. She looked younger than seventeen and wore the uniform of the girls high school located in a middle-class residential area, several miles from Kings Rise Comprehensive where Ricky was a pupil. Middleham Road ran between the two, parallel to the Birmingham to Bristol railway line. The two kids were quite literally from opposite sides of the track. 'Yasmin Akram,' Fiske announced, importantly. 'Last seen by her friends getting her train at Kingsmead Station yesterday afternoon to go home. It's worth bearing in mind that her parents have some influence within the Asian community. I think you'll find the risk assessment profile on this one rather more urgent.'

So that was how this one was different. Yasmin Akram had hit the jackpot. She was young, female and respectable middle class. At one time, being Asian might have counted against her, but not any more, not in the wake of the Macpherson report; the enquiry into police racism that had followed the bungled investigation into the murder of black student Stephen Lawrence. These days, being from a minority ethnic group could be a positive bonus. Mariner bit back his objections. On that score Fiske was right, it wouldn't do him any good. The pretty teenager smiling up at him had to be found. She was young, vulnerable and at risk. It just didn't meant that Ricky Skeet wasn't.

'Her parents, Shanila and Mohammed Raheem Akram, run an independent Islamic prep school, Allah T'ala, in Sparkhill,' said Fiske. 'And until we've established that this is a simple missing persons, we need to keep our options open.'

Mariner picked up the inference immediately. For

16

months now, right-wing nationalist groups had been taking advantage of the public fears of Islamic fundamentalist terrorist incidents to stir up unrest, and in recent weeks a number of Islamic institutions had themselves been under attack – from the eighty-six mosques in the city to countless businesses, large and small. Muslim schools in the city were amongst the obvious targets, mainly because of the threat posed by their academic success.

'If this does turn out to be politically sensitive,' Fiske went on, 'I need someone on it who knows what they're doing and will cover all the angles right from the beginning.'

Coming from Jack Coleman, that would have been a compliment, but Mariner wasn't naive enough to take it as such from Fiske. The DCI was simply covering his own back. Mariner had the distinct impression that Fiske was out of his depth already. His previous posting in rural East Anglia had been poor preparation for a city as huge and socially complex as Birmingham. And while he'd probably read a few textbooks and attended a couple of seminars on equalities, Mariner doubted that Fiske would have any real grasp of the issues involved.

At the turn of the millennium, Birmingham had become the first European city to no longer have a single ethnic majority and Mariner had lost count of the number of minority groups that made up the million plus population. The whole spectrum of racial integration was represented, from communities that remained closed and self-sufficient, to those individuals whose physical characteristics were the only indication that their ancestors weren't of Anglo-Saxon origin. Over the years, Mariner had worked with colleagues and members of the public from every background imaginable, but he still wouldn't presume to understand all the subtle implications of living inside a different coloured skin.

Added to that were the infinite configurations of family life, regardless of culture or class. He also wondered how much the DCI understood about handling the press on a case as potentially high profile as this. If Yasmin's disappearance should turn out to be racially motivated, then they would be eager to join the dots and draw their own conclusions.

Fiske buzzed through to his PA. 'Is WPC Khatoon here yet?' In response, the door opened and a young Asian woman came in. Almost matching Mariner for height she was generously proportioned, and Mariner was reminded of how unflattering the police uniform could sometimes be.

'This is Jamilla Khatoon, a family liaison officer who's going to be on loan to us from Operational Command Unit 2,' said Fiske. 'She'll be working with you on this for obvious reasons. Jamilla, this is DI Mariner.'

He didn't hang about, did he? As they shook hands, Jamilla's expression was guarded and Mariner was left wondering how Fiske had prepared her for this introduction. Mariner forced a smile. 'Nice to meet you, Jamilla.'

Her tentative smile stretched to one that was broad and white. 'It's Millie, sir.'

'OK.'

'I want you to keep this low key,' Fiske intervened. 'Just the two of you on the preliminaries until we know what's going on. Talk to the family, friends, the usual. If this does develop into anything, we're going to have the media and the politicians crawling all over us. So let's get it cleared up quickly and cleanly, whatever it takes.' Then if I do screw up, at least not too many people will know about it, Mariner tacked on, in his head. It was Fiske's dismissing remark.

18

Chapter Two

Mariner seethed with resentment on the walk down to his office. For the second time that day he was leaving an encounter feeling manipulated. First Anna and now Fiske, working him like a puppet on a string.

Although there was a strong possibility that Fiske could be right, he resented the dismissal of Ricky Skeet's disappearance as routine, and entirely down to the kind of home life the kid had. Never mind that he was bright. He didn't stand a chance. Colleen wasn't going to like this one little bit. Added to that was the clumsy assumption that as a white, male officer, Mariner needed help to handle the Akrams. He'd be the first to admit that he was far from being an expert on Asian conventions, but the initial interviews would be standard stuff, establishing the facts. This was far too much too soon.

'Congratulations on being hand-picked by Mr Fiske,' he said to Millie, not without sarcasm. 'The press would have a field day with this: prejudicial use of resources so early on. We haven't even filled out the risk assessment yet.'

'With respect, I'm not sure that it's—'

'How long have you been in the job, Millie?' Mariner ploughed on.

'Just over a year, sir.'

'Something you might want to remember. If you want the police and media to sit up and take notice when you disappear, you'd better be female and from a "good" family. Don't ever be male and from a broken home, with a dodgy dad, like Ricky Skeet, because then the media aren't interested and the police won't give a fuck.'

'Girls are more vulnerable,' Millie pointed out.

'Which doesn't means that boys aren't,' Mariner replied, with feeling.

'No, sir. Who's Ricky Skeet?' Millie asked.

'He's another kid who disappeared yesterday. I know the family so his mum contacted me. I've just been pulled off it. Not a good use of an inspector's time, as he's probably only a runaway. No fanfare of trumpets or special resources for Ricky Skeet, but then he's the wrong kind of MisPer.'

'I'm sure the officer it goes to will give it his best shot.'

'The officer it's gone to doesn't know the family and is up to his neck in other unsolveds.'

'And you're not? Sir?'

Said so innocently, Mariner couldn't help but smile. 'Let's get a drink, Millie. And then we'll see who knows anything.'

Fresh-faced PC Robbie Thorne knew more than anyone, having been the uniformed constable who responded to the initial missing persons call for Yasmin Akram. Summoned to Mariner's airless office, he sat down to form the apex of a human triangle with Mariner and Millie, and read from his notebook.

'Yasmin was last seen yesterday afternoon at around four thirty, when she left the girls school with a group of friends to go home,' Thorne said. 'She took her usual route: travelling three stops on the train to the university station where she gets off and walks several streets to her house. She was last seen by the friends, running for the train at Kingsmead.'

'And no one's heard from her since?'

Thorne shook his head. 'She carries a mobile, which as far as we know is working, but she hasn't used it. That's

20

partly why nobody was panicking at first. She wasn't even reported missing until this morning.'

'After she'd been gone all night?' said Mariner.

'The father is away and the mother thought she'd gone to stay with a friend. It wasn't until the school called her this morning to say that Yasmin hadn't turned up that she realised that wasn't the case. That's when she contacted us.'

'Since when did schools start ringing up parents to ask where their kids are?' Mariner asked, remembering that Ricky had been subject to the same checks.

Millie supplied the response. 'Since the truancy rates went through the roof and school attendance became a government issue,' she said.

'Christ, when I was at school if you wanted to bunk off, you just did it. The teachers were grateful to have fewer kids in the class.'

'That was before results and league tables got to be so important.'

'Shanila Akram seemed concerned about her husband's reaction to involving the police, too,' Thorne added.

'Where is he?'

'Away on business, she said. He's due back later this afternoon.'

'Do we know if Yasmin's ever done this kind of thing before?' asked Millie.

'Only the usual. Once when she was smaller, she threatened to run away to her auntie's, but only got as far as the end of the street.'

'This auntie has been contacted?'

'Yes, sir. Mrs Akram has been in touch with all other relevant family members.' Thorne glanced at his meticulously taken notes. 'The only thing Yasmin had with her was her school bag. She didn't even have dinner money.' He glanced up. 'The school operates some kind of credit card system so no cash is exchanged. All that we know she had on her was her travel card that covers West Midlands buses and trains.'

'So theoretically she can't have gone very far.'

'Tell us about the family set-up,' said Millie.

'The family is Pakistani Muslim. Yasmin's the second of three children. There's a sister in her twenties who now lives abroad, and a ten-year-old brother. Paternal grandmother also lives with them. The home language is a mix of Urdu and English but the mother speaks English fluently.'

'How did she seem?' asked Mariner.

'About what you'd expect: pretty distraught.'

Mariner looked over at Millie. 'So, let's go and see for ourselves.'

Yasmin may have disappeared on their patch, but both the family home and her parents' school were some distance away. The foundation grammar school system in the city meant that hundreds of kids travelled such journeys every day.

The drive over to the inner city suburb of Sparkhill was about as uncomfortable as it could be. In the mid-afternoon sun Birmingham smouldered, heat shimmering up from the road, melting and splitting the tarmac and condensing the air to a stinking, exhaust-laden smog. In the last few weeks the city had got noisy and overcrowded, too small and cramped for its one million inhabitants, causing more than the usual friction and conflict. There had been a sharp increase in the number of domestic and common assaults and the number of road-rage incidents had risen by a quarter.

Even the trees looked as if they'd had enough, their leaves limp and lacklustre. Traffic on the outer circle route this afternoon had virtually ground to a halt, leaving drivers to stew impatiently in their vehicles. Despite the full-on air conditioning, Mariner could feel his shoulders beginning to prickle and itch and he glanced up in despair at the cloudless blue sky. After five weeks the heat showed no sign of abating. News reports were full of dire warnings about

22

hosepipe bans and forest fires. Ironic, given that spring had been one of the wettest on record, submerging whole areas of the country beneath flood water for days at a time. Impossible to imagine now.

'What does it mean, Allah T'ala?' Mariner asked Millie, as they idled at yet another congested junction.

'Literally it means "God Most High".'

'So this is the school of God Most High.'

'That's right.'

'What do you think of segregated schools?'

Millie's answer was measured. 'Lots of parents, white and black, choose to send their children to private schools for many different reasons.'

'But these are primarily religious reasons. What kind of precedent are we setting for these kids? Already in this city we have Catholic schools, Jewish schools and Muslim schools, all telling these children that their religion makes them special and different from others. Then they leave school and we expect them to forget all that and take their place in a multicultural society.'

'The good schools also teach tolerance and respect for the religious beliefs and customs of others, whatever they may be. I don't think you'll find bigotry anywhere on the curriculum.'

As if to illustrate this crossover, the Allah T'ala turned out to be housed in an imposing ironstone building with white twin spires and a high arched window; a former Anglican parish church that dominated a meandering street of Edwardian townhouses. As they drove up they saw a man scrubbing at an illegible slogan that had been sprayed in red paint along one wall. Approaching from the same direction but on foot were two women in full *burkha*, the black robes leaving only their eyes exposed. A less common sight in the southern suburbs, Mariner was well aware of the connection between the mode of dress and the perceived oppression of women, and was surprised to find himself mildly unsettled by the sight.

23

As the women neared the door marked 'Entrance', it swung open as if by magic, just wide enough to admit them, and they were gone.

Mariner hoped that, as a man, he wouldn't have a problem gaining access. As much as he was prepared to trust Millie he wanted to be there himself to talk to the Akrams. But the school was co-educational, which presumably meant there were male teachers. Vehicles on the forecourt outside the school were of mixed vintage and power.

Despite finding a patch of shade cast by an ancient spreading beech, they stepped out of the car into what felt like a fan-assisted oven and it was with reluctance that Mariner retrieved his jacket from the hook behind the driver's seat and slipped it on. Millie rapped the door-knocker, simultaneously holding her warrant card up to the peep-hole below. Again, the door opened marginally, sucking them into a dim reception room before closing softly again behind them.

Once Mariner's eyes had adjusted from the brightness outside he could see that this was the main administration office, crowded with phones, computers and filing cabinets. The walls were decorated with childlike powder-paint creations annotated with quotations, most probably from the Koran. A small, brown-eyed child fidgeted on a chair beneath the proclamation that: 'In the remembrance of God do hearts find satisfaction.'

Millie offered a greeting *salaam* to the young girl behind the desk. 'I'm Liaison Officer Millie Khatoon, and this is Detective Inspector Tom Mariner,' she said. 'We have come to speak to Mr and Mrs Akram.'

The girl flashed a brief sympathetic smile. 'Of course. I'll tell Mrs Akram you're here.' Picking up the phone she spoke briefly in what Mariner surmised to be Urdu, before rising from her chair. 'Please come with me.'

She led them through into a small lobby and up two narrow flights of stairs, gliding with the kind of feminine

24

grace that her flowing robes seemed to induce. Behind closed doors they could hear the insistent chatter of children's voices. Shanila Akram's was a more orderly office and lighter, thanks to the broad window that overlooked the street. As they entered, she got to her feet and came towards them, extending a hand. Mariner took it. It was delicate and as cool as marble. Small and slight, she was also dressed all in black, her *hijab* head scarf, wrapped about her face like a nun's wimple. In ordinary circumstances she would be stunningly beautiful, with flawless olive skin, mahogany eyes and a full mouth, but today those features were clouded with tension and Mariner wondered how she was managing to work.

'Our school must continue for the children,' she explained apologetically when introductions had been made, as if she was party to his thoughts. 'And I felt it better to keep busy.' Busy was the word. Outwardly in command, she was a bundle of nervous energy, struggling to maintain eye contact for more than a few seconds at a time. As the conversation progressed she continually rearranged her robes, moved papers from one side of her desk to the other and then back again. She straightened a stack of books, opened and closed a drawer for no apparent reason, and her eyes rarely settled on anything for long.

The office girl had brought in chairs behind them and Shanila Akram asked them to sit. 'Would you like tea?' she asked.

'Yes, thank you.' This Mariner had expected from past experience. He was no great fan of the traditional sweet Masala tea, but knew that the atmosphere would be more conducive if the hospitality was accepted. However, when refreshment came, it was served Western style, for which he was grateful.

'My husband should be back very soon,' Shanila Akram told them. 'I haven't yet been able to contact him.'

Good, thought Mariner, we may be here when the news is broken. We'll be able to judge the reaction.

25

'Perhaps you could start by telling us about yesterday evening,' Millie began.

'Of course. I arrived home at a little after seven. It's a busy time of year, there is much to do here at the school. Preparations for the end of term. The children's *Amma*, my husband's mother, is at home all day so is there to welcome Yasmin and her brother. Sanjit was at home at the usual time. I had allowed Yasmin to go and stay with her friend—' She broke off uncertainly, as if she was going to say more of that but then changed her mind.

'And the friend's name?' Mariner prompted.

'Suzanne. Suzanne Perry. The arrangement was that Yasmin would phone from Suzanne's house to let me know that she was safe, but when I got home she hadn't yet phoned.'

'Did that concern you?'

Almost immediately Mariner regretted the insinuation. Shanila Akram's eyes filled with tears. 'Not unduly. I thought that perhaps Yasmin had forgotten, that she was having a good time. I tried to phone her friend's parents but that's when I discovered that their number isn't listed. By this time it was getting late and I just thought . . . Of course I know now that I should have persisted, but at the time I had no reason to think that anything was wrong.' She was on the verge of tears, but with effort of will she looked Mariner in the eye. 'It was a mistake. Of course I realise that now. I was ready to scold Yasmin for not keeping in touch, but I was shocked when the school contacted me this morning to say that she had not arrived and that her friends had not seen her since yesterday afternoon.'

'She she didn't go to stay with Suzanne?'

'No. At the last minute she changed her mind and told her friends that she was coming home instead.'

'But she didn't.'

'No.' The woman's voice had dropped to a whisper. Through the open window they heard a car pulling up on to the forecourt below. Shanila Akram turned to look out.

'My husband,' she said. But her body language conveyed anything but relief.

They heard voices below and moments later Mohammed Akram burst into the room, his face a mixture of anxiousness and bewilderment. In his mid to late forties he was unexpectedly dressed in a dark business suit with a crisp white shirt and striped tie.

Shanila Akram jumped to her feet. 'Moshi, this is Inspector Mariner and Constable Khatoon. They are from the police.'

Akram shook their hands. 'Fakhra told me you were here. What's happened now? Have there been more letters?' As he spoke Akram pulled up a seat beside his wife and they both sat.

'It's Yasmin,' Shanila said, a tremor in her voice.

'What about her?'

'She has disappeared.'

'What?'

Something subtly changed in the atmosphere. Something Mariner couldn't identify. Shanila Akram's fragile confidence had deserted her altogether and she seemed to shrink back from her husband, as if he might be angry with her. Perhaps he would. She had been left in charge of the family.

'It appears your daughter changed her mind about going to stay with her friend yesterday evening, but didn't return home either,' Mariner said. Now Akram seemed confused.

'Yasmin was to go and stay with Suzanne last night,' his wife reminded him.

'She—'

'They had to finish their project, the presentation they were doing together. Yasmin was desperate to go,' Shanila pressed on. 'But she must have decided against it after all.'

'I don't understand.'

'The school telephoned me this morning to say that Yasmin hadn't arrived there. That's when I called the police.'

27

Akram's full attention was on his wife, Mariner noticed. He seemed to have forgotten that they were there. 'Why didn't you wait – Never mind.' Mohammed Akram's eyes narrowed as he tried to make sense of what his wife had told him, and Mariner tried to read the emotion. Shanila Akram's demeanour had completely transformed. No mistaking who was the dominant person in this partnership. Only, it seemed, when he had swallowed his anger did Akram think to ask, 'Where has she gone? Have you spoken to her friends, to the rest of the family?' He reeled off a list of names.

His wife shook her head. 'I've tried them all. No one knows where she is.'

'It seems the last people to see her were her friends, yesterday afternoon,' said Mariner.

'So I'm to understand that she's been out all night?' Akram's anxiety was beginning to gain momentum, but again Mariner felt that there was more to it than that. 'How has this happened?' The demand was made of Shanila, who visibly flinched.

'I understand your concern, Mr Akram,' Mariner said, in an attempt to diffuse the tension. 'But the fact remains that it has happened, so we need to ask you some questions about Yasmin so that we can find her as quickly as possible.'

At that, Akram seemed to get a grip. 'Yes. Yes of course,' he shook his head slowly. 'It's just so hard to take in. I can't believe it. What is it that you need to know?'

'Your wife was talking us through the events of yesterday evening.'

'Well, as I'm sure she has told you, I have been away on business since yesterday afternoon.'

'May I ask where you've been, sir?'

'We are opening a school in Bradford. I went to meet with some of our staff up there for a planning meeting.'

'And you left Birmingham at what time?'

Akram thought for a moment. 'It was around four thirty

28

in the afternoon. I had an appointment with the printer and went on from there.'

'This friend, Suzanne. Has Yasmin stayed with her before?'

'No.' It was Mohammed Akram who answered, sharply, with a look to his wife that was clear disapproval and a frisson of conflict thickened the air again. They'd need to return to that.

'She has been to Suzanne's house for tea, but always came home later in the evening,' Shanila said, softly.

'And what did Yasmin take with her?'

'As far as I know the usual things: a change of under-clothes, toiletries. Other than that it's hard to tell.'

'And you have no idea where else Yasmin may have gone. Are there any friends or relatives she might have gone to stay with instead?'

'I've contacted everyone I can think of. We have family in London, Bradford.'

'What about your cousin Ameenah?' Mohammed Akram asked of his wife.

'I've called them.'

'I understand Yasmin's sister lives abroad.'

'In Lahore,' said Shanila Akram.

'Is there any chance that Yasmin would try to go there?'

'She doesn't have a passport yet. We are in the process of applying.'

'And she wouldn't have money for a ticket,' added Mohammed Akram.

'Mrs Akram, I'd like you to think back to Monday night; Yasmin's last evening at home. How did she seem then?'

'She was fine.'

'And nothing unusual occurred?'

'Nothing. Except ... she was late home. There had been a problem with the trains, but it's not uncommon.'

'Does Yasmin enjoy school?'

This was safer ground, easier to elaborate. 'Yes, she's a clever girl. Her teachers are pleased with her.'

29

'It was a big decision to allow Yasmin to go to a school outside our own religion,' Mohammed Akram added. 'But the high school has an excellent reputation and we felt it would benefit Yasmin's career prospects to go there, even though it involved extensive travelling.'

'And there was nothing bothering Yasmin that you can think of.'

A glance between them that Mariner tried in vain to read. Could have simply been a clumsy and belated attempt at mutual reassurance.

'Nothing.' It was Shanila who spoke.

'Yasmin hadn't fallen out with any of her friends?' Millie asked. 'It happens all the time with girls that age.'

Mohammed Akram spoke up. 'If there is anything on Yasmin's mind she would tell us. She's a sensible girl, and we are very close. The family is important to us and we always encourage our children to be open and honest with us, so that we can support them.' Recited like a mantra.

'Anything could have happened to her. She's so young—' Shanila Akram's voice cracked with emotion.

Millie leaned over and put a hand on the woman's arm, demonstrating the value of her presence. 'The vast majority of missing persons turn up alive and well within seventy-two hours, Mrs Akram,' she said. 'We'll do everything we can to find Yasmin.'

'We'll need to look at her room,' Mariner said, offering something practical to focus on. 'It's just routine, but the sooner we can do that the better.'

'I'll come with you,' Akram volunteered.

'That may not be necessary. You said that Yasmin's grandmother is at home? If she can let us in—'

'Yes, of course, I'll let her know you're coming.'

'Then we won't keep you any longer,' said Mariner. He took a business card from his inside pocket and handed it to Mohammed Akram. 'If Yasmin does contact you, or you think of anything, however small, that might help, give me a call at any time. And of course we, in turn, will keep you informed.'

'I'll keep in touch,' Millie reassured Shanila Akram.

'Thank you.'

It was Mohammed Akram who stood to show them out. Signalling for Millie to go on ahead, Mariner waited until he and Akram had descended the stairs and were alone in the lobby before saying, 'Mr Akram, when you first came in you seemed to think that we might be here about something else. You asked your wife about some letters. Do these relate to the graffiti outside?'

Akram rubbed a hand over his face. 'And the rest. It's become a way of life for us: graffiti, bricks through the windows, dog excrement through the letterbox. Recently my car was damaged.' His eyes lit up as he seized on an idea. 'Do you think Yasmin's disappearance is connected with these incidents? There are some sick people out there, Inspector,' he said, with growing fervour. 'After September eleventh we went through a bad time.'

'We can't jump to any conclusions at this stage,' Mariner said. The incidents would have been looked into, but it seemed a little premature to be making those kinds of assumptions, unless Akram knew something they didn't. 'Do you have any thoughts about who might be behind these attacks, Mr Akram? Or anyone who might have a specific motive to harm your family?'

'Apart from the usual?' Akram glanced up at Mariner. 'My wife and I built up this school from nothing. When we both left college as trained teachers we could see that the British education system was failing the children in our communities. Many of the children around here have little English when they enter the school system, so they are already at a disadvantage. We founded this school in an attempt to give them a better start. Now every year we are inundated with applications. We have expanded several times but still we don't have enough space to take all the children who want to come here.'

31

'And plenty of people resent success,' said Mariner.

'While others feel very threatened by Islam, as I'm sure you are aware, Inspector. Bad enough having the country overrun with Asians, let alone *educated* Asians.' He took a pamphlet from his pocket. 'We get these all the time.'

The red, white and blue flyer was being published by an organisation calling itself 'The Right Way'. Mariner had encountered it before: a right-wing organisation led by Peter Cox, a known racist and white supremacist based in the city. 'When was the last time?'

'It comes and goes.' Akram was suddenly uncomfortable. 'It's been worse since the letter.'

'What letter?'

He shifted uncomfortably. 'I belong to an Asian business consortium. We have all been targets and we were sick of the constant harassment. We wrote a letter to the local press denouncing the cowards who instigate race crimes and in particular The Right Way.'

'So you could have inflamed the situation.'

'It was impulsive, something I now regret. It seemed like the right thing to do at the time, but it probably hasn't helped.'

To put it mildly, thought Mariner.

'This came through the post at the end of last week.' Akram took from his pocket another sheet, this time of A4, word-processed on a computer, which he handed to Mariner.

al-Fath (The Victory)
Punish the hypocritical men and the hypocritical women. For them is the evil turn of fortune, and Allah is wroth against them and hath cursed them, and hath made ready for them hell ...

'It's from the Koran,' Akram said. 'My wife hasn't seen it. I didn't want to upset her, especially now—'

'It's powerful stuff. Do you know if anyone else has received anything similar?'

'I don't know. I haven't told anyone.'

'Not even the police?'

'What would be the point? It's completely anonymous. What could you do? It could have come from anywhere.'

'And the envelope?' Mariner asked, without hope.

'It was printed anyway, but I threw it away.'

'I'll need to take this to get it checked for fingerprints.' Akram shrugged. 'As you wish.' But they both knew that as it stood it was a long shot.

'If you get *any* further communication like this from anyone, please let me know immediately.'

'Is it possible that Yasmin could have been abducted?' Akram had clearly begun to give the idea some thought.

'I think in the circumstances it's a possibility we shouldn't discount.'

'Please help us to find her, Inspector.'

'We'll do everything we can. You said you were away from yesterday afternoon? Where did you stay last night?'

'We have family in Bradford.' As he spoke, Akram pushed open the door to the reception area, where Millie was chatting to the girl behind the desk. Seeing them, she drew the conversation to a close. Akram showed them out.

Outside on the forecourt another car had been added to the collection: Akram's top of the range black Mercedes with the registration MOH 1. It had a vicious scratch along one side. 'Yours is the Mercedes?'

Akram nodded.

'It's a distinctive car,' said Mariner.

A glint of irritation flashed in Akram's eyes and Mariner began to recognise him as a man with a short fuse. 'I work hard. I should be allowed to drive the car I choose.'

'Naturally,' said Mariner, calmly. 'I only meant that it makes it an easy target. We'll be in touch, Mr Akram.'

Chapter Three

While they'd been inside, the sun had moved round and their own vehicle was no longer shielded from its burning rays. The heat inside gusted out when they opened the doors. It wasn't until Mariner pulled out on to Highgate Middleway, where the traffic and the air moved more freely, that he asked, 'So what have we got here, simple absconder or something more sinister?'

'I thought it was interesting that Mr Akram made the point about his wife reporting Yasmin missing.'

'Implying that perhaps he wouldn't have? That she's over-reacting?'

'Could be. I thought his response was unusual. To begin with, he seemed angry, then once he'd calmed down he was almost businesslike.' Millie was perceptive.

'Maybe he's just a pragmatist: OK, this is the problem, so what can we do about it?'

'So far I can't see a clear reason why Yasmin would have run away.'

'Not one that they're telling us about. But does there have to be one? It could be that even Yasmin herself doesn't know. Perhaps she just needed some time away. Sometimes it happens.'

Millie turned to face him. 'Does it? That sounds like experience talking.'

Mariner shifted in his seat. Now wasn't the time. 'Think

about it,' he said. 'Yasmin's parents are both high achievers, which makes me wonder what sort of pressure they put on their children.'

'Without playing a particularly active part in their lives. They're "busy people". Sounds as if most of the parenting gets left to grandma.'

'Even worse then: at seventeen, having an elderly woman breathing down your neck.'

'Yasmin might have a great relationship with her grandmother,' Millie said.

'Yes, she might.' But the ensuing silence signalled that they both had doubts.

'Have a look in the inside pocket of my jacket.'

Reaching round to the back seat, Millie fished out the plastic wallet containing the sheet of A4. 'What's this?'

'It's the latest of a series.' Mariner took her briefly through his conversation with Mohammed Akram.

'So he was pretty quick off the mark to finger Cox's organisation.'

Mariner shrugged. 'If you've been subjected to that kind of campaign it would be only natural. Though I did wonder about their knowledge of the Koran.'

'It would be a clever tactic though: turning someone's religious beliefs back on them.'

'Maybe.'

'Alternatively, this could have come from inside the community. Sometimes the in-fighting can be worse than anything from the outside.'

Mariner turned to her. 'You've got a reason for saying that?'

'Fakhra in the office was less than discreet. Competition to get into Allah T'ala is fierce. There are forty-six places available for the new term, and they've already had a hundred and thirty-eight applications.'

'Mm, Akram said as much to me.'

'Did he also tell you that one family in particular was upset that their child didn't get a place for September.'

35

'Not specifically. But forty-six vacancies for a hundred and thirty-eight kids doesn't make for great odds. Not getting a place is pure bad luck, no worse than losing on the lottery. Why take it personally?'

'This child is very disabled. The father is bitter about this anyway and has turned his frustration on the school. According to Fakhra he's also religious fanatic and "a bit of a nutter". The consensus is that he was the one who damaged Akram's car.'

'Did you get a name and address?'

'Fakhra was reluctant. She said she'd want to speak to Mrs Akram first. They don't want to make more trouble for this man's family. I think she already felt she'd said too much.'

'All we'd want to do is eliminate him from the enquiry.'

Millie wafted the letter in mid-air. 'In the meantime, how seriously do we take this?'

'It's hard to say. After the quote, it all gets a bit vague, so I wouldn't want to automatically jump to any conclusions. And it's not much of a lead. It could have been written by anyone with access to a PC.'

'Even Mr Akram.'

'That had crossed my mind.'

'You didn't immediately warm to him, did you?' Millie said.

'That obvious? I agree with you that his reactions weren't quite right, anger seemed to outweigh anxiety.'

'It's not always an indicator. People can be very good at covering their feelings, can't they? His wife is clearly not coping, so he may feel it's important to try and appear in control, even though he's not.'

'I felt it was more than that. I thought he seemed annoyed with her.'

'She'd been left in charge.'

'But that shouldn't make her wholly responsible. There seemed to be some blaming going on.'

Millie didn't seem convinced. She turned her attention

36

back to the letter. 'But if this is a genuine threat we might be looking at abduction.'

'Could be. Akram was quick to suggest that too.'

'Wouldn't we expect a ransom demand?'

'Not necessarily right away. The timing would have to be right.'

'And in the meantime?'

'We continue to treat this as a missing persons and talk to the people who really know what Yasmin is thinking.'

In terms of location there could hardly have been a greater contrast between the small Islamic school and the girls high school that Yasmin attended. On the Granville Lane patch, it was more familiar to Mariner. Purpose built in the mid 1930s the red-brick building nestled snugly in leafy suburbia, surrounded by acres of what at any other time of year would have been lush green grass, but which had by now been scorched to a crusty, brownish yellow by the relentless sun.

Here Mariner really was glad of Millie's presence. Preadolescent girls had ceased to be one of his areas of expertise for going on for thirty years. In addition, these were likely to be worried adolescent girls, given that one of their friends had disappeared. The meeting with Yasmin's closest friends was to be supervised by the head of pastoral care but, even so, Mariner felt a certain apprehension as, in the middle of the afternoon, he and Millie drove slowly along the winding, tree-lined drive.

They were a little early, so were invited to take a seat in the reception area to wait.

With its coffee-table reading and lush green pot plants it was more like the lobby of a private corporation, though it lacked the comfort of air conditioning. The power of the connection between aroma and memory never failed to amaze Mariner, and the combined old-school smell of cleaning fluids and cooked food was one

37

of the most potent of all. His lightweight suit felt suddenly constrictive as he made a conscious effort not to let his own experiences affect his perceptions. His own schooldays had been far from the happiest of his life when he'd been a square peg in a round hole at the boys grammar school he'd attended.

Nearly six feet tall by the age of thirteen, he'd stood out, literally at first, and then socially too, when people had gradually discovered that his was a single-parent family. Lone parents back then were still a relative rarity, and amongst his particular strand of lower-middle-class population were virtually unheard of. Throw into the equation his mother's eccentric mode of dress and outspoken views and any attempts of his to blend in hadn't stood a chance. He and Anna had recently watched the video *About a Boy* and in the central character Mariner had seen shades of himself, from the bizarre dress code to the gross social ineptitude. He too had been a victim of hand-knitted pullovers and oversized home-made PE shorts. Even his lunches had been outside the norm, with sandwiches made from home-baked wholemeal bread at a time when white sliced Mother's Pride was all the rage. It was during those years, at the age when conforming meant everything, that his relationship with his mother had begun to deteriorate.

Mariner wondered how Yasmin fitted in here. Looking at the most recent school photo, displayed on the wall ahead of them, there weren't many other brown faces. Did it mean that Yasmin had a point to prove, or was she made to feel like an outsider? The staff line-up was interesting too: the proportion of men to women more evenly balanced than he might have expected and Mariner wondered not for the first time what would make any man want to work in a school full of young girls, exposing himself to unattainable temptation.

Unlike the displays at the Islamic school, here around the main photograph were displayed sketched portraits, drawn, the label announced, by members of the Year 12

38

A level art group: pencil sketches of body parts. The most striking one was of a male torso, from the waist to just below the chin, displaying a series of intricate tattoos on the biceps and shoulders. It was expertly drawn, the proportions just right.

'Robbie Williams,' said Millie, knowledgeably, at the same moment as the deputy head appeared. Small and trim, her powder-blue suit and bright turquoise and yellow blouse, offset by shoulder-length blond hair, Mrs Darrow stood out like an exotic bird amid the drab navy blues of the school uniforms. She apologised for keeping them waiting before setting off at a brisk, high-heeled pace along endless corridors, leading them through what seemed to be an impossible number of left turns. Occasionally, confident young women clomped by in heavy shoes and perilously short skirts, surreptitiously eyeing them up, perhaps thinking that they were parents, although Millie was way too young. Mariner took the opportunity of the lengthy trek to draw out Mrs Darrow's opinion of Yasmin.

'She's a popular girl,' was the somewhat trite reply. 'She came to us from her parents' Islamic school, which is a big leap, especially socially, but she seemed to take it absolutely in her stride.'

'Her parents implied that she's had a sheltered upbringing.'

'Relatively perhaps, but she's had the opportunity to spread her wings here. In many ways Yasmin's background is very different to some of the other girls, but because she's friendly and outgoing, she gets along with people. She's also not afraid to express her own opinions. Don't be misled into thinking of Yasmin as some "poor little black girl", Inspector.'

'Would anyone particularly resent that, an Asian girl being clever and popular?'

Mrs Darrow stopped and turned to face him. 'We don't tolerate racism or bullying in this school, if that's what you're implying.'

39

'That's not to say that it doesn't go on.' Mariner held her gaze. 'I can't imagine that there's any school that doesn't have a problem with bullying; some establishments are just more aware of it than others.'

Mrs Darrow's colour deepened before she walked on. 'You're right of course, Inspector, realistically it happens, but I've never known it to be an issue with Yasmin.'

'You have a high reputation in the area,' commented Millie.

Had she been a bird, Mrs Darrow would at that point have preened her feathers. 'Mm. We had an eighty-four per cent pass rate at A–C and a ninety-three per cent pass rate at A level last year. It put us into the top ten in the national league tables and this year we're on stream to do even better.' The numbers, largely meaningless to Mariner, fairly tripped off her tongue.

'And is Yasmin keeping up?'

'Her GCSE grades were excellent: six A stars, three As, one B.' She frowned. 'Although as with most of the girls, she's finding sixth form a little more of a challenge.'

'Why's that?' asked Mariner.

'The work is harder,' she said simply. 'Added to which these are adolescent girls, Inspector, at the mercy of their hormones. They get distracted. It's not an uncommon thing to happen. They're under an enormous amount of pressure, to be clever, pretty and popular. Some girls cope better than others. For Yasmin there's the additional conflict that what her parents want for her isn't necessarily what she wants.'

'And what does she want?'

'At present, just to keep her options open.'

'And her parents don't?'

'Like many of our parents, Mr and Mrs Akram have fairly fixed ideas about what constitutes a worthwhile career. Often those views can be quite traditional.'

'Medicine or law,' Millie chipped in.

Mrs Darrow smiled. 'Exactly.'

40

'What would be her teachers' response to a drop in standard?'

'We'd encourage her to put in that little bit more effort.'

'Would that worry Yasmin?'

'It's hard to tell, but I'd guess that it might unsettle her a bit. Yasmin's a bright girl, and I know her parents have high hopes for her.'

'Are they adding to the pressure?'

'No more than any other parents who want their child to do well,' Mrs Darrow responded quickly.

'What's your relationship with Yasmin's parents like?'

'They're very supportive. Many of the resources we acquire these days are accessed through specific government initiatives, often through matched funding.' Seeing the blank expressions she continued. 'We put up half and the DfES matches it.'

'Ah.'

'Yasmin's father has been very generous in our endeavour to acquire language college status.'

'What about friends? You said Yasmin is popular.'

'She's part of an established group.'

'And Suzanne Perry, the friend her mother thought she was staying with?'

'I was quite surprised about that, I must say. Their friendship has always been rather an unlikely alliance.'

'Why do you say that?'

'I'll let you find out for yourselves. Here we are.'

They had reached their destination and Mrs Darrow pushed open the door of what seemed to be some kind of recreational room. Low, comfortable chairs were grouped around a couple of square wood-effect utilitarian coffee tables. At least she'd taken on board Mariner's request to keep this informal. There were five girls present. They had been talking, but quietened politely when Mrs Darrow appeared. They weren't cocky and street-wise like the girls Mariner was used to dealing with. Even at this age, they seemed cool and sophisticated and more than a little intimidating as they appraised their visitors and Mariner wished he'd checked his flies before coming in. Each girl had put her individual stamp on the school uniform, but one in particular stood out. She looked older than the others, not just because of her spiky red hair or the heavy black eyeliner that circled her eyes. There was something about her demeanour. She was the only girl in the room to return Mariner's gaze, and some.

There were three vacant seats. Mrs Darrow offered one each to Mariner and Millie, before making introductions and taking the other herself.

As Mariner had agreed with her beforehand, Millie took the lead in the hope that the girls might be more relaxed with a woman nearer their age and therefore more inclined to open up. Mariner was impressed with the way she handled it, too: just the right proportion of friendly to professional.

'Hi. We're really glad that you agreed to meet with us today. If any of you has any idea where Yasmin might have gone, it's really important that you tell us now. It goes without saying that everyone's very concerned about her, and she may be in danger.' Silence. Time to be more specific.

'Yasmin told her mum that she was going for a sleepover with Suzanne. Is that right?' Millie scanned the room, inviting a response from Suzanne. When none came Mrs Darrow offered a gentle prompt. 'Suzanne?'

'That's right.' The sullen reply came from the spiky-haired girl, who addressed her answer to Mariner, at the same time shifting in her seat and conspicuously adjusting her tiny skirt.

'So what happened?' Millie asked.

'She changed her mind.' Her green eyes remained disconcertingly fixed on Mariner's, but Millie persevered.

'Why was that?'

'She said she wasn't feeling too well. And she felt bad about coming.'

42

'What about the project?'

Finally, Suzanne turned to face Millie. 'What project?'

'The project you and Yasmin were working on, that you had to finish?'

Suzanne frowned. 'First I've heard of it.'

'OK. Why do you think Yasmin changed her mind about coming?'

'Because of the row with her dad,' she said with exaggerated patience, finally switching eye contact to Millie.

'What row was that?'

'About the sleepover.' Mariner could imagine her tapping the side of her head in despair. What kind of thicko was she dealing with here? 'Her dad wouldn't let her come.'

Understandably, Millie was puzzled. 'I don't understand. I thought she'd had her parents' permission.'

'Her mum's,' Suzanne corrected. 'Her dad had said absolutely no, but when she knew he was going away, Yasmin talked her mum round. That's the whole point. That's why she changed her mind. She felt bad about going against her dad.'

So the Akrams were in conflict about Yasmin's sleepover with Suzanne. That explained a lot.

'So the two of you hadn't fallen out?'

'No. Yasmin just succumbed to emotional blackmail, as she was expected to do.' Her voice was heavy with contempt.

'And as far as you're aware, Yasmin went straight home from school?'

'Yes. She said it would keep.'

'What would?' Mariner asked. Suddenly he was interested and Suzanne knew it.

'She had something important to tell me, but that by the next day it would be better, there would be more to tell.'

'Have you any idea what this was all about?'

'No. But Yasmin was pretty wound up about it.' She was playing him like a violin.

43

'Wound up how? Excited or worried?'

Suzanne took her time. 'I'd say excited.'

'But she didn't give any hints about what it was?'

'No.'

'Who travels home with Yasmin regularly?' Millie asked. A couple of hands went up tentatively. Mariner had forgotten what a programmed response that was. 'Could you tell us about that journey, yesterday?'

At last a shrug from the girl called Emma, with dark hair tied back and an uneven, lumpy complexion. 'It was just the same as any other. We had graffiti club after school so we were late leaving.'

'Graffiti club?'

Mrs Darrow smiled. 'No, we're not encouraging vandalism, Constable. It's just the trendy name for our art club.' A couple of the girls rolled their eyes, smirking at her use of the word 'trendy'.

'What time was that?'

'About quarter to five,' the girl whose frizzy red hair was escaping from her ponytail spoke up. 'We had to go back into school because Yaz couldn't find her travel card. We had to retrace our steps, everywhere we'd been that day.'

'And did you find it?'

'It was on the floor in the art room. The last place we'd been. Typical.'

'Go on, Emma,' Millie encouraged.

'It was the same as usual. We all walked down the road together. Some of us carried on along the main road to get the bus, while Yaz went down the side road towards the station for her train. We could see it coming in as she got there, so she had to run.'

'Is Yasmin the only one to get the train?'

Another girl spoke up as confidence began to grow. 'Some other girls in the school do, but none of our crowd.'

'At that time in the afternoon, most of the girls would have already gone,' added Mrs Darrow. 'The only ones left

44

are those who stay for after-school activities. We've asked for anyone who might have seen Yasmin on the train to come forward, but they haven't as yet. It's quite possible that no one did.'

'And no one else lives near Yasmin?'

Shakes of the head, but it didn't come as any surprise. They already knew that.

'And Yasmin didn't say anything about doing anything different or going anywhere yesterday evening? Could she have gone into the city, for example?'

'Suzanne?' Mrs Darrow prompted.

Suzanne merely shrugged and it was Emma who supplied the answer. 'We had a piece of English homework that was going to be hard. Yaz was going to phone me later when she got home.'

'And Yasmin was excited rather than worried about anything. Other than the disagreement about the sleepover, nothing recently upset her?' Mariner asked Suzanne directly.

'She was pissed off with her parents, but what's new?' She glanced at Mrs Darrow to see if her language would be censured and was satisfied by a disapproving glare. Mariner could imagine Suzanne being pissed off with just about anyone. She behaved like a girl who was used to controlling adults for her own ends, and it was becoming glaringly obvious why Yasmin's parents didn't want to encourage the friendship between their daughter and this girl. He wondered what it was that made her so angry. But then he remembered that most teenagers were like that at some point – for no reason at all. He was just out of touch.

'Yasmin's old man doesn't give her an inch. She's always in trouble with him about something lately. He's a psycho.'

'Suzanne, that's going too far!' Mrs Darrow was looking not at all happy about the way this was going.

Shooting her a look that would fell an elephant at nine paces, Suzanne's 'what would you know?' remained unspoken, but it reverberated around the room nonethe-

45

less. 'Look at the fuss they made about her staying late for graffiti club.' It was quoted as evidence, making Mariner wonder if this girl might have a career in law ahead of her.

'They were unhappy about that?' said Millie.

'Her dad was unhappy about anything that wasn't work. "Go to school, go home, do your homework." Yaz is expected to be a good little Asian girl.'

'Does she resent that?'

'Sure she does, but not enough to do anything about it. She's not allowed to wear make-up, but instead of standing up to her parents she just puts it on while she's on the train coming into school and washes it off afterwards. She just gives in to them all the time.'

'But she comes to graffiti club.'

'Only because Sir stuck up for her.'

'Has anyone got anything else to add?' asked Millie after a respectable pause. More shakes of the head.

'Well, if there's anything else you think of, we'll be giving Mrs Darrow a contact number for us. And please remember, it's vital that you tell us anything you know, however small or unimportant it may seem.'

The teacher nodded in agreement. 'I'll put the number on the common room bulletin board.' And as there seemed nothing else forthcoming, she dismissed the girls back to their lessons.

'I'm sorry that wasn't more helpful,' said Mrs Darrow when they'd gone. 'And I would take Suzanne's last comments with a pinch of salt. Some of the girls at this age do have this "the whole world's against me" mentality, usually with parents and school at the top of the list. Added to that, their imaginations are fuelled by the constant confrontations they see on TV soaps. Suzanne in particular can be something of a drama queen.'

'Who runs this graffiti club?' Mariner wanted to know.

'The "Sir" Suzanne mentioned: Mr Goodway. He's the head of D & T.'

Mariner turned to Millie for clarification. 'Design and Technology,' she grinned, shaking her head sadly. 'I expect it was plain old woodwork in your day.'

'We could do with talking to him. It looks as if he may have been one of the last adults to see Yasmin yesterday afternoon.'

'We can see if he's free.'

Chapter Four

Brian Goodway blinked rapidly at them through dense wire-framed glasses. Although school was in session, he had what Mrs Darrow referred to as a 'non-contact' period, and they found him pottering about in the technology room, which Mariner discovered to be the home of wood- and metalwork, textiles and art. Picking him out on the school photo, Mariner wouldn't have attributed anything artistic to Brian Goodway. He was too tidy, more maths or geography, with his neatly knotted tie and one of those ubiquitous tweed jackets that had gone out of fashion years ago with everyone except a certain generation of teachers, although this one didn't extend quite as far as leather elbow patches.

The classroom was a different matter entirely: a chaotic arrangement of workbenches topped by the skeletal wire forms of half-finished sculptures and interspersed with spindly easels displaying adolescent creations in various stages of completion. Goodway himself seemed surprisingly unmarked by the fallout; several pairs of overalls hanging on the back of the door took the strain.

Mariner's eye was caught by a particularly ghoulish design, not unlike those on display in the entrance hall. 'Body art,' Goodway volunteered, seeing Mariner's interest. 'If you're going to motivate the kids you have to operate on their level. The days of sketching a vase of flowers or bowls of fruit are long gone. That particular effort was drawn by a young lady in class 9G. She's been working on it for three weeks now, mainly because of the problems she's had with the proportions of the eagle's head just here, getting those feathers to sit properly.' He ran a finger along the offending area, and Mariner had the impression that whichever of the creations he had picked on, Goodway would have been able to supply exactly the same amount of detail.

Goodway showed them some still life drawings that Yasmin had been working on. One was a pencil drawing of a hand, the veins and skin texture perfect. 'Yasmin is a very talented young girl,' he told them. 'Art is a discipline like any other. Along with creativity you must have an eye for precision.' He smoothed his sparse sandy hair over his scalp and took his glasses off to wipe them on a tissue. 'Occupational hazard,' he explained.

'I understand that you fought Yasmin's corner for her when her parents were reluctant to let her stay for the club.'

'It would have been a criminal waste if she hadn't been given the opportunity to develop her talents. As it is, she's been persuaded to give up art in favour of more academic subjects at A level. Graffiti club means that she can pursue both.'

'Would she make a living at it?' Mariner asked, wondering if this was the conflict of interests with what her parents had in mind for her.

Flattening his hair again, Goodway let out a sigh. 'As a freelance artist? Not necessarily. Art is a competitive world.' He gestured towards a photograph of three teenage children, two boys and a girl, that was pinned to the wall above the corner desk. 'That's my daughter Chloe,' he said. 'She's in her twenties now and was gifted enough to get a place at the Slade Art College in London, but she still struggles to make a living as an artist. I try to ensure that the girls here have a realistic view of what they can achieve. Encourage them to get their academic qualifications too, looking at a more structured career within the art world, perhaps within graphic design or illustration.'

'How did Yasmin seem at your class yesterday afternoon?'

'Fine. The girls seem to like the club. It's a chance to relax and shake off the shackles of prescribed coursework.' A twinkle gleamed in his eye. Despite appearances, maybe there was a rebellious streak in there after all.

'She hadn't fallen out with anyone?'

Goodway shook his head. 'You know what youngsters are like. Even if she had I doubt that I would know. It may be a more relaxed class, but I don't fool myself that any of the girls would share much with an old fogey like me.'

Mariner wasn't so sure. 'Why do you think Yasmin's parents weren't keen on her staying for the graffiti club?'

'They're naturally protective of her. The club runs throughout the year and in the winter months it can mean the girls getting home well after dark. Yasmin had a longer journey than most.'

'What changed their minds?'

Goodway shrugged as if it was no big deal. 'I had a chat with them and they're reasonable people.'

Not what Suzanne seemed to be saying, but then the adult perspective would be a different one. 'Thanks, Mr Goodway.'

They were nearly out of the door when Goodway called after them, uncertainly. 'Yasmin's a good kid. I hope she turns up soon.'

Mariner turned back. 'So do we, Mr Goodway. So do we.'

'He seems like a very committed teacher,' Mariner remarked, as Mrs Darrow walked them back through the school.

'He's inspirational, a real Mr Chips. We don't get many of those any more. I think having had his own teenage children helps him to stay in tune with the girls.' She was full of admiration. 'We'll be sorry when he goes.'

'Goes? He seems a little young for retirement.'

'Mr Goodway wants to spend more time with his family,' was all Mrs Darrow would say.

From the art department Mrs Darrow took them to Yasmin's locker, opening it with a master key. It revealed little. The inside of the door was lined with the ubiquitous teen posters of pop stars and TV presenters, none of whom Mariner recognised. A wad of drawings or a sketchpad fell out and scattered on the floor. The drawings were good. Some of the same 'body art' that they had seen in the classroom. On the face of it they'd learned little to progress their search, except perhaps to learn that Mr and Mrs Akram hadn't been entirely candid with them.

They were standing directly underneath the bell when it rang deafeningly, signalling the end of the day. Through the open door of the classroom opposite, they watched girls filing out, dipping into a bright red plastic crate on the way.

'Retrieving their mobile phones,' Mrs Darrow explained. 'The things are a nightmare. We tried banning them completely at first, but it was hopeless as practically all the girls have them. Parents complained too that they needed to know that their daughters were safe. Ironic, given this current situation. So, instead, most teachers collect them in at the beginning of each lesson, to remove any temptation to use them.'

'Couldn't the girls just switch them off?'

'Not with text messaging. The girls can be holding lengthy conversations without staff even knowing. It's a distraction we can do without.'

'Do any ever get left behind?'

Mrs Darrow knew what he was getting at. She shook her head. 'Very rarely. It's amazing. These girls might lose everything else: clothing, books, jewellery, you name it, but their phones seem to be surgically attached. The few that are get put in lost property. You're welcome to have a look.' They did, but of the couple of outdated units that were there, neither could be identified as Yasmin's.

51

'Well, thank you for your time.'

'Not at all, Inspector. Whatever we can do to help.'

'I don't get it,' said Millie as they drove from the school. 'How can someone just disappear?'

'If she wants to, it's easy.' Millie had guessed right. Mariner spoke from personal experience. He'd done it himself when he couldn't face another night of coming home to the Spanish Inquisition. His mother had taken his popularity with girls particularly hard. Although he had vague memories of the occasional short-term 'uncle' early on, latterly it had just been the two of them and, as Mariner grew, the dynamics of dependency had shifted as his mother had discarded the other facets of her life to concentrate on him. Her whole life became dedicated to her only child and, at the time when other parents were letting go, Mariner's mother clutched on with increasing desperation, until finally he had to take the initiative and break away completely. So instead of getting the bus to school one day, on an impulse he'd caught the train to Birmingham and gone to look for a job. Except for brief visits he'd never gone back.

'If what Suzanne told us is right though, it sounds as if everything wasn't as rosy in the Akram household as we were led to believe,' he said now.

'You think she was telling us the truth?'

'It would account for the tension between Mr and Mrs Akram, wouldn't it? I thought he was just annoyed that his wife had contacted us before telling him. And having left her in charge it may be natural to hold her responsible. But if she'd gone against his wishes as well ... Let's go and see what we can pick up at home.'

The two uniformed officers who were to help with the preliminary search met them at the Akrams' house, which turned out to be a detached red-brick, large and imposing, built at around the turn of the last century. It was the home

52

of successful people. With the shrinking of the nuclear family, these houses were normally too big to fulfil a useful purpose as a family home and several of the properties on this street displayed boards to indicate their conversion to business hotels and retirement residences. The Akrams' property was set back from the road behind a five-foot high decorative wall; the entire front of the house shaded by a dark umbrella of chestnut trees, creating a cool oasis of relief from the heat. Grandma, an elderly woman in white *mengha*, came to the door, her eyes watery, whether from age or from weeping it was hard to say.

'*Salaam Allah Kouom,*' Millie smiled, knowing that she spoke little English.

The old lady nodded. '*Walaik um-asalaam.*'

Millie explained in Urdu the reason for their visit. Scrutinising Mariner's ID, the old woman nodded word-lessly and indicated that they should follow her. Akram had phoned ahead to let her know they were coming. She led them through the house. Cool and dark with high ceilings, it was neat and tidy and deathly quiet in the absence of anyone else.

Leaving the rest of the house to the uniforms, Mariner and Millie focused their efforts on Yasmin's bedroom on the first floor. It was comfortably furnished, the décor in feminine pastels, but without extravagance. The giant desk that took up most of the room was clutter-free beneath a solid shelf of reference books, and there was no CD player, TV nor any of the other usual electronic paraphernalia that most kids were reported to have these days. Half a dozen cuddly toys were neatly arranged on the bed and a further shelf displayed a number of photographs, including a formal family group, presumably taken at her older sister's wedding. Millie picked up the photograph to verify this with Grandma. The two women embarked on an animated conversation, during which Millie successfully shepherded Grandma back downstairs, leaving Mariner to continue the search unobserved.

Yasmin's hair brushes were neatly aligned on the dressing table. If they were going to need DNA ... Mariner refused to let his mind move along that track. A small jewellery box contained a few simple gold chains and bracelets. Checking in the drawers, her clothes were neatly folded. The only hidden treasure Mariner found was a small pouch of eye shadows and mascara hidden under some T-shirts at the back of a drawer. Apart from the schoolwork there were no personal items: no diaries or letters that were going to help them out.

Mariner heard the front door slam and, moments later, a small figure appeared in the doorway. Yasmin's younger brother.

Mariner smiled. 'Hello. It's Sanjit, right?'

A nod. 'You're a policeman?'

'That's right.'

'Are you looking for Yaz?'

'Yes. Have you got any idea where she might have gone?'

The boy shrugged. 'She doesn't talk to me, except for a bit of verbal abuse.' He made a quacking gesture with his fingers and thumb and Mariner curbed a smile.

'What are you looking for?' Sanjit asked.

'Anything that might give us clues about where Yasmin is.'

'Have you found her secret box?'

'No.'

Without another word the boy dropped to the floor and wriggled on his belly under the bed, emerging minutes later with a small, cardboard shoebox. 'She doesn't think I know about it.' He handed it to Mariner. Inside were an ornately carved rubberwood chest and a ceramic moneybox in the shape of a teddy bear. Mariner lifted the lid of the first. It contained more make-up, a leaflet for the Tate Modern, illustrated with a Lucien Freud nude, and a couple of tickets for the London Underground dated March of that year. 'Did you go down to London too?' Mariner asked.

'No, she went with her school.'

Euston to Embankment. Must have been a special trip if she'd preserved the tickets. And why two tickets? Yasmin and Suzanne?

The moneybox, when he prised off the stopper in its base, contained three ten-pound notes and some loose change.

'It's her pocket money,' said Sanjit. And surely the sort of money Yasmin would have taken with her if the disappearance had been planned.

'Anything unusual happen lately?' Mariner asked, replacing the items. 'Yasmin fall out with anyone?'

Sanjit rolled his eyes. 'She's always arguing with Dad, stomping around and slamming doors. We have to walk on egg boxes all the time,' he said, in an approximation of the phrase.

The woodentops had given the house a good going-over but found no sign of Yasmin nor anything else unusual, and nearly an hour after their arrival, Mariner pulled out of the drive hardly any the wiser.

'Not much to help us then,' he said. 'All we know is that Yasmin had a row with her dad about staying at Suzanne's, then apparently Mum gives in while Dad's away and says she can go. Did you ask Grandma about that?'

'Yes, and she has views all right although she was coy about expressing them. Naturally she sides with her son and sees this as a direct consequence of Yasmin's mother flouting his wishes.'

'So she blames Shanila rather than Yasmin.'

'Not exactly. She just implied that Yasmin is no different from your average teenager, and that it's her parents' duty to give her strict boundaries. *Righteous women shall be obedient. And those you fear may be rebellious admonish.* It's what the Koran says.'

'Then perversely, when her mother lets her go beyond those boundaries, Yasmin decides not to go to Suzanne's after all, but for some reason doesn't make it home either.'

'Because she'd had enough of rules and wants out completely?'

'She didn't take any money with her.'

'It's not necessarily long term. It could just be a gesture. Giving her old man the finger because of the hard time he's been giving her?'

'Anything's possible.' And that was the whole problem. There was nothing to narrow the scope of the search.

Back at Granville Lane DS Tony Knox had requisitioned the CCTV footage from Kingsmead Station, where Yasmin boarded her train.

'What's it like?' Mariner asked as they settled down to watch.

Knox shrugged indifferently. 'See for yourself.'

The black and white image was crude and snowy. Knox perched on a desk behind Mariner and Millie as they watched a train draw into the station. A number of people alighted while a couple further down the platform climbed on. Then, at the last minute, to the bottom right-hand corner of the screen a figure could be seen running for and jumping on the train. A split second before the doors closed on her she turned and gave them a full facial shot. No question it was Yasmin.

Knox snapped off the film. 'The footage from the university station isn't quite so helpful.' This was the station at which Yasmin would have alighted. 'It's harder to see Yasmin: there's a lot of movement.' It was the understatement of the year. The platform was crowded and although several people left the train, they had to strain their eyes to pick Yasmin out as any of them.

'There,' said Millie, eventually. Reaching out, she pointed to a figure moving across the bottom of the screen.

'Right height and build,' Knox agreed. 'Same colour clothing from what you can see, and a bag over her shoulder.'

'Like just about everyone else,' said Mariner.

56

'She's walking pretty casually, too. In no particular hurry.'

'That's Yasmin Akram?' They all turned. They hadn't heard Fiske come into the room.

'We think it might be.' Mariner remained cautious.

'Good, so we know that she followed her normal route.'

'We're not—'

But Fiske didn't want uncertainty. 'Which means that she must have disappeared somewhere between the station and her house,' he cut in. 'I understand that from there she walks through part of the university campus to get home?'

'Yes, sir.'

'In that case let's do a search of the area between the station and her home. If that turns up nothing we'll do the railway track.'

'But—'

'You'll need to talk to the university security, too. Are we absolutely certain there's no one she could be staying with?'

'Her parents have spoken to anyone they can think of. Robbie Thorne is double-checking that. And we'll do the usual phone round of hospital emergency departments. I think we should—'

'So let's just get on with it, shall we? Organise the search for first thing in the morning. I'll make sure that there are uniformed officers at your disposal and we can bring in an additional search team if necessary.' He was halfway out of the door before he turned and added, 'That's good work all of you. Well done.'

'He's easily impressed,' remarked Millie when Fiske had gone.

'He's just hoping that he might be able to stop shitting himself sometime soon,' said Knox.

'That's what I'm afraid of,' said Mariner, getting up from his seat. He caught up with Fiske just outside the DCI's office. 'Arranging a search at this stage is a bit premature, sir,' he said.

57

'Nonsense,' said Fiske. 'We've got the CCTV footage. What more do you need?'

'It's not entirely clear. I'd like to get it enhanced to be sure.'

'But I saw it with my own eyes and your colleagues seemed pretty certain. What reason is there to delay? Superintendent Bourne is due to meet with community leaders later this afternoon and it would be beneficial to have something substantial to give them. Get it done, Mariner, first thing tomorrow.'

'I'll need to widen the investigation team,' said Mariner. 'Millie and I can't do this alone. And Charlie Glover's in the same boat.'

'Use whoever you need,' said Fiske. 'Charlie Glover's on a different enquiry. For the moment our priority is to find Yasmin Akram. If Charlie Glover doesn't like it he can come and talk to me.'

And giving Mariner no further opportunity to argue, he turned and went into his office, resolutely closing the door.

So that's what the hurry was all about: Fiske's desperation to impress Superintendent Bourne with the efficiency of his leadership. Mariner hoped that Yasmin Akram would turn up soon, alive and well. He also hoped that somewhere along the way Fiske would shoot himself comprehensively in the foot.

When he got back to the office Knox had gone.

'Isn't he a jolly soul?' said Millie. 'Not one word to me after you'd gone out.'

At the time Mariner had barely noticed but now he thought about it, Knox had seemed unusually subdued, and he hadn't been particularly welcoming to Millie. 'Promotion back to CID must be losing its novelty value,' he concluded, hoping he was right. After all, it had been a couple of months since Knox had returned to the fold following his digression, so the initial elation must be wearing off.

58

'Anything else?' he asked.

Picking up the phone, Millie shook her head. 'I'll start on the calls.' She'd be checking the usual: hospitals, hostels, and women's refuges, within a ten-mile radius. If that yielded nothing, they'd spread the net.

Meanwhile, Mariner ensured that the photograph of Yasmin was being circulated citywide, including to the press, and fixed a TV bulletin for the nine o'clock local news.

It was close to eleven when they both resurfaced. Now they had to sit back and wait for the results. 'We've done everything we can for now. We might as well knock it on the head for tonight,' said Mariner.

'I'll see you in the morning, sir.'

It being mid-week Anna would have her hands full with Jamie, so there was little point in Mariner calling round to see her tonight. Despite the heat, the aromas of Sparkhill had lingered with Mariner and were tweaking at his appetite, so when he drove past Yasser's, his local Balti house, and saw that it was still open, it was impossible to resist stopping.

Only when he was inside did he see that Tony Knox had fallen on the same idea. Nodding a greeting, Mariner placed his order and sat down beside Knox on the bench.

'Dinner's in the dog, eh?' he joked.

Knox looked momentarily blank. 'Oh yeah,' he said, eventually catching on.

'Tell Theresa it's my fault,' Mariner went on. 'Keeping you out all hours.'

'Sure.' But unusually for the otherwise gregarious Knox, he wasn't inclined to talk. Not that Mariner minded. He was tired himself, and there had been enough talking today. So they sat in companionable silence until Knox's order was called and he got wearily to his feet.

'See you in the morning,' said Mariner.

'Right, boss.'

But ten minutes later, as he left the restaurant himself, Mariner was surprised to see Knox with his carrier bag: standing, waiting at the bus stop. He pulled over and lowered a window. 'Want a lift?'

'Nah, you're all right, boss.' Knox glanced up the road hopefully, though it was late and Mariner could see in his rear-view mirror that there was no sign of any red, white and blue double decker.

Both men knew that Mariner would have to virtually drive past Knox's doorstep on his way home and by now Mariner was curious to know what was going on. 'This is ridiculous, Tony,' he said. 'Get in.'

Knox wouldn't meet his eye, but this time he concurred.

'I didn't know your car was off the road,' said Mariner conversationally as his own vehicle began to fill with the warm smell of cumin and coriander.

'The bus is fine.'

Drawing up outside Knox's house Mariner noted the complete darkness. Knox's kids were grown up now, his daughter living with her own child and partner and his son away at university. 'Theresa not home, then,' Mariner said.

'She's up in Liverpool, has been the last few weekends. Her mother's not well.'

'I'm sorry. How old is she?'

'Seventy-two.'

'Well, I hope she pulls through.'

'Thanks.' Knox pushed open the car door. 'I won't ask you in, boss, the place is a bit of a tip. But cheers for the lift.'

Chapter Five

Closing his front door on the world, Tony Knox bent to pick up the mail from the mat. He'd recovered from that first plunging disappointment he'd felt on seeing the empty driveway, but now anticipation rose again as he embarked on the emotional bungee jump that had become his end-of-the-day ritual. He sifted through the post, each letter stabbing at him anew as he passed over bills and junk mail and found none bearing her handwriting. Disgusted, he tossed them on to the growing stack. She hardly ever wrote to anyone so why would she suddenly take to writing him letters? Especially now.

For a moment he hovered over the phone, wondering whether to check call minder now, or to wait, in the superstitious hope that patience would be rewarded with a positive outcome. Superstition lost out. Leaving his supper on the kitchen table, he returned to the phone and keyed in the number of the answering service. Two new messages. His hopes soared again. 'Come on, come on!' he urged the recorded voice. But call one was from a call centre in Delhi, asking him to reconsider his mortgage arrangements and message two was a hang-up. Cresting the wave of optimism, he came tumbling down on the other side and the searing emptiness that had taken temporary residence somewhere above his diaphragm returned: the same black hole he'd woken up with every morning for the last two weeks.

Walking back into the kitchen, Knox stared at the plastic carrier bag, smelled the rich spices, and they made him want to gag. Instead, in the lounge he picked up the next in the neat row of Glenfiddichs that he'd stockpiled over the last few Christmases. For years they'd stood untouched in the cupboard. He didn't really even like Scotch, but the in-laws had got it into their heads years ago that he did. Now, after less than a fortnight, the shelf was nearly empty. Still, it needed using up and if it got him to sleep at night and helped him to face the day, that couldn't be a bad thing. The phone rang as he was swallowing the last dregs in the glass. He raced to pick it up.

'Dad? It's Sinead.' Knocked back again. 'Mum told me. Are you OK?' Asked out of concern or sense of duty?

'I'm fine.'

'Will you be able to sort this one out?'

'I don't know, love.'

'You have before.'

'This is different.'

'Well, if you need anything, you know where we are.' The offer was cool, the onus on him. The sub-text: this is your fault, you stupid old git. Well, he didn't need his daughter to tell him that.

'Dave and the kids OK?' he asked.

'We're all good; just worried about you.' Christ, when did that about face happen? So suddenly he hadn't even noticed it. 'See you, Dad.'

'Bye, love.' Cradling the phone, he looked around the room at the depressing mess: the accumulation of soiled mugs and glasses, items of clothing discarded from the nights when he couldn't face the bed they'd shared and had opted instead to sleep on the sofa. He'd clean it up later. But first he'd have another drink. He couldn't find his glass so he swigged straight from the bottle, the first mouthful burning a path to sweet oblivion.

Mariner, likewise, returned home to an uncharacteristically

empty house. His lodgers, Nat and Jenny, students at the university, were away backpacking in Eastern Europe for their summer vacation. After years of contentedly living alone, he was surprised to find how much he missed them. The top floor of the canal-side house was almost a self-contained unit, so it wasn't as if they were under each other's feet all the time. In fact, Mariner had seen more of them since he'd invested in a DVD player — they used it more than he did. But they'd given him an insight into the student life he'd missed out on, and he liked having them around.

Snug in the winter, in the summer the house could get stuffy, so he threw open all the windows in an attempt to entice in some stagnant air.

The light on his answer phone was flashing, so he pressed the play button. Two hang-ups and his mother: 'How are you, dear? It's so long since you've been to see me. Give me a call soon, would you? There's something I want to talk to you about.'

Mariner sighed. What scheme was she hatching now? Something, no doubt, that would involve him in endless discussion and research on her behalf, which would come to nothing when she changed her mind, like her idea of selling up and moving to a retirement property in Weston-super-Mare. That one had kept him busy for weeks. Three times inside a month he'd even taken her down there to get a feel for different areas. Then, on a whim, she'd dropped the idea and that was when he first developed the suspicion that she'd concocted the whole thing just to keep his attention focused on her.

When he'd left home as a teenager, he'd hurt her. He knew that and had come to regret the fact, even though at the time his leaving had been pure self-preservation. It was only a matter of three or four years before their relationship was re-established, but she'd never let him forget the digression. Since that time, she'd demanded assurances that though they had their separate lives, as long as he was able, he would be there to support her. And she'd held him to his word, making sure that at regular intervals some project or minor ailment would occur that required his attention. Projects that invariably failed to come to fruition, but were enough to keep him dangling. Over the last few years her demands had increased in frequency so that she seemed to be developing classic 'cry wolf' syndrome. With a stab of guilt, Mariner thought of Theresa Knox ploughing up and down the motorway to visit her mother on Merseyside. Funny, Tony hadn't mentioned that before. How long had it been going on?

Cracking open a bottle of home-brewed Woodford's Wherry, kept cool by storing it in the lowest depths of the old-fashioned scullery, Mariner took his dinner out on to the canal-side. The water was silent and still, with hardly any sound from the surrounding city and no breeze to sway the birches on the opposite bank. With the cooling of the air the smell of vegetation was strong: Mariner even caught a hint of perfume from the single strand of wild honey-suckle a few feet away. Screaming swallows had given way to bats and crane flies, but even now the air was mild and sultry. If Ricky or Yasmin were sleeping rough tonight, at least they'd be warm.

Usually at this time of the year there would be a couple of narrow boats parked a few hundred yards up river where the two canals joined, but the low water level was discouraging most, forcing them to steer a central line or risk being grounded in the mud. In some areas of the country stretches of the waterway had even been closed. It being the close season, fishermen, too, had given up on the dark, stagnant waters and even the ducks seemed lethargic in their quacking.

In the twilight he could just make out the perfect symmetry of the guillotine lock beyond the junction with the Stratford-on-Avon canal, put there years ago for just such circumstances as these. The two canals were on different levels and it was to prevent the water running from one into the other: one of the remnants from the city's industrial past as a contest was created between the canals and the river that ran alongside.

His meal finished, Mariner took a long shower to wash off the grime of the day, before tuning in to watch the late news report on TV.

'There are growing concerns for the safety of schoolgirl Yasmin Akram, who disappeared on her way home from school yesterday afternoon,' the anchorman said. The same smiling photograph that Mariner carried in his pocket was flashed up on the screen. 'She was last seen boarding a train for the university station, and police are appealing for anyone who may have any information about the schoolgirl's whereabouts to get in touch.' The bulletin ended with the Granville Lane telephone number. It would prompt the usual flurry of crank calls. Some anorak was bound to have seen Yasmin abducted on to a spacecraft by aliens, at the very least. An incident information centre had been set up at Granville Lane to weed out the genuine stuff.

Mariner wondered if Colleen Skeet was watching. If so, she'd want to know why there was no mention of Ricky. He'd deal with that one tomorrow.

He tried Anna's number a couple of times but strangely her line was engaged. A bit late to be canvassing for donations, he thought, but he didn't like to consider any other possibilities. And now he'd left it too long to think about calling his mother. That one would have to wait, too. Checking that his mobile was charged and switched on, Mariner went to bed.

It was an undisturbed night and Mariner woke early to another blistering morning: the sun pushing up over the skyline, already dazzlingly bright. He got to the office to find, among other things, a call from Colleen Skeet waiting to be returned. Millie was already at her desk, deep in a phone conversation; trawling the hospitals once again, just in case. Mariner gestured 'drink' and got a thumbs up in reply.

On his way to the water cooler he had to pass DS Charlie Glover's desk. Glover too was on the phone, shirtsleeves up, tie hanging loose and a thin sheen of sweat coating his pale features. He looked as if he'd been up for hours. Without breaking the conversation, he looked on warily as Mariner sorted through his in-tray, finding the file he wanted two thirds of the way down the pile.

'That's great. I'll look forward to hearing from you soon,' said Glover, concluding the call. He replaced the receiver. 'Can I help you, sir?' he asked mildly.

Mariner was reading the top sheet of the chosen file. 'Not much progress,' he observed.

Glover leaned back in his chair. 'I'm doing the best I can with just the one pair of hands, one pair of legs and a desk full of other crap.' He wasn't being insubordinate, merely stating the facts.

It's not enough though, is it? Mariner wanted to retort, even now picturing Colleen sitting at home, poised by the phone, longing for it to ring. But he kept quiet, because Glover was right. It was just one case among dozens. And it wasn't Charlie's fault that it had been pulled from Mariner and given to him.

'I've talked to the lad's friends,' Glover went on. 'Not that he's got too many of those. He seems to be a bit of a loner. According to the school, he's a bright kid with a promising future. Nobody saw him beyond Tuesday afternoon when he left school. He went off on his bike. And we've checked the places his mum says he usually hangs out.'

'Fido thinks he's a runner.'

Glover shrugged. 'Could be. He's taken his life savings with him.'

'Has he?'

'All seven quid of it. Did you know he'd been talking to his mum about joining the army?'

'The army?'

'Apparently she didn't take him too seriously.'

'I'm not surprised. He's not that sort of kid.'

'Maybe he wants to be that sort of kid: a hero.' To make up for the times he hadn't quite managed it before.

'Colleen has phoned me. OK with you if I return it?'

'Sure.'

Back at his desk, Mariner made the call. Colleen picked up before the phone had even rung.

'Why have they taken you off it?' she demanded immediately.

'Something else came up.'

'Something more important than Ricky?'

'Something different.'

But she wasn't listening. 'Is it that girl? She went missing round here, too. I saw it on the telly last night.'

'Charlie Glover's a good bloke,' said Mariner, sidestepping the question. 'He'll do a thorough job. He's talking to Ricky's friends—'

'Huh. That won't take long. Why can't they put Ricky's picture on the telly?'

'They still might. They're doing a search of the places you suggested first. Plus, we've issued a description of Ricky and his bike. We're doing all we can, Colleen.' But it wasn't enough, and it wouldn't be enough until Colleen had her son back safe and sound. That twinge of guilt returned, remembering what he'd put his own mother through all those years ago.

The knock on the door preceded Fiske. Mariner groaned inwardly.

'Anything?' Fiske demanded. 'Any results from last night's appeal?'

'It's still too early.'

'But there's nothing? I thought not, which is why we need to push on.'

Tony Knox appeared.

'The search volunteers are awaiting your briefing, boss.' he told Mariner.

'What search volunteers?'

Fiske smiled knowingly. 'I've enlisted the help of the Operational Support Unit and their team of specialist "search-trained" offices. We need to up the ante,' he said. 'Yasmin's been missing for two nights now. As you so rightly said, you need to widen the investigation team, so I thought it would be helpful if I put in a word on your behalf. Uniform have rounded up some volunteers to help do the search, too. It seems they're awaiting your instructions.'

'But as I said yesterday, sir, we still don't know for certain where Yasmin got off the train. The last people with a definite sighting of her were the friends who saw her running for the train at Kingsmead. We don't have—'

'You have the CCTV footage.'

'I don't think it's conclusive.'

'It's enough.' Fiske's abrupt departure said the debate was over.

'They're all waiting for the party to start,' prompted Knox.

Mariner glared at him. 'Well, we'd better get on with it then.' He didn't like this one little bit. 'Either he lets me run this or he doesn't,' he muttered, on the walk to the briefing room. 'We don't have enough clear evidence that Yasmin even got as far as the university. Next thing, we'll have finance on our backs telling us we've run out of money.'

'He has to be seen to be doing something,' Jamilla said, trailing behind.

'Even if that something could be a complete waste of fucking time?'

'Look on the bright side, boss,' said Knox. 'There's an outside chance it might not be.'

Because the main search area was on the university campus, as a courtesy they had to get permission from the Dean to go ahead. Before going to see her, taking Millie and Tony Knox, Mariner parked by the university railway station and walked the route that Yasmin would have taken, to give them an idea of the general lie of the land. Emerging from the station, a tarmac footpath took them through well-groomed park land that ran for several hundred yards alongside a piece of rougher, untamed ground before climbing a slight incline towards the central cluster of mock-Elizabethan buildings that was dominated by the clock tower pushing up into the cornflower sky. Outward from the core, buildings encompassing every architectural era of the twentieth century had grown up. The path emerged on to a network of roads, just along from the stripy arm of a security barrier. Some of the roads were public thoroughfares: connecting the main routes that ran either side of the campus, and linking the different faculties of the university.

From there, Yasmin would have walked past the main student union building and out on to a well-populated public highway. Looking back, it was plain that the most vulnerable section of Yasmin's journey would be between leaving the railway station and getting to the main body of the campus. And that would be where they would concentrate their search.

Dean Angela Woolley's office was situated on the first floor of one of the original university buildings that surrounded the impressive Chancellor's court, and was overlooked by the three-hundred-foot tall Chamberlain clock tower; affectionately known as Old Joe. An information board outside told them that they were on the site of one of the original red-brick universities, built at the turn of the twentieth century with the intention of educating those who would manage the Midlands' burgeoning manufacturing industries. Not much call for that any more, thought Mariner. But its reputation had lived on and now the university seemed to serve as many students from overseas as it did local youngsters. The main building reeked of academia, an atmosphere that Mariner found at once comfortable and intimidating.

'You ever wish you'd gone to university?' he asked Knox, as they stood cooling their heels outside Woolley's office.

The vacant response said that the thought had never entered Knox's mind. 'You?' he asked. Mariner wasn't so certain. Sometimes he wondered how different his career path might have been had he taken that route. How different his whole life might have been. People like Fiske met their life partners at university, or emerged with a core group of friends. It was certainly an opportunity that would have been open to him. 'No,' he said. 'I don't.'

Angela Woolley was sturdily into middle age, her hair set in a rigid perm, the colour of honey. They didn't need to explain their purpose in being there: she was fully abreast of current events.

'Anything we can do to help, Inspector. Though I'm sure nothing untoward could have happened here in the university without someone noticing. There aren't many students on campus now because of summer recess, but there are some and I'll make sure that word gets round to the relevant departments to cooperate with your officers.'

Along with all the search team from the operational command unit, a handful of students had also come forward to help, mostly postgraduates. The summer exams were over and many of the students had gone down, but a straggling line of about forty strong swept across the ground like an ill-disciplined advancing army.

After issuing instructions, Mariner left Sergeant Pete Welford to supervise the search, while he and Knox walked along to the hut at the barrier to talk to the security guards who had been on duty on Tuesday afternoon. Not that Knox was much help. He seemed to be having problems focusing on anything today. One of the security guards thought he remembered having seen Yasmin on occasions but not every day, and he couldn't recall seeing her on Tuesday.

70

The problem was that this wasn't unusual. The guards didn't stay in their hut all afternoon, especially in this sort of weather, when the flimsy structure offered little relief from the heat. And at this time of year, when there were fewer students, most people coming in and out would have their own passes. The rules were more relaxed and it was not unusual for them to leave the barrier raised for lengthy periods of time. Neither man had noticed anything out of the ordinary on Tuesday afternoon. And this was not an area covered by CCTV so the police were entirely reliant on the vigilance of the security personnel. Leaving the booth, Mariner was immediately accosted by a young woman.

'Are you here about the girl who's gone missing?' Speaking with the upward inflection at the end of the sentence that placed her as a native of the antipodes. She was in full Bondi beach ensemble: low cut denim shorts that were a good eight inches off joining company with the cropped T-shirt that strained over an ample bosom; all off-set by a rich, caramel tan. Instinctively, Mariner glanced across at Knox for signs of awakening interest. On any other day his tongue would have been practically hanging out. But for once there were none.

Mariner nodded. 'We're the investigating officers.'

'They've told you about the flasher, right?'

Mariner looked towards the security guard who squirmed uncomfortably.

She shook her head knowingly. 'I thought as much. A couple of months ago, back in May, one of my roommates, Lizzie, got flashed at.'

'Do you know exactly what happened?'

'Oh yeah. I mean it was a bit of a giggle, but it shook her up.'

'What time of day was this?'

'Early evening; about five, half five. She was coming back over the meadow.'

'The meadow?'

'It's what we call that rough ground down there.' She pointed down the hill from where they stood to the area that the search party had just left – the area that Yasmin would have crossed immediately after leaving the station.

'Go on.'

'Well, the way she told it, Lizzie was just walking along the path minding her own when this guy jogged past her. She thought nothing of it but then as she rounded the corner and into the trees there he was again, standing with his back to the path like he was taking a leak. But as she approached he turned around and it was all sticking out there. He grinned this nasty little grin and mumbled something about getting "caught short".'

'Did Lizzie think that could have been genuine?'

She shook her head. 'Not a bit. She said, "No guy I know pees with a stiffy like that."'

'So what did Lizzie do?'

'She said something like, "Get a life, saddo," and got past him as fast as she could. She came straight home and told me all about it.'

'Did she report it to the police?'

'She didn't think it was necessary. Just some perve getting his kicks. And I think she felt pretty stupid too, you know? It upset her more that she thought it would and she just wanted to forget it. I think she was kind of ashamed that it had got to her.'

'It's nothing to be ashamed of.'

'I know but I guess you always think if you're in that situation you'd be cool and just laugh it off, because it's so pathetic. But I think it shocked her, and she knew that this guy could see that. So she'd given him what he wanted, hadn't she?'

'Did Lizzie feel physically threatened in any way?'

'No. It was like her reaction was enough. That's why she felt so stupid.'

'There's nothing stupid about flashing.' It was always the same story. Even with the progress made in forensic psychology, flashing had never lost its reputation as one step down from an old music hall joke. 'Did Lizzie tell you what he looked like?'

'Not really. I don't think she got a good look. It was turning to dusk and she said he was facing sort of sideways, with a baseball cap pulled low.' She gave a wry smile. 'And I guess she wasn't exactly focused on his face, you know?'

'Did she tell anyone else about it?'

'She didn't want to. But I made her write it all down, just in case, and she was going to think about it. In the end she chickened out and mentioned it to one of her tutors, who said she'd pass it on. They told her security would deal with it – issue a warning to students and let the Dean know and to be honest, I think that suited Lizzie.'

'And?'

'We heard nothing more. Than a couple of weeks ago there was this rumour going round that it had happened again to a couple of other girls, in practically the same spot. I wondered if it could be the same guy. I know Lizzie did too.'

'Where's Lizzie now? We may want to talk to her.'

She pulled a face. 'I can't be very specific. She's hitching in France with her boyfriend.'

Mariner was sure none of this had got as far as the police. Incidents like these would show up on the monthly Intranet bulletin. There had been a spate of indecent exposures, as there often was when the weather got warmer, but nothing that he could remember having been reported on or around the university. He turned to the guard. 'You knew about this?'

He shrugged. 'I'd heard something, but we were told not to make an issue of it.'

'It already is an issue. What makes it worse is that we weren't told.' Angela Woolley would have to be confronted about that.

'Do you know the names of any of the other girls?'

73

She shook her head. 'Sorry.'

Mariner knocked and walked into Angela Woolley's office, leaving the Dean little opportunity to protest. She was packing things into a briefcase. 'I'm sorry, Inspector, I'm due at a—'

'I think that might have to wait.' Now he had her attention. 'Do you understand why we're here today?' he demanded. 'That we're here searching for a seventeen-year-old girl who may well have vanished less than a mile from this office? Why didn't you tell us about the indecent exposures that have been occurring next to this campus for the last two months and more? Of course, that's not counting any incidents that haven't been reported because the victim is completely unaware that it's happened to anyone else but her. Ms Woolley, you seem to have a sexual deviant operating on your campus. I think you'd better tell me everything you know.'

In effect, they'd had the better account from the student and Angela Woolley's version demonstrated that she'd barely attended to the facts. At least now though, she had the grace to be embarrassed.

'I'd really like to know whose idea it was to suppress this information,' Mariner said.

'It wasn't a question of suppressing it. We just felt it was better that only a limited number of people should know. What we didn't want to do was cause panic among the students, or deter any prospective students. Miss Greenwood was offered counselling, as were the other three young women—'

'You mean there are at least four?'

'Really, Inspector, this all happened weeks ago and I'm sure it was just a harmless student prank. There haven't been any incidents since the end of—'

'You mean, there haven't been any *reported* incidents. And why would students report it when none of this information is acted on? These incidents are never just "harmless pranks". Have you ever met any sexual deviants, Ms Woolley? Any convicted rapists among your acquaintances?'

'I don't know what—'

'Let me tell you something about rapists then, because in my line of work I've met one or two. And guess what? They don't wake up one morning and decide that today they are going to rape. Rape is just one stage in a progressive pattern of sexually deviant behaviour. And that pattern starts, more often than not, with flashing: indecent exposure; an unsolicited demonstration of naked sexual power to an unsuspecting victim. Then, when the buzz begins to wear off from that relatively harmless little pursuit, and believe me, it nearly always does, that's when things start to turn nasty. If you're so concerned about adverse publicity, I wonder what prospective students would make of the fact that for the last few months failure to disclose information to the police has exposed existing female students at this university to the risk of being attacked by a potential rapist.'

Angela Woolley did not have a reply.

'Christ. Since when did education become an exercise in PR?' Mariner boiled as they left the building. Short of any response from Knox, he answered his own question. 'Since it became a commercial enterprise, that's when. It's all about reputation and money.' He took a deep breath. 'We'll need to track down all the girls who've been victims to this flasher and take statements from them. It might not have anything to do with Yasmin, but they need to be investigated just the same.'

They had been given one other name. Helen Greenwood was a library assistant who fortunately remained on campus throughout the holidays.

'Go and get a detailed statement from her,' Mariner said to Knox. 'Then I want you to go back to the station to follow up on any other similar incidents there have been locally and see if there are any links.'

'Yes, boss,' said Knox, with about as much enthusiasm as a bloodhound on valium.

Librarian Helen Greenwood was thirty-three, so she said, but to Knox she could have been anything up to fifty. Her mousy brown hair was held off her face by an old-fashioned Alice band and her blouse and skirt could only be described as 'sensible'. All that was missing Knox thought were the horn-rimmed glasses. He really didn't want to do this. He'd other things on his mind. Greenwood was already behaving as if she was afraid of him, but then, he was a man so she probably was. He couldn't imagine her having had much experience of the opposite sex.

She was about to take her lunch break. 'I've brought sandwiches and I usually go out for a bit of fresh air,' she told Knox apologetically.

'Well, perhaps you could walk me to where it happened,' Knox suggested. 'Then you can tell me about it.'

'Oh, I don't know...'

'We'll take it slowly. You can stop any time you like.'

'All right,' she said, sounding as if it was anything but.

It was going to be a waste of time, thought Knox. She was scared of her own shadow. She led him down the footpath, back towards the railway station until it almost reached the meadow, where the path went briefly through an area of shrubs and there was plenty of scope for concealment. She stopped abruptly. 'It was about here.'

'So he could easily have been waiting over there on the rough ground until you came along, then hopped over the wire. Was there anyone else about?'

'Not here. I mean, the campus wasn't deserted, but there was no one down here at the time.'

'Do you take the same route every day at the same time?'

'I did then, yes, but not any more. If it's quiet I walk all the way round on the road now.'

'Can you describe exactly what happened?' Knox took out his notebook, partly because his memory didn't seem to

76

be all that reliable at present, but also so that she wouldn't have to look at him while she talked.

'I was just walking down to the station to catch the train, along here. It was one of the first nice warm days we had. He just stepped out from the bushes in that way that everyone says they do. I didn't notice at first, then he smiled at me so I smiled back but his smile was sort of ... lewd, and then we were almost level when I happened to glance down. I don't know what made me do it, and I saw that he had his, his ... thing out'

'His pri— His penis?'

'Yes. He was holding it. And it was huge, and horrible. I just felt sick.' Glancing up, Knox saw that she'd flushed scarlet. He looked back at his notebook.

'What did you do?' he asked.

'I just got past him, around him, as fast as I could and hurried down towards the station.'

'Did he follow you?'

'I don't know. I didn't dare to look back, but I don't think so.'

'So what was he like?'

'That's the silly thing. I don't really know. I didn't notice. I only glanced at him for a second.'

Great. 'Was he white or black?'

'White.'

'You're sure?'

'Yes, he seemed to have a very high colour, from the little I could see. He had this cap pulled down low so I couldn't really see his eyes, but his cheeks and his chin were—'

'What?'

'Sunburnt, I think. His chin was very red.'

'What colour was the cap?'

'Dark. Blue or green, I think. One of those that most young men seem to wear these days.'

A baseball cap. 'How tall was he? Same as me?'

She looked Knox up and down. 'Taller, I think. And thinner.'

Knox pulled in his stomach. This was better than he'd expected. 'You're doing well,' he told her. The other overriding image, she said, was the powerful smell of his cologne. 'It smelled sort of cheap and nasty. It was much too strong.'

Taking the statement and getting back to the car took Knox around an hour. A couple of times he'd had to ask Helen Greenwood to repeat what she'd said because he'd missed it. Now, back in the office, he was finding it difficult to concentrate on what was on the screen in front of him. He'd some detective work of his own to do and wouldn't be able to settle until he'd done it. The office was quiet, everyone taken up with the two investigations. Knox reached for the thermos he'd brought with him. He needed a bit of Dutch courage for this.

Minimising the program he was in, he connected to the Internet.

'It's someone I've known for years,' Theresa had told him during that painfully brief conversation on the phone.

'Do I know him?' he'd asked. She hadn't answered, which meant that maybe he did.

'Where did you meet?'

'It's not important.' But Knox had already worked it out. The only someone she could have known a long time who they both knew could be someone from school. Theresa used the computer all the time. She'd been on courses and could find her way round it better than he could. He also knew that she visited the various school reunion sites that were springing up. Once she'd urged him to have a look.

'It's fun,' she'd said. 'You get to find out what's happened to all those spotty oiks.' But Knox had declined. He didn't have the same enthusiasm for the past as Theresa did. It must be a woman thing.

There were half a dozen sites offering to put people in contact with old acquaintances. Knox logged on to the first and typed in the name of the secondary school they'd gone to and the year they'd both left. By the time he clicked to proceed, his palms were sweating and his heart pounding. Would he know who it was? Would he recognise the name?

'Anything?' Mariner's voice behind him sent the mouse skidding across the desk. He hadn't heard anyone come in.

'No. Nothing yet, boss.' Knox minimised the screen but Mariner was already looking over his shoulder.

'Are we sure we're looking in the right place?' But it was curiosity more than anything else.

Knox fumbled for the notes he'd made. 'Checking back over the indecent exposure incidents in the south of the city during the last six months, there have been two others as well as the unreported ones at the university, bringing the total to six,' he said. 'All occurred at different times of the day, and on the surface there seems little to connect them.' He'd plotted the incidents on a map, which they now pored over. 'As you can see, boss, they all happened in secluded areas, but then the flasher is hardly likely to strike in the middle of a busy shopping centre, is he?'

'It would be a first.'

'One common thread seems to be that a lot of them take place fairly near railway stations.'

'Like Kingsmead. OK. How did you get on with Helen Greenwood?'

Knox reported what she'd told him.

'Sunburnt, eh,' said Mariner. 'That might be helpful.'

Calling in at the incident centre revealed that the news bulletin had been less fruitful. Although there were a handful of possible sightings of Yasmin to follow up, the descriptions were vague and there didn't appear to be anything that held any great significance. Mariner could safely leave Knox to follow those up. As the search of the university campus had turned up nothing either, apart from

79

a handful of spent spliffs, the logical thing to do was to widen the search to the stretch of railway track between Kingsmead Station and the point at which Yasmin left the train. That would be a much bigger operation requiring far more manpower, which Mariner didn't like to think about just yet. As far as he was concerned, they were already jumping the gun. Instead, he wanted to concentrate on the information they had got. On an investigation like this it was important to be systematic, starting at the core and working gradually outwards, making sure not to miss anything.

DCI Fiske, however, was like a dog with a bone and any decision on how to prioritise this was all but taken out of Mariner's hands. Now that Yasmin's disappearance had been on TV, the press were on to it, presenting exactly the sort of case that would capture the public's imagination. Always on the lookout for an 'angle', the media were playing up the possibility of a racially motivated abduction and, ever helpful, Fiske was equally taken with the idea and was making noises about a press conference for the parents.

'What about this letter?' he demanded at the daily update he'd insisted on. 'If it's genuine, it was a pretty open threat.'

'Forensics have found nothing on it,' said Mariner. 'And it's hard to tell how genuine it is, given that it's such an indistinguishable note. The Akrams have had similar stuff in the past.'

'But this follows the consortium letter to the press: a provocative act if ever there was one. If the initial campaign has failed to subdue them – which it patently has – then the perpetrators might feel that it's time to do something more dramatic. And so far, you don't seem to have come up with any other logical reason why Yasmin should have gone missing.'

'We're still exploring all the possibilities.'

'Like what?'

80

'Well, for one thing we've learned that everything in the Akram household wasn't as rosy as we'd been led to believe. Mr Akram and his daughter had disagreed.'

'I'm not saying you shouldn't keep the family under scrutiny, but you can do that while following up other avenues. The racist incidents have to be examined. Mohammed Akram has sent us a list of dates and occurrences going back over three years.'

'I haven't seen that.'

'It was passed directly to the superintendent. This is a copy.'

Mariner took the sheet. The incidents were as Akram had described them to him yesterday, fairly low level: excreta through the letterbox, windows broken, graffiti sprayed, sometimes as often as weekly and usually at night. Up until now the school had always been the target. Attached to the list was a copy of the letter written to the local press, by Akram and several other business owners in the area, denouncing what they called 'terrorism by stealth' perpetrated by 'those too weak to reveal themselves'. It described The Right Way as a club for cowards who indulged in covert, petty crime instead of openly confronting the issues. The question was whether it was enough to prompt such drastic action from The Right Way and, if so, could they expect a ransom note at any time?

'And that, Inspector, should be your next line of enquiry.'

Mariner opened his mouth to complain, but stopped himself. It was a valid route that would have to be pursued at some time. They may as well do it now and with any luck, his deference would keep Fiske off his back for a few hours.

But before entering the lion's den, Mariner wanted a bit more information about the man they might be dealing with. Detective Sergeant Bev Jordan came over from the

81

Racial Crimes Unit at Lloyd House to talk to him and Millie.

'What do you need to know?' she asked when they were installed in Mariner's office.

'Everything there is to know about Peter Cox.'

Jordan grimaced. 'He's a nasty piece of work in every respect. He runs a very active cell of The Right Way who hold extreme views on repatriation, birth control programmes and all the rest of it. He's denounced the BNP for being too moderate.'

'What a charmer.'

'You said it.'

Mariner handed Jordan the leaflet Mohammed Akram had given him. 'Is this one of his?'

Jordan nodded. 'This is exactly the sort of stuff he writes. In the past there have been various threats against groups and individuals. And he has his own little band of fanatically loyal followers in the south of the city and beyond, mainly recruited via the Internet, though not exclusively. He spreads the word in local pubs, particularly those on white, working class housing estates: areas of high social deprivation where white kids are pretty frustrated with their lot, but generally powerless to do anything about it. One of his main themes is the threat of Islamic fundamentalism. Muslims taking over jobs, local businesses—'

'And schools.'

'Particularly schools, because that's where it's all seen to be taught. He'd be encouraged by the current climate, too. Since September eleventh there's been a huge rise in the membership of these types of organisation.'

'And beyond the leafleting and general incitement?'

'Oh, the usual petty harassment: damage to property, disgusting things sent through the post. We have a couple of informants on the inside, but Cox is clever, he's very careful not to be directly involved. He relies mainly on the mental instability of his recruits. He provides the ideas, they carry them out. So far we've only ever been able to charge a few individuals with criminal damage. There's one in particular, David Waldron, who's a real fall guy for Cox.'

'Are you aware of the antagonism with the Asian business consortium?'

'Oh yes. That's been brewing for a couple of years and the letter to the press won't have helped the situation, but again, Cox is too smart to let something like that get to him. It was only a letter, after all. It's his followers who would be more upset by it.'

'Do you think any of them would go as far as abduction?'

'Up until recently I'd have said no, but there has been a worrying trend lately, which is that – thanks to the Internet – these groups are developing international links and are being increasingly influenced by their counterparts across the pond.'

'In what way?'

'A spate of letter bomb attacks in the South of the US was followed, weeks later, by the letter bomb attacks here, in Manchester and Leeds last month, remember?'

'And?'

'Three weeks ago there was a high profile abduction of a black senator's daughter by right-wing activists in Savannah, Georgia. The senator was proposing legislation to curb the distribution of certain right-wing propaganda.'

'And has the girl been found?' asked Knox.

'Oh yes. Strangled and dumped in a garbage skip. It's believed that there was no intention to release her alive.'

'Christ Almighty. Do you think there's anyone in The Right Way who would go that far?'

'It only takes one. We know that the case has been discussed among them and Cox likes his followers to "prove themselves" by using their initiative, so it would only take one of them with a particular bent for this kind of activity, and we have our abduction.'

'And Waldron?'

83

'He's on remand at present, so effectively out of the picture. It might be worth a chat with Peter Cox, though. Find out if he's hired any new recruits lately. Yasmin was last seen at four forty-five on Tuesday afternoon, wasn't she? It would be interesting to know what Cox was doing then, too.'

'I can't wait to meet the animal who causes so much misery.'

'He's not what you'd expect,' said Jordan. 'He might not put it to any great use by working for a living, but he's bright; a graduate. He just prefers to utilise his talents for stirring up trouble.'

The other surprise was that Peter Cox lived in a smart neighbourhood in a homely 1930s semi with bay windows and a porch. Given what Jordan had told them, Mariner guessed that it was his parents' house, the one he'd been born and raised in. What set it apart from its neighbours was the jungle of a garden and the limp, discoloured curtains hanging behind grimy windows. It was a neighbourhood for young families. As there were no garages, Mariner drove the length of the street, looking in vain for a parking place, and was eventually compelled to settle for a neighbouring street.

He craned his neck to concentrate on a reverse park, which he executed smoothly.

'Very neat,' said Knox. It was the only time he'd spoken on the entire journey. His words seemed to sweeten the air somehow, but Mariner dismissed the sensation as his own over-active imagination. They climbed out of the car and walked back to number forty-eight, where the warm smell of decaying refuse became stronger.

The doorbell showed little indication of being connected to anything, but Mariner pressed it anyway and beside them at the bay window the faded velvet drape was pulled aside and a round, white face peered at them.

'Mr Cox?' Mariner called out, politely, holding up his

warrant card. 'Could you spare us a few minutes?'

The face regarded them with distaste, but the curtain dropped back and moments later the door was opened.

'Can we come in?' Mariner asked. It was obviously the last thing Peter Cox wanted, but he nevertheless stepped back to allow them in.

What sprang out first at Mariner from the gloomy hallway were the framed posters on the walls. From his limited knowledge of the Third Reich, Mariner thought one of them might have been Rudolf Hess. The other was unmistakable: Adolf Hitler's eyes focused purposefully on something in the middle distance, one hand on his hip in a pose which, in Mariner's opinion, made the Führer look rather camp. He thought it best not to mention this. The atmosphere inside the house was acrid: stale cigarette smoke with an underlying feral smell. Cox took them into a small, front living room that was piled high with books and papers, in the centre of which was an old battered sofa. A computer monitor hummed gently from the corner of the room.

Cox himself was small and weedy, as unhealthy as a plant starved of natural light, as if he never ventured out of his dark and dingy lair. Balding slightly, he was pale as uncooked pastry and the amber-coloured stain on the index finger of his right hand tallied with the pile of home-rolled dog-ends in the makeshift ashtray. 'How can I help you, Officers?' he asked politely, with what sounded more than anything like bored resignation.

'Just a simple question,' said Mariner. 'Where were you on Tuesday afternoon at around four forty-five?'

'Now, why would you want to know that?' But before they could answer, he laughed out loud. 'This is about that little Paki, isn't it?' He shook his head sadly. 'Dear me, you must be desperate if you've come to me about that.'

'Her family seems to be on the mailing list for your enlightening pamphlets.'

85

'I hardly think that's significant. We have an extensive target audience.'

'And David Waldron, one of your party members, was caught inflicting damage on property in the area.'

'As I said at the time, I can't be responsible for the actions of all our members. All I do is provide a forum for like-minded people to share their views and concerns.'

'In the same way that the National Socialist Party of Germany provided a forum?'

'I repeat, Waldron was acting independently. I had nothing to do with any of that.'

'Until Mohammed Akram brought your name into it. He said some not very nice things about you publicly, some highly provocative things.'

'Do you seriously think a bit of name-calling's going to bother me? It's what you get when you're prepared to stand up for what you believe in. Goes with the territory. Our territory.' He noticed Knox looking around. 'Want to search the house, do you?'

'It would help us to—'

'Well, you'll need a warrant and a fucking good reason,' Cox said, mildly.

'So maybe you could answer the question, just for the record.'

But disappointingly, Cox did have an alibi, and a fairly unassailable one at that: at the crucial time he'd been speaking at a meeting of 'like-minded people' in Walsall. He travelled on the train. And if, as he said, the meeting didn't end until four thirty, it would have been practically impossible for him to have been anywhere near Yasmin Akram when she disappeared. It would be easy enough to verify.

'It still doesn't mean that he hasn't put someone else up to it,' Mariner said to Knox, as they traipsed back along the street.

'Mm.' Knox grunted.

Back at the car Mariner saw he had a message on his mobile. He rang back. It was Millie. 'I've got a name for you. Fakhra has coughed up the identity of that disgruntled parent: a guy called Abdul Sheron. Oh and another thing—' Suddenly she sounded uncomfortable. 'DCI Fiske is organising a press conference.'

Chapter Six

'Police Constable Khatoon should get her facts straight before she comes bleating to you.' Pacing the floor of his office, DCI Fiske was angry. Very angry, if the colour of his face was anything to go by. Even so he seemed keen to defend his actions, Mariner thought with some satisfaction. 'I am not organising a press conference, I have merely indicated to the press that one is imminent, and asked the TV station to be on standby.'

'Which, with respect, sir, is as good as declaring it where the media are concerned,' said Mariner, seriously wondering if Fiske was beginning to lose it already. More than accustomed to keeping the press at bay, he'd never had to fend off an over-zealous commanding officer before. 'The timing of press conferences is crucial and I'd have preferred to hold it when I was ready. If you want me to continue as SIO then I need to be able to do things my way.' His powers of diplomacy were being stretched to the limit.

'That seems to involve doing very little, as far as I can make out. This case is developing a high profile—'

Yes, and who have we to thank for that? thought Mariner.

'We need to be seen to be acting. We should be looking at running a reconstruction, too. People expect it.'

That was the problem with having all these bloody crime

programmes on TV. The public thought they knew better how to do the job. 'It's much too soon. We're following up outside leads, and after a week, we'll get someone to walk the route to encourage any new witnesses to come forward, but we can't discount Yasmin's family and immediate friends yet. We already know that the parents aren't telling us everything.'

'So having them in for a press conference would provide you with an opportunity. TV cameras are an excellent way of stripping away any pretence.'

'Yes, sir.' Mariner turned to go, thinking that in some cases just the opposite was true. 'And maybe, sometime, you could go over that egg sucking thing with me again, sir,' he murmured under his breath.

'Let's bring them in,' Mariner said to Jamilla on his return to the office.

'Any particular way you want me to steer things, sir?'

'No, save that for afterwards. Keep it all light and conversational on the journey in. That way, Akram's guard won't be up – if it needs to be.'

As the Senior Investigating Officer, Mariner had no choice but to accompany Fiske at the appeal, which passed in a blur of flash-bulbs and quick-fire questions. Afterwards, he, Knox and Millie watched the playback. Mohammed Akram was calm and dignified while even his wife, clinging to her husband for support, remained composed, despite the obvious strain. She seemed smaller than she'd looked two days ago, as if she'd lost about half a stone, and all of it from around her face, where the skin was pale and sagging. Mohammed Akram did all the talking, reading from the prepared statement he'd been given by the press officer, appealing to Yasmin to come home, or to anyone who may be holding her to please let her go. Throughout, his voice was clear and steady, his gaze straight into the camera.

'He's a cool one,' Mariner conceded.

'Don't be fooled,' said Millie. She was right to be

89

cautious. Even when parents had made an emotional public appeal for the return of their offspring, they couldn't be eliminated from the enquiry. Distress and guilt had the habit of manifesting themselves in very similar ways and in recent years, increasing numbers of murderers had successfully, at least for a while, concealed one with the other.

Before being returned home, the Akrams were taken into a side room and offered refreshments. Having fielded the inevitable questions from reporters, Mariner went to talk to them. Two sets of eyes turned hopefully on him as he went into the room. He shook his head. 'I'm sorry, there's nothing new. But I do need to clarify a couple of things with you.'

'Anything,' said Akram, looking shaken now that the ordeal was over.

'We've spoken to Yasmin's friends and I understand that you were not entirely happy about Yasmin staying the night with Suzanne.'

Mohammed Akram responded instantly. 'It was nothing. It was the kind of thing every parent and child goes through.'

'Is that why it didn't seem important enough to mention?' asked Mariner. 'I must impress on you that anything out of the ordinary, however small, could be of help. Tell me what happened exactly.'

'Yasmin asked to go and stay with her friend, overnight. I said no.'

'Why was that?'

'It was a school night and she would have homework. It was inappropriate.' More to it than that, but Mariner wouldn't push it now. Was Akram just trying to be diplomatic about his dislike of Suzanne, or was it power games between Mum and Dad?

He looked from one to the other parent. 'So am I to understand that Yasmin was defying you by going to Suzanne's?'

'She was defying me, not her mother.' Akram glanced at his wife. 'After I had left the house on Tuesday morning, Shanila allowed Yasmin to go.' The accusation was there along with the obvious source of that additional tension.

Shanila Akram made a weak show of sticking up for herself. 'Yasmin was threatening to go to Suzanne's anyway. I thought it much better that she should go with our blessing than deceive us. I thought if she was allowed to go once she would get it out of her system.'

'So you encouraged her to collude with you in deception.' Mohammed Akram's anger was building.

But his wife was equal to it. 'I would have told you when you returned.'

'Do you approve of Suzanne, Mr Akram?' Mariner asked. There followed enough of a hesitation to confirm the antagonism that existed there.

'It's not a question of approval.'

'Then what is it?'

'You went to see Yasmin's friends. You've met Suzanne?'

'Yes.'

'Then you'll know that she is very different from Yasmin.' Full marks for tact.

'And does that bother you?'

'As we've already told you, Yasmin is relatively inexperienced at life. It would be easy for her to be influenced by a stronger, more . . . worldly personality, someone who has different values.'

'So you've discouraged the friendship.'

'We have been realistic. We can't prevent Yasmin from mixing with whoever she wants to at school. Let's just say that we haven't done anything to encourage it.'

'How does Yasmin feel about that?'

'Kids get angry, you know, especially if they can't get their way.'

'She said—' Shanila Akram stopped abruptly.

'What did she say, Mrs Akram?'

91

'She said we might regret it if we tried to prevent her from doing things.'

'Like staying with her friends. So then, Mrs Akram, you decided to allow Yasmin to go and stay with Suzanne.'

'Yes.' She addressed her husband. 'I was concerned that we were being too strict on Yasmin and that she might rebel. I thought that once it had happened, when my husband saw no harm had been done and that Yasmin appreciated the gesture, it would be for the best.'

'For the best? How can you possibly say that now? Look at what has happened. Now we have no idea where Yasmin has gone.'

'Of course I can see that now, but at the time—' Mrs Akram's eyes filled with tears. Her husband reacted with a contemptuous snort.

'How did Yasmin react when you told her she *could* go to stay with Suzanne after all?' Mariner pushed on, keen to maintain the momentum.

'She was excited, happy. She hugged me. But I know she was mindful of her dad's feelings, too.'

'Mindful how? Do you think Yasmin really intended to stay with Suzanne, or could she have decided to get back at you for making life difficult for her? Could she have run away?'

Akram was unequivocal. 'Yasmin isn't like that. Even if she was still angry she wouldn't take it this far. If she decided to punish us it would be a gesture, that's all. She would go somewhere safe; to someone within our family. I believe Yasmin thought of her duty to me, and was intending to come home. Something prevented her from doing so. Something has happened to her, Inspector, and I really think your time would be better spent out there looking for her instead of dissecting our family life. I don't understand why you are persisting with this. I told you about the trouble we've been having. Why aren't you talking to Peter Cox?'

'We are following that line of enquiry, but we have to

ensure that all possibilities are covered. Tell me about Abdul Sheron.'

'How did you know about him?'

'That doesn't really matter. Just tell me.'

'Abdul is an old friend. Things have been a little strained because we felt that we couldn't meet the needs of his youngest child in our school. It can be hard to accept but it is for the good of the child.'

'I understand he was angry about that.'

'At first he was, yes, and that was to be expected. His daughter has lots of problems and it is hard. But our families have known each other for years. Abdul would not do anything to hurt us. It's out of the question.'

And on that note, Mariner allowed Millie to take them home.

'What do you think?' Mariner asked Knox after they'd gone.

'He's working very hard at trying to steer us towards the racist angle,' said Knox with rare lucidity.

'And away from anything else? My thoughts exactly.'

As a follow up, Mariner had suggested a few directions for Millie to take with the 'informal conversation' on the way back, and was waiting for a debrief when she returned to the station.

'What else did you find out?'

'About as much as I would if I'd been making a social call. But I do think Shanila is beginning to open up and talk to me more as if I was a friend of the family than a police officer.'

'Surely that can be far more productive.'

'Sometimes. Depends on how much they decide to patronise me and how much they disapprove of my role.'

'What do you think?'

'They still hold a fairly traditional view of the female role. Not outright disapproval, but probably not what they'd want for their girls.'

93

'Yasmin's older sister lives abroad?'

'Yes, we talked about her; she was married earlier this year, apparently.'

'Fairly recently then. And how often does she see Yasmin?'

'Quite often, according to Mum and Dad. Her husband is a successful lawyer and travels extensively. They were over here just a few weeks ago.'

'Was it an arranged marriage?'

'Sounds like it, in that the two families already knew each other and the match was obviously approved by both sets of parents.'

'Might Yasmin have wanted to escape from that scenario?'

'It depends on how strictly they follow it through. Arranged marriage is not always a bad thing. Usually these days, the son or daughter has the right of veto. This couple are a mix, like their dress: her in traditional, him in Western. On the one hand, Shanila Akram seems very Western and liberal, but at the same time I get the impression that Mohammed likes to keep Yasmin on a tight rein.'

'By not allowing her to stay overnight with her friend,' said Mariner. 'Although I can see why Suzanne would be a less than ideal playmate.'

'It's not that uncommon, of course. Yasmin's parents want her to have all the advantages of growing up in Western society, as they so successfully have, but within the confines of their religious rules. Problem is, the two are not always compatible and it's hard to find a balance. It can present quite a tension. To Yasmin, at her age, it probably seems as if she gets the worst of both worlds. She gets to work hard to achieve what her parents want her to, but without the social life enjoyed by her friends.'

'So they limit her.'

'They'd say they're protecting her. Family life is important to them.'

'Doesn't make it any easier for Yasmin.'

94

Millie shook her head. 'You have no idea.' She spoke with feeling, and Mariner realised for the first time how little he knew about his colleague's own background.

'I asked them again about Abdul Sheron too,' Millie said. 'Neither of them believes he'd be involved but they have at least agreed that we can go and talk to him.'

'No time like the present.'

Millie pulled a face. 'Sorry, sir, I've a few calls to make.'

'That's OK. Knox!'

Chapter Seven

Sheron's address turned out to be a hardware store down the Stratford Road from Allah T'ala, between a shop selling wedding sarees, and an Indian sweet shop. At ground-floor level was a family-run hardware business that flowed on to the pavement outside, with stacks of plastic buckets and storage boxes arranged in neat rows alongside mops, brooms, cleaning cloths and tubs of cheap batteries. The family lived in the flat above the shop. Mariner's opening words established that Sheron didn't speak English, so one of his brothers agreed to interpret for him. Mariner kicked himself that he hadn't waited for Millie instead of bringing Knox, who was chewing grimly on some menthol-smelling gum.

They followed the two men through the shop and up a flight of dark, narrow stairs. The flat at the top was grubby and dismal, the floor uncarpeted and strewn with piles of newspaper and a few broken toys. From one corner, a huge wide-screen TV dominated the room, the sound turned down so as to be virtually inaudible. A long sofa was arranged directly opposite and beside the sofa, on the bare floorboards, sat a child of about three or four: pretty, with dark curls framing a delicate face. Her head wobbled as she balanced uncertainly and her limbs occasionally twitched violently. As they went in, their footsteps echoing on the wooden floor, she seemed to look up at them and smile, but Mariner could tell that her eyes were unfocused. Transparent tubes were taped under her nose, the other end connected to a tank that leaned against the wall. Sheron and his brother completely ignored both the child and the elderly matriarch who sat at the end of the sofa, her eyes fixed on the giant screen, and the conversation was conducted with all four men standing in the corner of the room. Most of the communication was with the man who introduced himself as Hasan, Sheron's brother.

'I'd like Mr Sheron to tell us about his involvement with the school, Allah T'ala,' said Mariner.

The brother spoke and for a few minutes, they jabbered an exchange in their native language. Then for the first time Hasan acknowledged the child. 'This is his daughter, Shebana,' he said. 'He put her name down for the school two years ago. His other children went there and he has given them money. Now it's time for Shebana to go they are saying that they can't help her. It's because she has problems, but they say they haven't got enough teachers or enough room for her oxygen. All her siblings and cousins have gone to the school, but not Shebana. Now you see she is here, she will have no school to go to and it's the fault of the Akrams. They have been unfair and it made him angry.'

Still muttering, Sheron walked across the room and retrieved something from a drawer. It was a glossy magazine, a prospectus. He thrust it in front of Mariner, rapping a forefinger angrily down on the page.

'He's saying, "Look at this. See what it says here,"' Hasan told them. 'It's written in this fancy book but the words don't mean anything.' Sheron was becoming angry and more agitated as his brother spoke.

Mariner looked. The brochure talked about welcoming all children of all different abilities. He turned the booklet over in his hand. At the bottom of the last page was the name of the printer, presumably the one Akram had been to see on the day when Yasmin disappeared.

'It is an insult to his whole family. That's why he's so angry.'

97

'Angry enough to damage Mohammed Akram's car?' Mariner asked.

'He knows nothing about that,' said Hasan immediately, and Mariner suddenly wondered if the deed had been carried out on Abdul's behalf. It was pointless to pursue it further, though. It would be impossible to prove. The significant thing was that this was clearly still an open wound, the situation unresolved. The question was: how far would Sheron's demonstrable anger drive him? The Akrams had made a victim of his daughter, would he want to do the same to the Akrams?

'Does Mr Sheron know Yasmin Akram?'

'Of course we do. She was friends with my daughter,' said Hasan.

'Was?' Mariner picked it up straight away.

'Going to that school has corrupted her. Now she thinks she is better than her old friends.'

'Does he know anything about her disappearance?'

Hasan spoke to his brother. The response came back immediately: more anger.

'How would he know that? He doesn't really care. Now they can know what it feels like to fear for their child.'

Hardly the same thing, but Mariner hadn't really expected anything different. 'Where was he on Tuesday afternoon at around four forty-five?'

'Abdul was here in the shop. You can see we have a business to run.'

Thanking Sheron and his brother for their time, they walked back out on to the busy street to the sound of voices raised in Urdu; the discussion continuing beyond their departure.

'Akram certainly seems to have got up his nose,' said Knox.

'Yasmin herself doesn't seem that popular with them, either. I thought "corrupted" was an interesting choice of word.'

'He just meant she's got too big for her boots. Yasmin

goes to a posh school. Maybe she flaunts it.'

'Another reason to wipe the smirk off Akram's face,' Mariner pointed out.

'But if they've abducted her, where is she and where are the demands?'

'There might not be any. The Akrams' distress might be enough.'

'But Yasmin disappeared a good six or seven miles away from here, near the university.'

'That's what I was thinking. Sheron would have had to be highly organised to operate in a part of the city that he's not familiar with. Where would he get the means?'

'That's where,' said Knox. His eyes were on the opposite side of the street as they watched Hasan Sheron emerge from the shop and climb in behind the wheel of the private hire vehicle that was parked on the kerb outside. 'How convenient is that?'

Impulsively, on their way back, Mariner asked Knox to wait in the car while he called in on Colleen. The house had had a sparkling new coat of white emulsion since his last visit, and the rotten windows had been replaced with uPVC, ill-disguising the fact that the house was basically structurally unsound and riddled with damp and should have been condemned years ago.

The front door was open so he called out, 'Hello. Anyone about?' She came to the door, her hair hanging lank and unwashed, the inevitable cigarette on the go. Her face, when she saw him, was a mixture of hope and fear. It was a mistake to have come.

'I've no news,' he said straight away.

'So why are you here?' She was dressed unflatteringly in a loose white T-shirt over faded black leggings, her bare feet in cheap velour slippers, worn through at the toe. 'To tell me that you've found that missing girl?'

'I can't talk to you about other cases that we're handling.'

'How come her parents get to go on the telly? All they've done for my Ricky is put up a few posters. Why can't I go on to ask him to come home?' The belligerence in her voice belied the desperation.

'It's not always appropriate. It depends on the circumstances.' How could Mariner tell her that she just wasn't TV material? That the success of a press conference depended on the public identifying and sympathising with the parents, and that neither of those was likely for a single mother on her third partner in as many years. They would make the same assumptions that his DCI had.

'You think that girl's more important than my Ricky.'

'I think nothing of the sort, Colleen, and you know it.'

'Maybe not you, but the others. Just because she comes from a rich, Asian family. I'm not stupid, you know. I get what's going on here.'

'We're doing what we can, Colleen,' Mariner said. It was true, to a degree.

'So where is he?' She took a step back. 'Where's my Ricky? Come and see me when you've found him.' And then she carefully closed the door in his face.

If it did transpire that Ricky had simply run away, Mariner would personally lynch the boy when he turned up, for having put his mother through hell.

The blatant hypocrisy of such thoughts was spelled out immediately he got home, with yet another message from his own mother on the answering machine.

'There's something I want to talk to you about,' she said again. 'I suppose it will have to keep until next time I see you.' Implying that it ought to be soon. He wondered if this 'something' was what he'd been waiting all his life to find out, but then that's what she'd be hoping he'd think. She was playing games with him again; one of the things she did for fun to get back at him for what he did all those years ago. Not that he could really blame her. He'd once asked her how she felt when, as a fifteen-year-old, he'd run away from home.

'I just wanted you back, unconditionally,' she'd replied. Only then did Mariner fully realise how much he must have hurt her. It had taken him weeks before he'd contacted her to tell her he was safe. What kind of torture had he inflicted on her in the meantime? It was something else on the list of things that they never talked about. Instead, she had other ways of making him pay. Well, he didn't have time for her games right now, or time to comply with what would be her excessive demands. He couldn't face that tonight, but at the same time, he couldn't help wondering how Shanila Akram would be holding up right now. Had Yasmin run away, for the same reasons he had: because she'd felt stifled by her family, or because she didn't like what they had planned for her?

He got through to Anna first time.

'How's the fund raising going?' he asked, out of politeness.

His restraint didn't wilt her enthusiasm. 'It's great. People are being so generous, though we're still waiting for some contributions.' It was a blatant hint.

'I'm thinking about it.'

'Yeah, well don't think too long, eh? How are things going with the missing girl?'

'Don't count on my company for the weekend, will you?'

'Interestingly enough, I never count on much where you're concerned, but that's OK,' Anna said, cheerfully. 'Good thing we both know the score, isn't it?'

'Sure.' Mariner's chest tightened.

'I know you're not allowed to say, but how's it going?'

'Even if I could say there'd be nothing to tell. It's frustrating, to say the least.'

'Mm, well,' she said slowly, her voice dropping half an octave. 'We can't have you frustrated, can we? There ought to be something I can do about that. What you need is a few soothing words to help you relax.'

'How's Jamie?'

'Jamie's fine. Glued to the TV as we speak. Want to know what I'm wearing?'

'Go on, then.'

'Is that better?' she asked him afterwards.

'Infinitely,' he said, although he didn't like to dwell too much on the fact that this was what their relationship had come to.

The next morning, Mariner gathered the team to review what they'd got so far. It wasn't much. The incident board displayed a blown-up version of Yasmin's photograph; an enlarged section of the street map covering the area where she'd disappeared; and a time line, leading nowhere. Colleen's complaint about the absence of a press conference for Ricky seemed unfounded. Yasmin's had yielded little in the way of new leads. Only one call received had produced anything of substance to follow up, and then that had turned out to be a dud too.

'What are the options?' Since he looked more like his usual lively self this morning, Mariner addressed the question to Tony Knox.

'If we rule out accidents, basically there appear to be three possibilities at this stage, boss: first possibility – Yasmin has gone off of her own accord.'

'Why would she do that?'

'She'd had a row with her parents,' said Millie.

'Not her mother. Her mother has given in to her,' Mariner reminded them.

'She'd rowed with her dad though, and he seems to be the one who wields the power.'

'And maybe she's just had enough,' offered Knox. 'From what we've heard, it's not the first time the old man's been down on her.'

'OK. But if that is the case, would Yasmin let things go this far? She's an intelligent and, so we're told, considerate girl. Surely wherever she was she'd eventually let her parents know that she's safe. We're three days in now and nothing. And she doesn't appear to have taken any money with her, so how is she living?'

'All right then. Second possibility: she's been abducted and is being held against her will.'

'Who by?'

'Peter Cox and his mates?'

Mariner was doubtful. 'Having talked to him, I don't quite see it. It's not really Cox's style, and if it was one of his followers, I'm not convinced that they'd be well organised enough. Cox may be clever, but according to DS Jordan most of his honchos are pretty inadequate people.'

'Could be just a random pick-up,' offered Knox. 'Someone offering her a lift home from the station.'

'But we keep being told that she's a bright, sensible kid,' countered Millie. 'She wouldn't have gone off with a complete stranger.'

'And why would she need a lift? It's a short walk to her house from there, and it's a warm sunny evening. What reason would she have to get into a car with just anyone?'

'Might not have been a stranger. Yasmin would know the Sheron family. We haven't ruled them out yet and Hasan drives a minicab. It would be the most natural thing in the world for him to offer her a lift.'

'It's risky, though, in broad daylight. Chances are that someone would remember seeing him.'

'Except that it's exactly the kind of commonplace occurrence that most people don't notice. The alternative leaves us looking at a total unknown, perhaps connected to the earlier attacks on the university campus, which would be even more noticeable.'

'There are no reports of anyone in the area seeing or hearing anything out of the ordinary on Tuesday afternoon, implying that Yasmin did nothing to draw attention. Even though term has ended there are still quite a few students around.'

In the silence that followed, Mariner held an internal mental debate about whether he should voice his thoughts.

103

Eventually, he had to come out with it. 'What we haven't yet given any thought to is the possibility that Yasmin could have stayed on the train and got off at a different stop.' No one had thought about it because they didn't want to and because Fiske had effectively put them off that particular scent.

'Jesus,' said Knox. 'If Yasmin had stayed on the train she could have gone into the city. That would open up a whole new set of possibilities.'

'But we saw her on the CCTV,' Millie reminded them. 'We watched her get off the train at the university.'

'I'm not so sure about that,' confessed Mariner. 'I'd like to see it again.'

To humour him they loaded the video and watched once more, comparing the two clips.

'See, to me it doesn't look like the same person. The gait is different.'

'How can you tell? She's running on the first, walking on the second.'

'I know, but it still doesn't look right to me. The second one has a slightly bigger build.'

'There's not much in it.'

'No, that's true.'

'So it could just be camera angle.'

Mariner was getting the distinct impression that he was alone on this. Everyone else wanted, understandably, to believe that Yasmin had alighted from the train as usual at the university. It would make their lives so very much simpler.

'If she went into the city she could have gone anywhere.' Knox put their thoughts into words. It opened up the possibilities of London, Glasgow, anywhere in Britain, in fact. And it didn't bear thinking about that Birmingham International Airport could have been on the agenda.

'But she had no money and as far as we know wasn't planning to meet anyone.'

'As far as we know.' But Mariner was increasingly

beginning to feel that where Yasmin Akram was concerned they'd barely even scratched the surface.

'It still brings us back to the *likelihood* of it being someone she knew,' said Knox. Making for safer ground.

'Sure, statistically we have to consider the immediate family,' conceded Mariner. 'Mum and Dad were cagey about the row they'd had. In fact, they've been less than forthcoming all the way along, which makes me wonder what else they haven't told us. But it's a long way off any kind of motive. We need to do some more digging, folks.'

Mariner's phone rang and Millie picked it up. Her face broke into a smile. 'I think we might have something,' she said.

Chapter Eight

The call nearly hadn't made it past the incident room, due to the perceived reticence of the caller, who'd had a change of heart halfway through. One of the less experienced civilian staff had fielded it, and almost logged it as a time-waster. It was only the quick thinking of a more experienced girl named Tanya that recognised its importance. She played back the recording of the initial contact.

'Hello, is that the police?' It was the voice of a young woman, timid and hesitant. It didn't sound to Mariner like any of Yasmin's schoolfriends. His heart rate quickened. Was it Yasmin?

'You're through to the incident room, yes.' A pause. 'How can I help? Do you have some information?'

'Yes. No. I don't know.'

'Who's speaking please?'

'I can't tell you that.'

'That's OK. Is it about Yasmin Akram?'

'There's something you should know.' Another long pause, broken only by the uneven rasp of shallow breathing; someone poised on the brink of a decision.

'What did you want to tell me?'

'Nothing. No, it's nothing—' A click and then the empty line hummed.

Mariner exhaled, suddenly aware that he'd been holding his breath throughout the exchange.

'You said you'd traced it?' he asked Tanya.

'It's a doctor's surgery in Edgbaston.' She gave them the address. So probably not Yasmin.

'It's a couple of streets away from the Akrams,' remarked Millie. 'The family GP?'

'I bet the doctor didn't make that call. The voice was young, lacking in confidence.'

Praising Tanya for her vigilance, Mariner verified the number and checked the surgery's opening hours. He didn't want to scare anyone off so he'd do this alone. By ten-thirty he had parked outside the converted bungalow and was watching the last of the patients leave. When he'd seen no one enter or exit for ten minutes, he locked the car and walked up the footpath. The waiting room was empty and behind the desk only a receptionist remained, her faced creased with concentration as she entered data into a computer. She was young and of mixed race, with a smooth complexion the colour of milky coffee.

Taking a gamble, Mariner walked up to the desk and showed her his warrant card along with what he hoped was a friendly smile. 'Hi. Did you make a telephone call at eight fifty-four this morning?'

Wide brown eyes looked up into his and her lower lip began to twitch and tremble. 'How did you . . . ?' Her voice was just a whisper but Mariner recognised it at once. He heard a door open behind him.

'Is everything all right, Nadine?' The woman who spoke was in her mid-forties with dark, penetrating eyes; she barely reached Mariner's shoulder. More Middle Eastern than Asian continent, her short, greying hair was swept back off her forehead. She was casually but immaculately dressed in slacks and a sleeveless blouse. 'I'm Dr Shah. This is my practice,' she said.

'DI Mariner. I'm the senior officer investigating the disappearance of Yasmin Akram,' Mariner explained. 'I have reason to think Nadine contacted our incident room this morning with some information, but, unfortunately, the

107

call was terminated before she was able to pass it on.'

'Nadine?'

The girl's eyes flicked from one to the other of them until her face crumpled and she finally succumbed to tears.

'Come into the consulting room,' said Dr Shah. 'I'll make some tea.' She turned to Mariner. 'I don't know what's going on here but I'd like to talk to Nadine alone first. Yasmin is a patient here, so I have to ensure that anything Nadine has to tell you is not likely to be a breach of confidentiality.'

Mariner fought down his frustration. 'If Yasmin is in some kind of danger then patient confidentiality may be an irrelevance,' he said. 'It's important that we have access to any information that will help us to find her.'

'I appreciate that, Inspector, but I would ask you to respect my professional judgement. Yasmin is my patient and needs to know that she can trust me. Any decision about what to tell you is mine and mine alone. I will listen to what Nadine has to say. If I consider that there is anything that will help in your investigation without compromising my relationship with Yasmin Akram, then I will allow her to pass it on.'

Mariner had no option other than to wait and hope. While the two women were closeted in the doctor's consulting room, he placed the waiting room outside like an expectant father. He was flicking through a leaflet on heart disease when the door abruptly opened. Dr Shah appeared, looking grim-faced. 'Inspector, I think you need to come in.'

In the tiny room Mariner pulled up a chair, so that his knees were almost touching Dr Shah's.

'It is with reluctance that I tell you this,' said Dr Shah. 'But if it does, as you say, put Yasmin in danger then I would be unable to forgive myself for not passing on this information. I would just ask that you use it judiciously.'

'You have my word.'

'I've been the GP for Yasmin and her family for nearly

ten years, so I know Yasmin very well. Just over a month ago Yasmin came to see me because she wanted to begin taking the contraceptive pill.'

'The pill?' Mariner could bearly contain his surprise. It flew in the face of everything they'd been told so far about the girl.

'You understand that, ordinarily, I would not be telling you this.' It was obvious that the doctor was still wrestling with the dilemma.

'Of course. You're doing the right thing.'

Dr Shah seemed less convinced, but she continued. 'At seventeen Yasmin is of course above the age of consent, but knowing her family's traditional views I was more than a little surprised by her request. She openly told me that she had not discussed this with either of her parents and felt unable to do so. But, as we talked it over, it became clear that Yasmin was already seeing someone and intended to proceed with or without my help.'

'I see,' was all that Mariner could muster. So much for honesty and openness with her parents, he thought.

'She seemed a little apprehensive,' Dr Shah continued. 'But made it clear that she was going ahead with the physical relationship and wanted to have some control over protecting herself. Yasmin is a bright girl and had clearly thought this through. The logical thing for me to do was at least prevent her from getting into trouble. I also agreed that I would respect her privacy in this matter.'

'So her parents don't know.'

'That's right.'

'And you're sure that Yasmin is in a relationship?'

'Of course I can't be absolutely certain, but that's what she told me. I had no reason to disbelieve her.'

'Did she mention any names?'

'That side of it really isn't my business, but no, she didn't.'

'Well, thank you, Dr Shah. That certainly adds a new dimension to our investigation.'

109

Dr Shah looked over at Nadine, who had dried her tears and sat silent throughout. 'There's more to it than that,' she said. 'Contraceptive pills affect women differently and I wanted to ensure that Yasmin would have no side effects with the one I prescribed, so initially, she had only a month's course as a kind of trial. The plan was that if she was happy with it she would come back for a full six months' prescription, which she did, at the beginning of last week.

'On the day Yasmin came in for her repeat prescription our computer system was down so I wasn't issuing any non-urgent prescriptions. I feel that those printed are preferable as there can be no query about the interpretation of handwriting. Yasmin didn't need the pills immediately so we agreed that as soon as it was ready the prescription would be left at reception for Yasmin to collect when she could. The following day our computer was working again, so I prepared the prescription and it was put in the envelope marked with Yasmin's name to await collection.' She turned to the receptionist. 'Tell the inspector what happened, Nadine.'

The girl cast Mariner an anxious look. 'Mr Akram has also been having ongoing treatment for high blood pressure.' Somehow that didn't come as any surprise to Mariner.

'He came into the surgery to collect a repeat prescription and saw the envelope with Yasmin's name alongside his. He asked if it was for his daughter. He gave me her address and date of birth and I checked and found that it was hers, so I gave it to him to pass on to her.'

'Isn't that against the rules?'

Nadine's face told him that it was. Her tears had subsided, but weren't far away. 'I'm really sorry.'

'She is new to the job,' Dr Shah said. 'We had talked about this, but clearly I didn't place enough emphasis. I must take full responsibility.'

'So you handed Mr Akram a prescription for his daughter for the contraceptive pill that he had no idea she was taking? Did he look at it?'

110

'No, he left the surgery. But he must have opened it outside. He came back in and wanted to know why Yasmin had been to the doctor and what was wrong. I said I didn't know and he started to get angry. He took out the prescription and demanded to know what it was.'

'And you told him.'

'I recognised it and I didn't think. I said I thought it was for a contraceptive pill.' The girl was dying inside and Mariner almost felt sorry for her.

The doctor rushed to her defence. 'To be fair, that is almost irrelevant. Mr Akram could have walked into any pharmacy or accessed any Internet site to find out what the drug was for. The damage had already been done.'

'What was Mr Akram's reaction when you told him what the prescription was?'

'He was furious. He didn't say much but I could see from his face. I told him that the pills could be to help regulate Yasmin's menstrual cycle and help with period pain. I had to do the same thing once. But he didn't listen. He wanted to speak to Dr Shah, and when I said she was out on her rounds, he stormed out.'

'Did he come back?'

'No.' Dr Shah provided the answer.

'Who did you think he was angry with, Nadine?'

'Me; Dr Shah; Yasmin maybe? I don't know.' Being forced to face the implications of what had happened for the first time, Nadine's voice cracked and again she dissolved into tears. Dr Shah put a protective arm around her.

'Thank you,' Mariner said to the doctor. 'I appreciate your sharing this with me. I understand what a difficult decision it has been.'

When Nadine was calm again, Dr Shah walked him out. 'I may never know if I've done the right thing, but that's something I'll have to live with.'

'I feel sure that you have,' said Mariner. 'If it helps us to find Yasmin. . .'

'When I saw the news of her disappearance I recognised

111

her, of course, but the talk has been of racially motivated abduction, and I thought you would naturally find out about any boyfriend through Yasmin's friends. Nadine didn't even tell me about her mistake because she was afraid she would lose her job.'

'And will she?'

'I think everyone should be allowed to get things wrong at least once, don't you?'

Given the number of times he'd fouled up over the years, Mariner felt he was hardly in a position to argue.

Back at Granville Lane, Mariner was keen to have Millie's take on this news, and asked the key question: 'How do you think Akram would have reacted to this?'

'He'd have gone ballistic,' she said, bluntly.

'Hm, that's what I thought.'

'Several things would have upset him: the fact that Yasmin was in a relationship—'

'The receptionist didn't tell him that. He might have accepted her explanation that Yasmin was taking the pill for other reasons.'

'But he'd be annoyed that Yasmin had gone behind his or his wife's back to arrange contraception and that the surgery had complied.'

'So as Nadine said, his anger could have been directed at the doctor's practice?'

'He didn't get back to Dr Shah to complain though, did he? I think he'd have been far more upset about the fact that Yasmin might be seeing someone. If he didn't buy Nadine's explanation for the pill then there's probably little worse that Yasmin can have done to anger him. He's already told us how "innocent" she is and now he's suddenly being told he might be wrong about that. There's a lot of pressure on girls in our communities to keep themselves pure for their future husbands, and we know that arranged marriage is one aspect of Muslim life that the Akrams subscribe to. If it became public knowledge that Yasmin was sleeping around it would

112

make it harder for her parents to find her a husband of any standing. And that would be important to a family like the Akrams. They value their reputation in the community and made a good match for their older daughter. They'd want the same for Yasmin. Previous relationships would limit the possibilities. She would be soiled goods.'

'And this is more information they've chosen not to share with us.'

'This would be quite a blow to the family pride and repu- tation. They wouldn't be keen to share it with anyone. It wouldn't be great publicity for their school either, to have their own daughter flouting fundamental Islamic beliefs. Part of the reason many parents choose Islamic schools is to protect their children from exactly this kind of thing: the corruption of the outside world.'

'Hasan Sheron wasn't so very far off the mark after all. How strongly do you think Akram would react to this knowledge?'

'Well, we already know that Mohammed Akram doesn't take things lying down,' said Millie. 'That would be espe- cially true where his daughter's concerned. And we know that he has a short temper.'

'So now, suddenly, we're presented with a fat, juicy motive. No wonder he's been trying to divert our attention elsewhere. Do you think this would give Akram enough reason to harm Yasmin?'

'You've heard of so-called honour killings?' Millie asked.

'Like Abdullah Yones?'

'He stabbed his sixteen-year-old daughter eleven times in a frenzied attack because she had started to wear make-up and had a boyfriend and others in the community began referring to her as a prostitute. He saw her behaviour as an affront to his honour.'

'But Yones was Kurdish, wasn't he?'

'There are plenty of examples of similar situations across other cultures. In Pakistan, Samia Sarwar was shot dead

113

with a gun disguised as her mother's walking stick, right in front of her lawyer. Islam doesn't condone such violence, but like any religion, honour can be used as a justification.'

'You think Mohammed Akram is capable of that?'

'I'm saying it happens, that's all. Perhaps Akram wouldn't need to go that far.'

'What do you mean?' Mariner asked.

'Well, on that Tuesday afternoon Akram travelled up to the school in Bradford. He's got contacts up there. Maybe it would be enough to get Yasmin away for a time. It may even be that he's planning to spirit her away abroad into an arranged marriage before her reputation becomes public knowledge. Remember, it was the school who reported Yasmin missing, and when we first went to talk to the Akrams he seemed almost irritated with his wife that the alarm had been raised. He said, "You should have waited?" We took it as being a control thing, but perhaps he had planned to let Mum in on it.'

'So why doesn't he just come clean about it now? Christ, he knows what we're putting into this investigation.'

'Because the timing's wrong. If it hasn't been followed through he can't afford to yet. And he wouldn't tell his wife because she might give the game away or she may not approve of or support such actions. By reporting Yasmin missing and involving us straight away, Shanila could have provided her husband with the perfect smoke screen, but one he'd have to keep in place until the job is done.'

'If Akram knows that Yasmin is safe, he's a hell of an actor. Remember the appeal? Where does all that angst come from?'

'It has different roots. In any other circumstances Akram is a law-abiding man. What he's doing is the best thing for his daughter and family, and he wouldn't hesitate to bend the rules, but he'd also know that at the very least, it's a gross act of deception. He wouldn't be comfortable with that.'

'But family come first.' Mariner couldn't deny that there

114

was a certain logic to what Millie was saying. 'So Dad plays along with the general view that Yasmin has gone missing until she is married off and it's too late to do anything about it. Forcing Yasmin into a marriage against her will is hardly likely to be what she wants.'

Millie agreed. 'And it's a major human rights issue. There are all kinds of pressure groups who'd have a field day if he was exposed. None of which would enhance Akram's image as a liberal, Westernised Muslim.'

'The other alternative is that Akram genuinely doesn't know where Yasmin is because she has run away. From what we're finding out about her, Yasmin doesn't sound like the kind of girl who's going to sit around and let herself be coerced into a marriage she doesn't want, however necessary her parents might think it is.'

'Either way we need to get Akram's side of the story on this,' said Millie.

'One thing we haven't found out yet.'

'What?'

'If Yasmin is on the pill because she's in a relationship – who the hell is it with? Someone's keeping a low profile.'

'The relationship was obviously a secret one. Probably the boyfriend knows the way Akram would react too.'

Chapter Nine

Mariner was put straight through to Mohammed Akram. 'You have some news, Inspector?' His hope was palpable. If he was covering up he was doing a brilliant acting job.

'No, I'm sorry, Mr Akram. But I do need to speak to you again. I wondered if I could meet you at your home. You may prefer to speak to us without your wife.'

'Why would I want to do that?'

'I'd like to talk to you about an incident that occurred at your doctor's surgery last week.'

Silence, then: 'I see. I'll meet you at the house.'

Akram's Mercedes was already parked on the looped tarmac drive when Mariner pulled in behind it. He was surprised when the door was answered by a pretty young woman in purple and black salwaar kameez. 'I'm Amira,' she said. 'Yasmin's older sister. I flew in this morning to give some support to my parents until Yasmin is found.' So the tired eyes in such a young face could have been jet-lag or worry. If this was some kind of scam, Mariner doubted that Amira was in on it. 'My father is in the garden. I'll take you to him.'

Mohammed Akram was sitting on a wooden bench in a shaded patch at the bottom of an expanse of lawn that was crowded on all sides with bulging shrubs. He was tie-less and the sleeves of his dress shirt were rolled up. A variety of garden chairs was scattered around him and Mariner took his chance on a flimsy, white plastic affair. Amira did the same.

Mariner glanced up at the elder daughter. 'Mr Akram, what we have to talk about may be a little sensitive—' he began, but Akram stopped him.

'I want Amira to hear it. At some time I have to tell my wife, so I would like Amira to know.' He seemed fidgety and unrelaxed, but then he already knew that this was going to be a difficult conversation.

'All right then. As I indicated on the phone, I have some questions regarding your visit to Dr Shah's surgery. I understand that you had an appointment there last Friday?'

Akram's eyes narrowed. 'How did you find out about this?'

'We have been in touch with Dr Shah.' No need to tell him who initiated the contact.

'She had no right—'

'Mr Akram, how we came by this information at this stage is irrelevant. We would have got to it eventually through routine checks on Yasmin's medical history. For Dr Shah it was a difficult decision to make. Like the rest of us, she is worried about Yasmin's whereabouts, but she only found out today what had happened. Would you like to tell me now, in your own words, what occurred, and then after that, you may want to explain why you kept this from me.'

Akram looked suddenly exhausted. 'That one's easy,' he said. 'I didn't tell you because this is our family business. I'm not proud of how I reacted – over-reacted – at the surgery and it really has nothing to do with Yasmin's disappearance. We had discussed the situation and resolved it.'

Just like that, thought Mariner. 'I'd still like you to tell me.'

Akram sighed. 'It's only what I expect you already know. On Friday afternoon I went to Dr Shah's surgery to collect my repeat prescription. I was making a further

117

appointment when I noticed an envelope with Yasmin's name on it. I asked if it was for my daughter. I had no idea that it contained a prescription. Girls, women, they have regular health checks and I thought that perhaps it was some kind of reminder. The receptionist asked my address and Yasmin's date of birth. When the details corresponded with those on the prescription she let me have it.'

'And you opened the envelope.'

To his credit, Akram didn't looked pleased with himself, but then he'd had ample time to concoct this little charade. 'There was nothing on the envelope to say that it was confidential and I thought if it was an appointment, Shanila and I would need to think about how we would get Yasmin to it.'

'And when you saw that it was a prescription?'

'I was surprised. I wasn't aware that there was anything wrong with Yasmin or that she had been to see the doctor. Normally, Shanila would tell me about anything like that.'

'Did you know what the prescription was for?'

'Not right away. I went back into the surgery and asked the receptionist. She said she thought it was for a type of contraceptive pill.'

'And you were surprised?'

'Inspector, I was everything you would expect me to be: shocked, horrified, angry and disappointed. Do you have children, Inspector? A daughter?'

'No.'

'I couldn't understand why Yasmin would need this and I was angry with our GP for having written such a prescription without telling me or my wife. She's just a child.'

'You were certain your wife didn't know?'

'Shanila and I don't have secrets, especially about our children.'

Yet Shanila allowed Yasmin to go to her friend's against your wishes, thought Mariner. He tried to catch Amira's eye but she was gazing intently towards the house, her face troubled. Instead he said, 'Doctors have certain rules of confidentiality they must—'

Again the anger flared up. 'Yasmin is only seventeen. She doesn't mix with boys. What would she want with the contraceptive pill? What sort of country is this where professionals can make decisions about a child's life without the knowledge of her parents?'

'So you were angry, Mr Akram.'

'At first, yes.'

'Who were you angry with?'

'The receptionist, the doctor, for writing this prescription without my knowledge and, I felt sure, without my wife's knowledge too.'

'And Yasmin?'

'Yes.'

'You said you were angry "at first"?'

'The girl told me that the pills could have been prescribed to control Yasmin's menstrual cycle, that it could be perfectly innocent.'

'And did you believe that?'

'When I took some time to consider it, thought rationally about the facts, it seemed the only logical explanation.'

'So you accepted it.'

'It was obviously something I needed to discuss with Yasmin.'

'And when did you do that?'

'I went to meet her from school. I thought we would be able to talk about it in the car on the way home.'

'And did you?'

'When I arrived outside the school Yasmin came out with her friends: Suzanne and some other girls. She wasn't pleased to see me. She didn't want a lift, she wanted to walk with her friends. Yasmin doesn't like to show how much she cares about her family in front of her friends. I told her I wanted to talk to her about something, but she said we had the whole weekend. Suzanne said something to her.'

'Did you speak to Suzanne?'

119

'She is an interfering b—' He stopped himself. 'She had probably put Yasmin up to it.'

'What made you think that?'

'The girl has a reputation.'

'For what?'

'For being easy with the boys. You only have to look at her clothing; it's indecent. She was encouraging Yasmin to behave the same way.'

'Is that the real reason you wouldn't let Yasmin go to Suzanne's house?'

'That girl is a bad influence.'

'So did you give Yasmin a lift?'

'Only from the university station. I went and waited for her there when she got off the train. I drove her home and we talked about it then. I didn't want that conversation brought into the house.'

'And what did Yasmin tell you?'

'She told me the same thing as the receptionist, that she was on the pill to control her periods. They had been irregular and uncomfortable and that the doctor thought the pill would alleviate those symptoms. She hadn't thought it necessary to tell her mother or me.'

'Did you believe her?'

'I wanted to. Yasmin is growing up. There are certain ways in which we must respect her privacy.'

'That doesn't answer my question. Mr Akram, what would you say if I told you that Yasmin had given the doctor a different story?'

'What do you mean?'

'Yasmin told Dr Shah that she needed to go on the pill to protect herself. That she was in a relationship that was already physical.' He was deliberately testing out Akram to measure the reaction, but to his credit Akram looked genuinely shocked.

'Yasmin denied it and I believed her.'

'So you believed that she was taking the pill for medical reasons and your anger with Yasmin passed, and yet you

120

didn't confront Dr Shah about this.'

'It was the weekend. The doctor wouldn't be available.'

'Did you give Yasmin the impression that you were angry with her? Did you, say, raise your voice to her?'

'I might have. I was upset.'

'Is it possible that your behaviour could have prompted Yasmin to run away?'

'Yes, of course it's possible. Do you think I haven't already thought of that?'

'If Yasmin was seeing someone, a boy, have you any idea who that might be?'

'When I asked her outright Yasmin denied it, and she wouldn't lie to me. As far as I'm concerned she has no contact with any boys.'

'Thank you, Mr Akram.'

Amira got to her feet. 'I'll show you out.' She took Mariner back up the garden and round the side of the house to his car. When they were out of earshot of her father she said, 'Inspector, it might be helpful for you to know that I can't be as sure as my father that Yasmin wasn't in a relationship. I know that for some months she had been coming under pressure from her friends to have some fun. She couldn't talk to my parents about it, but she often rang me for my advice.'

'And what did you advise her to do?'

'I told her to relax. That virginity isn't as important as our parents seem to think, and that if an opportunity comes along that she wants to take, then she should take it.'

'And did an opportunity come along?'

She flashed an apologetic smile. 'That's what I don't know.'

Millie met Mariner as he came back into the building. 'How did it go?'

'He certainly seemed upset by it all.'

'Guilt.'

'Trouble is, what kind of guilt? Is he feeling guilty

121

because he knows what's happened to Yasmin and he's stringing us along, or feeling guilty because he may have caused his daughter to run away?' Mariner fed back what Amira had told him, too.

'It would be interesting to get Suzanne's perspective on that story,' said Millie. 'If Yasmin has been seeing someone, she'll be the one to know.'

'We'll talk to her on Monday.'

'Yes, sir.' Jamilla hesitated, about to say something else.

'And?' prompted Mariner.

'Tony Knox,' she said. 'Is he all right?'

'In what way?' asked Mariner, regretting the hint of defensiveness that he knew had crept into his voice. It was enough to put her off.

'It's OK. Nothing, I'm sure.'

'His mother-in-law's ill and his wife's away. He's distracted, that's all.' Mariner hoped it was true. He wasn't oblivious to the fact that Knox and Millie didn't seem to have established much of a working relationship when he wasn't there. He'd never seen Tony Knox as a racist, but then the situation had never previously arisen.

Millie shrugged. 'Like I said, it's nothing.'

Nonetheless, Mariner took the next opportunity to quiz Knox. 'How are you getting on with Millie?'

Knox seemed surprised by the question. 'Fine,' he said.

'She's a good officer. I think she's brought an added dimension to the investigation.'

'Yeah.'

Mariner had successfully backed himself into a corner. The next question was: And do you have a problem with her being Asian? Instead he took the easy way out. 'How's Theresa's mother?' he asked.

'What?'

'Theresa's mother. I take it she's still up there, looking after her?'

'Oh. She's up and down, you know, but Theresa just

wants to be there.' Knox stared into space, lost for a moment in his own thoughts, before turning his attention back to the database he was working on. That was definitely it, Mariner thought. It was Theresa's mother that was the problem. Touching that a bloke could be so concerned about the mother-in-law.

A walk-through was scheduled for late Tuesday afternoon, one week after Yasmin's disappearance, and would provide an opportunity for the press and media to assemble and publicise the event to anyone who may have been in the area on the day that Yasmin vanished. Local newspapers, radio and TV were well represented and now that the case was gathering momentum there would be national coverage too. To maximise the potential for witnesses to come forward, they had to take the most likely option, based on Yasmin getting off the train at the university station as she would normally have done, and walking home. The length and complexity of the journey turned everything into a major production, with three different camera crews on the train and at either end of the walk.

Mariner was pleased with the turn-out, though. Even considering that many of the onlookers were simply there to rubber-neck, the more people there were, the greater the chance that Yasmin would continue to be the topic of everyday conversation and the greater the chance that someone, somewhere, would recall seeing something of relevance last Tuesday afternoon. Posters of the seventeen-year-old peppered the walls of the station and officers distributed more of the flyers among the small crowd that had gathered, though Mariner couldn't imagine anyone who hadn't just jetted in from Mars being unfamiliar with that smiling snapshot.

The group of young girls from a neighbouring school, including the one who was to be Yasmin's double, had been carefully primed and taken several times through each step of the journey as Yasmin would have made it.

Miraculously, at the appointed time everything was ready and Mariner was able to give the instruction to begin. On cue, the girls left the high school and began the walk down towards the railway station. A small crowd followed them, supervised by uniformed constables, but despite the numbers an unnatural hush had descended, interrupted only by the staccato snapping of camera shutters.

On instruction the girls waited at the top of the road leading down to the station until the train was seen approaching so that 'Yasmin' could run for the train in the way that 'she' had done on Tuesday. Today, the train was several minutes late, causing tense moments while everyone stood about waiting for it. They'd been able to arrange for the original driver of the train to be back on duty, in the hope that his memory would be jogged, but as there was no routine ticket check on board they were relying on other passengers to have seen Yasmin. This was likely to prove difficult as, at this time of the afternoon, the trains going into the city were almost deserted; all the passenger traffic going in the opposite direction, at the beginning of the rush hour.

An additional carriage had been laid on for press only – based on the assumption that Yasmin had got on the train and continued her journey home, they followed her to the university station from where she would have walked home. The route took them along the walkway through the university grounds and past the meadow where Helen Greenwood had encountered the flasher, confirming that it would have been all too easy for Yasmin to draw attention to herself and solicit an unwelcome approach from a stranger. It seemed more implausible than ever that anyone with a gramme of common sense would attempt a random abduction in these surroundings, and in broad daylight.

A film crew from the regional TV station was there to film this part of the journey and a clip would be broadcast the following evening on the regular 'Crimestoppers' slot. Before long, the story would be national news, too. That would really open the floodgates to the cranks.

Mariner watched the beginning of the reconstruction before he and Knox drove across to the university to pick up the end. Despite his reservations, Mariner felt that it was going well, and that they would have done enough to stir the memories of anyone who was around that Tuesday afternoon. What they really needed was one good, solid lead.

Mariner's wish was granted, but not from the expected source. The walk-through successfully concluded, he and Knox were on their way back to Granville Lane when the radio crackled into life.

'The manager at Comet electrical superstore has just phoned. He's got something you might be interested in.'

'Like what?'

'Yasmin Akram's mobile phone.'

In a move worthy of Starsky and Hutch, Knox made an illegal U-turn at the next traffic lights and they drove to the retail park where the store was based. Even at this time on a weekday there was a steady stream of traffic in and out of the park. The garden centre next door was displaying everything to enhance the summer experience and they had to pick their way through barbecues, garden furniture and pot plants.

Inside the store, Mariner showed his warrant card and asked to speak to the manager. Mark Williams looked about fifteen, clean cut in a dazzling white shirt with the company logo on the pocket. With a dramatic flourish, he put a plastic bag down on the counter. Mariner opened the bag and removed the only item: a purple mobile phone. 'A Nokia 3100 with a mauve oil and water removable cover,' said Williams, though whether the pride was in the phone itself or his own professional knowledge, was hard to tell. 'The bloke who brought it in had found it. He came in to check the registration, so that he could return it.'

'He couldn't get that from the phone?'

William shook his head. 'It's "pay as you go" so we had to track the owner on the system. Every time one of these is bought, it's logged with the company: in this case, Nokia. You can check it out with anyone who sells the brand of phones. This one is registered to Miss Yasmin Akram,' he said. 'As soon as I saw that I knew whose it was, so I thought we should call you.'

'You thought right,' Mariner said. He looked around at the customers browsing the displays. 'Where's the guy who brought it in?'

'Mr Hewitt? He couldn't wait, but he left his address and his mobile number.'

'You let him go?'

Williams's face fell. 'He had to get back to work. I'm pretty sure he's kosher.'

'He'd better be, for your sake.'

Mariner called the mobile number. When it was picked up, after several rings, there was noise and disturbance in the background: animals yelping.

'Mr Hewitt?' Mariner enquired, over the din.

'Yes.'

'You handed in a phone belonging to Yasmin Akram.'

'That's right.'

'We need to speak to you urgently. Where are you?'

'The animal rescue centre on Barnes Hill.' It explained the soundtrack.

'We'll be with you right away. Don't go anywhere.'

'I wasn't planning to.'

Meanwhile, Knox had bagged up the phone so that they could drop it in at Granville Lane to be sent on to forensics without delay. That tiny device could prove invaluable in the search for Yasmin Akram.

In this heat you could navigate the city with your eyes shut, from the acrid Longbridge paint shop to the sickly-sweet halo surrounding the Cadbury factory. The aroma that lingered over Barnes Hill was a not entirely pleasant antiseptic with a hint of dog crap. The pound was quiet, but for the persistent yapping of some kind of small breed dog. It was getting on Mariner's nerves before they even reached the office, but he guessed the staff working there must be immune to it.

'Be with you in a sec.' Paul Hewitt was processing paperwork in a tiny office just behind the reception desk. As they waited, a lethargic Labrador wandered in out of the heat and plopped itself down in a basket in a corner of the room.

When Hewitt finally appeared, Mariner had a visual impression of a kind of understated Friar Tuck: medium height and rotund, his shiny bald scalp circled by a fringe that resembled a monk's tonsure. Large, square-framed glasses rested on the bridge of his nose and his cheery smile completed the image. 'We'll go in the training room,' he said. 'It'll be cooler in there.'

The room was indeed airier and had a table large enough to spread out the map that Mariner and Knox had brought with them.

'So, where did you find it?'

'Kingsmead Reservoir,' Hewitt said. 'Right here.' Hewitt jabbed a finger at a spot right on the edge of the map, just beside the blue blob that symbolised water.

Although he'd heard of it, Mariner's knowledge of Kingsmead Reservoir extended no further than a label on the incident room map: an uninhabited wilderness on the other side of the railway track to the station, between the main Birmingham to Bristol line and Birchill Lane. The reservoir itself, though once functional, had ceased to be useful after Birmingham began drawing water from the Elan Valley, storing it in the much larger Bartley Green reservoir. 'But that's in the middle of nowhere,' he said.

'I know,' agreed Hewitt.

'So what were you doing there?' asked Knox, more than a little pointedly.

Hewitt was unruffled. 'We got a call from St Clare's, the old folk's home that backs on to it, just here.' He put an index finger on the map. 'One of the old biddies had got it

127

into her head that she'd seen a man there beating a dog. She thought he might have killed it.'

Hairs stood up on the back of Mariner's neck. 'When was this?'

'She mentioned it to the staff a few days ago, apparently, but nobody took her seriously at first. The old girl has her "senior" days, if you know what I mean. But she wouldn't let it drop. I think she must have driven them mad over the weekend with it, so to humour her, they gave us a call, first thing this morning. I drove over with Sue, my partner, and had a look at the place she described. It took some finding, I can tell you. Even though Lily, that's Lily Cooper, showed us from her window where she saw it happen, it was still difficult to find a way in. We had to use the *A–Z*.'

'I'm not surprised,' said Mariner, looking again at the map. There was no obvious access to the site.

'When we got to it, there was no sign of any dog where the old dear said, but just to make sure we had a good hunt around, as far as we could – most of it's like untamed jungle – and that was when we found the phone, lying there in the grass. We brought it back to the office, charged it up then keyed in to find the user identity. But because it's one of those "pay as you go" phones I had to take it to a dealer so they could look up the name and address of the person who bought it. The Comet store's not far away. We've all seen the news bulletins so once they'd looked it up, it didn't take long to put two and two together.'

'Well, I'm very glad that you did,' said Mariner. 'This could be quite a breakthrough.' Suddenly he sensed that there was more. 'Was there anything else you wanted to tell us?'

Hewitt lowered his voice. 'I wouldn't want to be alarmist, but near where we found it there was brown stuff, sort of staining on the grass. I didn't say anything to Sue, but it looked to me like blood.'

'We'll need you to take us to the exact spot, Mr Hewitt.'

Hewitt slapped his thighs, a little nervously Mariner thought. 'Whenever you like.'

Chapter Ten

They followed the same route that Hewitt had taken to get to the reservoir, past the railway station, over the line, past a pub called the Bridge and on to Birchill Lane, flanked on one side by a public park and on the other by wild woodland, broken only by a tall and rambling building that looked as if it had once been a country residence of some kind.

'That's the nursing home.' Hewitt said, just as the sign for 'St Clare's' came into view. Just along from the home they passed the entrance road to a small industrial park, which was followed by another half a mile or so of sparse, unhealthy looking woodland, to a row of four derelict cottages. The houses were fenced in by heavy-duty spike-topped railings, with a huge pair of steel-framed, chain-link gates padlocked against trespassers. A board in the entrance announced that the enclosed land was on the market for development.

To the side, a narrow, unmetalled service road curled round to the back of the cottages into what once might have been their gardens, with perhaps an orchard, but was now an open piece of rough ground of about a quarter of an acre. And it was here that Hewitt took them, Knox easing the car cautiously over the uneven terrain to avoid damaging the suspension. They drew to a halt in a small grassy clearing, pock-marked with litter and the sort of detritus left behind by glue sniffers. Here and there were areas of blackened grass where fires had been lit and an old, filthy mattress lay on its side, springs spilling out of it like guts from a dead animal. Even in daylight any vehicle parking here would have been shielded from the view of houses on the opposite side of Birchill Lane by the cottages themselves, the trees and the rampant, overgrown shrubs.

'This was the nearest place I could find to park,' Hewitt said. 'I was hoping to find a way through somehow. I was encouraged by the fact that other people obviously use it.' He was referring to the tyre tracks carved out of the hard earth and the little heaps of dog-ends. 'When I looked around I saw that opening, there in the trees.'

He'd done well to spot that, thought Mariner. It was nothing more than a small gap in the undergrowth. 'Lead the way,' he said.

By now it was well after seven, but time had drawn none of the heat or humidity out of the day and even in shirt-sleeves they sweltered. Knox and Mariner followed Hewitt through the wasteland, along the only clear path that cut a swathe through the low undergrowth, and straggling birches that had undoubtedly provided the adjacent road with its name. The dirt underfoot had been dried solid by the long, hot summer, but at one point, Mariner stopped at a small patch where water drained across its width, throwing up a couple of distinct footprints and a narrow tyre track, possibly belonging to a bike.

They smelled it before they saw it: a thick, peaty methane smell. Then, as the path meandered from one side to another, the trees began to thin to low shrubbery, then long grasses, and finally the path broke out again into the glare of the evening sun, at the edge of the reservoir, if that's what you could call it. Today it was simply an expanse of black mud, shrunken and dried by the drought, with a single broad channel flowing sluggishly across the centre from the far side, maybe five hundred yards away, towards where they were standing now. 'Kingsmead Reservoir,' Hewitt announced.

Mariner marvelled at how such an expanse could exist on their patch without any of them really knowing about it. The size of three football fields, it was a vast and untamed open space, the water's edge crowded with willows and reeds and shoulder-high grass. The land was bordered along the far side by the Birmingham to Bristol railway line and beyond that, a high bank of distant houses; the 'cottages on the ridge' from which the community of Cotteridge had taken its name. The factory site took up much of the near side, almost as far as the trees they'd walked through, though it finished four hundred yards away, behind substantial wood-panelled fencing. The only building that had any kind of direct view of the area was St Clare's.

'How could we not know about this?' Knox said.

'I'd heard about it.' Mariner admitted. 'It's part of the River Rea that runs down from the Waseley Hills right though the city and to Spaghetti Junction at the other end. It's been neglected for years but there has been a conservation group, Birmingham Riverside Trust, working on areas further up stream to try and clear it and create more of a leisure area: footpaths and cycle tracks, that kind of thing. I've seen posters around advertising for volunteers.'

As they surveyed the scene, a train thundered by on the opposite side of the water; not the local train that Yasmin would have caught, but the Birmingham to Bristol express. They heard rather than saw it, the wooden fence hiding it from view, and equally preventing any passengers from seeing anything on the reservoir. Anyone operating down here would know that they had almost complete privacy from prying eyes. The thought made Mariner shiver, despite the heat. Alongside the railway were the long production hangars of a glass manufacturer, separated from the track by a fifteen-foot wall topped with broken glass and razor wire. Anything along that stretch could be discounted as means of access.

They had come to a junction of sorts in the footpath: to the right was the rickety bridge that crossed the out-flow

131

stream at the back of St Clare's, but going round to the left, skirting the edge of the reservoir, there were also clear signs that other feet had trodden.

'Lily had mentioned the bridge, so we went this way,' said Hewitt, leading them round to the rotting structure. Constructed from wooden planks, it was in a state of disrepair, the boards mottled with holes, though still sound enough to take their combined weight. On one side the railings were snapped in two. Underneath the structure the water moved reluctantly on to a square plate of deeply rusted metal, accumulating at a pair of wooden gates. Though firmly shut, there were enough rotten crevices to allow the pathetic dribble of water to slowly insinuate itself through them to where it barrelled and cascaded limply over a concrete shelf and down into a narrow tunnel.

'So what's all this about?' Knox asked, peering over the edge.

'It looks like some kind of slow-release mechanism to make sure the reservoir doesn't go completely dry or flood,' Mariner said. 'They have them on some canals. As the reservoir fills, the pressure builds on that plate until it eventually gets unlocked by the weight and volume of water, the gates open and the water surges down the spillway into the tunnel.' But he was talking to himself. Knox had already lost interest.

Hewitt crossed the bridge to where the path broadened out slightly on the other side. 'This is where Lily said she saw the action, and that was where we found the phone, lying just there,' he said, pointing to an area of longish grass just to the side of what would have been a path. 'And that's what I thought might be blood.' Initially camouflaged, on closer inspection there was no missing the brownish stains, some of which were as dark as creosote on the yellowing grass. Mariner's first thought was how Sue, Hewitt's partner, could have overlooked them.

'But where's our dog?' he murmured to himself. 'Is there a way down here from the station?' he asked, looking up at the chain-link fence that separated them from the platforms and car park, two hundred or so yards away.

'I think there used to be,' said Hewitt. 'But I wouldn't know where exactly it comes out. I can't imagine that anybody uses it any more because, since the factory was demolished, it wouldn't go anywhere. The industrial units block off the other side. If you wanted to get to Birchill Lane it would be much simpler to walk along the road instead.'

But longer, thought Mariner, making a visual sweep through 360 degrees. As a walker, he was accustomed to scouring overgrown tracts of land for signs of a thoroughfare. Many times he'd come to a so-called public footpath across a field that some uncooperative farmer had planted over in the hope of discouraging ramblers. Only a few weekends ago, he'd had to battle his way through a field of maize that had grown taller than him, completely obscuring the right of way.

Generally speaking, he wasn't alone in his determination and there were others who wouldn't be deterred, which meant that usually, as in this case, a soft line marking out the faintest traces of human disturbance could be seen. Nettles and cow parsley stems that elsewhere were waist high had been snapped and crushed, the long grass swept over. He struck out along it a little way and was proved right: though not well-used and with hardly a break in the solid foliage, it was a definite path; recently forged down from the back of the station to where they now stood, and passed through, perhaps three or four times, since the early summer. The logical destination would be the cluster of low-level pre-fabricated units a quarter of a mile away, but the greenery in that direction looked untouched. 'What have we got there?' Mariner asked.

'Small businesses, that sort of thing,' Hewitt replied. 'There's a sign on up the road.'

'We should have a closer look,' Mariner told Knox. 'Meanwhile, I don't want everyone tramping around here

133

like a herd of elephants just yet. We need to cordon off the area and get a team down here ASAP to do a thorough search.' He scanned the area. It wasn't going to be easy. The surrounding ground had been left to go wild for years and the grass was dense and impenetrable, with some vicious-looking brambles and nettles. Added to which they'd need to cover the disused cottages. It was all going to take valuable time and manpower. Meanwhile, forensics could get down here and verify that the staining was indeed blood, though Mariner, from experience, was pretty sure that it was.

He looked at his watch. Gone eight o'clock. By the time they could get anything organised it would be going on for nine and even at this time of year the light would start going. In this hostile terrain it would be a nightmare. Despite the urgency it would be better to have the light on their side to avoid missing anything. In only a few hours the sun would be coming up again.

'OK, let's get off here. We'll need to get the area sealed off and do a thorough search first thing tomorrow.' They trekked back along the narrow path to where the car was parked and Knox could call through to Granville Lane to organise securing the site. They were just about to leave when a distant roar greeted their ears and another vehicle appeared in the mouth of the clearing, with a lone driver. Seeing the assembled group he applied his brakes, clearly considering whether to continue or to turn and retreat. Before he could, Mariner approached, arm outstretched, holding out his warrant card, Knox at his heels. When he was near enough to be clearly identified, the car driver reacted with a resigned movement of the head and put on the handbrake.

'DI Mariner, Mr—?'

'Pryce, Shaun Pryce,' the man obliged, indicating a degree of familiarity with this routine. 'It's all right. I'll come back another time.' He glanced up into the rear-view mirror as if to go, but Mariner was close enough to place

134

both hands on the sill of the door.

'Would you mind getting out of the car a minute, Mr Pryce?'

Standing alongside Mariner, Shaun Pryce was considerably shorter than him, a wiry young man of about thirty, his platinum hair edged with lethal-looking ginger sideburns. Testosterone oozed from every pore, his stylishly crumpled combats and a faded black tank top displaying his muscular arms and shoulders to their fullest advantage, including a couple of elaborate tattoos. He saw Mariner looking at them.

'My personal *hommage* to the Robster,' he said, pronouncing the word with an exaggerated French accent. 'That's where you've seen them before. So what's going on then?' He grinned, exposing perfect, gleaming white teeth, his eyes roving from one to another of the policemen, distinctly cagey despite the outward charm. Leaning back on the car door, he was a picture of relaxation but, folding his arms, he kept a wary eye on Knox who was prowling around the battered VW Golf. Old and scruffy, the vehicle had bits of electrical equipment lying on the parcel shelf, including several coils of plastic sheathed wire. A St George's flag sticker decorated the rear window.

Mariner ignored the question. 'What brings you here?' he asked.

'I saw the car and came to see what's going on. I wanted to make sure it wasn't kids messing about. One day they'll set fire to the trees and the whole lot will go up.'

No kids Mariner knew had access to a top of the range Vauxhall Vectra, he thought, but he didn't pursue it.

'So you've been here before,' he said instead.

Pryce shrugged. 'A couple of times. It's peaceful. Somewhere to come and unwind a bit.' As if to sanction the rustic image, an evening blackbird chose that moment to begin its repetitive song. For many people, Mariner included, it might have been a credible response, but Shaun Pryce just didn't look the type to derive his relaxation from a patch of scrubby, rubbish-strewn grass.

Knox leaned in through the car's passenger window and retrieved something from the back seat. 'Come being the operative word, eh, Mr Pryce?' The magazine he'd retrieved displayed a full montage of photographs of naked women striking far from modest poses. That was more like it.

Unembarrassed by the find, Pryce smirked. 'You know how it is. I have a high sex drive,' he said. 'I'm sure you can be a bit of a wanker sometimes, Officer.' He was deliberately baiting Knox. He was playing with fire. Muscles bunched around Knox's jaw, but he kept control.

'Where exactly do you do this unwinding?' Mariner asked. 'It must be a bit stuffy in the car in this weather.'

'Just around.' Pryce glanced around the general area, none of which looked the least bit inviting.

'Ever go on to the reservoir itself?' Mariner nodded towards the path they'd found.

Pryce shook his head. 'No.'

'Never? Why not?'

'No point. Why walk half a mile through the jungle when everything I need is here.'

'When was the last time you were here?'

'I couldn't really say. Like I told you, it's only occasionally.'

'Try to think.'

'Couple of weeks ago, maybe.'

'Can you be a bit more precise?'

'I can't honestly remember.' He glanced at his watch, a hint that he'd like to go now.

'What time of day was it?'

'After work.'

'And what sort of work is it that you do, Mr Pryce?'

'Actually, I'm an actor.' So that as why he was enjoying this so much. Kid thought he was in an episode of *The Bill*. 'I'm resting at the moment, except for a bit of modelling but—'

136

'Been in anything I'd have seen?' challenged Knox.

'As I said, mostly modelling work, although I've been up for an audition for Jimmy Porter at the Rep.'

'I thought you said you came down here after work.'

'When I'm resting I do electrics. I'm working on an extension.'

'Nearby?'

'Just up the road.'

'Ever seen anyone else down here?'

Pryce laughed. 'That's the whole fucking point. It's *private*.'

'Have you ever owned a dog, Mr Pryce?'

Understandably perhaps, the question took Pryce by surprise. 'No.'

Knox opened the driver's door for Pryce to get in.

'Aren't you going to tell me what's going on?' he asked.

'No.'

But Knox did take details of where he was working before they allowed him to get into his car and watch him reverse skilfully out of the clearing, right hand down at precisely the right point.

'Thinks he's God's gift,' said Knox, bitterly.

'Were you thinking what I was thinking?'

'That flag of St George was conspicuous in the back window of his car.'

'He might not have put it there of course,' said Mariner. 'It's a pretty old car. He seemed more New Age than National Front to me.'

'That hair, though. Would have made any Aryan proud.'

'Even though it was dyed. What do you think?'

'He admitted himself, he's a little tosser. He didn't come down to check us out, he was surprised to see us. He braked as he came into the clearing.'

'And he's been here more than a few times,' Mariner agreed. 'That space isn't an easy one to reverse out of, avoiding the potholes, and he did it like a pro. Nor would I rule out him going on to the reservoir itself. How else

137

would he know it's a half a mile of jungle unless he's been through it? No. Shaun Pryce wasn't telling us anything like the truth. The question is, is it because he knows something or is he hiding something? Just for the record, check whether we've got him on our books.'

'What for?'

'I don't know, but I think Shaun Pryce might be the kind of cocky little bugger who likes to play games.'

They took a last look around, but there was nothing more to be gained here. 'OK, let's knock it on the head for tonight and get some sleep while we still can,' said Mariner. 'We'll start the search first thing in the morning.' Knox didn't offer any resistance.

It was nearly ten when Mariner was ready to leave Granville Lane. He tried to phone Anna to let her know what was going on, but was wasting his time: all he got was her answering machine. It irritated him disproportionately. He looked up to see Tony Knox doing nothing more useful than staring into space. 'Do you want a lift home?' he asked. Mariner half expected a rebuttal, but for once Knox took the sensible option.

'Fancy a drink?' Mariner added, when they got to the car.

'All right.'

'Spoken like a man who has nothing better to do,' said Mariner. 'How could I fail to be flattered?'

They stopped off at the Boat, Mariner's local, where tonight the garden seemed the most comfortable option. Even with a pint in front of him, Knox's reticence continued and ten minutes in, Mariner half-wished they hadn't bothered. 'We've been married too long,' he said, in an attempt at levity. 'Nothing to say to each other any more.'

Knox grimaced, before draining his glass. 'One more before the bell?'

Mariner had hardly started his. 'OK,' he said, and

gulped it down. What a waste. Minutes later, Knox was back with two pints and a whisky chaser for himself. 'It's been a long day,' he said.

Mariner wasn't about to disagree. 'Cheers,' he said, before the silence set in again.

'So how do you think it got there?' said Knox suddenly.

'What?' Mariner was startled by the unprecedented verbosity.

'Yasmin Akram's phone,' Knox went on. 'It's on the other side of the track from where she would catch the Birmingham train.'

Mariner pounced on the interest. 'I've been thinking about that. She must have dropped it,' he said. 'Someone else picked it up and took it there. If we're certain that she got on the train it's the only possibility.'

At last Knox appeared to engage. 'Well, we are certain, aren't we? The CCTV footage at this end is pretty clear. We all saw her getting on the train. You can't argue with that.'

'I wouldn't mind looking at it again.'

'What for? We've no reason to think that she didn't board that train. Why the hell would she have been going down to the reservoir? There's nothing there.'

'Bearing in mind what Dr Shah has now told us, there already seems to be plenty we don't know about Yasmin. And what did you think about Paul Hewitt? Is he straight?'

'It was just a chance discovery. He and his partner were led to it and there must be plenty of other people involved who'll be able to corroborate that.'

Mariner was inclined to agree. 'It will be easy enough to check with the nursing home and with his partner, Sue.'

'Your version's much more likely. Someone else picked up Yasmin's phone and took it to the bridge.'

'So how does that fit with what Lily saw?'

'If she saw anything. Hewitt implied that the old girl might not have all her marbles.'

'The bloodstains are there all right.'

139

'Except that we don't know for certain that they are blood.'

Knox was right. They'd need forensic confirmation that it was blood. If it was human blood, the next step would be to get a DNA sample from the Akrams to make a comparison. He didn't relish that prospect one little bit.

'It could just be that whoever picked up Yasmin's phone was the guy who Lily saw beating the dog,' Knox said, now fully engaged in the discussion.

'And I wouldn't rule out Shaun Pryce from all this, either.'

'Do you think he's the mystery man? We now know that Yasmin could have been seeing someone. She could have arranged to meet him anywhere between here and the station.'

But Knox picked on the obvious flaw. 'Except how would Pryce have known Yasmin? She's a schoolkid, he's an out of work actor and part time leckie.'

Mariner sighed. 'And we don't know for certain that there is any mystery man. Yasmin could have invented him in an attempt to be more sophisticated than she really is. We haven't talked to Suzanne yet and I got the impression of some pretty fierce competition going on between the two of them.'

'I do love a simple, straightforward case,' said Knox, wryly.

Mariner frowned. 'Ever had one?'

The thought was enough to render Knox sullen and morose all over again, and by the time Mariner dropped him off outside his house he was back to his monosyllabic self. Mariner offered a silent plea for Theresa to come back soon.

Mariner himself took the briefing at six the next morning at the entrance to what had become, overnight, the official reservoir car park. As much manpower as was possible had been mustered to conduct the second search, packing the areas with bodies. A new buzz in the air had been created by the discovery of the phone: introducing, thank God, a point of focus at last. As DCI Fiske was quick to point out, if didn't negate the possibility of Yasmin getting on the train as usual, but suddenly the options had opened up again. The relevant portion of the map showing the reservoir had been enlarged, circulated and apportioned, and Mariner split the group into teams of three to ensure that every square metre would be covered. 'We'll start with the more accessible areas: the land around, then if we need to, the water itself.'

Protective overalls, scythes and secateurs had been provided to assist with the mammoth task of hacking back the undergrowth, making the search party took like *Ground Force* on the rampage. The sun was already climbing steadily and Mariner had arranged for bottled water to be delivered: he didn't want anyone collapsing with dehydration.

Yasmin's phone was already at the lab where it would be checked for fingerprints and any messages analysed. Fortunately, on a case like this, it would take priority and could be rushed through in twenty-four hours. Mariner sincerely hoped they wouldn't come across anything more sinister or conclusive first.

With the search begun under the supervisory eye of DS Mark 'Jack' Russell, Mariner took Knox and went to the nursing home to talk to Lily, the woman who had witnessed the attack. St Clare's retirement home had exactly the kind of stale hint-of-urine aroma that seemed to go with the territory. 'God, I hate these places,' Knox said.

'One of our fastest growing industries,' remarked Mariner.

'But what's the point of festering away for years in a place like this. What kind of life is it? We're all living too long.'

His supporting argument was right in front of them. The

141

office they'd been asked to wait in overlooked a kind of sun lounge, where high-backed easy chairs were clustered, most accommodating an elderly resident, even at this early hour. It was probably the same as hospitals, Mariner thought, everyone roused at the crack of dawn whether they liked it or not. Close to the TV, two elderly ladies stared fixedly at some kind of morning chat show, although whether either of them was actually watching it was impossible to tell. A uniformed nurse came and spoke to one of them. Painfully slowly, she helped the old woman to her feet and they shuffled out of the room, arm in arm. The girl looked about sixteen. What age was that to be carrying out intimate tasks for people old enough to be her grandparents? Mariner tried to envisage his mother in a place like this, but he couldn't. She'd be the world's worst resident. 'They're all white,' he said, suddenly noticing the fact. 'Mohammed Akram's mother won't end up in one of these.'

'Mr Mariner? I'm Nora.' The woman who breezed in was the member of staff Lily had confided in. A solid woman of around fifty, Norah's substantial bulk and bosom were held in by the starched blue nurse's uniform apparently worn by all the staff. 'Do you mind if we go outside? I'm gasping for a fag.' Gasping was the word. As they walked, she wheezed in rhythm with her stride, leaving Mariner wondering how she could cope with such a physically demanding job. They stood outside the front door, under a dripping lime, as traffic roared by on Birchill Road just a few yards away.

'Can you tell us what happened last Tuesday afternoon?'

Nora tapped half an inch of ash on to the path. 'It was tea-time. Lily was in the dining room, along with all the other residents when she said she didn't feel well. As she's still fairly independent we suggested that she should go back to her room and have a lie down. When I went up a little later to check on her, she was standing transfixed, in the middle of the room, staring out of the window. She was in some distress. I thought she'd had a funny turn or something, but when I asked if she was all right she grabbed my arm and said we mustn't under any circumstances let Casper out because she'd just seen a wicked man beating a dog to death down by the reservoir. I got her to show me, but of course, when we looked out of the window there was nothing to see.

'I didn't think any more of it then because although, generally speaking, Lily's one of our more lucid clients, she does have her moments. Casper was the cat she left behind when she moved in here four years ago, so she was clearly getting a bit confused. When I reminded her of this she realised her mistake, but I could see that something had upset her. I thought it was over and forgotten but a few days later, Lily said she hadn't been able to sleep for thinking about it, so I asked her to show me again where she'd seen it.

'She told me exactly the same story and the description of what she saw didn't change. She insisted that she'd seen this man and that the poor dog could only be dead. As it was bothering her so much, I thought the least I could do was humour her and call the RSPCA. They'd be able to go and have a look and confirm that there was no dead dog. And Lily would be reassured to know that she'd been mistaken. There was nothing to lose.' She looked from one to the other of them and her voice dropped to a whisper. 'The man I spoke to said they found blood.'

'Well, we haven't established what it is just yet, but it would be helpful if we could speak to Lily herself, in case there's anything else she remembers. Would she be up to that?'

'I think so.'

'Would any other of the residents or staff have seen anything?'

'No, everyone else was in the dining room on the ground floor, which looks out over the side garden.'

'You said this happened at tea-time. What time would that have been?'

'About quarter to five.'

Twenty minutes after Yasmin had said goodbye to her friends and disappeared off the face of the earth. Mariner didn't like that timing one little bit.

Back inside, they trooped up a winding staircase to Lily's room, a twelve by twelve box of floral wallpaper and chintzy fabrics. The bed was covered with the kind of peach-coloured candlewick bedspread Mariner hadn't seen for years. On top of the mahogany chest of drawers were the assorted remnants of Lily's life: a few photographs and a couple of pieces of cheap porcelain; a varnished seashell purporting to be a gift from Bridlington. Not much left to show for more than seventy years on the planet.

The view from the window wasn't much to speak of either, overlooking as it did the jungle of yellowing scrubland that encircled the reservoir. Naturally, Lily had her windows open and even up here you could smell the sour, stagnant water. Mariner feared another setback when Lily turned out to be a frail old woman with whiskers sprouting from a face that was as lined and furrowed as the dry ground outside. Her sparse silvery hair had been permed into tight curls, exposing patches of scalp as pink and smooth as a baby's flesh, and the cotton frock she wore hung loosely on her withered frame. She was perched on an armchair, her eyes closed, but she opened them as they arrived, huge blue irises staring at them through the magnifying lenses of her glasses.

'Lily, these are the policemen I told you about. They just want to ask you some questions,' Nora said gently.

'Anything you like,' said Lily, encouragingly alert, once she'd come round. 'I know what I saw.' Perhaps she would turn out to be a decent witness, after all.

'I'll get some chairs,' said Nora, returning moments later with a couple of the moulded plastic variety, which she arranged beside the old lady. Mariner sat, but Knox maintained a disinterested distance, staring out of the window.

'Can you tell us exactly what you did see?' Mariner asked.

144

'It was tea-time, but I didn't feel like eating, especially the rubbish that they give us here; ratty-twee or some such foreign muck.' Mariner waited for Nora to contradict her, but then saw the game glint in Lily's eye. Why had he assumed that because she was old there would be no sense of mischief? 'Anyway, I came into my room and I could see someone down there on the bridge. He caught my attention because there's never anyone down there and the movement was ... well ... violent. He was swinging his arm up and down, up and down, hitting something on the ground.'

'Can you show me exactly where?' Mariner asked.

Using the armrests for support, Lily pushed herself up from the chair shakily and they joined Knox at the window, looking out at where the yellowing field with its dark kernel swarmed with police officers, moving laboriously through the undergrowth, heads bowed as if performing some ancient religious ritual.

'He was right next to that little wooden bridge, the one with the broken railings, to the left of it where the long grass starts again.' Nothing wrong with her eyesight, then.

'Was he standing or kneeling?' Mariner asked.

'He was standing, his legs apart, but he was bent over, low.'

'Could you see his face?'

'No, because he had his back turned to me. He just kept swinging his arm up and down, up and down.' Her eyes filled with tears. 'That poor little defenceless creature.'

'The dog.'

'Yes.'

'Could you see what colour the dog was?' Mariner peered out. It was unlikely that she could have. If what she said was right, the creature would have been hidden by the tall grass.

Lily shook her head. 'Not very well, the grass was too long.'

'But you're sure it was a dog?'

'What else—?'

145

'Could it have been that he was say, banging his shoe on the ground to dislodge something that was in it?'

Lily gave him a withering look. 'I know what I saw. The way he was hunched over, you could see the hate in him. He sort of stood back to look at what he'd done. The creature was moving, then it stopped moving.' She looked out at the search. 'I must say, it's very good of you to have all those people looking for a dog.'

'Is there anything else you can tell us about this man?' Mariner asked. 'The colour of his hair, say? What he was wearing perhaps?'

'I think his hair was brown and he was wearing a suit, like yours.' She looked at Mariner. 'A nice summer suit, except yours is lighter. The one he wore was darker, more of a light brown. I remember thinking that he would spoil it, and how warm he must be, too.'

Gazing out of the window, Mariner tried to establish whether Lily would have seen the comings and goings of Shaun Pryce.

'You said you never see anyone down there, Lily. Do you mean that? Never?'

'Never.' She was adamant.

'Have you ever seen a young girl down there? Or a young man, over on the other side?'

'No.' On that point she stood firm.

'Up until about a week ago she wouldn't have been able to see much at all from up here,' put in Nora. 'That row of cypress trees was so tall it used to completely block the view.'

It was only then that Mariner noticed the line of tree stumps at the bottom of the garden, the timber inside freshly exposed.

'They were lovely trees,' said Lily. 'I was sad to see them go.'

'Lucky for us that they did,' said Mariner. 'Thank you very much, Mrs Cooper,' he said, absently. 'You've been very helpful.'

He turned to Nora. 'We'll need to come and take a written statement.'

'Of—'

Suddenly, as they watched, a shout went up and the figures working below began converging on an area a couple of hundred yards away from the bridge, where the foliage was at its most dense. Seconds later, Knox's mobile rang and Mariner felt a sudden weight in the pit of his stomach. Knox took the call out in the corridor, returning moments later, his face grim. 'We're needed down there, boss.'

Chapter Eleven

It was only a few hundred yards away as the crow flies, but the drive around to the reservoir was nearly a mile in the car and seemed to take them an adrenaline-fuelled eternity. By the time they got there, the reservoir itself had been cleared of all but the essential personnel, the search parties had retreated to avoid contaminating the area and were congregating in the parking area to await further instructions. As Mariner and Knox bumped towards them over the uneven ground the mood was sombre, voices low. Russell greeted them at the edge of the wood. Beneath his tan he was white faced, his eyes dull with shock.

'We didn't find it until we were almost on it, despite the smell,' he said. 'The stink of the reservoir masked it.'

'Is it her?' Mariner asked, but Russell had already set off, eager to get this over with and pass on the find to a more senior officer.

This time they followed the initial path over the bridge, continuing around on the other side of the water. On their last visit this had been uncharted territory, where the searchers before them had been forced to slash away the grass and brambles to create a narrow passage. Even now, the thorns clawed at their trousers, their feet tripped on loops of tangled grass. It was heavy going, speed impossible and the hike around the edge of the water seemed interminable. The heat beat sickeningly down on Mariner's skull, while his imagination conjured up every possible variation on the horror he was about to see, the psyche's desperate effort to prepare and defend. Even then, it came nowhere close.

As Russell had warned, rounding a clump of burgeoning shrubs, it was the smell that hit first, the cloying stench that smelled like nothing else on earth, the unmistakable odour of human decay. After the smell came the noise: the high-pitched, triumphant buzzing of busy insects. Finally, the grotesque discovery came into view.

'Jesus Christ.' Bile rose in Mariner's throat and behind him he heard the glug of Tony Knox's involuntary retch.

Bizarrely, what first held Mariner's attention were the many different shades and shapes of grass that had moulded themselves around the body, as if his brain was forcing him to focus on the peripheral detail to avoid the unspeakable. To begin with, it was hard to make sense of, obscured as it was by the dense foilage, where an attempt seemed to have had been made to bury it under the thick strands of grass.

The soles of the shoes were visible first of all. They were the easy part: normal, like any pair of shoes on any pair of feet. Pulling away the grassy coverage, Mariner forced himself to work his way visually up the battered, bloody and decaying form, and by the time his eyes reached the insect-infested skull he already knew. 'Turn it over,' he instructed Russell. Russell did so. 'Christ.' Although the face and side of the head had been half eaten away, it didn't matter. The Nike tracksuit and Manchester United football shirt were unmistakable from the description he'd been given only days earlier. 'It's Ricky Skeet,' he said, dully, while inside he wanted to bellow all the breath from his lungs. Why hadn't he listened to Colleen? Why had he let Fiske bully him into believing that Ricky had just run away? He'd never be able to live with himself over this.

'Call Charlie Glover and get SOCO—'

'They're on their way, sir.'

Mariner forced himself to take another look. SOCO

149

would confirm it but the state of Ricky's body would indicate that he was the 'dog' Lily had seen being beaten to death.

'We haven't found his bike yet,' said Russell. 'It must be around here somewhere and it might give us a clue about how he got in here in the first place.'

'It might lead us to a witness, as well.'

'There's something else interesting the lads came across, sir.' Russell walked them back over the bridge, towards where they'd left their cars. This time though, he passed by their entry point and kept right, skirting under the trees to around the edge of what, at wetter times, would have been the lake's edge. The flattened area was perfectly concealed by the high grasses around it, like a small arena. They were standing now on the opposite side of the water to the side where Ricky's body lay, and the reason for the location was obvious. Unlike the other side of the reservoir, this area would have been bathed in sunshine for most of the afternoon. 'They guys have found a couple of used condoms too,' Russell said. 'We've bagged them up. But there's no other sign of activity.' Like blood, he might have added.

It was the side nearest to the clearing where they had met Shaun Pryce. Knox stooped to retrieve something from the ground. 'Good place to relax, eh?' He held up a home-rolled dog-end, putting it to his nose. 'Most animals don't shit in their own back yard,' said Knox, grimly. 'Shaun Pryce doesn't come down here on his own and he doesn't settle for the clearing, either.'

Even as Mariner saw Charlie Glover approaching from twenty yards away, leading a procession of white-boiler-suited SOCOs, he could read the expression on his face. It told Mariner that he was racked with the same guilt. He waited on the bridge while Charlie went to look at the body.

Five minutes later Glover returned, a man in a daze.

150

'Christ, it's like the arsehole of hell,' he said, numbly. 'What in God's name was Ricky Skeet doing down here? It must be what, three or four miles from his house? And how did he get in?'

'God knows. Good place to hide out, though. No one would think to look here for him.'

'Well, we didn't, did we? But how would he even know it existed?'

Mariner gazed out over the dark, cracked mud. 'Ricky's dad used to take him fishing. Maybe there were fish in here once.' They were back on the bridge, close to where Yasmin's phone had been found. 'This whole thing makes no sense. Yasmin's phone here and Ricky's body way over there.'

Glover looked around, saw the brown stains on the grass. 'If it's his blood then Ricky was killed here. He could have somehow come by Yasmin's phone.'

'That's the only plausible explanation. There's the possibility that Yasmin was seeing someone, a boy, or man. Do you think there's any chance it could have been Ricky?'

Glover thought about that. 'I don't see how. How would they have met? They're at different schools, from different parts of the city. He's two years younger.'

'That's what I thought. Unless it was a chance meeting. They could have met down here, or at the station,' Mariner offered.

'What would have taken Ricky to the station?'

Mariner shared his scepticism. 'All we found was Yasmin's phone. I think a more likely explanation would be that she dropped it and someone – Ricky perhaps – found it and brought it here.'

'Or he stole it.'

'Ricky doesn't do that. And anyway, when would he have had the opportunity? It's much more likely that Yasmin dropped it. The afternoon she disappeared, she had to run for the train. It could have happened then.'

'Haven't you got CCTV on that? It may have picked it

151

up and might also show us if Ricky was at the station.'

'Sure,' Mariner said, absently, his mind not really on it. He knew he should be focusing on Yasmin but now all he could think about was Colleen waiting at home in hopeful ignorance. He didn't want to leave all that to Charlie Glover.

Tony Knox was hovering. 'Shall we bring in Pryce?'

'Who?' Glover's ears pricked up.

'A guy called Shaun Pryce turned up while we were here yesterday, back in the clearing, but claims that he doesn't come on to the reservoir itself.' Mariner filled Glover in on the main points of the conversation with Pryce.

'But I think he's a more regular visitor there than he told us. That flattened area of grass looks tailor-made for him. He wasn't telling us the truth about that, and he doesn't come here alone, either.'

'Judging everyone by your own standards, Tony?' said Glover.

Mariner cringed on Knox's behalf at the reference to his colourful past, but he took it well enough. Would have been something of a double standard not to. 'There were a hell of a lot of fresh dog-ends for one person,' he said.

'The weather's been dry for weeks. They could have built up over a period of time. And if he's down here screwing some girl, why didn't he just say so? It's no big deal. In fact I'd have thought it was something he'd want to brag about.'

'She'll be married, won't she? Didn't you ever see *Confessions of an Electrician*? He'll be having it away with someone else's missus.' There was a bitter edge to Knox's voice. 'Maybe Ricky saw Pryce knocking off some woman and threatened to let it out, so Pryce had to shut him up.'

'How would Ricky know that what he saw was illicit? For all Ricky knew it could have been Pryce and his wife having a bit of open-air fun.'

'Maybe Pryce didn't like having an audience.'

Mariner shook his head. 'Oh no, Shaun Pryce would love

152

it. He's an actor,' he added, for Glover's benefit.

'He might not be so keen on being watched if things aren't going his way,' Glover said.

'Can't imagine that,' said Knox, sourly.

'Perhaps Ricky was a regular visitor down here, too. Had seen what Pryce was up to and been blackmailing him?'

'Well, right now Pryce is the only other person we can place down here, so we at least need to talk to him.'

'Yes, we do,' Mariner agreed. 'We need to know *exactly* what he did down here, when he was here and for how long – going back for the last couple of months. But I don't think there's any urgency. I get the feeling that Shaun Pryce might be in a more talkative mood once news leaks out about where we've found Yasmin's phone.'

'You're sure he won't disappear?'

'Oh no, judging by yesterday's performance, if he is involved, he'll want to be around for his bit of the lime-light.'

'I'd better go and tell Ricky's mother. Do you want to come?'

Mariner winced. Running the scene in his head, he could hear Colleen's screaming and sobbing as if it was real, and see her beating her fists against Glover. 'Not yet. She needs to know that you're in charge. And we've got things to do.' Or was he taking the coward's way out, unable to face Colleen after letting her down so badly, afraid of the hysteria that would ensue? Later, Charlie told him it hadn't run like that at all. She'd taken the news in a stunned silence. Somehow that had been even worse.

As they left the site, a low loader bearing a Portakabin was driving on. The incident room would be set up here to maximise the use of local intelligence and deepen the search. One of the first tasks would be a door to door to try and establish when and where Ricky was last seen. The Murder Investigation Unit would support Charlie Glover's

OCU investigation and a team would be put on to searching the reservoir area for the murder weapon. The diving team would have to be contracted in from a neighbouring force, since their own divers had gone the way of the mounted division and fallen victim to budget cuts. Trawling the reservoir would be a mammoth task in all that thick black mud. Close behind the truck was a couple of unmarked vehicles, one of them a grey Transit.

'The vultures moving in,' observed Knox. Inevitably, the press would have picked up news of the discovery from the morning's activities over the air waves. 'Want me to get rid of them, boss?'

'Be as unpleasant as you like,' said Mariner.

What Mariner was less prepared for was the mob of reporters already assembled outside the entrance to Granville Lane. News had travelled fast and they were not a happy throng. Knox and Mariner got out of the car just as Fiske appeared at the main doors to read a prepared statement. 'We will do everything within our power to bring the killer of Ricky Skeet to justice,' he concluded.

'Is that the same kind of everything you did to find him when he went missing?' someone called out.

'We followed all possible lines of enquiry. I have no doubt that my officers did all they possibly could to prevent this situation from occurring.'

'Mrs Skeet doesn't seem to agree with you on that.'

Fiske was getting hot under the collar. 'Any complaints about the way this enquiry has been handled will be dealt with through the usual channels.'

'Whitewashed, you mean.'

Mariner signalled to Knox and they slipped round the building and into a side door. Along the corridor they ran into Fiske, making his escape. 'Bloody press,' he grumbled.

'Perhaps they've got a point this time,' said Mariner.

'And what the hell's that supposed to mean?'

'We didn't exactly pull out all the stops for Ricky, did we?' Mariner reminded him.

154

'Given his profile we followed the correct procedures.'

'I'll tell his mum that. I'm sure she'll feel greatly reassured. "Your son's dead, but given his profile, we did everything by the book, Colleen."' Deep down, Mariner recognised that he was more angry with himself than he was with Fiske. If he'd made more of a stand against the arrogant bastard instead of caving in at the beginning this might not have happened. 'We've got a kid we hardly looked for dead and another we've wasted energy on looking for who might have eloped with her lover.'

'We got it wrong. Sometimes it happens.'

'You can say that again.'

Millie was up in the office. 'You heard?' Mariner asked. Her face said it. 'I'm sorry.'

'Yeah. But we have to turn our attention back to Yasmin. There's always the chance that the two cases aren't linked. I know the probability has slumped a bit, but still the only two people we can definitely place down at the reservoir at any time are Shaun Pryce and Ricky Skeet. Yasmin's phone was there but that's all. We still don't know for sure that she was too: let's deal with the reality first, before we go off speculating about other things.' She'd been gone more than a week now and their one breakthrough had led them nowhere.

'Let's see the CCTV footage again. We might be able to establish if Yasmin dropped her phone, and I want to be absolutely sure that it's her getting on that train.'

'But we've been over that, boss,' Knox groused.

Brushing aside his complaints they played the tape yet again. They watched as Yasmin boarded the train and the door closed behind her, as on every previous occasion. As the train began to draw away, Knox switched the tape off.

'That's definitely Yasmin,' said Millie, swivelling on her chair to face Mariner. 'She looks right into the camera.'

'And no sign of her dropping her phone,' said Mariner.

'But she started running from the top of the road. She could have dropped it anywhere before she comes into

155

view.' Her disappointment was tangible.

'Well, we may soon find out about that, anyway. Her phone should be back from—'

'Look, boss.' Tony Knox had suddenly become animated. While Mariner and Millie were talking he'd turned the tape on again, watching it with half an eye.

Mariner turned his attention back to the screen as Knox wound back the film at speed. 'But we've already seen—'

'Look, for Christ sake!' At the point at which Yasmin boarded the train, Knox pressed the play button again. The train began to move off, and as it did so, a door further down the carriage reopened, a figure appeared and after a second's hesitation, leaped from the moving train on to the platform. It stumbled and almost fell before regaining its feet and, when it straightened, was unmistakable.

'She got off the train,' said Knox, with a degree of satisfaction.

'Nearly killing herself in the process,' observed Mariner. 'Christ. Why didn't we think of that?'

'Think of what?' They were so caught up in their find that Fiske's voice startled them. Sneaking up on them was becoming a speciality.

'Yasmin Akram had us all fooled,' said Mariner. 'Play it back, Tony.'

'What ag—?' Mariner glared at him and dutifully Knox reran the tape yet again. As they watched, Mariner provided the commentary. 'She runs for the train, giving her friends – and us – the impression that she was going as usual, but gets off again before the train pulls out. He looked up at Fiske, calculating how far he could go. 'She never even got as far as the university.'

A muscle bulged in Fiske's jaw. 'Are you trying to make some kind of point, Mariner?'

'Only that perhaps we could have saved ourselves considerable time and resources if we'd been a bit less hasty with the search, sir,' said Mariner calmly.

But Fiske wasn't so easily beaten. 'We did the right thing

156

based on the information available at the time,' he replied, icily. 'Not forgetting that in the course of those actions, we've exposed a sex attacker operating in that area.'

'Oh, very good, sir.' Knox grinned inanely, before realising, along with everyone else, that the pun had been unintentional.

'Given that new information has come to light, I'd have thought your time would more usefully be spent following it up rather than playing games of "I told you so".' And with that, Fiske turned and walked out.

'Fucking moron,' muttered Knox. Mariner should really have reminded him about respect for senior officers, but it was good to have Tony Knox back on the planet again, however fleetingly. Instead, he brought them back to task. 'So why does Yasmin get off the train?'

'Because she has other plans?'

Having recovered from her leap from the moving train, they watched as Yasmin walked along the platfrom, towards the footbridge and off the screen. 'What it doesn't tell us is where she went next.'

'Except that there's a camera positioned at the back of the station too,' Knox remembered. 'It would be worth checking out the tape from that now. She's going towards the footbridge. She could be crossing the line.'

'In more ways than one.'

'Yasmin's just full of surprises, isn't she?'

'Let's get the tape.'

Yasmin did indeed appear on the footage from the back of the station, descending the pedestrian bridge and moving across the screen towards the station car park, but that was the extent of the camera's coverage.

'So where's she off to?'

'Suddenly, it's not beyond the realms of possibility that Yasmin dropped her phone at the reservoir.'

But as Knox went to switch off the TV, Mariner spotted something else on the screen. 'Look at that; bottom right-hand corner.' Next to the kerb was the offside wing and part of the bonnet of a dark vehicle.

'A Merc,' said Knox. 'You can tell from that radiator grille.'

'Is there anyone in it?' asked Millie, as they all squinted at the screen.

'Hard to see; it's from the wrong angle. Can we home in on that licence plate?'

They could, but it was still too blurry to be of any use.

'Mohammed Akram drives a black Mercedes,' Mariner reminded them.

'That's neat. Maybe Yasmin got off the train again because she saw someone she knew.'

The time on the corner of the screen said: 16.29. 'How accurate is that?'

'According to Akram, he'd been to the printer and by half past four was on the motorway on his way up to Bradford by that time,' said Mariner.

'Is the printer in the city?' asked Knox.

'I assumed it was in Sparkhill, near the school. TMR Printers, it's called. It was on the prospectus Hasan Sheron showed us.'

Knox reached for the *Yellow Pages* and flicked through until he found 'printers'.

'Here we are: TMR Reprographics. Two branches, one in the city and another—' He looked up for dramatic effect. 'On Birch Close.'

'Shit,' said Millie.

'Thanks for that valuable contribution,' Knox said. But he did seem to be joking.

'And from there it's just a short drive up to the station where the CCTV picks up his car,' said Mariner. 'If it is his car.'

'And it would be no problem to get on to the motorway from here. There's nothing stopping him from going back out through the city centre and up to Spaghetti Junction, or even up the Wolverhampton Road to the M5, then M6. The fact that Yasmin stayed for the art club and left school late would have helped him out. He'd also probably have known that she was on her own so it would have been the ideal place if he didn't want to confront Yasmin in front of her friends, or back at home.'

'So he could easily have picked her up from the station and taken her with him.'

'What time did he check in with the family in Bradford?' Knox wanted to know.

'Not until nearly eight. But he says he stopped off at Sandbach Services for something to eat on his way and that there were roadworks on the M62, which there are.'

'It doesn't rule him out, though. It's still a bloody big coincidence if he was in the area at all at around that time.'

'An appeal for the driver on local news can rule out anyone else.'

'When did he say he'd confronted Yasmin about the pills?' Millie asked.

'On Friday. He said they'd sorted it out. But there might have been unfinished business.'

'What if Akram had talked Yasmin into going up to Bradford with him?'

Mariner was dubious. 'Without telling her mother what was going on?'

'They probably wouldn't have wanted her to know about the contraception.'

'But that doesn't tie in with Akram forbidding Yasmin to go to Suzanne's. He couldn't have known that his wife would give in and let her go.'

'He might know his wife better than she thinks.'

'The receipt from the service station only indicates a meal for one.'

Mariner sighed. 'OK, folks, we're wandering into the realms of speculation again. Let's get back to the facts.' *Just the facts, Jack.*

'We have Ricky, Yasmin and Akram all in the same area at the same time,' said Knox. 'That's fact.'

159

'Only if it is Akram's car.'

'And I still don't get where Ricky comes into this,' Millie said.

'He might not,' said Mariner. 'We could still be looking at two entirely unconnected events. Maybe all Ricky did was to find Yasmin's phone at the station and take it with him to the reservoir, where he was attacked and he dropped it, simple as that. Meanwhile, Yasmin, unaware that she's even lost her phone, meets her dad at the station.'

'Are we absolutely certain that Yasmin and Ricky didn't know each other?' Knox asked.

'I just don't see how they would,' said Millie.

'But we don't know for sure that they didn't,' Knox insisted, the tension in the room thickening.

'They don't need to have done. If Ricky was in the wrong place at the wrong time, Akram could have just jumped to the wrong conclusion.'

'What are you talking about?'

'Maybe the phone does provide the link. How about if Ricky found the phone, as we thought. Yasmin's home number must be on it. Ricky phones that number to establish its owner, gets Akram who arranges to meet him to collect it. Akram's at the printer, Ricky knows the reservoir, so they arrange to meet at a mutually convenient spot. Akram is still wound up about Yasmin being on the pill, jumps to the wrong conclusion about Ricky having her phone and loses it.'

Knox's facial expression fell just short of contempt. 'That's a hell of a conclusion to jump to. A kid finds his daughter's phone so he assumes he's having sex with her?'

'We don't know what's on that phone.' Millie stood her ground. 'There might be some interesting messages. Could be that Ricky tried blackmailing Akram: perhaps he demanded money before giving it up. Akram's already pissed off about all the hassle he's been getting. This could've been the final straw.'

Seeing Knox's colour rising, Mariner spoke up. 'It's an

160

interesting idea, but knowing Ricky, I'm not sure that he'd have done that kind of thing,' he said, calmly.

Millie shrugged. 'He'd run away from home. I didn't think that was his kind of thing, either. And if he wasn't planning on going back he was going to need more money.'

'So why did Paul Hewitt find the phone still lying there?' Knox almost sneered. 'Akram would have taken it with him.'

'Ricky was in a bad way, wasn't he? The attack must have been violent, impulsive even. Maybe he just lost it and in the heat of the moment he dropped the phone and it got forgotten. He'd have been pretty caught up in what he was doing. Or somebody disturbed him.'

'Down there?'

'OK. He looked up and saw Lily watching him.'

'I doubt that he'd see her from that distance,' said Mariner. 'And even so, if the phone was what this was all about, he'd hardly leave it behind, would he?'

'Or go in bloodstained clothing back to the station to meet his daughter.'

'He was going away overnight. He would have had a change of clothing in the car.'

'That's crazy. If that *is* what happened, Ricky would have had hardly any time to find the phone, alert Akram and arrange to meet him. I'd say it was virtually impossible.' Knox glared at Millie, who refused to be intimidated. It was a stand-off.

'And I think we're getting a bit carried away here, folks,' Mariner intervened, quietly. 'We need to look at it from every angle, but this isn't getting us any nearer to knowing where Yasmin's gone.'

'I think we need to check her dad's movements up in Bradford,' Millie insisted. 'If she has simply been spirited away, it would explain why he didn't seem so anxious at the start.'

'Look into that, will you?' said Mariner. 'It remains a possibility, but one of many. At the moment all we have is

161

Yasmin's phone, Ricky dead and Yasmin vanished.'

'Like one of those lateral thinking problems,' said Knox.

Millie pulled a face. 'I was always rubbish at them.'

'I need some fresh air,' said Knox.

When he'd left the room, Millie asked the question Mariner had been dreading. 'Are you sure it's not me?'

'Tony just takes the job seriously,' said Mariner, brushing it off.

'Implying that we don't?' She had a point.

Mariner was saved from making any further crass remarks by the news that Charlie Glover was back from the Pathologist's office with the preliminary findings.

Chapter Twelve

Glover cut to the chase. 'Everything so far says the blood on the grass is definitely Ricky's,' he said. 'It was a frenzied attack involving repeated blows to the skull with a blunt instrument. It would have been messy.'

'So the clothing the killer was wearing—'

'—would be pretty well covered in blood.'

'According to Lily, it was some kind of brown suit.'

'Yeah, I've spoken to her. Her eyesight seems pretty sharp and what she's told us seems accurate so I think we can go with that. So the brown suit would have needed to go to the cleaner's or even more likely to have been destroyed. Hard to explain to Sketchley's why your suit is covered in someone else's blood.'

'Have we got a time of death?'

'Thanks to the weather the body was pretty ripe, as you saw. But they're saying it's been there about seven days. That would put it at sometime late on Tuesday afternoon.'

Lining it up nicely with the last time that Yasmin was seen alive. 'Anything else?'

'Only what Lily's already said: she's pretty certain that the man she saw had dark hair.' Like Mohammed Akram, thought Mariner. Did he own a brown suit? 'It could, of course, depend on the angle of the sun at that time,' Glover went on. 'If the sun was behind or overhead it could be the one detail that she's mistaken on.'

'It's possible,' agreed Mariner. 'What about Colleen's boyfriend, Steve?'

'We're checking him out, but so far his alibi looks sound. He was still at work.'

'That's a pity.'

'Yeah, isn't it? And so that you know, Ronnie Skeet was in Wolverhampton.'

'Any thoughts on how it played out?' Mariner asked.

'Well, we've got blood on the grass by the bridge, but around that, nothing, and no sign of disturbance. However, working back from where the body was found is a kind of tunnel through the grass, leading almost back to the bridge, and also smeared with blood. It makes it look as if Ricky was killed at the bridge, then his killer, probably thinking he was dead, carried him into the long grass and dumped him, coming back to the path to cover his tracks. It looks as if Ricky could have dragged himself further through the grass, creating a kind of tunnel, to the point where we found him.'

'Christ, so he wasn't dead.'

'And crawling even further from the path did his killer a favour by delaying the discovery of his body. We're continuing the search in the direction he was going: to see if he was making for anything in particular. But he may just have been trying to get away. And you were right about the reason for Ricky being there,' Glover added. 'I asked Colleen. His dad did used to take him fishing on the reservoir, but not for years. We still haven't found his bike, but did they tell you about the Anderson?'

'I didn't get time to check in yesterday.'

'Further round still from where Ricky's body was found we came across an old Anderson shelter. From all the empty cans and crisp packets it looks as if Ricky had been there before.'

'He used to go off for the day at weekends,' Mariner said, recalling the conversation with Colleen. 'Is this all going to the press?'

'It might have to. Fiske is desperate to get them off his

164

back. How does a berk like him get to be in his position?'

'Gift of the gab,' said Mariner. 'Did you ask Colleen about Yasmin?'

'Yeah, and nearly got a black eye for it.' Glover recounted the conversation conducted under the beady gaze of Steven Marsh. 'He didn't seem to appreciate the timing.'

Mariner grimaced.

'And Colleen, of course, took it as further proof that we were more concerned with Yasmin than with Ricky, but basically the answer was no. She couldn't see how Ricky would have known that "posh little Asian kid", even when I told her about the phone.' Glover paused. 'Question is, though: would Colleen have even known?'

Mariner reported back on what Glover had said as he and Knox drove over to Allah T'ala. For once, Knox seemed unnaturally chipper, his jaws working hard on a gobbet of chewing gum, which he'd lately taken to chewing almost constantly. They were shown up to the same office where Mariner and Millie had first gone, and where Mohammed Akram, in shirtsleeves, his tie hanging loose, was poring over some architect's drawings. He jumped up as they went in, his face a turmoil of emotions. 'You've found something?'

'Nothing more. I'm sorry,' said Mariner, wishing that he could read that face. 'PC Khatoon has kept you up to date?'

'She told us about the boy, and that Yasmin's phone was nearby. Do you think—?'

'We're trying to establish the facts,' said Mariner, 'which is why we need to clarify a couple of things with you.'

'My wife is teaching a class.'

'That's fine, I think you should be able to help us. The printer you were at in Kingsmead on Tuesday afternoon,' said Mariner. 'It's some distance from your school. Why there?'

'My last supplier closed about a year ago. I happened to

165

mention this to Yasmin's teacher one parents' evening. Yasmin had been awarded a certificate and I asked where they had got it printed. She recommended the place. I decided to try them.'

'And tell me again, what time were you there on that Tuesday afternoon?'

'Around four o'clock. I left twenty or thirty minutes later. The meeting didn't take long. I just needed to look at some proofs. But you know all this. I already told you.'

'Will the printer be able to confirm that timing?'

'I'm sure that he will.'

'And from there you drove up to Bradford.'

'As I've already told you,' said Akram, irritably.

'Did you go anywhere near Kingsmead Station?'

'No. I had no reason to do that.'

'Yasmin would have just been leaving school at that time.'

'I suppose she was. I didn't really think about it.'

'You weren't tempted to meet her to discuss your recent disagreement?'

'As I said before, that matter had been resolved.'

'Mr Akram, do you own a brown suit?'

A slight pause. Surprised about the question or thinking about an answer? 'Yes, I do. As a matter of fact I have it here. It's due to be dry-cleaned.'

That was a piece of luck. 'Could we see it?'

'Er, yes.' Akram left the room and after several minutes returned with the suit, protected in a plastic cover. It was a shade of mid-brown. For a suit that was going to the cleaner's it seemed spotlessly clean.

'Mr Akram, I'm going to ask you again. Do you have any idea about the whereabouts of your daughter?'

Akram looked him straight in the eye. 'And I will tell you again, Inspector. No, I have not.'

*

166

'That suit looked OK to me,' said Knox as they cooked again in the car.

'We didn't ask him if he owns more than one.'

Knox gave him a sidelong look. 'Just because all your suits are exactly the same colour—'

'Two colours, actually,' Mariner corrected him.

'All I'm saying is: most of us have a bit more imagination.'

'Thanks.'

'Any time.'

'Akram is consistent about the timing, though,' conceded Mariner. 'Did the printer verify it?'

'Over the phone, yes.'

Mariner sighed. 'Even with the techies' enhancements on the CCTV footage, I'm not sure that we'll be able to determine the licence plates or the driver of that car.'

'And if he's telling the truth, he'd have left the city before that was filmed.'

'Did you believe him, that he didn't realise that Yasmin would be at the station at that time?'

'Yeah.' Knox nodded. 'You're not thinking about your kids all day long, especially when they get to that age. You're starting to lead separate lives.'

'Some more than others,' said Mariner. 'It just would be nice to know for sure.'

As it turned out, they soon did. The appeal the night before had brought forward a young woman.

'A Miss Devreaux called in just after you left,' Millie told them. 'Her fiancé met her from the station in his midnight-blue Mercedes. He parked exactly where the camera is pointed. They even had a row because she was late.'

'Shit.'

'Does it rule Akram out?' Millie asked.

'It confirms that he wasn't at the station then.' Mariner sighed. 'But Yasmin's phone was found *between* the station and the printer. I want to go and talk to the printer.'

'Nothing like going over old ground,' muttered Knox.

'It's called being thorough,' said Mariner.

'Yes, boss.'

Printer Tim Randall was pretty certain about the timing of Akram's visit. On arrival, they'd walked through the warm and humid prefabricated hangar, where the dominant smell was of warm plastic. Stepping around an obstacle course of thrumming computers and boxy digital printers, they ducked under the spaghetti tangle of cables and wires tossed carelessly over the fragile steel beams and into the quieter design office, where a couple of graphic artists were laying out proofs on long tables. 'We were in the middle of a big print run,' Randall went on, 'and as he left, I remember looking at the clock to see how much time we'd got left to finish up. We were cutting it a bit fine.'

'And what time was it?'

'A couple of minutes off half past four, give or take. That clock probably isn't a hundred per cent accurate.'

So that was that.

'He didn't drive off straight away.' The young man who spoke up was leaning over the drawings, cornrows sprouting from his head.

'Are you sure?' asked Mariner.

'I went out for a fag about quarter to five and he was still there, his flashy Mercedes parked down at the end of the loop, by the bins.'

The lad wasn't wearing a watch, Mariner noticed. 'How can you be so sure of the timing?'

He grinned. 'I'm trying to quit, so I'm spacing them out. This week I'm out there at five o'clock, last week it was quarter to.'

'Did you see him drive off?'

'No. He was still out there when I came back in. Doesn't take long to smoke a fag and I'm only allowed the one.'

'Was Mr Akram definitely in his car? Was there anyone with him?'

He swayed his head doubtfully. 'All I saw was the car.'

Outside, they looked down towards 'the loop'- the neck of the cul-de-sac – to the row of industrial-sized steel bins. They were backed up against the wood-panelled fence, on the other side of which was the reservoir.

'The kid saw Akram's car parked outside at quarter to five. It doesn't mean that he was in it. He could have easily been down there with Yasmin.'

'When we were on the bridge we didn't look to see if you could get on to the reservoir from this industrial estate.'

'If there was a way through, surely we'd have noticed it.'

'Not if we weren't looking for it. And it may only have been used once or twice. If Akram did have unfinished business with Yasmin, it would have been a much more private place to meet her.'

They found what they were looking for in minutes. Behind the giant bins a panel of fencing had split, creating an opening easily large enough for someone to squeeze through. Standing on the concrete plinth, Mariner could look down towards the bridge and the sludge beyond. Running through the long grass was the unmistakable pale line caused by a single passage through it.

'So what now? Back to Mr Akram?' Knox asked.

But Mariner shook his head. 'We need to keep on to everything else, too. I'd like to have a closer look at what you found on Shaun Pryce first.'

But the database had turned up little of interest. 'Only one minor offence in the past, boss: possession of cannabis.' Knox closed the record sheet. 'I thought this was more interesting.' He'd book-marked a site and when he double-clicked it, a whole web page appeared devoted to Shaun Pryce: actor and model. On it, Pryce was described as a 'talented and versatile' character actor who'd played a

169

range of diverse and challenging roles, most notably as a romantic lead, and who was also available for modelling and voice-over work. 'I bet he wrote that himself,' said Knox. 'Shame we can't bring him in for blatant self-promotion.'

'I want to talk to him again, though,' said Mariner. 'He frequents the reservoir area and I'd like to know what he really does there. SOCO found spliffs and condoms. I want to see if there's anything else we can shake out of him. I wonder if Charlie Glover would like to come.'

'Sounds like fun,' was Glover's reaction.

The daytime contact Shaun Pryce had given them belonged to a property about three quarters of a mile from the reservoir; a collection of houses in what estate agents would refer to as a 'much sought after area'. Consequently, most had been extended in one way or another. The addition Pryce was working on was huge, almost doubling the size of the property. Plenty of electrical work here to keep him busy. There was no sign of his VW Golf in the line of assorted vehicles parked outside, but when they asked Mrs Paleczcki, the owner of the house, she took them through to where Pryce was working alone, in what looked like a newly created ground-floor room.

'Shaun, there's someone to see you.'

Their footsteps echoed as they went in. Pryce turned from where he was kneeling on the bare floorboards, screwing a double socket to a freshly plastered wall. Raw wires sprouted from the walls elsewhere around the room, waiting for his attention, and the air was clouded with fine dust. A tinny radio blared some kind of phone-in progamme that ricocheted around the emptiness. Elsewhere in the house were the sounds of other work progressing.

'Would you like a cup of tea, love?' Today Pryce was in T-shirt and shorts, his tattoos standing out vividly against his bronzed skin, and there was no mistaking the look on Mrs Paleczcki's face as she spoke to him. Knox had guessed

170

right: it was *Confessions of an Electrician* all over again.

Pryce grinned at her. 'You know just what to say to a man.'

The hospitality wasn't extended to Mariner or Glover: Mrs Paleczcki not encouraging them to hang around any longer than was necessary.

'How can I help?' Pryce asked, his demeanour casual, but the voice guarded. He seemed to have lost some of the confidence he had a couple of days ago. But then a lot had happened since then, and he would know that they'd found Ricky.

'By stop pissing us around and telling us what you really get up to at the reservoir,' said Mariner, without ceremony.

'Is that where they found that kid?'

'You know that very well. We've found your little retreat, too.'

'Oh.'

'So? What is it you do there?'

'I go there to top up my tan.'

'Most people sunbathe in their own gardens or in the park.'

'I haven't got a garden. I live in a flat. And anyway, some of the modelling work I do, my tan needs to be . . . comprehensive.'

'You sunbathe nude.'

'I'm not harming anyone.'

Mrs Paleczcki came back in with a mug of tea. Mariner wondered if she knew about Pryce's all-over tan. He decided that she probably did. When she'd gone he asked:

'When was the last time you were there? And this time we'd like the truth.'

Pryce hesitated. Debating what to say to avoid incriminating himself?

'The day I met you lot.'

'Don't be a smart arse, I mean before that.'

'The week before.'

'Day?'

'Tuesday.'

171

Bingo. 'What time?'

'About one o'clock.'

'Till when?'

'I don't know. Half one, two.'

'Is there anyone who can verify that?'

'The rest of the crew here can vouch for me.'

Mariner looked around him pointedly. 'And they are?'

'Upstairs right now. We started on the loft conversion this week.'

Mariner could only guess at the motley bunch that comprised Pryce's co-workers. He'd have laid bets that, like Pryce, they'd be mainly casual labourers with more than a couple of criminal records between them. He didn't have much confidence in any of them as a solid alibi. Nonetheless, Glover went up to check it out.

'So what were you doing for nearly an hour? And don't give me any bird-watching bullshit. We all know you wouldn't know a redshank from a shag.'

'I was chilling out. It may not look like it to you but this is bloody hard work, especially in the heat. Sometimes I have to help with the labouring too.'

'My heart bleeds. Take Mrs Paleczcki with you?'

'She's a married woman.'

'But you've taken women there before. Either that or you're the only man I know who practises safe sex with himself.'

'You sure they're mine? I'm a good Catholic boy, me.'

'When's the last time you took a woman there?' repeated Mariner.

'Not for a while.'

'Oh? What about your insatiable sexual appetite? Losing your touch?'

'The last one I took there didn't like the long grass. Said it scratched her. Got into all those uncomfortable little places. So I haven't bothered since.'

'When was that?'

'Ages ago. Probably sometime back in May. It's hard to remember.'

'See a lot of women, do you?'

'I can't help it if they find me irresistible.'

'Anything else? Had a smoke, did you?'

He could see that they'd found the cannabis. No point in denying it. 'I might have smoked a couple of joints.'

'Does your employer know about your habit? It must improve your wiring skills no end.'

'I know what I'm doing. I'm careful.'

'Do you know a boy called Ricky Skeet?'

'Is that—?'

'—the boy whose body we found yesterday afternoon by the reservoir? Yes. He'd been bludgeoned to death. We have the time of death as sometime on Tuesday afternoon.'

Shaun Pryce looked as if he was about to throw up. 'Did you know him?'

Pryce's voice dropped to a whisper. 'No.'

'What do you wear when you're working?' Mariner asked suddenly.

'What?'

'What do you wear? Your clothes?'

Pryce splayed his arms. 'What you see. Jeans, T-shirt, shorts if it's a hot day.'

'Do you own a brown suit?'

Pryce sneered. 'Shit colour, you mean? No thanks.'

'What about overalls?'

'Too restrictive.'

Glover appeared in the doorway and gave the faintest nod.

'Right,' said Mariner. 'That's all for now. Thanks for your time.'

'What do you mean "for now"?' said Pryce, uneasily.

'You've admitted to being close to the scene of a murder at around the time it was committed. We may have some further questions. Don't worry, we'll see ourselves out.'

As they were leaving, Mariner turned back to Pryce. 'Where's the car today?'

'I left it at home. Came on my bike. I do, when I get up

early enough. Helps keep me fit.'

'Is that what you did on Tuesday? Were you on your bike then?'

'I might have been. I don't honestly remember.'

Glover and Mariner got reluctantly back into their sweltering car.

'He seems pretty cool,' Glover observed.

'Meaning, he has nothing to do with this?' Mariner was disappointed.

'Or that he's good at covering up. He's an actor, after all.'

'He didn't hesitate about owning up to being at the reservoir on that Tuesday.'

'He must know we'd find that out, anyway. Yeah. As long as he sticks to the timing there's not much we can do about it. What about his alibi?'

'The other guys are saying that he was back after lunch and then they didn't knock off until nearly six,' Glover said.

'So we may have to accept that Pryce probably wasn't there when Ricky was killed.'

'If we choose to believe them. Or if they even know. The other three have been working on the loft all week while Pryce has been downstairs, more or less on his own. Would they even know if he disappeared on his bike for an hour? He could easily get down to the reservoir in that time. I can't shake off the feeling that he knows something, that there's something he's not telling us. Do you believe the nude sunbathing?'

'Yes, it fits in with the image.'

'But he denied having a brown suit. We could have pushed him on that.'

Mariner turned to face Glover. 'We've seen his suit already, most of it: a light brown suit? It's this famous all-over tan he keeps bragging about. Wouldn't have to take that to the dry-cleaner's, would he?'

*

When Mariner got home late that night, he realised he still hadn't contacted his mother, but when he tried, the phone just rang on and she had no answering service. She'd probably got the TV on too loud to hear it. He thought about calling one of her neighbours but he wouldn't want to risk getting anyone out of bed, so he didn't bother.

Chapter Thirteen

Next morning, the lab report on Yasmin's phone had come back, along with the analysis of the calls made, and Mike Finlay, the technician who would be able to clarify anything that didn't make sense. Mariner asked Knox and Millie to sit in on it. Most of the fingerprints on the handset matched with those taken from Yasmin's room at home. A couple of larger, smeared prints were as yet unidentified. 'But could belong to the parents,' Finlay said. 'We're re-checking that.'

A transcript of all the saved messages was attached. Mariner had never signed up to the text message culture, continuing to use his own mobile like a traditional tele-phone, and to his unfamiliar eyes the calls read like the Enigma Code.

'These are all messages?' Mariner asked the technician, feeling ignorant.

'It's on a save cycle of about a month,' Finlay told him. 'But this is quite a sophisticated phone and works a bit like e-mail, automatically saving the messages sent, too.'

'So we've got everything she sent and received over the last month?'

'Not quite. Some messages have been deliberately deleted. I'm not surprised, either, given the content of some of the others.'

'Oh?'

'A bit on the racy side.' Confirming that Yasmin wasn't quite the innocent they'd first thought her to be. 'Where we can, we've linked the phone numbers to Yasmin's phone book, so most of the messages, though not all, can be attributed. Messages to and from her parents and sister were easy to identify, especially as there aren't that many. Some of them also have only an initial or what looks like a nickname to identify them.'

'And the hot ones?' Tony Knox asked.

'They all appear to be to or from someone known as Lee.'

Lee. So Amira was right. Yasmin could have been seeing someone after all. The contraceptive pill wasn't just trying to be grown up in front of her friends. She really needed it. But why had none of her friends mentioned Lee?

'The one you'll be most interested is this one. It's the last message sent, on Tuesday at around lunchtime.'

'CU @4 things 2 TL U'

'What does it mean?'

'It makes more sense if you read it out loud: "See you at four. Things to tell you."'

'That was what she said to Suzanne. I'd thought that Lee was the something. Maybe she was telling him that she was on the pill, so it was all systems go.'

Finlay nodded sagely. 'It looks as if Yasmin had arranged to meet this Lee at four o'clock on the day she disappeared. I think you need to speak to him.'

'Do you reckon?' Knox was straight faced.

'There's one other message received after that, in the middle of the afternoon, but she's deleted it.'

'Christ, how can you tell that?'

'It leaves a trace, a bit like the imaging you get on a computer hard drive. Perhaps she deleted it because it was a bit strong for her parents' eyes again.'

'Thanks,' said Knox. 'We'll bear it in mind.'

'Can we be sure from this that Yasmin had her phone right up until Tuesday afternoon?' Mariner asked.

177

'Somebody did. The prints would indicate that it was probably her, because those are the clearest. The rest is for you to find out.'

'Thanks,' said Millie quickly, before Knox could get in. 'You've been very helpful.'

'OK,' said Mariner, when Finlay had gone. 'At least we now have the boy Yasmin was seeing, and we know it wasn't Ricky.'

'Unless he was using an alias.'

'Let's not complicate things for the sake of it. We should go and talk to her family about this.'

'I think we'd be better off talking to her friends, sir,' Millie suggested. 'They're more likely to know who she's been texting, especially given the content of some of these. It's not the kind of stuff she'd want to share with her mum and dad.'

On their return to the school, Mariner took with him photographs of Akram and Pryce. A cluster of girls was gathered outside the school gates. 'Isn't that Suzanne?' said Millie.

'Yes, let's get her on her own. She may be more inclined to talk.'

Millie was driving, so pulled over to the kerb to let Mariner out of the car.

'Suzanne. Can I have a word?'

The girl turned and gave her friends a knowing smile before breaking away from them and sashaying over to Mariner, obviously pleased to have been singled out for special attention. 'What can I do for you, Inspector?' The suggestion in those few words made Mariner's skin crawl.

He pretended not to notice. 'You've probably heard, we've found Yasmin's phone. There are several text messages on it from someone calling himself Lee. Do you know who that might be?'

'I might.' Suzanne shrugged and raised her eyebrows at her friends, eliciting a bout of giggling. Another one playing hard to get. Mariner snapped. 'Suzanne, a boy has been murdered. And not far from where we found his body we also found Yasmin's phone. You need to tell us everything you know. Loyalty to friends is commendable but it's not going to help Yasmin. At the very least, she may be in serious trouble, so we need to find out where she is.'

His tone shocked her out of her complacency. 'Lee is a boy Yasmin knows,' she pouted. 'And it's not really Lee. That's just his tag.'

'What is his real name?'

'Lewis Everett. He just calls himself Lee.'

'Are you sure about that? Did Yasmin know a boy called Ricky Skeet?'

'Is that the boy who—' The veneer of confidence was all but gone now.

'Yes. Did Yasmin know him?'

'I don't think so. I've never heard that name before.'

'How well does Yasmin know this Lee?'

'They sort of went out for a while.'

Finlay had been close to the mark. 'Why didn't you tell us about him before?'

She wrinkled her nose. 'It's history. Yaz hasn't seen him for weeks.'

Except, thought Mariner, that he was still texting her as recently as the day she disappeared. And Yasmin had recently gone to the doctor's to go on the pill.

'He goes to the boys school up the road. We met them on a school trip, to London.'

The tickets in Yasmin's treasure box.

'Them?'

'He's mates with my boyfriend, Sam. We all met up on the same trip. Yaz and Lee started it, really. We all went off to see the London Eye, then we couldn't find our way back to the bus. We got on the wrong Underground train. It was wicked. All the teachers were going crazy because me and Yasmin had gone off with "*boys*". They were worried about what her parents would say.'

179

'What about your parents?'

'Mine don't give a toss. It was Yaz's they were worried about. Pretty rich coming from them.'

'What do you mean by that?'

'Darrow and Goodway. They were all over each other. It was disgusting. Mr Goodway's wife had only left him a couple of weeks before, but she couldn't keep her hands off him.'

Was this a further example of teenage fantasy? 'But surely Mrs Darrow is—'

'Ms, actually.' The self-satisfaction crept back. 'She's divorced.'

'How did Yasmin's parents react to what happened?'

'They never found out. In the end Yaz persuaded the teachers not to tell. She promised that she wouldn't see Lee again so she had to meet him in secret, after school.'

'But you said she isn't seeing him now.'

'She isn't. It's over.'

'Who finished it?'

'Lee did.'

'Why?'

'Yasmin hadn't got the guts.'

'For what?'

'What do you think? What do all boys want? You're all the same.' She looked Mariner up and down with eyes that were experienced beyond her years. 'Eventually, Lee got the message that it wasn't going anywhere.'

'That Yasmin wouldn't sleep with him.'

'Yeah. She was "saving herself" for the right man, the one her parents were going to choose for her. Silly cow.'

'When did all this happen?'

'Ages ago.'

'Was Yasmin upset about the split?'

'Yeah. She wanted me to come out in sympathy and finish with Sam, too.'

'And did you?'

'No. It was totally unreasonable.'

180

'So you're still seeing Sam?'

'Yeah. He rocks.'

'Do you think Yasmin could be jealous of you and Sam? Did she think she was missing out?'

'It was up to her, wasn't it? She'd made her choice between her parents and Lee. She chose her parents.'

'Do you and Sam have a full relationship?'

'Do you mean sex? Of course we do.' Treating the question with the disdain it deserved. 'Sammy's hot. But I'm not stupid. I've been on the pill for months.'

'Did you ever suggest to Yasmin that she should go on the pill?'

'We talked about it, sure: we all know guys don't like skins, but it was too late for that. Yaz blew it.'

'What would you say if I told you that Yasmin was texting Lee as recently as the day she disappeared, and that she'd asked her GP to prescribe the pill?'

Suzanne's eyes widened. 'I'd say fucking good for you, Yaz. She finally decided to do it. That must have been what she was going to tell me.'

'That's what we think, too. But why would Yasmin suddenly change her mind about sleeping with Lee? Has anyone been putting her under pressure?'

'Yaz doesn't need anyone else to do that. She's well good at doing it for herself.'

'If Yasmin was going to meet Lee again, where would she have met him?'

'I don't know. When they were going out he sometimes used to meet Yaz from school, or they'd meet down near the station where she gets her train. Lee gets the train home too. He lives in this big posh house in Barnt Green with a pool and everything. There's a pub down by the station called the Bridge. Yaz used to talk about seeing Lee at the Bridge.'

Except Yasmin could have meant another bridge. Maybe it was she who had dropped her mobile phone there. But was it before or after Ricky had been attacked? And did the

181

two occurrences really have anything to do with each other?

Millie had parked the car, so Mariner caught up with her outside reception, and reported back on the conversation. 'So perhaps that's what it's all about: Yasmin trying to keep up with her friends. The status of being on the contraceptive pill.'

'Better than the status symbol of being landed with a baby at seventeen,' said Millie. 'Like Finlay said: we need to go and talk to Lewis Everett.'

'I'd like to get the official take on what Suzanne told us too. Let's see if *Ms* Darrow is around.'

The deputy head was in her office, and they were shown in just as Mr Goodway was leaving. Mariner couldn't help but see them in a new light, though it was hard to tell if what Suzanne had said was true. As Ms Darrow herself had said, teenage girls could be prone to overactive imaginations.

'Can you tell us anything about the Year 12 trip to London in the spring?' Mariner asked, when they were settled.

'That was months ago,' said Ms Darrow. 'Some of the girls went on an art trip to the Tate Modern with students from the boys school. Mr Goodway and I took them, along with a teacher from the boys school. We run quite a few joint trips. It cuts down on the expense and also allows the youngsters to mix, which is an important part of their social development.'

'From what I understand, the trip certainly enhanced Yasmin's social development.'

'Ah. You know about the incident, then.'

'We've heard one version but would be interested in your account of events.'

'It's very simple. When the time came to leave, all the girls were accounted for except Yasmin and Suzanne, and two of the boys were also missing. They eventually turned up at the coach, almost two hours late. People were beginning to get worried.'

'Where had they been?'

'Sightseeing. It was all perfectly innocent. They simply got lost and had to get the Tube back to the meeting place. London's a big place, Inspector. I wouldn't be taken in by any embroidery that might have been added.'

'Why didn't you tell us about this before?'

'As I said, it was months ago. Why would it be relevant? It seemed unnecessary to drag it all up again.'

'Did you tell Yasmin's parents about what happened?'

The smile went and the defences went up. 'We didn't think it necessary.'

'Because you knew how they would react.'

'We didn't want to jeopardise Yasmin's education because of one foolish episode.'

'Or jeopardise the generous donations Yasmin's father was making to the school.'

'That's a very cynical view, Inspector. The truth is that it was just one of these passing crushes girls have: completely normal and harmless, and over before it had begun. It had run its course so there seemed no need to rock the boat.'

'It wasn't quite over, though.'

'What do you mean?'

'Yasmin was still in contact with the boy in question, Lee, up until last Tuesday. And she had begun taking the contraceptive pill. Her father found all this out shortly before Yasmin disappeared. I wonder how he would feel if he knew that you had been responsible for introducing Yasmin to her lover and had let things "run their course"?'

The colour drained from Ms Darrow's face.

'Thanks, Ms Darrow. That's been helpful. We will naturally have to discuss this with Yasmin's parents. You may want to prepare for the fallout.'

Subdued by the revelations, Ms Darrow showed them out into reception again, where Mariner's attention was caught anew by the body art sketches. This time though, they triggered a recent memory. He'd seen some of those designs somewhere else, only yesterday afternoon.

Digging it from his inside pocket he held up the picture of Shaun Pryce in front of Ms Darrow. 'Has this young man been here, to the school?'

'Sorry? Oh, yes, he's an actor. He came and did some modelling for us about a year ago. We try and include life portraits in the syllabus where we can. It was a mistake though, really.'

'Why?' Millie was surprised. 'The pictures are very good.'

'The young man in question liked to flirt with the girls. He seemed to get them rather excited.'

'I'll bet he did,' murmured Mariner. 'Did he model for Yasmin's class?'

'He might have.'

'Think!' barked Mariner. 'Did he?'

'Yes. I think so.'

'So Shaun Pryce has a link with the girls school and may have known Yasmin. Now why the hell didn't he tell us that?'

'Do you want to go and talk to him again?'

'Not yet. Let's get Lee out of the way first.'

Built during the same era, the boys school was structurally a mirror image of the girls, but there the similarity ended. Less well cared for, soft greenery gave way to show cases full of competition trophies, and raw testosterone hung in the air. Mariner identified himself to the matronly receptionist. 'We need to speak to one of your students: Lewis Everett.'

'I'll just need to check with Mr Blyth. One moment, please.'

Head Teacher Gordon Blyth, a small man with thinning black hair and a voice from the valleys of South Wales, came out to speak to them in person. 'I'm afraid Lewis isn't here at the moment,' he said. 'He's doing work experience.'

'Where?'

Blyth had to go away and consult with the person responsible for organising these things. He was back moments later. 'At a place that makes kitchen units, on Birch Close. It's—'

'I know where it is,' said Mariner. He looked at Millie. 'Now we are going round in bloody circles.'

Within a few minutes they were back on the small industrial estate, four units down from TMR Reprographics. The manager of Dunhill's Kitchen Design was not a happy man.

'Work experience, is that what they call it? Little bugger hasn't turned in for work again today. He cleared off last Tuesday afternoon and I haven't seen him since.'

'What time on Tuesday afternoon?'

'About half one. The kid's a waste of space. He's hardly put in a full day's work since he started here. I ask you. What kind of a worker is he going to make?'

'Have you rung the school to find out where he is?'

'I haven't got time to go chasing round after him, I've got a business to run. It'll just go on his report at the end of the week. He wasn't much use, anyway. He's a spoilt little rich kid who doesn't like getting his hands dirty.'

Outside, just a few yards away were the refuse bins that concealed the gap in the fence.

Mariner put through a call on his mobile to the head of the boys school. 'We're at the kitchen workshop, but Lewis isn't. In fact, he hasn't been here since last Tuesday. I trust you didn't know that.' The pause at the other end of the line confirmed it. 'I'd like Lewis's home address, please.'

Lewis Everett's daily train journey home terminated at the exclusive hamlet of Barnt Green that nestled complacently at the foot of the Lickey Hills. The Everetts' house was 'big and posh' as Suzanne had described it, hemmed in on all sides by woodland on a private road that wasn't even graced with a proper street name. Hawthorns here had rather more to do with the shrub than it did the home of

185

West Bromwich Albion. Mariner tried to picture the Akram family living round here. He couldn't. Number 5, Hawthorns, consisted of five room widths of 1950s mock-Georgian with a broad double garage, behind impressive wrought-iron gates and a paved drive. Burgeoning ten-foot leylandii divided the property from its neighbours. A side gate was unlocked and they pushed through and approached the building. Mariner stepped over a dark stain that marked the otherwise flawless drive, but closer inspection revealed only engine oil. Pushing the button on the studded oak front door prompted nothing more than the jangle of a bell deep inside the house. Millie peered in through the window to see a neat and tidy sitting room, plush carpeting, gleaming antique reproduction furniture, everything in its place.

'At work, I suppose,' Millie said. 'We'll have to come back later.'

'On holiday,' called a disembodied voice from behind the hedge. The rhythmic chopping in the background that they hadn't even noticed, abruptly ceased. Mariner followed Millie back out through the gates and round to the adjacent property, an equally imposing edifice with tall windows and curving bays, in the style of Rennie Mackintosh. A man, tall and white haired, with a weathered face and sinewy arms, stood mid-way up an aluminium stepladder, brandishing a pair of garden shears. 'I do their garden, too,' he said. 'And they've gone away. Mr and Mrs have, anyway. Three weeks in the Bahamas. They do it every year at about this time. Due back early hours of Thursday morning.'

'It wasn't Mr or Mrs we were looking for,' Mariner said. 'It was Lee. Lewis.'

The man thought for a minute before slowly shaking his head. 'Haven't seen him for a few days, either.'

'You're here every day?' asked Millie.

'Look at the size of these gardens. This street is a full-time job for me. This time of year I get here at seven in the morning and don't go home until at least six, sometimes later if I've a job to finish. And by the time I get to the end

I have to start all over again.'

'So when was the last time you saw Lee Everett?'

He thought for a moment. 'Monday. He was around then, driving that car of his too fast up and down the road. Only a matter of time before he kills someone.'

Mariner and Millie exchanged a look. 'You didn't see him on Tuesday?'

'Let me think. Tuesday I was doing the back lawn at Number 8. I'd have been round there for most of the day. They've got more grass there than Wentworth.'

'And you definitely haven't seen him since?'

'No, but you might want to check with Margaret.'

'Margaret?'

'Margaret Ashworth, their daily help.'

'Do you have her phone number?'

'No.' He shook his head, before nodding an acknowledgement towards a green Land Rover Discovery that had driven up and was pulling into the driveway opposite. 'But Mrs Goldman would.'

Dashing across the road, Mariner and Millie sneaked in before the electric gates could close. Mrs Goldman was stepping down from her Land Rover Discovery, stretching out long legs clad in gleaming white cotton jeans, her equally dazzling blouse highlighting the deep tanning on her arms. On seeing Mariner's warrant card, the friendly smile on her immaculately made-up face dissolved to a troubled frown. 'Not another burglary,' she said, opening up the boot of the vehicle to retrieve Waitrose carrier bags. 'Who this time?'

'It's nothing like that,' Mariner reassured her. 'We need to get in touch with your cleaner, Margaret Ashworth.'

'Margaret? Why? What's happened?'

'We're trying to track down Lewis Everett.'

'Oh. Do you have to?' she said with feeling, slamming shut the tailgate. 'It's been so peaceful these last few days.'

Mariner offered to carry one of the bags.

'Thanks.'

187

They followed her round to the side of the house where she let them into a kitchen the size of Mariner's entire ground floor. It was sparse and modern, with wall-to-wall limed oak cupboards, and a wide central station that held a butcher's block. Another wall was dominated by a huge green-enamelled Aga; otherwise the appliances were in clinical stainless steel, everything as spotless as Mrs Goldman herself. Margaret was clearly a treasure.

'Can I offer you something to drink, something cold, perhaps?'

Mariner placed the bag alongside the others she'd deposited on the counter top. 'That would be very welcome. Thank you.'

Opening a fridge the size of a wardrobe, she dropped chunks from an ice dispenser into beautifully crafted crystal tumblers, topping them up with an orange-coloured fruit juice.

'You remarked on how quiet things have been over the last few days,' said Mariner. 'Implying that it's not always the case.'

'Lewis takes full advantage of his parents being away,' she said with feeling. 'We get treated to the latest rock bands at full volume most evenings. The warm weather encourages him to keep all the windows open too, of course, which makes it worse.'

'No one complains?'

'Oh, one or two of the neighbours have tried talking to him. It's a question of getting through, though. Lewis is a very intense young man. The sulky and broody type, a regular Liam Gallagher – or is it Noel? You never quite know what's going on inside his head. To be truthful, I think his parents may be a bit afraid of him, and they're lovely people, so nobody really wants to upset them. We just all put up with it. When you live in a little community like this one it's important to get along. And to be fair, Lewis isn't that much trouble when his parents are around.'

'When was the last time you saw him?'

188

She thought about that. 'I haven't seen him – or heard him – for about a week. Last Monday or Tuesday, I think.'

'If we could just have Margaret Ashworth's number—'

'Yes, of course. I'll get it for you.' Mrs Goldman was also good enough to let Mariner use her phone, but Margaret Ashworth was out shopping. Her daughter was expecting her back in a couple of hours.

'We may as well go back to the shop,' Mariner said. 'Thanks for the drink, Mrs Goldman.'

'Not at all. Good luck with Lewis.'

On their way back to the station, they had to drive past the girls school. It was the end of the afternoon and they saw Suzanne Perry arguing with a man beside a big flashy car, as girls swarmed out past them.

'Look at that,' said Millie. 'What do you think's going on there?'

Mariner put a call through to Knox back at OCU 4. 'Could you run a vehicle check on a Volvo estate, personalised plate SDP 2.'

Moments later Knox came back. 'The car is registered to a Mr Stephen Perry, 39 Silvermere Road, Kingsmead.'

'She's being shown up in front of her friends by an over-protective father,' Millie concluded. 'Now who's being paranoid?'

Charlie Glover was also checking in at Granville Lane, where they found him brooding over the incident room map.

'How's it going?'

'Slowly. There's still nothing to indicate that Ricky would have known Yasmin. It's looking more and more like sheer coincidence that they were around there at the same time.'

'So nothing new?'

Glover shook his head. 'We're still looking for a murder weapon. How about you?'

189

For the benefit of Knox, too, Mariner filled Glover in on the afternoon's developments. 'So now we have Yasmin and the boyfriend missing. The boyfriend works at the industrial units and Yasmin's phone is found between the station and there. It gives us a whole new scenario.'

'If Yasmin was trying to prove to Suzanne that she could cut it in the romance stakes, and if she wanted to get away from her parents, what better way to do both simultaneously than to elope with her boyfriend? She could have planned the whole thing, including the sleepover at Suzanne's, which she never had any intention of following through.'

'But Suzanne seemed certain that the relationship with Lee was finished,' Millie reminded him.

'That's what Yasmin told her. The bigger the surprise then, when her friend finds out what she's done. Suzanne said that Yasmin was excited, had something to tell her. Might have been rather more than we thought.'

'If Yasmin's eloped she hasn't taken much with her,' Millie said, quietly.

'She wouldn't need to. Boyfriend Lee isn't short of a bob or two.'

'Where does that leave us with Pryce?' asked Glover. 'Potentially, we now have four people on or around the reservoir that afternoon, three of whom know each other. Akram knows Yasmin, Yasmin knows Lee.'

'And as we found out this afternoon, Shaun Pryce probably knows Yasmin.'

'Pryce insists he was there much earlier. Surely we can rule him out now.'

'If we believe him.' Mariner was sceptical. 'I'm sure there's something going on with him.'

'And Akram's still in the picture, but only in the background.'

'Which leaves us with Yasmin, Lee and Ricky as the most likely – in that order. As far as we know, Ricky doesn't know Lee or Yasmin, but perhaps he saw something, tried to stop it and Lee turned on him.'

190

'Perhaps eloping wasn't on the agenda,' Millie put in. 'We know for sure that Yasmin had just gone on the pill, and that she was all set to lose her virginity. Maybe that's what they were meeting for. Shaun Pryce could have even suggested the location. We don't know how he gets his kicks. Perhaps he was planning to watch. So Yasmin gets there. Lee turns up with high expectations, but Yasmin then gets cold feet and won't play. Lee gets rough with her and Ricky, there by sheer coincidence, intervenes to help her—'

'And Lee turns on him.'

'Mrs Goldman said he's a bit of a sullen bastard.'

'And Randall called him a spoilt kid. Implying that he's used to getting what he wants.'

'Then Lee and Yasmin panic about what's happened and disappear together.'

'Or Lee panics and forces Yasmin to go with him.'

'And Pryce?'

'Pryce witnessed the whole thing, which is why he's playing silly buggers with us.'

'So why doesn't he just tell us?'

'Because he could be implicated on some level: especially if he just stood back and watched it all happen.'

'Or more than that, it turned him on.'

Mariner sighed. He couldn't ever remember standing on such fast-shifting sand. The phone rang.

'Margaret Ashworth,' said Millie. 'She'll meet us at the house.'

191

Chapter Fourteen

'Have you got a search warrant?' were Margaret Ashworth's first words to them when they arrived. Fortunately, Mariner was able to persuade her that it wasn't necessary since she was merely cooperating with the police enquiry. 'We don't want to search the premises,' he said, 'only see for ourselves that the place has been uninhabited for a few days.' They had to wait while she disarmed a complex security alarm and then carefully removed her shoes in favour of fluffy pink mules just in front of the door, glancing disapprovingly at their own heavy footwear.

'You wouldn't want me to take them off, love, believe me,' said Knox.

Margaret took them up a sweeping staircase to Lee's room, just off the first landing at the back of the house. The curtains were drawn, rendering it almost pitch black inside.

'He likes them kept closed at all times,' Margaret Ashworth told them. Switching on the ceiling spotlights revealed a room that was a far cry from the single bed, nightstand and wardrobe that had furnished Mariner's room at the same age. There was a double bed, a bank of technology including PC, games console, TV, video recorder and DVD player, even a kettle, fridge and a microwave. It was virtually a self-contained flat with everything a young man could want. 'Christ, if I had a place like this and the folks were away I wouldn't do a disappearing act,' was Knox's comment.

Spaces on the purple-painted walls were covered with posters of surfers riding massive waves, along with some of Lee's own gruesome drawings. A battered skateboard leaned against the wardrobe. Mariner picked over the untidy desk, a jumble of papers, books, CDs and lad magazines. He was itching to rifle through the drawers too, but Margaret was keeping a beady eye on them from the doorway.

'How about a cup of tea, love?' Knox asked, summoning the best of his scouse charm. 'I'm parched. I'll bet you make a smashing cuppa.' But Margaret wasn't having any of it and her arms remained resolutely folded.

'You're losing your touch, mate,' murmured Mariner.

'Tell me about it,' Knox retorted. The rubbish bin had been emptied so there were no clues there, but tucked behind it, Knox found a small silver tin of the kind that normally holds travel sweets. This one didn't. Knox sniffed the dried green substance. 'He's got something in common with Shaun Pryce, then.'

Mariner wasn't that surprised. He walked over to inspect the computer that was switched off and his eye was caught by a glossy scrap of paper that had slid underneath the monitor. He edged it out with a fingernail. Dusty and slightly bent at one corner, it was a strip of photographs of the kind taken in an instant photo booth. 'Tony.' He held it up to show Knox. Lewis Everett and Yasmin Akram; grinning broadly, their faces squashed together to fit into the shot. 'At least it confirms that they've been an item.'

'Not much care taken with preserving it,' said Knox. 'A one sided relationship, d'you think?'

'Could be,' said Mariner. Another one, he thought, with feeling. Downstairs, a kitchen memo board bore postcards from various locations around the world, along with a number of business cards for local tradesmen and a couple of dental appointment cards. The answering machine might have been a source of additional information, but until they had permission it was off-limits.

'Have you any idea where Lewis might have gone?' Mariner asked Margaret, who was hovering, ever vigilant, watching over them. 'Did he say anything to you?'

She snorted. 'He doesn't even tell his parents what he's up to. He's a law unto himself.'

They did, however, get from Margaret a good description of Lewis's car and its registration, and she even, if a little reluctantly, allowed them to borrow a more naturally posed recent photograph of the man himself from a display in the lounge. He was as Mrs Goldman described him, scruffy and staring defiantly into the camera, a frown where the smile should have been.

'It'll help us to eliminate him from our enquiries,' Mariner said, as a sop, though in reality Lewis was inching nearer by the minute to the main frame. It would have been good to be able to delve a little deeper but, until Mr and Mrs Everett returned, their hands were tied. Mr Everett was, apparently, a director of several small companies, so would certainly have some legal connections. He wouldn't be too pleased about coming home to find his house had been ransacked when there was no concrete evidence for doing so. They had little choice but to wait a day or so and hopefully do it with his blessing.

What they could do, meanwhile, was issue a nationwide description of Lee and his car, highlighting to colleagues in other forces the possible link with Yasmin. Mariner would go with Millie to talk to the Akrams as well. Their reaction to all this information would be educational.

Mariner wanted both parents together, so they went back to the house in the early evening. Amira was present too, giving her mother some much needed support. Shanila Akram was displaying increasing signs of strain. Her eyes seemed sunken in her pale face, and Mariner would have guessed that food and sleep had become irrelevancies.

194

Mohammed Akram was fairing better, because he knew that his daughter was safe, or was it just that he was able to put on a better show for them?

'We're fairly certain now that Yasmin may have been seeing a boy called Lee or Lewis,' Mariner said, when they were gathered in the garden. 'Has she ever mentioned him to you?'

'Yasmin doesn't know any boys, only her cousins.' Mohammed Akram was calm but firm.

Mariner had no choice but to hand over the photo booth snaps and watch shock and bewilderment creep over their faces once again. 'As you can see, there's no doubt that Yasmin knows this particular boy. She met him on a school trip when they spent some time together. We've also confirmed this with the school. It means that we have to consider the possibility that Yasmin could be with him now. They have both disappeared.'

In an unprecedented outburst, Shanila Akram turned on her husband. 'Do you see what we've done? We've pushed her into the arms of a boy. If we had let her do this out in the open, and if you hadn't—' She stopped herself, and for a moment the air was thick with the unspoken.

'Hadn't what, Mrs Akram?' Mariner prompted.

'I was going to say "argued with her",' Shanila Akram replied, weakly. Mariner didn't believe her, but the moment had passed and she was no longer prepared to say what she'd intended.

'It's my fault,' said Amira, shakily. 'I encouraged her.'

Her mother stared. 'But why? Yasmin is so young, and she should be pure for her husband.'

'Amma, that's ridiculous, antiquated nonsense,' said Amira, her voice strengthening. 'I had been with several men before Ravi and I married.'

'Amira!'

'It's true. But Ravi doesn't mind. In fact, he liked that I had some experience and knew what to do. Yasmin is the

195

same. She needs some experience. She should get to know some boys.'

'So you told her to make a whore of herself?' Mohammed Akram was beside himself with fury.

'Of course not. I just said that if a chance presented itself she should take it. Virginity is overrated. And I know that Yasmin was under pressure from her friends. She felt excluded.'

'It takes a special kind of courage to stand by your principles,' said Akram coldly. 'And this is the price we pay for giving in to temptation.'

Amira dissolved into tears and this time it was her mother who moved across to offer comfort.

Mohammed Akram glanced at Mariner. 'We would like to be left alone now, Inspector.'

'Whatever other skills she has, Yasmin's pretty adept at keeping all the different facets of her life separate from one another,' said Millie as they drove away.

'It's something we all learn to do, some more efficiently than others,' said Mariner, thinking that he'd managed to get it down to a fine art: his work, mother and Anna all running on separate, parallel tracks.

Kings Rise was holding a memorial service for Ricky the next morning at a local church, to assist pupils through the grieving process, though how many of them would genuinely be mourning the boy was open to debate. It was another unrelentingly hot and dry day, and it was obscene to Mariner that the sun could shine so cheerfully over such an event. Fiske had insisted on accompanying him and Charlie Glover, keeping the police presence to a minimum. The three of them slipped into the back of the church and had to stand in the unbearable heat: the place was so packed with family and schoolfriends. If this lot was anything to go by, Ricky had more mates than his mother knew. Half the church seemed to be filled with spotty adolescent kids. Mariner tried not to think that it might just be a sick excuse for a day off school.

One of Ricky's uncles spoke nervously, and with hesitance, about the 'grand lad' Ricky had been, while Colleen's sobbing seemed to echo throughout the whole chapel. Mariner detested the indignity of these manufactured occasions and, as the congregation rose falteringly to its feet and began an uneasy rendition of the final hymn, he noticed one or two of the kids stifling giggles. When Fiske's pager went off, he wanted to punch his superior officer in the face.

Afterwards, they joined the long line that filed past the family to pay their respects.

'What the hell is he doing here?' demanded Colleen emotionally as Fiske appeared in front of her. 'You did nothing. Nothing!' Suddenly she lunged for him. Mariner heard camera shutters clunk behind them and knew that this would not be Fiske's finest hour. Turning his back on the debacle, Mariner walked over to where Charlie Glover stood, lighting up a cigarette. At least Colleen would appreciate that particular brand of camaraderie.

They drove in an uncomfortable silence back to Granville Lane, where Tony Knox had mixed news. 'Lewis Everett's parents are home. They flew in from the Bahamas in the early hours of this morning, boss. But they don't know where he is either. As far as they were concerned their precious son was looking after the house and doing his work experience. They admit that he can be a bit wild but they don't see him eloping with anyone. Too selfish for that, so they say.'

The vestibule they'd entered the previous day was, this afternoon, cluttered with matching Luis Vuitton luggage and a bulging sack of golf clubs. Mr and Mrs Everett were nicely tanned, but they no longer looked very relaxed.

'Thank you for seeing us so promptly,' Mariner said. 'I realise you must be tired and jet-lagged and have things to do.'

'This is not the kind of reception you expect or want on return from a peaceful holiday,' admitted Mr Everett, with slight irritation. 'But we'd like to sort it out as soon as we can.'

'You'll be aware by now that a young girl has gone missing in the area. We have reason to believe that she was having a relationship with your son.' Mariner produced the photo. 'This is Yasmin Akram. Did you know that Lewis was seeing her?'

Everett gave the picture a perfunctory glance before passing it to his wife. 'Lewis has had various girlfriends. We don't always meet them.'

'And Yasmin?'

'I don't recall her, do you, darling?'

Mrs Everett was studying the snapshot more carefully. 'No.'

'And have you any idea where Lewis may have gone? We need to find him. He may be the last person to have seen Yasmin before she disappeared.'

'I've had a look round,' Everett said. 'Some of his camping gear has gone from the garage, but as to where he's gone, I wouldn't know.'

'We'd like to do a more thorough search of his room, if that's all right.'

Everett flattened a yawn. 'If you must.'

'Do you know if Lewis kept any kind of diary?' Mariner asked Mrs Everett.

'I don't think so.'

'Perhaps we could have a look on his computer.'

Even on the more thorough search, the only paperwork they could find was a school planner, but it contained nothing personal. On his PC they looked for traces of records on Outlook but there was nothing.

'What would Lewis do for money while he's away?'

'He has an allowance paid into his bank account and a debit card that he can use to withdraw cash from ATMs. He has a credit card too,' Everett told them.

'We'll need the details. The credit card company may be able to help us track his movements.'

Lewis's credit card records provided the break they needed. A phone call to the company revealed that since the day of his disappearance, Lewis had been spending heavily at petrol stations, restaurants and surfing shops in the area around Newquay in Cornwall.

Knox contacted local police with the description of Lewis and his car, with a request to publicise it widely, especially around the camp-sites in the area.

'That could take some time,' he was told. 'There's hundreds of them and in this weather they're pretty full, too.'

'Do what you can, will you?' Then it was back to the waiting game.

When Mariner got home that evening, he found that his answering machine had been working overtime. An unexpected message from Anna told him that she had the chance of a night's respite from Jamie if he felt like calling round. It happened occasionally when Manor Park had an overnight vacancy. Mariner looked at his watch: it was ten fifteen. It didn't take long to make up his mind.

The house was dark: Anna making the most of the opportunity for an early night. So often was her sleep disturbed by Jamie's nocturnal wanderings that she took a full night when ever she could. Mariner let himself in and, after taking a long, cleansing shower, eventually slipped into bed beside Anna.

'Hello, you,' she murmured, sleepily.

'Hi.' In the heat of the night she'd thrown off the duvet and he could make out the luscious curves of her body. He slid a hand round over her stomach and up towards her breasts, feeling his own body starting to respond.

But Anna wriggled away. 'Mm, I'm really tired.'

Pity. Sighing heavily, Mariner had to content himself with moulding his body to hers and breathing her scent. He

199

lay there for a while, trying to drift off, but sleep just wouldn't come. Eventually, he got up and prowled the rooms, coming to rest at the bedroom window where he stared out at the eerie orange glow cast over the street by the sodium light, until at last it was faded out by the dawn. The next morning he felt like death warmed up while Anna was full of energy. 'I've got a meeting with Simon about the festival this evening,' she bubbled. 'Any chance you could sit with Jamie for me?' Suddenly, irrationally Mariner began to question the motives for that late night phone call.

'Sure,' he said, indifferently.

She picked up the undertone. 'Is that going to be a problem?'

'Of course not.' But he wasn't convincing.

She was still watching him carefully when the phone rang. 'It's the wife,' she said, handing it over.

In fact it was Tony Knox. 'Cornwall police have come back to us. They've found Lewis Everett. But he's not there with Yasmin. He's there with his mate Daniel who's also skiving off work experience.'

'Really gives you confidence in the future generation, doesn't it? Are they are on their way?'

'They're being escorted back this afternoon.'

'We'll talk to Lewis as soon as he gets here.' Which, he realised, might mean interviewing him through the evening. He gave Anna an apologetic look. 'I'm sorry, I won't be able to make it tonight after all, something's come up.'

She studied him for a moment. 'That's OK, I can take Jamie with me. Simon won't mind.'

Mariner picked up his jacket. 'I'll see you later, then.'

'Sure, have a good day.' No hint of disappointment, not even the demand for further explanation, so why, as he walked out to his car, did Mariner feel so piqued? Because Simon *wouldn't mind*. He wouldn't, would he? Bastard. In all honesty, what Mariner had really wanted her to say was that she would cancel the appointment. Knowing that he was being unreasonable, he recognised the growing feeling inside him for what it was. He was jealous, of Simon Meadows, with whom Anna seemed to spend ever-increasing amounts of time.

It was essential to her autistic brother's well-being that Anna and Meadows should get on, so it came as a bit of a shock to Mariner that he should begin to resent their relationship. But it was turning into something he couldn't deny, even to himself. After all these years of bearing witness to the devastating impact of human jealousy, a tiny part of him was beginning to appreciate its power.

Lewis Everett arrived back in the city in the early afternoon and had legal representation right from the start. His father made sure of that, and insisted on being present, too.

Approaching six feet tall, Everett was lean and lanky in that gangling, post-adolescent way, his hair fashionably mussed and with a few days' fuzzy growth on his chin. The first thing to draw Mariner's attention, as they faced each other across the interview room table, was the tattoo on his left forearm. Mariner wondered if he'd got it at the same tattoo parlour as Shaun Pryce.

'I understand you're seeing Yasmin Akram,' Mariner began.

'Was seeing, past tense. It was months ago.'

'How did it start?'

'We met on a school trip.'

'Oh yes, the trip to the Tate. You were late back to the bus.'

'We went sightseeing. Got carried away.'

'And lost. You continued to see Yasmin after that?'

'Not for long.'

'Who broke it off?'

'I did. She was a prick tease.'

'Lewis!'

'Please, Mr Everett. We agreed: no interruptions. What do you mean by that, Lewis?'

'She used to wind me up. All over me, hands going

201

everywhere, then suddenly the parents and their religious beliefs would come into her head and she'd want me to stop. She'd say she couldn't go any further. I got fed up with it.'

'But you saw her again recently.'

'I see her sometimes across the platform at the station, waiting for her train. One day a couple of weeks ago, she sent me a text. Said she wanted to meet me again. She had something important to tell me. She asked me to meet her from school.'

'And?'

'I told her I wouldn't be at school the next week. I was doing work experience up at the factory centre.'

'Huh.' Lewis's father couldn't stop himself. Mariner silenced him with a glare.

'I told her she could come over to the centre on Monday after school. She'd be finished before me.'

'And did she come?'

'Eventually.'

'What do you mean?'

'She was late. She'd walked all the way round on the road. It's miles.'

'She didn't know about the short cut over the reservoir.'

'No.'

'Did you tell her about it?'

'Yeah, so she'd know next time. Anyway, by the time she got to Dung Heap's it was nearly time for her to catch her train.'

'But did she tell you?'

'What?'

'The "something important" she wanted to say.'

Lewis snorted. 'She said she really missed me and that she'd changed her mind.'

'About what?'

'About doing it – sleeping with me.'

'What had brought this on?'

Everett lifted his bony shoulders. 'Who knows? Her mate

202

Suzanne had been giving her a hard time. And there was something about her sister, too.'

'So she was planning to go through with it this time.'

'I said, great, but what was she going to do about protection. I said it would be easier if she just went on the pill.'

'That's very considerate of you,' put in Tony Knox.

'If you must know, I thought when I said that she'd back down again.'

'But she didn't.'

'No. She'd already sorted it. I was pretty stunned. Her dad had even found out, but she'd fixed him too.'

'She told him she was on the pill for medical reasons.'

'Whatever.'

'So what did you do?'

'We arranged to meet again on the Tuesday afternoon, after school. I was going to get off work early and we'd go back to my place. She was going to tell her parents she was staying at her mate's house for the night.'

'So what happened?'

'Monday night, Dan called with this big plan about going down to Cornwall. But it was cool. I could meet Yasmin as planned then we'd go down afterwards, drop her off at the station or something on the way.'

'Have your cake and eat it.'

'Then, Tuesday morning, Dan called to say we'd have to go earlier or we wouldn't get a pitch at the camp-site. I texted Yasmin to let her know I wouldn't make it, and that I'd see her when I got back.'

'Just like that.'

Lewis shrugged again. 'I felt bad letting her down. She'd gone out on a limb for me but, well, you know—'

'Girls in Cornwall more of a certainty?'

'Less complicated. Yasmin had messed me around before, so she could easily do it again.'

'What time did you send the text?'

'Some time that morning.'

'What exactly did your message say?'

203

'I'm going to Cornwall with Dan, don't bother turning up at the reservoir. To be honest, I was pretty convinced she wouldn't come. I thought she'd bottle it at the last minute like before.'

'Is there any chance that Yasmin could have misunderstood your message?' The shrugged responses were beginning to get on Mariner's nerves. 'And what time did you leave to go to Cornwall?'

'I left the workshop at lunchtime, about one o'clock. I told them I didn't feel well—'

'Christ, Lewis, when are you ever going to do a decent day's work?'

'Mr Everett, please.' He turned back to Lewis. 'Then what did you do?'

'I went home and packed my stuff, and waited for Dan. But his car was leaking oil—'

'All over my drive, I notice,' Lewis's father interrupted.

Mariner lost patience. 'Mr Everett, if you can't remain silent, I'll have to ask you to leave. Go on, Lewis.'

'We didn't get it fixed till nearly four.'

'And you went on the motorway?'

'Straight down the M5.' He sliced through the air with the edge of a hand.

'Did Yasmin ever talk to you about her parents?'

'Only to moan about how strict they are.'

'She ever talk about running away?'

'Not for real.'

'But she had mentioned it.' A nod. 'Did she say where she would go if she did?'

'No.'

'Did you think about taking her to Cornwall with you?'

'No way.'

'Will anyone be able to corroborate the time you left?' A shrug. 'Dan?'

'Your best pal? Not much of a back-up,' said Knox.

'The traffic cameras might pick up the car.' Lewis was hopeful.

But Mariner kept pushing. 'I still don't understand why you turned down a perfectly good opportunity on your doorstep to drive all the way down to Cornwall. Especially given that Yasmin had started contraception for your benefit. Was she too tame for you?'

Lewis's face screwed up in a flash of irritation. 'She was using me too, man. All of a sudden she had this thing about losing her virginity. That's all she wanted me for. Listen, I really like Yasmin, but like I said, she's a mess. When we were going out she didn't really know what she wanted. And I've heard about her dad, too. He sounds seriously scary. Cornwall was just a laugh, a chance to get away from all that.'

'Without the responsibility,' put in Mr Everett.

His son stared back insolently. 'Yeah, that's right.'

'Ever heard of a boy called Ricky Skeet?' Mariner slid the photograph across the table. 'This is him.'

Lewis looked at the picture, at ease with the question. 'No.'

Knox produced the grass. 'We found this in your room.'

'It's for personal use. To be honest, it's been there ages. I'd forgotten all about it.'

'Where did you get it?'

'A friend got it for me.'

'What's his name?'

'John Smith.'

'You sure it wasn't Shaun Pryce?'

Again, it was a smooth response. No hint of recognition. 'No.'

Mariner put the second photograph on the table. 'This is him.' Lewis frowned.

'What?' said Mariner.

'It's just – weird. I'm pretty sure I don't know that guy, but it's like I've seen that picture before.'

'This picture? Or one like it?'

'Could be one like it.'

'Have you ever been into the girls school?'

205

'No.'

'That is weird, then.'

They were able to let Lewis go home with his father in the late afternoon. His car was impounded for fingerprinting but Mariner was pretty sure they were wasting their time.

'Young lad like him, you'd have thought that he'd jump at the chance of a girl offered to him on a plate,' Mariner said to Knox afterwards. 'Would he really forgo that opportunity?'

'He was hedging his bets. Yasmin had messed him around, hadn't she? Like I said, the girls in Cornwall must have seemed more of a cert.'

'He seems relaxed enough talking about Yasmin. On balance, I think he's telling the truth. And it will be easy enough to check out his story with this Dan.'

'They've had the whole drive back here to get their stories straight.'

Knox followed up by talking to Dan, who was able to confirm Lewis's version of events in every detail. And though the occupants were a blur, Lee's Grand Vitara could be picked out on motorway CCTV, passing Bromsgrove at 4.09 on that Tuesday afternoon.

In all probability they'd drawn another blank and Mariner could reasonably have taken the rest of the evening off to help out Anna. But he chose not to.

Instead, he went back to Finlay.

'Is there any way of knowing the content of Lee's last message, even if Yasmin deleted it afterwards?'

'There is one deleted message: the last one received, which would have been it. As I said before, the ghosting is there. But there's no way of knowing what that message said.' So they had Lee's word that the text was calling off the meeting. For all they knew he could have been calling to confirm it.

'If she got the message from Lee, why did she still go there?' Knox wanted to know.

'We still don't know for certain that she did,' said Mariner. 'All we know for sure is that she got off the train again.'

'And her phone found its way to the bridge,' said Millie.

'But supposing she did go to the bridge,' Mariner said. 'Say, somehow, she misunderstood what Lee had said. What would she do when he didn't turn up?'

'I'd expect her to wait around a bit, then when it's clear he's not coming, go back to the train station.'

'Unless she saw it was the opportunity she'd been waiting for,' said Mariner. 'She's getting grief at home and with her friends. Suddenly she's in a position where she's accountable to no one. Her mum thinks she's with Suzanne. Her dad's far enough away not to be giving her much thought. A window opens up of a few hours when no one's going to miss her: a chance to get away.'

'On a West Midlands travel card?' Knox was doubtful.

'Don't forget that this is all at about the same time Ricky is killed on that very spot. We've thought about Ricky witnessing something and being killed for it, but what about if Yasmin saw what happened to Ricky and it scared her into running away.'

'Which brings us back to where we came in last Wednesday: where has she gone?' Mariner got up from where he'd been sitting, massaging his temples to ease the headache he was developing. 'Potentially, we've got several people at the reservoir at that time and now we have photographs to go with them. Let's go and talk to Lily again, see if we can prompt her into remembering anything new.'

The air felt as if it was closing in on them as Knox drove them back to St Clare's, armed now with photographs of Yasmin, Lee, Mohammed Akram and Shaun Pryce. Dusk was a couple of hours away but the sky had dulled to a misty grey and, when they got out of the car, Mariner noticed his shirt speckled with tiny storm flies. He was hoping that Lily would recognise at least one of the photographs, but she simply shook her head at each of them.

207

'Are you saying you don't know?' Mariner asked.

'No. I'm saying it's not him.'

'None of them? You're sure?'

'Absolutely.'

'Well, thanks for looking.' It was not what he wanted to hear.

'Not at all.' Lily smiled. 'You were lucky to catch me again, Inspector. I shan't be here for much longer.'

'Oh?'

She beamed with pride. 'I've won a competition. Twenty-five thousand pounds.'

Mariner was impressed. 'That's fantastic. What competition was that?' Going over to the little table in her room, she handed him a letter. It was the sort of 'Congratulations! You have been selected to receive one of our stunning prizes' variety of junk mail that every household receives on a weekly basis. All it required in return was that the recipient sign up to a monthly magazine to be entered into a prize draw.

'Lily, this isn't—' Mariner began gently, but Nora caught his eye and gave a tiny, warning shake of the head.

'I'm going to buy a nice little flat,' Lily went on, enthusiastically. 'And I'm going to have a party for all my family and friends too. You must come, Inspector.'

'I'd love to,' said Mariner, with a sudden sinking feeling.

Nora showed them out of the building. 'I know what you're thinking and yes, it's true, she does have days when she's confused, but not every day. She still saw what she saw.'

'I know.' But now Mariner was beginning to wonder exactly what it was that Lily saw. On the way home, the pain that had been moving round his skull throughout most of the day began to tighten like a vice, as thoughts bounced around his head, seeking out connections. He considered again whether he should go to Anna's but something stopped him. What he needed was some time on his own to

208

think. In the cottage, he washed back a couple of painkillers, sat back in the armchair and closed his eyes.

Mariner was woken at around midnight by what he at first thought were fireworks: these days, especially in summer, the universal way to celebrate any special event by waking all the neighbours. But the air had grown stickier still, and the next rumble he heard was preceded by the unmistakable flicker of lightning. The storm crept slowly on to the city like a slothful beast, grumbling and complaining, building in strength until the thunder shook the house and lightning flashed with dazzling intensity. Then the rain came, pounding on the water and trees like no rain Mariner had heard before. He leaned on the sill of the open window to breathe it in. Mesmerised by the cool freshness after the weeks of intolerable heat, Mariner took his keys from the shelf and stepped outside into a puddle that covered his shoes, and just walked. Shining under the streetlights, the gutters had become rivers, gardens vast ornamental ponds, as the water sought to find an outlet through the hard, dry earth.

Within seconds, his clothes were soaked through and his hair plastered to his head, but the heavy drops beat soothingly on his head and shoulders as he walked the deserted streets, while the storm raged overhead, before finally admitting defeat and moving off to terrorise elsewhere. As the rain weakened to a light drizzle, Mariner let himself back into the house, where he stripped off his wet clothes in the hall, climbed the stairs and collapsed into a restless, dream-ridden sleep as dawn was beginning to prise open the sky.

He was woken from a deep, heavy sleep by the phone. It was Fiske. 'Yasmin Akram,' he said abruptly. 'There's been a development.'

Chapter Fifteen

Not 'breakthrough', Mariner noted, but 'development'. It didn't sound good. Fiske, playing the drama queen again, couldn't just come out and tell him. But it was serious, judging from the number of people who had been contacted and brought in on this Sunday morning. With everyone crammed into the small and stifling briefing room, Fiske broke it to them. 'The body of a young Asian girl has been found in the river that runs through Kingsmead Park,' he said. 'We think it's Yasmin Akram.'

Missing person to murder victim, in two simple sentences. Murmurs of disgust rippled round the room, an odious Mexican wave.

'She was discovered early this morning by a park ranger.'

'How close is that to where her phone was found?' someone asked.

'It's about a mile away, down from the station but on the other side of Birchill Road. We'll be setting up an incident room as soon as identity is confirmed.' He turned to Mariner. 'DI Mariner, who has been investigating her disappearance, will continue to lead on the ground.'

The flash storms had caused chaos across the whole of the Midlands area. Towns along the Severn, like Bewdley that had seemed to be almost permanently under water last autumn and spring had fallen victim yet again. And in Birmingham itself, they drove through streets that were still several inches under water. But the freshness the rain brought was short-lived. It continued to be a sticky and stormy day; the sun a white smear against the grey-yellow sky, the peculiar half-light threatening more showers.

It was a slow drive down past the railway station and to the park, in a convoy of cars that inched its way through patches of deep flooding. In the car park, a small group had already gathered and uniform were having a nightmare task keeping kids away from what had become an instant water park. 'Who found the body?' Mariner asked the nearest officer.

'Andy Pritchard.' He pointed over to a young lad in khaki shirt, trousers and high waders, standing isolated from the pack. 'Park ranger. There's a couple of them cycle around all the local parks, dealing with vandalism, that kind of stuff. Today he's on his own.'

'The Lone Ranger,' observed Knox.

'He's pretty shaken up,' the officer added.

'Who wouldn't be?'

Andy Pritchard had one of the worst cases of acne Mariner had ever seen. He was virtually hiding under the peak of his green ranger's cap. Nearby, two more officers were transferring soggy books and papers into evidence bags. A saturated, dark-blue back-pack lay at their feet. Mariner recognised it from the description they'd had of Yasmin's. Putting on waders, he and Knox went with Pritchard to where he'd found the body, in a remote corner of the park.

'I saw the books first of all,' he told them as they sloshed through water eight inches deep, 'floating along on the surface. I couldn't work out where they would have come from. Then I saw the bag. So I went upstream to see if there was anything else, and that was when I noticed what I thought were clothes caught on the tree roots on the other bank. When I had a closer look—' he lifted the binoculars,

'—I could see that it was something more.' They had come to the main channel of the river: although there was no distinguishing it from the pond they'd just waded through. Stopping abruptly, Pritchard pointed across to the opposite bank a couple of yards away, where they could now see a dark, sodden bundle of clothing, long black hair fanning out behind. 'Then I saw her face.'

'Now I'm a believer,' muttered Knox under his breath.

As if to confirm Pritchard's story, the water suddenly bulged, turning the body and for a split second they looked into what was unmistakably the pale, lifeless face of Yasmin Akram.

'What time was this?' asked Mariner.

'About seven o'clock. We work dawn till dusk in the summer months.'

'But you didn't call it in until nearly eight,' said Knox. 'Why was that?'

Pritchard flushed. 'I wasn't sure what to do. I thought about trying to get across to her but the water was too deep and too fast flowing. I thought I might lose my footing. It's gone down a bit since then. I thought the best thing was to call you.'

'It was the best thing,' said Mariner, though preserving this scene was going to be a joke. 'Is there a way round on the other side?' He looked up at the steep embankment, knowing the answer already.

Pritchard shook his head. 'This is the closest we can get. You'll have to wade across.'

Here, the main course of the stream was six or seven feet wide. From where they stood, the level had risen to Mariner's knees, and now and again he had to lean into the powerful current.

'OK. Thanks, Andy, we'll take it from here,' said Mariner. 'If you go back up to the road someone will take a full statement from you.'

Pritchard on his way, Mariner turned to Knox. 'Want to try and get a bit nearer?'

212

'After you, boss,' said Knox.

They edged out towards the middle of the fast-flowing brown water, dodging the debris that rushed by, until the level was up to their thighs. The floor of the stream was soft and yielding and a sudden surge caught them unawares. Knox staggered, and almost fell, but found his footing again. 'The flow is uneven,' said Mariner, bracing himself. 'We just need to get the timing right to get across the deepest section.' He watched and waited. 'OK – now!'

Taking advantage of the next lull, they pushed across the mid-stream, grabbing at sodden vegetation to steady themselves in the shallower water on the opposite bank. Now they were standing directly over the deceptively animated body as it danced and swayed on the water, the clothing grasped firmly by the exposed roots of an overhanging willow. Despite the bloating effects, there was no doubt about the identity. Several dark blemishes on Yasmin's face threw up the possibility that her death had been accompanied by violence. For Shanila and Mohammed Akram, the agonising wait was over, but about to be replaced by something infinitely worse. Millie would be dealing with that. She was probably there right now. Mariner forced himself to not think about it.

Straining to keep his feet in the surging water, Mariner looked around him. It was unlikely, as far as he could see, that Yasmin would have been put in here. He voiced the thought to Knox. 'To get to this point she'd have had to be carried the way we came through the park, which, in the sort of weather we've been having, would have been busy on into the late evening, and far too public. The only time to have done it would have been under cover of night.'

'Even then it would have been risky,' said Knox. 'People walk through this park to get from the main Pershore Road through to Birchill Road.'

'We need to look further up.'

They were hailed by a shout from the other side of the stream. SOCO had arrived in overalls and waders. Mariner talked them across the river.

'It's definitely her?' asked DC Chris Sharp.

'No question,' said Mariner.

Sharp shook his head sadly. 'Trouble is now, that after last night's rain, all your physical evidence will have been washed away.'

'No kidding?' said Mariner. 'Just do what you can, eh?'

Mariner and Knox left SOCO to do their work. Battling against the rushing torrent and clutching at the overhanging bushes, they staggered upstream as far as they could get, to where the stream emerged from a tunnel beneath the road.

Knox looked up towards the parapet: a brick wall topped with waist-high railings. 'She could have gone in here,' he said. 'It would only take a couple of minutes. Stop the car, open the boot and tip her over the edge, she then gets carried downstream.'

'It's a busy road,' said Mariner. 'Late at night would be easier, but you'd still run the risk of someone driving past and seeing.' Looking up on the other side of the road, he noticed they'd come out opposite St Clare's retirement home.

'This stream must connect to the reservoir,' he said.

Knox foraged in his pocket and produced the rather crumpled map. 'You're right, boss. It looks as if we're just further downstream from the wooden footbridge.' Where Ricky Skeet was killed and where Yasmin had arranged a rendezvous with Lewis Everett.

'How does the river progress down to here?'

Knox traced a finger down the map and Mariner couldn't help noticing how chewed his fingernail was. 'It looks as if it must be under the ground, through some kind of tunnel,' Knox said.

'And above the ground it's all green, so more of what we can see: rough woodland, and pretty impenetrable at that. And the river doesn't surface at all?'

They both studied the map. 'Doesn't look like it, boss. The next place it appears on the map is at the spillway next

214

to the reservoir.' Knox looked up. 'You think she could have been put in there?'

'It's where we found her phone.'

'She travelled all this way underground?' Knox was doubtful.

'Let's go and have a look. And get hold of someone who knows more about the river.'

Millie had been adamant at the time. She could handle this on her own. The Akrams had got to know her, and Shanila, in particular, she felt, trusted her. But now she was here it was different. She'd spent the drive over going through all the different possible strategies for breaking the news; set pieces she'd previously rehearsed only during training. Prepare the way but don't prolong the agony, use their names and make it personal. She needed none of it. Taking one look at Millie's face, Shanila knew why she'd come. 'You've found her, haven't you? Oh God, you've found her!' Before she let out a horrible, gut-wrenching howl, that went on as long and as hard as her lungs would allow.

The reservoir had undergone subtle changes since their last visit: where it hadn't been cut down, the foliage had been beaten flat; there was a higher tide mark; and the rank, sulphurous smell had been replaced by a fresher one of damp plant life. Looking more closely they could see that the channel down the middle was moving faster and a torrent of water gushed noisily down the spillway. From the bridge the damage was clearer. The wooden gates, there to control the flow of water, had been cast aside and lay in a jumbled heap at the base of the concrete shelf, along with bricks that had broken loose from the mouth of the half collapsed tunnel.

'It's flowing pretty fast now, fast enough to take a pretty big object with it,' Mariner said.

'But you saw how it was on the day Hewitt brought us here. It was barely a trickle because we'd had no rain. It

215

would hardly have carried a feather down with it.'

'But Hewitt also said something about the water collecting and releasing every so often. Maybe the day Yasmin was killed was one of those days. We need to find out more about this.'

'Mr Mariner?' The elderly gentleman who approached them looked as if he was almost ready to join Lily in St Clare's. He came unsteadily along the path, using a stick for support. When he got almost to them he proffered a hand. 'Eric Dwyer,' he said. 'One of your colleagues asked me to meet you here. I'm the chairman of the local river conservation group.' Dwyer's cheeks were weathered a rosy pink, but much of the rest of his face was obscured by glasses and a pair of extravagant mutton chop whiskers.

'So you know all about this reservoir,' said Mariner, shaking the bony hand.

'I dare say I know as much as anyone.' He looked out over the water. 'It was built at the turn of the century to top up the canal system in times of drought. It's what's known as a feeder lake: the water diverting away from and back into the canal.' He peered over the bridge. 'My, my, that's taken a battering.'

'I understand that these gates were meant to open under pressure.'

'That's right.' He went on to describe what Mariner had already surmised.

'How big a release is it when it goes? Enough to carry something big with it, say seven or eight stone in weight?' Mariner wondered if Dwyer had any idea what kind of object they were talking about.

If he did he wasn't curious enough to ask. 'Given the gradient of the incline, I'd say easily. I've never seen this one in full spate, but I've seen other similar mechanisms and they usually flow at about ten cubic feet per second. That's quite a force.'

'How often does this release occur?'

'At this time of year, as you'd expect, not very often.

The drier the weather the longer it takes for the pressure to build. It'd be once a day, if you're lucky.'

'And would there be any way of telling what time of day this was occurring recently?'

'Unfortunately not. It would depend entirely on the flow into the reservoir.'

'And after heavy rain, such as we had the other night?'

'After heavy rain the water would just flow straight through, much as it's doing now. The gates would be permanently open, almost as if the reservoir were just part of the river. The river flows to here from its source in the Waseley Hills right through to Spaghetti Junction. After last night's storms, by the time it got to this point it would be torrential, hence the damage. That will take some sorting out.'

'So what's down there?' Mariner pointed into the tunnel.

'At this end, a series of valves and valve vaults to control the flow.'

'Would they hinder anything passing through?'

'To a degree. The mechanisms are old, have been there for decades and under no particular pressure: but the sudden influx of last night's rain was clearly enough to break the sluice gates and could have equally damaged or destroyed the valves too.'

'But we've had rain like this before. Why would this happen now?'

'Probably because of the work we've been doing upstream, clearing all the rubbish and dredging out where the river has got clogged up.' He shook his head regretfully. 'We've been too thorough.' He looked back over the pool itself. 'The water hasn't had such a clear run for years.'

'Sounds like hard work.'

'It's not always. We're quite a sociable group, too.'

'Ever had a guy called Shaun Pryce in the group?'

'Shaun Pryce? I don't remember the name.' Mariner described Pryce to Dwyer.

217

'He doesn't fit our profile. We're mainly middle-aged, retired folk with too much time on our hands and a concern for the preservation of our city. But that said, people come and go. Occasionally we get more ecologically aware students who come and join us.'

'I wonder if you could let me have a list of your members some time.'

'Consider it done.'

Mariner looked out over the wasteland of the reservoir. 'So your work hadn't brought you as far as this, then?' Mariner asked.

'Not yet. We're running a bit behind schedule, dependent as we are on volunteers. But we did all the prep work some time ago.'

'What does that involve?'

'Myself and another member coming down here with someone from the rivers authority to look at what there is and what needs doing. That's how I know about the tunnel.'

'When did you come here?'

'It would have been in about March, I suppose. We were being somewhat optimistic, as it turns out.'

'And who came with you?'

'Sheila Carr was the other member. It's interesting because I'm sure that at that time the railings weren't broken. It's not something we put on our work list.'

'Well, thanks for coming down here, Mr Dwyer, it's been very helpful.'

Watching him go, Mariner took another look around, noticing anew the break in the timber railings. 'Lily mentioned that,' he recalled.

'It's not that recent,' Knox was examining them. 'The wood on the inside of the break is weathered too.'

'I think we do have to consider it a probability that Yasmin was put in the water here,' Mariner said.

Knox nodded agreement. 'But is this where she was killed?'

*

218

Arriving at the Newton Street mortuary later that afternoon, Mariner's stomach began to bubble gently. Outside, the temperature had soared again: a signal that the storms had been just a blip on the meteorological radar.

'Lucky for us that they happened at all,' remarked pathologist Stuart Croghan. 'Or Yasmin's body might have remained hidden.'

This wasn't the first child murder Mariner had worked on, but contrary to popular belief, the average detective rarely deals with murder cases, children or otherwise. The experience was always guaranteed to be traumatic, even though the meeting would be conducted in Croghan's office with reference to photographs, rather than walking around the cadaver itself, in the manner of all good TV detectives.

Croghan had been working non-stop since the body had been brought in a couple of hours ago and already the file on Yasmin Akram was thick with detailed notes. Much of this information would be saved for the inquest, so Croghan confined himself to the salient points, knowing exactly what would be of practical use to Mariner now.

'Death was by asphyxiation,' Croghan told him. 'She was strangled with some kind of ligature, probably some kind of wire. There's no apparent discolouration or abrasion in the ligature wound so it was a clean or treated wire.'

'Plastic coated?'

'Could be. It was quite soft, around a twenty-eight gauge – about three millimetres thick. You can tell that from the shape and depth of the groove.'

'Some kind of electrical wire, perhaps?' Mariner was hopeful.

'It's possible but I couldn't be certain.'

'But not an accident, then.'

'Absolutely not. She was already dead when she went into the water. There are diatoms in the throat area but not in the bloodstream, heart or lungs.' Meaning, she hadn't inhaled water. The microscopic algae were reliable indicators.

'Decomposition is patchy though, which is unusual, not

219

in keeping with being totally submerged throughout. Different areas of the body seem to have decomposed at different rates.'

'Consistent with spending a few days in a drainage tunnel with an irregular through-flow?'

'That would probably do it, yes.'

'How long had she been exposed to the water?' he asked.

'I'd say several days. The decomposition pattern is going to make it hard to pinpoint the time of death very accurately. We'll analyse stomach contents but there's a limit to what that can tell us, too.'

'But we're looking at her being killed roughly when?'

'It's more than a week ago.'

Mariner gave Croghan a look that said, 'Thanks for nothing'.

'I did warn you,' the pathologist said.

'Anything else that would help?' asked Mariner.

'Quite a bit of post-mortem bruising that would imply that she had a rough journey after she was put in the water.' Yasmin progressing through that underground tunnel.

'Any sign of a sexual assault?' asked Mariner.

'No physical signs, as far as I can see. And from the internal I'd have said that she wasn't sexually active. However, she's not wearing any underwear. Curious.'

Croghan was right, that was curious.

'So Lee's message could have been confirming their meeting,' said Millie. She looked shattered after the visit to the Akrams, but had insisted on being present for the debrief. They'd gathered again in Mariner's office: it was becoming a regular club meeting. 'Yasmin disappeared at around the time Lee left. He could have done it before he went. Perhaps he wanted her to go with him and she refused.'

'And the missing underwear would mean some kind of sexual activity, or the start of it,' Knox added.

'But as Croghan said, this doesn't look like a spur of the

220

moment thing. It smacks of premeditation. I can't imagine that Lee would set out to kill Yasmin.'

'No. It would have to be someone who just happened to have about their person a piece of electrical wire,' put in Knox. 'Like Shaun Pryce.'

'Maybe that's what Ricky saw,' said Millie. 'Someone assaulting and killing Yasmin.'

'So why didn't the killer tip him over the bridge too?'

There were still so many questions. 'I should go and talk to Yasmin's parents,' said Mariner. 'They'll want to know what comes next.'

'I'll come with you, sir.'

The smiling face of Yasmin Akram beamed at Mariner from where the photo sat at the centre of the shrine for family and friends to pay their respects in the sitting room, where Millie and Mariner had been shunted to wait. Bypassing the huddle of people on the pavement outside, they'd been shown directly into the cool, formal room that was lavishly furnished and spotlessly clean and, Mariner guessed, rarely used.

The house was busy, but in here an eerie silence reigned. If the body were not still being held at the mortuary, they would, Millie told him, be looking into an open coffin. A knock on the door preceded Amira, her dark mourning clothes emphasising the paleness of her skin. Millie got up and gave her a hug. 'How's your mother bearing up?'

'She's OK. My father's taking care of her.' Her face crumpled. 'All this is my fault,' Amira said. 'If I hadn't encouraged her—'

'That's not true, Amira,' said Millie firmly. 'Someone else did this. They are responsible. You only wanted what was best for Yasmin.'

'I've let them all down.' Overcome with grief, she began to weep, and while Millie attempted to console her, Mariner was suddenly struck by the inappropriateness of his presence here. This intrusion on the family's grief, bringing the constant reminder of unnatural death was one of the most repulsive aspects of the job. He got up suddenly. 'I'll come back another time,' he said.

Millie chose to stay, and when Mariner drove away he found himself close to Anna's house. Suddenly he was aware that he'd been letting down a number of people too. The Akrams he could do little about for now, but he could make amends with Anna. He took a chance and stopped by her house, but was disconcerted to see an unfamiliar car on the drive. Laid across the parcel shelf was a green sweatshirt bearing the embroidered Manor Park logo. He parked and walked round to the side of the house, from where he could smell the charcoal fumes from a barbecue and hear the sound of music and laughing, as if a party was in full swing. The voices were predominantly male.

Mariner opened the side gate. The first person he saw was Jamie, typically detached from the group, pacing the edge of the lawn, head down, muttering to himself and wringing the hem of his polo shirt in his hands. He was wearing shorts: something that even a few months ago he wouldn't have countenanced. Good old Manor Park.

Clustered at the far end of the patio, nearest the kitchen door, Anna stood, leaning back against the picnic table, wine glass in hand and deep in conversation with a man lounging below her on a garden chair, his back to Mariner. Anna wore a scrap of a vest and a denim skirt short enough to offer the Kingsmead girls some strong competition. Her face was open and smiling and attention focused one hundred per cent on her guest, whose gaze would have been at about the level of her smooth, lightly tanned thighs. No marks for guessing where his mind would be.

'Any more drinks out there?' called another man's voice from the kitchen; someone else clearly at home.

Sickened, Mariner turned to go, but he was too late. Without even seeming to glance in his direction, Jamie had seen him.

'Spectre Man,' he said loudly.

In those early days when Anna had addressed him as 'Inspector Mariner', Jamie had found it impossible to get his mouth around it, Spectre Man being the closest he could get. Highly appropriate today when Mariner felt exactly that: the spectre appearing at the feast.

'Hi, Jamie,' Mariner said.

Hearing Jamie speak Anna had immediately looked up and Mariner tried to read her face. Surprise certainly, but anything else? Hard to tell. She left her guest and came over. Big smile but no kiss: maybe he was giving off the wrong signals, or maybe not. 'Hi. We weren't expecting you. Coming in?'

We? 'You've got visitors.'

'That's OK. Come and join us. You can meet Simon and—'

'I'm not much in a party mood. We found Yasmin Akram.'

'Yes, I heard about it on the news. I'm sorry. Why don't you stay anyway and have a drink?'

He did consider it, but only for a split second. 'No. It's fine. There's a lot to do.'

'All right.'

It was one of those occasions when she disappointed him. It had been a tough day and Mariner wanted to share it with someone. He was restless, and for once his own company wasn't enough, so short of anything better to do, he went back to Granville Lane. After a while Millie returned from the Akrams' house, looking drained, and by nine thirty only the two of them remained in the incident room.

'Come on,' Mariner said, 'I'll buy you a curry.' Then he realised what he'd said.

Millie just laughed. 'I know a place where you can get the best,' she said. The place turned out to be her ground floor flat, in Acocks Green.

'This is fantastic,' said Mariner as he scooped up rogan

223

josh with a spicy naan that was as light as a feather. He hadn't eaten all day, and until now hadn't realised how hungry he was.

'Don't get too excited,' Millie said. 'I didn't cook it myself. My mum sends it over now and again. I think it helps to salve her conscience when the rest of the family won't have anything to do with me. Dad doesn't know she does it.'

'Oh?'

'Long story,' Millie said.

'I've got time. If you want to, that is.'

'Why not?' She dropped her chunk of bread into her dish and sighed. 'My parents aren't quite so enlightened as Yasmin's. They always expected me to be a traditional Pakistani wife. I had to learn to cook and sew – all the usual. But when I got to about Yasmin's age, I started to realise that there could be more to life than that. I was doing pretty well at school and decided I wanted to go to university. I fancied being a forensic scientist. But my dad has a rather more traditional view of the female role than the Akrams. Within our community the whole *raison d'être* of a woman is to look after her husband and produce lots of healthy children. I would have to do it the hard way. Over a number of years, I saved enough money to start paying my way through college, but a few weeks before I was due to go, Dad got hold of my building society book, confiscated my savings and that was the end of it.'

'Christ, I had no idea.'

'Naturally, this led to a massive row with my dad. I called him a lot of things that I shouldn't have and my family and the rest of the community shunned me. I left home and came to live with a sympathetic auntie in Alum Rock, and this job was the nearest I could get to what I really want to be.' Partly to conceal her emotion she got up and carried her plate to the kitchen.

Mariner followed her through. 'Do you still have ambitions for forensics?' he asked as they stacked dishes in the dishwasher.

224

'I don't know. I like what I do now.'

'You're bloody good at it,' he said.

'Thanks.'

'I mean it. You've built a great relationship with the family.'

'Today was horrible, having to tell them.'

'It was always going to be. It's one of the bits that doesn't get any easier.'

'I keep trying to imagine what they must be going through. Their own child. It must be—' Her eyes watered and she wiped at them crossly.

Mariner put a hand on her shoulder. 'You made it as easy for them as you could,' he said. 'You supported them. It's all you can do. You can't bring her back.'

'No, but I still wish I could.'

Afterwards, Mariner couldn't really be sure how it happened. One minute he had his arm around Millie comforting her, the next her lips were fused to his, her tongue, sweet and spicy, probing his mouth. Maybe the curry had aphrodisiacal properties, or perhaps seeing Anna like that had left him gagging for it. Whatever it was it seemed like the most natural thing in the world that he should kiss her back, his hands roaming her shapely body. And by the time her hand slid down to unzip him he was already hard.

They made love urgently, only making it as far as the sofa, Mariner's trousers shoved down to his thighs. For him it was over in minutes, too soon for Millie, who continued her frenzied pumping on his softening member for what seemed like an eternity, until spasms rocked her and she finally allowed him to withdraw, deflated and sore.

'Sorry,' Mariner said. 'That wasn't up to much.'

'No.' She seemed not to mind. 'But probably about what you'd expect from a couple of drunks. I'll call you a cab.'

Thankfully, Mariner made it inside his own front door before his bowels decided to erupt. He awoke the next morning, still half-clothed, mind and body feeling lousy in

225

equal measures. His system clearly wasn't accustomed to industrial-strength curry and Millie's mother's, good though it was at the time, had consigned him to the bathroom for much of the night. He'd a thumping hangover and his dick hurt about as much as his ego. He didn't think Millie was the type to broadcast details of their pathetic encounter around the station, but you could never really tell with women.

When the phone rang, he really hoped it wasn't Anna. It wasn't. It was Mark Russell. 'I thought you'd want to know, sir, we've got another body.'

Somehow Mariner dragged himself under the shower. Every time he moved his head, pain jangled round it like the vibrations in a bell. Forcing down coffee and painkillers, he put on his sunglasses against the agonising glare of sunlight and got a taxi to Granville Lane, where he saw that his own car had miraculously materialised in the station car park. The movement of the journey in had made him feel queasy again, but somehow he managed to stagger upstairs, roll down the blinds in his office and make it to his desk, where Mark Russell came to brief him on the latest discovery.

'She was found a little way downstream from where Yasmin was found.' Russell was saying, but Mariner was momentarily distracted by Millie walking into the bull pen. She smiled a brief 'good morning' to them both through the glass partition, but her face gave nothing away.

'Sir?' Russell said.

'I'm listening.'

'She was found by Ben: a liver and white springer spaniel who's apparently a keen swimmer. His owner, a Mr Lovell, took him to the park this morning as usual, and Ben had what I s'pose you'd call a "swamp day". Mr Lovell had to go looking for him, and that was when he saw the woman's body, caught on an old bit of fencing that runs alongside the stream. Yesterday, that part of the park would have been completely under water but the flooding has subsided overnight.'

'And what do we know about her?' Mariner forced himself to concentrate.

'Not much yet. She's an older woman: late forties or fifties. The pathologist at the scene said she's been in the water a lot longer than Yasmin: could be weeks or even months. She's got similar kinds of bruising, though.'

'So she could have been released at the same time, when the mechanism disintegrated.'

'It's likely. They think there won't be much in the way of forensics, thanks to decomposition, but we've got a pair of earrings that may help in identification, and there was a large splinter of wood caught in her cardigan.'

'From the bridge?' Mariner thought of the railings.

'SOCO are down there now.'

'Do we know how she died?'

'Her skull has been smashed, but Croghan seemed to think that may have happened when she felt into the water.'

Mariner fought down a wave of nausea. 'Any ID?'

'Not yet. Tony Knox is going through the missing persons.'

'OK, let me know when you find anything.'

The best solution to avoid throwing up, Mariner found, was to remain as inactive as possible. There were things to do but, for once, he'd let the answers come to him. He got Russell to bring him some water, then began sifting through the messages that had accumulated on his desk. He didn't trust himself to return any of the three calls from Anna and consigned the yellow message slips to the bin. The next was from a Sahira Masud. Mariner couldn't place the name, not even in connection with Yasmin Akram, so began sifting through the thousands of names on file in his head, in an attempt to attach meaning to this one. In the end he had to pick up the telephone to find out.

'I live next door but one to your mother,' Mrs Masud

227

reminded him, patiently. 'I'm afraid she's had a slight stroke.'

The words had more of an impact than Mariner could ever have imagined, temporarily displacing his own fragility. As the contact between himself and his mother had dwindled over a number of years, Mariner had always thought that he would be quite detached from any such news. He'd been wrong. Now he felt bad that he hadn't returned her calls. Was that what she'd been ringing about, to tell him she wasn't feeling well? 'Will she be all right?' he asked, with far more anxiety in his voice than he would have expected.

'She's fine.' Mrs Masud was instantly reassuring. 'But they've taken her into Warwick Hospital to keep an eye on her overnight. You might want to—'

'Yes. Thanks for letting me know.' Any decisions about visiting her he would make himself, after weighing up whether it was likely to make her worse or better.

'She's on ward eight.'

'Thanks.' Mariner looked up to see Millie standing in the doorway, swinging his car keys. She came and laid them on his desk, all the time studying his face, which Mariner guessed was probably an interesting shade of grey.

'Everything OK, sir?' she asked.

Mariner nodded and instantly regretted it. 'Look, about last night,' he said. 'I was pretty pissed.'

She returned a wan smile. 'You and me both, sir. To be honest I can't remember much about it. Probably best forgotten.'

'Yes, I'm sure you're right.' Mariner was weak with relief.

'In my job I move around a lot,' she went on. 'I try to bag an Inspector at every OCU I'm assigned to. You did enough.' Mariner gaped at her. 'Joke,' she said, deadpan, before walking away.

Tony Knox was next in line. The bacon sandwich in his fist

228

nearly had Mariner reaching for the bin, but he was oblivious to Mariner's state. Then again, he didn't look all that hot himself. His shirt was creased and slightly grimy and he didn't appear to have had time for a shave today.

'We've got a possible match on the body, boss. Barbara Kincaid. IC 1 female, aged forty-four, reported missing back in March from an address on Banbury Road.'

'That's what? About half a mile from the reservoir?'

'The other side of the station. According to the husband's statement at the time, she'd been suffering mental health problems: depression. She left the house sometime late one night and didn't come back. The description of what she was wearing on the day she disappeared matches clothing on the body, and we've asked him to come in and identify some jewellery she was wearing.'

'Russell said something about a splinter of wood?'

'Yeah. It's a possible match with the wooden railings of the reservoir bridge.'

'So she went in at the same place Yasmin did.'

'It looks like it.'

'She could have been the one who leaned on them and broke them. It wouldn't have taken much. They were pretty well rotten through. What do you think?'

'Either that or she threw herself in, got tangled up in the drainage mechanism. It's a bit desperate though.'

'Desperate feelings lead you to do desperate things. Let me know when identity's confirmed.'

The final straw was Fiske, who hovered in the doorway, distinctly reticent, and Mariner was soon to find out why. 'The Skeet family have made a complaint,' he said.

'About what?'

'About the way the disappearance of their son was handled, that it wasn't given enough of a priority. How far do you think they'd take it?'

'What do you mean?'

'Is Colleen Skeet the vindictive type?'

229

If it hadn't required the effort of standing up, Mariner would have been tempted to walk over and punch his smarmy face. 'Colleen Skeet isn't any "type", sir. As I seem to remember it was thinking of her family as a "type" that got us into trouble. Right now, she's a woman grieving for her son. I couldn't begin to understand what's going on in her head.'

'I thought you said you knew her.'

'I know Colleen, sir. I know very little about those who might have any influence over her, especially at a time like this.'

'Will you talk to her?'

'I'm not sure that that's a very good idea.'

'I do hope that as a fellow officer I will be able to count on your support, Inspector.'

Not a request, just a statement. That was a hard one. Mariner felt not a shred of fellowship for the man.

Chapter Sixteen

Fiske had given Mariner the nudge he needed though, and by mid-afternoon, having exhausted all the paperwork he could reasonably do at this time, and starting to feel halfway human again, he ran out of options. He hadn't had the guts to face Colleen directly since Ricky's death. Now was as good a time as any, and from there, he could go over to see his mother. Moving very carefully, Mariner picked up his jacket and keys and walked out to his car.

He went to pass through an exit door at the same moment as someone else, being escorted from the building by Mark Russell.

'I'm sorry.' To avoid a collision the other man stepped back, exactly mirroring Mariner's action.

'After you.' Mariner found himself looking into a vaguely familiar face, but there was no reciprocal recognition and he dismissed it. It happened all the time in this job, as a consequence of meeting so many people. Then, crossing the car park, it came to him. He went back to reception.

'That man who just left. What was he doing here with Russell?' he asked Ella.

'I think he's the guy who came in to identify his wife's jewellery. The second body that was found. Poor bloke.'

'Can I use the phone?' Mariner called up to Russell. 'The body found today, I thought her name was Kincaid.'

'Ms,' said Russell. 'She kept her maiden name when she

got married.' He told Mariner her married name.

Poor bloke indeed, thought Mariner.

He found Colleen sitting smoking on her front step in the yellow late afternoon sunshine, a grotesque pastiche of contentment. 'You've got a bloody nerve,' was all she said as he walked up the path.

'I'm sorry, Colleen: really sorry.' Was there ever a way of instilling those words with adequate feeling? Mariner doubted it.

'I bet you are,' she said. 'Sorry that you're all in the shit.'

She was wrong about that, but there was no point in arguing. 'Are you really going through with it?'

'Yes she fucking is,' snarled a voice from behind her. It belonged to a giant of a man with thick muscles and apparently no neck. Steve, Mariner guessed. 'So why don't you piss off out of here and stop harassing her?'

Yeah, why didn't he? 'I'm sorry, Colleen,' Mariner said again. 'Ricky was a great kid.' And he turned and walked back to his car.

'Tom?' she called after him, her voice smaller than before. He looked back. 'I know it wasn't your fault.'

Mariner nodded briefly and walked on.

Back in the car, Mariner thought again about the connection he'd learned about from Russell. The reservoir, Yasmin Akram, Barbara Kincaid and, through her husband, the link between them all: Shaun Pryce, with his predilection for middle-aged housewives. Mariner wondered if there was any way Barbara Kincaid could have known Shaun Pryce too. He must know her husband. He'd have to drive along Banbury Road on his way out to Leamington to visit his mother. That was fortuitous.

There was a considerably delayed response when he rang the doorbell of the three-floor terrace, but eventually the door opened on Brian Goodway. His shoulders were hunched, and even on this warm afternoon he wore a thick cardigan over his open-collared shirt, his body temperature thrown off balance by delayed shock. He was apologetic. 'I was upstairs. The kids are at home but they never answer the door, even though it's usually for them. Teenagers, eh?' He shook his head despairingly but his heart wasn't in it, he hadn't got the energy.

Mariner felt another flush of sympathy for the man. 'Mr Goodway, I know this is a difficult time for you, but I understand you identified your wife's jewellery this afternoon.'

'That's right.'

'As you know, I'm investigating Yasmin Akram's death. This may be important. I wonder if you could spare a few minutes.'

'Um, yes, of course.' He seemed disorientated and vague and Mariner almost changed his mind. But he was here now and followed Goodway past bikes propped in the hallway into an untidy lounge with a high ceiling and a wide bay with sash windows. Like the Akrams' sitting room, it felt cool and unlived in, probably because most of the space was taken up by a polished walnut baby grand piano.

'Barbara's,' Brian Goodway said, although Mariner hadn't asked. 'She used to teach piano part-time. The number of pupils had dwindled over the years but she liked to do it. It was something for herself.' Already used to speaking about his wife in the past tense, but then she'd been missing from his life for months.

'Is that why she kept her maiden name?'

'It was like a stage name. Barbara was a performer: music, amateur theatre, that kind of thing.'

For the first time, Mariner saw the black and white portrait photograph. The subject was stunningly glamorous. 'Is that her?'

'Yes, taken a few years ago now.' Not the woman Mariner would have identified as the natural partner for Goodway.

'The teaching was supplementary,' he was saying. 'At the time we married she had quite a reputation locally,

233

so understandably didn't want to lose that. Inevitably though, once the children came along, the family became more of a priority and she had to put her other ambitions on hold.'

'That can't have been easy.'

'No. I know she found it frustrating at times. She was very artistic. But she continued to provide accompaniment for a local drama group from time to time. Please sit down, Inspector. Can I get you anything? A cup of tea?'

'That would be good, thank you.' It was the last thing Mariner wanted, but it would give Brian Goodway something else to focus on while they talked. He sat down on a lumpy sofa, draped with an Indian print throw. Somewhere in the house, a low bass throbbed a steady beat. Looking around it was clear that this room wasn't a priority for decoration, being papered with ivory-coloured anaglypta that had gone out of fashion ten years ago. There was a vertical strip from the light switch to the ceiling that had been torn away, and fresh pink plasterwork inserted. It was precisely what Mariner had been hoping for.

Goodway returned with two mugs, handing one awkwardly to Mariner, before perching on the piano stool opposite.

'They said they found her downstream from the reservoir,' he said, talking into his tea mug. 'Near to where Yasmin was found.'

'So I gather,' said Mariner.

'Oh God.' Dropping his gaze, Goodway fumbled in his pockets, coming out with a handkerchief, which he used to noisily blow his nose and conceal the fact that he was weeping. 'I'm sorry.'

'No, I'm sorry, Mr Goodway. I realise how hard this must be for you. But I won't keep you any longer than necessary.' Mariner turned his attention to his tea, to give Goodway time to compose himself. The dark green mug had seen better days and Mariner could barely pick out what was left of the design: the row of cartoonish trees that

234

had succumbed to the regular abrasion of a dishwasher. He took a scalding mouthful.

Goodway sighed. 'It wasn't a huge surprise when Barbara went missing, you know,' he said. 'She'd been depressed on and off for years, and since Christmas it had got much worse. We've got the children, of course, and for the last five years we've been looking after my mother, too. Sometimes it got on top of her. It was exhausting. Barbara said more than once that she could fully sympathise with these women who just walked away from it all and never came back. But I never thought she'd really—'

'Did your wife often walk near the reservoir?'

Goodway shook his head. 'I don't know. I didn't even know there was a reservoir there until the body of that boy was found there and I saw it on the news.'

Just like the rest of us then, thought Mariner.

'Barbara went out walking a lot, particularly in the evenings. She needed to, to get a break from everything. But I didn't really know where she went. There are parks around, and I suppose I just thought that she walked around the streets.'

'Did your wife ever talk about meeting anyone?'

'No,' said Goodway instantly, then he seemed to recon- sider. 'It did cross my mind once or twice. Barbara had been an attractive woman, but I'm sure—'

'I'm sorry,' said Mariner. 'I'm just exploring the possi- bilities.'

Goodway frowned into his mug. 'The thing I don't understand is that the reservoir is miles from here.'

'There's a quicker way down to it from behind the station,' said Mariner. 'Your wife must have known about it.'

'She lived in this area all her life,' said Goodway, as if that explained it. He looked up at Mariner hopefully. 'I keep wondering if perhaps it could have been an accident,' he said. 'The children ... it would be so much easier ...'

Mariner thought of the broken railings but he didn't want

to give the man false hope. 'There will have to be an inquest of course. But it's possible, Mr Goodway. The coroner will consider all the evidence.'

'Barbara was taking anti-depressants at the time. She wasn't always thinking clearly.'

'I understand,' said Mariner. 'Thanks for your time, Mr Goodway.' He got up to go, pausing by the strip of fresh plasterwork. 'You've had some electrical work done.'

'Actually, it was months ago. I'm not very practical around the house and rewiring was long overdue. I haven't quite got round to decorating again.'

'Looks like quite a job. Did you do it yourself?'

'Heavens no. I'm hopeless, I'm afraid. We had a proper electrician come in to do it.'

'Was it by any chance Shaun Pryce?'

For a moment Goodway looked startled. 'Yes, it was. How—?'

'He modelled for students at your school.'

Then Goodway remembered. 'Ah, of course, you've seen the art work on the walls.' He hesitated. 'It was Barbara who discovered him, you know, at one of her drama productions. I got home from school one day and here he was. We got talking and he said that really he was an actor. I thought he was so striking that I asked him to come and model for the girls at school.'

'Did Shaun Pryce model for Yasmin's class?' Mariner asked.

'Not her class, but I think he sat for the art club on one occasion.'

'Your head said he was quite friendly with the girls.'

'Yes. In fact it became a bit of a problem. He was a bit too friendly.'

And what about your wife? Mariner wanted to ask. How friendly was Shaun Pryce with her? But now was not the time. The man had more than enough to contend with.

Mariner would have liked to report this latest news back to

the team and get on to Shaun Pryce right away, but he had put off seeing his mother for long enough.

He decided to drive over, taking the M42. Even though the rush hour was officially over, it was still heaving with traffic. Hard to believe that just a few years ago this was the open, green countryside of the North Worcestershire way. On one of his frequent Sunday walks, he'd had the dubious pleasure of peeing on the foundations, right where the services were now.

His mother had rarely been ill. Not enough to be hospitalised, anyway. She wouldn't make a good patient. Maybe this episode would make her consider her own mortality and think about tying up any loose ends. His gut tingled with an edge of anticipation. Maybe now she would finally give in and tell him.

He'd been seven years old when he'd first confronted his mother with the question that had been increasingly bothering him, and that he was being asked by some of his schoolfriends. 'How come everyone else has got a mum and a dad, but I've only got a mum?' Over time, of course, he'd come to realise that somewhere on the planet he must have a dad like everyone else, but that for some unknown reason, the man had failed to take any active part in Mariner's life. Nor did his mother ever talk about him. When he was a kid, it had opened the way for all kinds of romantic notions, but with adulthood came the realisation that the truth was likely to be far more mundane: that his father had simply been married to another woman.

It had crossed his mind on occasions that his mother could have been bluffing all these years, and that in reality she didn't have any idea who his father was, but in the midst of her vagueness there had always been consistency. And once, when she'd thought he was too young to notice, he remembered overhearing her say to a friend how much like his father he looked.

It took him just over half an hour to get to Warwick. The

237

hospital was a little way out of the town, sandwiched between a housing estate and a business park: the hybrid collection of buildings a reflection of the town itself. He could have been driving into the car park of a supermarket with its brash Pizza Hut style building squatting alongside its darker Victorian predecessors. Ward eight, Coronary Care, was on the second floor of the old hospital and he'd arrived with a cluster of friends and relatives just at the start of visiting hours. He spotted his mother right away. A nurse was at her bedside, checking her blood pressure.

'This is a turn-up,' Rose said, when she saw him approaching. 'West Midlands police having a quiet spell, are they?' The whiplash sarcasm reminded Mariner of where he'd developed a taste for it.

'Hello, son, how nice to see you,' he countered.

She was unyielding. 'I don't have to spell it out, do I?'

'If you did I'd really think something was wrong.'

'This is my son,' she told the nurse. 'He's a policeman.' Most mothers would have instilled the statement with some degree of pride, but Mariner's managed to imbue it with savoured distaste. Mariner could recall with great clarity the look on her face the first time he'd turned up unannounced at her house, in uniform. It had been his intention to shock her, of course, and he'd succeeded. 'You've done this to spite me, haven't you?' she'd said.

'Don't flatter yourself. Why does everything have to be about you? Perhaps I've actually done this because it's what I want.' How could he begin to explain that after the unlimited freedoms of his unruly childhood he craved discipline, order and routine. Only after he'd had that grounding was he ready to flex his individuality again, when CID had offered him the chance.

'So how are you?' he asked now. 'What happened?'

'I went a bit dizzy and my arm went numb, that's all. But now it's passed and I'm ready to go home. Except, of course, they won't let me until the man from del Monte says "yes". So I'm stuck here until the morning.' Any speculation about

238

the origins of his own belligerent nature was always instantly dispelled by any conversation with his mother.

'What were you doing?' he asked.

'I was up a stepladder, decorating the hall.' Said so casually, it was easy to forget that she was a woman fast approaching seventy. Once she'd got used to the fact that he'd left home for good, she'd reverted to her youthful independence.

'Was that what you were ringing me about?'

'There was something I wanted to tell you.'

'What?'

'Well, obviously it's nothing important enough for you to call me back. So it'll keep.'

Which probably meant it was nothing at all. She was punishing him for the time it had taken him to respond. Mariner was tired of his mother's games, and he could be as stubborn as she was. He wasn't going to give her the satisfaction of begging her to tell him. Or reveal the extent of the guilt he felt because he hadn't returned her calls. She seemed about to tell him anyway but changed her mind. Sod it. She'd do it when she was ready.

'I have been busy,' he said.

'I know. I saw you on the local news. But even a phone call would have been nice.'

'Yes.'

'Anyway, now you're here you may as well make yourself useful.' She leaned over and opened the cabinet by the bed. 'Mrs Masud has brought me all these things that I don't really need. It was kind of her but will you take some of it back to the house?'

'Yes, of course.'

She sorted out a plastic carrier bag of things that were surplus to requirement.

'I'll come and see you tomorrow.'

'Twice in two days, eh? Must be a record. My cup runneth over.'

*

239

Outwardly, the tiny, neat cul-de-sac in Leamington where his mother still lived had barely changed since he was resident there too. The two of them had moved suddenly from their London home when Mariner was about three and it was the only place he could remember living as a child. Built between the wars, it originally belonged to his grandparents and they'd shared it right up until Granny and Grandpa had retired to a bungalow in Pembrokeshire, where he'd then spent some summer holidays. Tonight, he could hardly get down the road, which like many was coping badly with the increase in car usage. Even with all them parked half on the pavement, a practice of which Mariner strongly disapproved, there was barely enough room for another to pass.

The street rang to the shouts of the usual motley gang of neighbourhood kids playing and getting along, or not, regardless of shape, size or skin colour. One or two adults were out too, tending their gardens as dusk fell on the balmy summer evening. Mariner pushed open the iron gate, which sported a recent coat of paint, as did the glossy white windowsills of his mother's house. Guilt nibbled at him again. Rose had given up waiting for him and got on with it herself, which had put her where she was. It surprised him. His mother had always eschewed the trappings of constant acquisition and modernisation, so it was unusual that she'd have bothered with decorating at all.

Walking up the drive, he saw Mrs Masud and thanked her for ringing him.

'I wasn't sure if anyone else would have contacted you.' Mariner wondered what she meant by 'anyone else'. Who else was there?

His mother was one of the few remaining white residents in the street. During the late 60s and early 70s Asian families had begun moving in, prompting a mass exodus of whites, and leaving his mother in the minority. She'd barely even noticed. He let himself in the front door. The house smelled overwhelmingly of emulsion and white spirit

240

and it took him a couple of minutes to work out what it was that looked different. The hall stairs and landing were coated in fresh paint, but then he'd known about that already. Then he realised: it was the tidiness.

Following his grandparents' departure, the house that he'd grown up in had always been awash with clutter. Treasures collected along the way from every conceivable source, saved for a rainy day, or in case they came in useful; mementoes and keepsakes, all randomly arranged on shelves and furniture, with barely a space between them. The genes responsible for orderliness were something else he'd inherited from his father.

Now, many of the shelves and surfaces were bare in preparation for more decorating. She was blitzing the place. He walked through the downstairs rooms and each one was the same. It was not before time. The place hadn't been touched in years, but even so, he couldn't help wondering what had prompted the sudden burst of activity. It crossed his mind that there could be more to the hospital admission than he'd thought, but rejected the idea almost immediately. Everything had been too relaxed.

Upstairs in her bedroom was a more familiar scene, the dressing table crowded with trinkets. He put away the things that he'd brought home for her and, out of habit, checked each of the other rooms. In the spare room he found a stack of black bin liners stuffed full to bursting, with what had once taken up shelf space downstairs; there were old clothes and bric à brac; artefacts that stirred memories of Mariner's childhood. Some of it was from the second large bedroom, the one that nobody had used since he left home. It too had been decorated. It was still a far cry from Lewis Everett's room. His mother was putting things in order for something, but right now he had little capacity for another mystery. Mariner returned the rest of the items he'd brought with him to what he deemed to be the most appropriate places, and left.

*

241

On the way home he had to drive very near to Tony Knox's house. Following the visit to Brian Goodway, Mariner wanted to sound him out. The ground floor lights were encouraging, but the look on Knox's face when he came to the door was not. The fumes nearly knocked Mariner off his feet.

'All right, boss?' Knox was surly and suspicious to an identical degree.

'I wanted to talk to you about something. Can I come in?'

With great reluctance, Knox stepped aside to let Mariner pass. Mariner almost wished he hadn't bothered. The living room looked just that. A lot of living had been going on in here and some clean air wouldn't go amiss. Knox repositioned himself in the dent in the sofa opposite the TV that had been permanently created by a lot of sitting. Around him was the detritus that could only have accrued over considerable time: a handful of mugs, several squat, green beer bottles, a plate bearing the remains of an unappetising looking sandwich. Even Knox himself looked lived in, wearing a stained T-shirt over scruffy, faded jeans. And Mariner noticed that the trademark buzz-cut was beginning to grow into a crew.

'Theresa not back yet?' Mariner asked, unnecessarily.

Knox grunted. 'She's not coming back.'

'Her mum's taken a turn for the worse?' Mariner asked, struck by what a strange coincidence that was.

But Knox blew that one out of the water. 'It's our marriage that's taken a turn for the worse,' he said. 'Theresa's left me.'

'Christ. Are you sure?'

Knox gave him the withering look the question deserved.

'I mean, are you sure this isn't just another temporary thing?'

'I'm sure. It hasn't happened overnight.'

'So what have you been up to this time?' Mariner had already had personal experience of Knox's extra-marital activities over a year ago, when Knox had hooked up with

242

Jenny. When Theresa had kicked him out, he and Jenny had ended up staying at Mariner's place. It wasn't the first time Knox had strayed and, although at the time it had seemed like their marriage was over, happily it was only a matter of weeks until Knox saw sense, and Theresa found it somewhere within herself to forgive him.

Mariner wasn't aware that Knox had been dipping his wick again but it didn't mean that he hadn't. He'd never really understood what made Tony Knox tick. But surely, even he was bright enough to grasp the obvious truth: that a woman will only put up with so much. 'I thought you were meant to have given all that up,' he said.

'Not guilty, boss.' Knox held up his hands in defence. 'I haven't played away from home since Jenny. Then, just as the halo was polishing up to a nice shine, Theresa told me she was leaving.'

'Maybe she just needs some space,' Mariner said, cringing inwardly at his choice of words.

'She's moved in with another bloke. Does that sound to you like she needs space?'

'Bloody hell,' was the best response Mariner could come up with. 'Why didn't you say?'

'It's not something I'm that proud of. She met him over the Internet. It makes it worse, somehow. It's so bloody tacky.'

'Only because of what you and I both know. I'm sure there are plenty of responsible people who use the Internet as a legitimate means of communication.'

'Is this what you'd call legitimate? They've been at it for months, years even, for all I know. All the while I thought she was going back up to Liverpool to visit her sick mum she was really busy rekindling an old flame. Romantic, isn't it? All she was waiting for was for Gary to leave home before she followed suit. She doesn't need me any more. She said that her job with the kids was done so there was no other reason to stick around.' He faltered. 'When I asked her what about us, she said, "What us?".'

Mariner thought the word was ironic but all he could muster was: 'Christ. I mean: Christ.'

Knox grimaced. 'That the best you can do? No "poetic justice" lecture?'

'You know me better than that. And I'm not about to feed the gossip mill either.'

'Doesn't matter, does it? It won't be long before it's all round the canteen. There'll be a few sides splitting over this. The sad old fart's got what he deserved.'

'I'm sorry, mate.'

'Not half as fuckin' sorry as I am,' Knox retorted, bitterly. 'It's like there was this whole other little parallel world going on that I never even knew existed, but suddenly, hindsight opened the door and there it was. Suddenly, I can see what a total shit I've been. I thought I had it all under control and meanwhile, Theresa's the one pulling all the strings. This must be the first time in my life when I've looked forward to the prospect of overtime. And do you know what the biggest fuckin' irony of all is? Now that I'm free to go out with any woman I like, I'm just not interested.'

'Do you know who this other bloke is?'

'Oh yes.'

'She told you?'

'She didn't have to. Come and look at this.'

Mariner followed Knox up the stairs to a small back bedroom where a PC sat on a small desk. He logged on to the Internet and typed in a web address. 'Old Friends' said the banner that unfurled before them.

'What's this?' asked Mariner.

'It's one of these school reunion websites. Watch.'

Mariner watched as Knox typed in the name of a school and a date and a list of names appeared on the screen. Theresa Fitzpatrick (Knox) was among them. But he ignored it, instead clicking on Stephen Lamb. Up came the details for Stephen Lamb. A brief paragraph revealing that Lamb, now forty-nine, had built up a successful construction business and, after a recent divorce, was single again. The end of the message asked if anyone knew the whereabouts of Theresa Fitzpatrick. It was followed by an e-mail address and a crystal clear invitation.

'Do you think somebody told her?' Mariner surmised.

'She was well capable of finding it herself. She's been e-mailing him for months. And all that time, not a hint of what was going on.'

'When did you find out?'

'Thirteen days ago. She went up to her mother's, so I thought. But then she sent me the letter saying that she isn't coming back.'

'Christ.' The silence that followed seemed to stretch for hours.

'Want a drink?' Knox asked. He'd clearly already had more than enough, but now wasn't the time to point that out.

'All right.'

Knox poured him a generous measure of Scotch and the silence resumed. 'How long have you been together?' asked Mariner eventually.

'Since we were fifteen. We met at the Coconut Grove in nineteen seventy-nine.'

'That what?'

'It was a nightclub in Tuebrook. There she was, dancing round the handbags with her mates. She was the most gorgeous thing I'd ever seen. But she was a good Catholic girl. She made me wait.'

'What, until you got married?'

'Till she knew I was serious. Jesus, the number of nights I went home with my nuts on fire.'

'How many times were you unfaithful?'

Knox visibly flinched. 'You mean the number of other women? Four in total. The first one was the hardest. I felt really bad about it. But after I'd done it that once it got easier, easier to convince myself that I wasn't doing any harm. Theresa was busy with the kids. She was shattered all the time. I convinced myself I was doing her a favour, taking the pressure off.'

'Did you ever do it out of spite?'

'No. Why?' He looked up at Mariner.

'Nothing. Forget it.'

But Knox couldn't. The cogs were turning. 'Christ, you haven't—' he said at last, having figured it out.

Mariner's silence said it all.

Knox raised an eyebrow. 'You've cheated on the gorgeous Anna? What the hell would you want to do that for? I thought she was hot.'

'She is, when she's available.'

'You knew about Jamie before you started it.'

'That's the thing. It's not Jamie. His respite hours are increasing all the time. And anyway, just because he's there doesn't mean I can't see her. Jamie's OK with me. He always has been. It's all the other stuff.'

'Like?'

'Well, right now we're organising a stall for the Bournville Festival.'

'What's that when it's at home?'

'It's like a fair: home-grown leeks and maypole dancing.'

'Nothing wrong with a bit of pole dancing.'

'*Maypole* dancing; this is sweet little girls in pretty dresses skipping around waving bits of ribbon.' They both thought about that. Then Mariner said, 'They probably attract the same kind of spectator, of course.'

'And this is what you're jealous of. Sounds to me like you're getting serious about our Anna.'

'Not really.'

'But you don't like it when she plays hard to get.'

'I don't know if she really is. It's just as if what we've got isn't that important to her. It's just one small aspect of her life.'

'Does she know how important it is to you?'

'What do you mean?'

246

'I mean, have you told her?'

Mariner had to think for a minute. 'Not in so many words.'

Knox laughed. 'You really don't get it, you pathetic loser, do you? I can tell you've never read a woman's magazine.'

'I haven't.'

'Not even in the dentist's waiting room?'

'My dentist gets the *Great Outdoors*.'

'Talk to Anna! Tell her what you've told me. How else is she supposed to know that you want more of a commitment?'

'I'm not sure that I do.'

'Oh, you do.'

'What is this? Your new career as Mary Knox: Agony Aunt?'

'Oh yeah. I'm a real expert, me. I bet you've never told her that you love her, either.'

Mariner couldn't answer him.

Knox shook his head in disbelief. 'Christ, what does she see in you?'

'I'm dynamite between the sheets,' said Mariner, looking on sheepishly as finally, combined with the whisky, he reduced Knox to uncontrollable mirth.

'So who is it?' asked Knox, when he'd wiped his eyes.

'What does it matter? It was only once. An abberation.'

'Who?'

'Millie.'

'With respect, sir, you're a fucking moron.'

'Millie's a great—'

'I didn't mean that.'

'No.' Mariner turned his attention back to the monitor. 'So this is your old school?'

'For its sins. The entries go back for years. There are people who were at my old school in nineteen forty-three. Can you believe that?'

'Are you on here?'

247

'You have to be joking. I wouldn't want to own up to my career choice. There's a few people I recognise though, kids and teachers. Some of the stuff about the teachers gets pretty libellous. You should have a go. Look up your old school.'

'No thanks.' Mariner could think of nothing worse. There wasn't a single person from his time at school that he would have the slightest desire to make contact with again. And he had other, more pressing, things on his mind. When they'd had strong coffee and Knox seemed almost human again, Mariner expounded his theory.

'It all just keeps coming back to Shaun Pryce,' he said. 'I don't think it was only electrical work that he did. I think he was offering Barbara Goodway another kind of service.'

'He really fancies himself. I wouldn't be surprised,' Knox agreed. 'He was very keen to tell us about his high sex drive, and from what we see he doesn't have a steady girlfriend, so how else does he get by?'

'Do you think Yasmin would have gone for a bloke like Shaun Pryce?'

'Yasmin?'

'I was just thinking: Pryce might have been useful to her. If Yasmin was still in love with Lee, Shaun would have come in useful for winding him up. She knew Lee was working at the industrial units and they used to meet on the bridge. Perhaps she arranged to meet Lee to show him what she was getting up to with Shaun. Maybe she wasn't going on the pill for Lee at all, but for Shaun Pryce.'

'Except that Lee's insisting that he didn't show that afternoon. I don't really buy that.'

'OK. Let's try the pure coincidence theory. Maybe Lee confirmed their date but had decided to stand Yasmin up. He told us he thought she was leading him on. Yasmin turns up at the bridge but no Lee. However, the guy who is there, lurking in the grass, getting his rocks off, is Shaun Pryce. Pryce recognises Yasmin from the school art classes and he's horny anyway, so he decides to try it on. But

248

Yasmin isn't interested, so Pryce loses it. The river, or at least the spillway, is in full spate so he dumps her over the edge.'

'Lucky with the timing.'

'Pryce could have known about the water release, though. He goes there regularly. He could have easily concealed her in the short term before coming back at the right time to dispose of her properly.'

'But Pryce wasn't there that late in the afternoon.'

'So he says. That day we met him in the clearing, he was saying he went there after work. Then suddenly it's one o'clock? You saw him at the reservoir. He was loving it. And at that time he must have thought he was safe. Yasmin's body was well concealed. Barbara Goodway's had been there for months, and this time there was Lee in the background to deflect our attention too. Yasmin probably told him that she was meant to be meeting Lee.'

'The PM indicated a degree of premeditation.'

'Not if he just happened to have a length of wire in his pocket. Whichever way you look at this, Shaun Pryce is in it up to his ears. He's the one who connects Yasmin to Barbara Goodway and he's admitted to frequenting the reservoir. I think we should bring him in.'

'You'll have to see what Fiske says about that.'

Chapter Seventeen

But DCI Fiske had other things to occupy him. In response to the formal complaint from the Skeet family, the Police Complaints Authority team had arrived to begin their investigation and for once, the DCI was happy to let Mariner get on with his job and take the initiative. Thus, when Shaun Pryce arrived at Mrs Paleczcki's the next morning, he found a two-man welcoming committee waiting for him. Half an hour later, Pryce was installed in an interview room while a search warrant was sought and his flat and car turned upside down. Mariner thought he looked even more jittery than the last time they'd met. His actor's mask was beginning to slip.

'I want you to tell me again when, exactly, on Tuesday the third of July you were at the reservoir and exactly what it is you were doing there.'

To settle his nerves, Pryce made a show of a heavy sigh. 'Aren't you lot getting bored with this, too? I went there at about one o'clock. I stayed half an hour. I sunbathed, I smoked a bit of weed. What's the big deal?'

'And you say you were on your own.'

'Yes.' Exasperation was creeping in to his voice.

'You're not always alone though, are you?' Pryce shifted in his chair and for a split second Mariner thought they might have him. 'When was the last time you had a woman down there?'

'I've told you. Weeks ago. They don't like the grass.'

'And who was it, Shaun? Was it Barbara Kincaid?'

'What?' They'd got him. He hadn't seen it coming.

Knox went in for the kill, unleashing the vitriol that should have been directed elsewhere. 'We know, you see, Shaun,' he said, leaning towards Pryce. 'We know that you're the link. We also know that you're a randy little bastard who can't keep his dick in his trousers. You have very eclectic taste, I'll say that for you. Middle-aged house-wives to seventeen-year-old schoolgirls. Very inclusive. Were they both threatening to abandon you? Is that what made you mad? Mad enough to kill them? Or is that just part of the turn on for you?'

Pryce was like a rabbit caught in the headlights. 'That's rubbish. I don't know what you're talking about,' he insisted, but the outburst had rattled him.

Knox leaned forward threateningly. 'Are you denying that you knew Barbara Kincaid?'

Pryce hesitated. 'No,' he said, petulantly.

'All right, then. Tell us about her. How did you two meet?'

'I thought she killed herself,' Pryce whined.

Mariner shrugged non-committally.

'So why are you asking these questions?'

'To find out exactly what happened. Just answer the question.'

'I used to do this amateur dramatics thing. She played the piano for rehearsals of *West Side Story*. There was a problem with the electrics one night and I fixed it. Afterwards, in the bar, she came up to me and said her house hadn't ever been rewired and she thought it might be dangerous. She asked me to go and have a look at it. After the run was finished I was resting again so I said I would.'

'When was this?'

'About March time, I suppose.' Around the time that Barbara Kincaid began threatening suicide, thought Mariner.

'Was that the only reason she asked you to go to her house?'

'What do you mean?'

'Did she fancy you?'

'A lot of women do.'

'That must be such a burden,' said Knox sarcastically. 'Was Barbara Kincaid one of them?'

'So you went to the house,' said Mariner. 'Was her husband around?'

'No. It was in the day. He's a teacher. He was at work.'

'That's handy. So what happened?'

'I did the rewiring.'

'That's all?'

'If you must know, she nearly fucking killed me. I was up a stepladder connecting up a ceiling rose and she came up behind me, giving me all the usual crap about her old man being useless in bed. Then she—'

'What?'

'Touched me up.'

'Very delicately put.'

'I nearly fell off the bloody ladder and took the light fitting with me.'

'But did you respond? Barbara Kincaid was an attractive woman. And we all know about your famous high sex drive.' Pryce didn't know what to say. 'Or was she too old for you?' said Knox.

'Luckily for me, her old man turned up.'

'So you met Brian Goodway, too. Did you tell him you were a model, or had Barbara already done that?'

'It just came up in conversation, you know.'

'And whose idea was it that you should go and model at the school?'

'I can't remember. His, I think.'

'I bet you jumped at it. All those young girls.'

'It was a modelling job. It's what I do.'

'Did you get paid for it?'

'Why else would I have done it?'

'Mm. Why else would you have chosen to spend your time surrounded by attractive adolescent girls? I can't think. I heard you got pretty friendly with some of them.'

'I like kids.'

'Particularly teenage girls. Was Yasmin Akram one of them?'

'I don't remember. There were a lot of them.'

'You offered to take your clothes off, didn't you?'

'It was one of the kids suggested that. "Show us what's underneath," she said.'

'Who said?'

'Tall, skinny kid. Susan.' Suzanne.

'It was just a laugh.'

'A laugh? These kids were seventeen.'

'It was a joke.'

They took a break. Results from the search of Pryce's flat sounded promising so far and they were building a good circumstantial case. Not surprisingly, the items included electrical wires of every gauge imaginable. His car had also yielded a grass-speckled blanket and samples from it could be tested with soil and grass from the flattened area at the reservoir. Condoms found were of the same brand as the used ones that had been picked up.

While they were taking a break, Delrose phoned up to say that Mariner had a visitor; a woman. He expected Colleen and dreaded having to face her. Instead, Anna was waiting for him in reception. Lesser of two evils. But only just.

'Hi,' she said, cheerfully. 'I wondered when I'd see you again. You look terrible.'

'Had a curry that didn't agree with me.' It didn't explain why he couldn't look her in the eye, but if she noticed she made no comment. 'What are you doing here?'

'I tried phoning, but you're a hard man to get hold of. I thought I might stand a better chance of talking to you if I came in person. I've missed you.'

'I've been busy.' Mariner rubbed the back of his neck.

253

'We're in the middle of something—'

'I know. But I think we need to talk. Can you spare a few minutes?'

'All right.'

They crossed the road and went into the park opposite, where they began a circuit of the boating pond. A couple of little kids with their grandparents were trying in vain to encourage their toy yachts to sail on the smooth expanse of water. Mariner knew how they felt. For days now it had seemed as if the wind had gone out of the sails of their investigation leaving it stale and stagnant as the water around them. Then, today, the first hint of a breeze. He hardly dared hope.

'I just wondered what's going on,' Anna said. 'The other evening you wouldn't stay and now I'm beginning to get the idea that you're avoiding me.'

'It's not that—' Mariner began, too tired for this now.

She moved towards him and made as if to take his arm, but some reflex made him move away, putting a distance between them. Their eyes met and as they exchanged a look he saw the flash of understanding cross her features.

'Just so that you know,' she said, using that phrase of hers that always preceded any straight talking, 'I'd be really hurt to find out that you're shagging someone else, too.'

It cut him to the core. 'I know,' he said helplessly, staring ahead.

She was astute enough to take this as confirmation. 'So you are sleeping with someone else.'

'Not exactly.'

'What the hell does that mean?'

'It means past tense. I slept with someone else, a couple of nights ago.'

'Well, thanks for telling me.' She hadn't been lying. He could hear the pain in her voice. It sliced right through him.

'It's not what you think.'

She stopped and turned to face him with the same anger he'd witnessed the first time they'd met. 'So what is it, then?'

'When I couldn't see you. I worked late instead, and afterwards, Millie Khatoon, she's our—'

'I know who she is.'

'Right, well, Millie asked me back to her place for a curry and we ended up getting drunk and having sex. It was terrible sex. Millie would tell you the same thing. We didn't go to bed, we didn't even take our clothes off and it was over in ten minutes. It will never happen again.'

An elderly couple walked by, gazing at them with interest.

'Well, that's all right, then,' Anna said, tightly.

Righteous anger rose in Mariner's chest. 'Oh, and I suppose you and Simon are above all that.'

'Simon?'

'You can't seem to stay away from him. Not that I blame you. He's young, not bad-looking from what I could see—'

'—and apart from me, the most important person in Jamie's life.' Anna rounded on him. 'We're talking about Jamie here, who can't communicate, and for whom consistency is a lifeline. That could explain why I spend so much time with Simon.'

'Even on a Friday night, when you're meant to be having a break from Jamie?'

'Sure, that was more of a social call, but if you hadn't walked away, you would have found out what it was all about.'

'I wasn't invited.'

'What, you need a written invitation now? I asked you to stay.'

Mariner gazed out across the pond. 'So what was it about?' Why was it that her questioning of him had sounded entirely reasonable and calm, but he just sounded like a petulant schoolboy?

'Simon has asked me to help with the stall on the day of the festival, so he and Martin had come round to discuss—'

'Martin too? That was a cosy threesome.'

'Actually, it was fun,' she responded, evenly. 'Martin

255

and Simon make a great couple.' She paused to allow that to sink in. 'Simon is gay, Martin is his partner. And if I'd thought that it was in the least bit relevant, I would have told you.'

But even then, when she'd handed it to him on a plate, he couldn't let go. 'That's convenient, isn't it?' he said.

'Oh, fuck off, Tom.' And she turned and walked away from him.

Even if he'd had the energy it would be pointless going after her, he could see that. He would only make things worse. So he went back to the nick and to Shaun Pryce.

They spent all afternoon on Pryce, covering the same ground but not really making any progress. Mariner was distracted and, if anything, Pryce seemed to be gaining control. He was certainly more relaxed than he had been a few hours earlier. In the end they had to let him go. As he stalked up to the office again, Mariner was ready to kill someone. Unfortunately the first person he ran into was Millie, typing at her desk.

'Has the search team come back yet?' he demanded.

'Not yet,' she said glancing up briefly before returning to the report.

Mariner banged his hand down hard on her desk, making everyone in the office turn round. 'So why the hell aren't you out there, chasing them up?' And he strode into his office and slammed the door, leaving Millie staring after him. After a few moments she tentatively went in.

Mariner stood with his back to the room looking out of the window. 'I'm sorry,' he said. 'It's been a long day.'

'Don't let Pryce get to you, sir. If it is him we'll find out in the end.'

Mariner swung round to face her. 'Anna found out about what happened with us.'

'Oh God. How? You don't think I—?'

'I told her.'

'Oh. Good move, sir.'

'I had to. It was gnawing away at me.'

'You have got it bad, haven't you?'

And that was the problem. He had. For the first time in his life Mariner had found a woman he could envisage growing old with. Someone he was finding it hard to imagine being without.

But the deal with Anna had always been no commitment. And now he was in danger of blowing the whole thing sky high.

Mariner's conscience told him that he ought to go over to see his mother again tonight, but after the sort of day he'd had, he couldn't face her. In any case, it was late and by the time he could get there, visiting would be over. Instead, he phoned and spoke to the duty nurse.

'She's fine,' the girl reassured him. 'Though I expect she'll be disappointed not to see you.' I wouldn't count on it, thought Mariner.

Knox had already left and in any case, Mariner didn't feel much like company, so he went home. The evening was warm and sticky again, the air heavy with unresolved tension. Opening up a bottle of home-brew, Mariner went to sit on the bench outside his front door, overlooking the canal. Towards dusk, the sky darkened ominously and thunder rumbled in the distance. A few spots of rain followed, temporarily making the air smell a little fresher, but this time the storm never quite broke.

The next morning he was in the shower, considering their next move with Shaun Pryce, when away in the distance he heard the phone. When he got out there was a message from the hospital on the answering machine, asking him to call back as soon as possible. He hoped it wasn't that they were letting his mother go home early. That was a diversion he could do without today.

'Mr Mariner, I'm afraid your mother has suffered a slight heart attack. You may want to come in.' The voice was calm and unruffled, implying nothing more than a setback, though this would inevitably delay her discharge from the hospital.

On the drive over, Mariner could visualise his mother's frustration as she was wired up to monitors and drips that would further restrict her independence. This had obvious implications for her after-care, too. He'd need to play a more active role, something he didn't relish, but it might mean getting to know each other again, which in turn may present new opportunities too. The nursing sister met him on reception and took him into a side room to explain what was happening. 'I'm sorry, Mr Mariner, we weren't able to resuscitate her.'

For several seconds her words didn't make any sense. Then, one by one, their meaning hit him like a forty-foot wave, almost physically knocking him off-balance.

'She died at just after nine o'clock,' the nurse went on, gently. 'It was very sudden, so it's unlikely that she knew anything about it. She wouldn't have been in any pain.' Her carefully chosen words were designed to offer comfort and consolation. They were words of the kind that had spouted from Mariner's own mouth a hundred times before, when he'd broken bad news to the relatives of crime victims. In all that time it had never occurred to him that one day, he might be on the receiving end. So this was what it was like. A feeling of complete disorientation, as if time had suddenly slowed to nothing.

'Would you like to see her?' the nurse repeated when he failed to respond the first time.

He had to wait a few minutes, while they made her presentable, presumably. But it made no difference. When he went in he didn't see Rose. They hadn't succeeded in making her look as if she was sleeping, as was the desired outcome. The life in her was gone, leaving only an empty shell. In the past he'd watched families say their last good-byes, to kiss the cold cheek of their loved ones, but Mariner couldn't bring himself to do that. His mother

258

wasn't there. Why was he so upset? It wasn't as though he would miss his mother's daily presence. They'd hardly seen each other in recent years. And it wasn't that he was suddenly brought face to face with death. Any reminders he might need of his own mortality came regularly at work. Perhaps it was because now he had to accept the possibility that he would never know.

He realised too how much he'd taken her for granted, expecting her to never not be there. He'd always assumed that she'd be one of these women who lived well into her nineties. An afterthought struck him: she'd never meet Anna now.

They were still holding some of his mother's personal effects at the nursing station on the ward so he went to fetch them. 'You've just missed your dad,' said the nurse. 'I think he's gone home.'

Mariner gawped. 'My what?'

Had he been thinking rationally and stopped to consider, Mariner would have recognised the unlikelihood, but suddenly, in a warped kind of way, everything began to make sense. The 'something to tell him', was that his father had reappeared on the scene. It might explain why she was doing up the house, too.

He dashed back to his mother's house, where an old style pushbike was leaning against the wall. That hadn't been there two days ago. He let himself in with the key, his heart pounding in anticipation. 'Hello?'

'Hello. You must be Tom.'

Harry turned out to be a softly spoken widower who had worked for years as an engineer at Potterton's boilers in Coventry and had lost his wife soon after his retirement.

'How long have you known Rose?' Mariner asked.

'About a year. I was planning to move in with her.'

'Were you?' Mariner's surprise was genuine. He was struggling to get his head round the idea that his mother had met another man after all this time. If there had been liaisons over the years Mariner had not been aware of them. As far as he knew, there had been nobody since his father who hadn't stuck around long enough to see his son born. Just like the Akrams with Yasmin, this was where he'd find out how little he knew about his mother.

Harry was flustered now. 'No, it wasn't like that. We were just friends, but I was coming to stay here with her. She'd offered me a room.'

'A room?'

'I'm living in rented accommodation at present but the lease expires at the end of the month and the landlord wants me out, so your mother had said I could have her spare room. It was all above board. We had agreed rent.'

'I see.' Typical of his mother to be adopting waifs and strays, even at her age. As he spoke, Mariner recognised that Harry and his mother had espoused the kind of pragmatic approach to life that is the privilege of the older generation. They'd reached the point where, having taken their share of knocks, they've realised that there's too little time left to waste it arguing about the minutiae. Harry was about to lose his home. Mariner's mother had a spare room. The two things fitted logically together, end of story.

'I'm not a con man,' said Harry, answering the very question that Mariner had moments before dismissed inside his head.

'No.' And you're not my dad.

Harry 'liked to keep busy' as he put it, hence the fresh coat of paint on the house. Mariner's mother had been helping him, but mainly by providing cups of tea, from the sound of it. 'I didn't want her to be up ladders. I don't know why she was.' Harry had come to collect his overalls and brushes. 'I expect you'll want to sell the house and I wouldn't want them to be in the way. No time like the present.'

When Harry had gone, Mariner called the office from his mother's old Bakelite phone and spoke to Fiske.

'I'm very sorry, Tom,' he said, formally. 'Is there anything we can do?'

'No thanks, sir.'

'Police Complaints are still here.' Fiske couldn't resist mentioning it, even though the timing was completely inappropriate. 'They're going through all the paperwork with a fine-tooth comb.'

'That's what they do, sir.'

'Yes. They'll want to talk to you, too.' Fiske paused. 'Tom, I hope—'

'Not really the right moment, sir.'

'Of course. Well, take as much time as you need.'

'Thank you, sir.' I won't be hurrying back on your account. He'd let Fiske squirm. Even if the DCI were vindicated, the fact that there had been an investigation in the first place could blight his career. With any luck, the mud would stick.

The truth was that Mariner was still uneasy about his own part in the fiasco. He should have been more assertive about keeping Ricky's case, and more proactive, both with Ricky and with his mother. Now he'd paid the price for both.

He went to the registry office to record his mother's death. Technically, it had been a sudden death, so there would have to be a post mortem, but it would be routine. The people around her when she died had all been fighting to save her life. Nothing suspicious about that.

Sitting on the hard plastic seat, waiting his turn, it occurred to Mariner that to all intents and purposes he was now an orphan, with very little family to speak of. His mother had a couple of cousins as far as he remembered, but there were no family gatherings when he'd been a kid. It gave him something else in common with Anna, too. She'd lost her parents several years ago, except of course that he didn't really know about the one, and perhaps now never would.

Ironically, if he'd been adopted it would have been simple. These days, there were routes to follow. But not for him. The only way of solving this particular puzzle would

261

be if there was some clue remaining at his mother's house, something she'd hung onto. He thought about the bond between the father of a child and the mother. Ronnie Skeet was a nasty piece of work but it still didn't stop Colleen from letting him back into the house time after time. *'He's the father of my kids,'* she'd said.

Mariner's mother had never given him any reason to doubt that she knew the identity of his father. Was there an unbreakable bond there, too, however tenuous? However effectively she managed to keep him a secret, would there still be some fine strand connecting them? If there was then there would be a trace of it at her house. It was the only place to start. Hours later he was back there.

For the sake of being thorough, he began with all the obvious places, but knowing beforehand that there would be nothing in the bureau in the dining room or in her drawer in the bedroom. It was too accessible. He found all her current paperwork: bank and building society accounts, letters from the last few years. Most of the numbers in her address book were local: friends and contacts made when she moved back up to Leamington. There was nothing from before that time.

Amongst the documents was his birth certificate, but he'd seen that years ago and it gave nothing away. He was officially a bastard. That would amuse some of the crooks he'd put away in the past. She'd kept all his old school reports too, most of them a variation on a 'could try harder' theme. But it was futile. She'd kept a secret for this long. She'd never leave anything around down here that would give it away. Mariner knew where the important stuff was. The past had literally been hanging over his head all the time he'd lived in this house.

When they'd moved in with his grandparents, space was at a premium and, consequently, much of their stuff had vanished up into the loft, and had never, to his knowledge, come down again. Rose had always vehemently discouraged him from going up there on the grounds that he might

262

clumsily put a foot through the fragile floor and into the ceiling of the rooms below, but Mariner suspected the real reason lay deeper than that.

No one had been up there for years, mainly because it was such a production to get up there, involving balancing precariously at the very top of the stepladder before launching off into the narrow aperture. But in adulthood, Mariner had height on his side and the manoeuvre was relatively easy. The loft space was stifling and dirty, everything coated in a layer of black dust. A bare bulb draped over one of the rough timbers provided the minimum amount of light and in the yellow gloom, Mariner could see the enormity of the task: boxes and trunks, rolls of yellowing wallpaper, a collection of old camping equipment that could have belonged to Edmund Hillary, complete with rusting tartan vacuum flasks and heavy canvas groundsheets.

Opening a cardboard carton, he found old crockery and cutlery, including a child's porcelain Peter Rabbit dish that had probably been his. In another, a whole willow-patterned bone-china dinner service. There was a suitcase full of dusty, dun-coloured blankets. Finally, he found what he was looking for in a brown cardboard suitcase with catches that had almost rusted solid. Working them back and forth finally slid them across and the lid flipped open to reveal yellowing paper: letters, cards, newspaper cuttings and photographs. The faded and peeling address label stuck to the inside of the lid had written on it: Rosemary Ellen Mariner, in neat italic ink-penned script. This was his mother's life in London.

She'd been twenty-four when he was born in that other long hot summer of 1959, which left him looking for anything dated 1958–59. Her twenty-first birthday cards were bundled together, as were letters from his grand-mother, even a few birth congratulations cards, most from women or couples. There were black-and-white photographs of him as a baby, wrapped in a woollen shawl. There were mementoes from special occasions: tickets from

London Zoo, a programme from the Henry Wood Promenade Concert in September 1958: an evening of Sibelius, conducted by Malcolm Sargent.

The only things that might reveal any clues were the letters. He sat on an old crate and strained his eyes to read. The letters were addressed to several different places in London, where his mother had lived an apparently nomadic existence. Mostly, his grandmother described trivial events in Leamington, though occasionally she made reference to things that Rose must have mentioned in her letters home. It was these brief glimpses that Mariner clung to. In the dim light, the curling italic handwriting wasn't easy to decipher and he took his time, anxious not to miss anything.

But he realised as he came to the last, with overwhelming disappointment, that there was nothing to miss. His neck ached and his eyes were sore with the dust and effort. It had gone cooler. When he had emerged back on to the ladder he found out why. It was dark and almost eleven at night. Turning on the landing light, he left a black fingerprint on the switch. He looked as if he'd been up a chimney. He was filthy.

His mother had never gone in for showers so he ran a hot bath and lay in it, soaking. He had a decision to make. He could either waste further endless time and energy trying to uncover something that was probably unattainable, or he could get back to his life. Later, he crawled into the spare room to sleep on it.

Chapter Eighteen

The morning brought with it a firm decision. Mariner locked his mother's house. He'd get on to the estate agent soon and arrange a skip and some visits to a local charity shop. At home he found a message from Anna on the answer phone. It wasn't exactly an olive branch, but carefully handled, it might have the potential to become one. He called her back straight away, half expecting her recorded message. To his surprise she was there, but the conversation didn't go according to plan. 'Where have you been?' Anna asked. 'I've been trying to contact you.'

'My mother's dead.'

'Oh God, Tom, I'm so sorry. What happened?'

'A heart attack, Thursday morning.'

'Why didn't you call me? Are you all right?'

'I'm OK.'

'Do you want me to come over? I can see if Simon could—'

'No!' he snapped. 'It's all right, I'm fine, really.'

'OK, then.'

So the experience hadn't changed him. In an emotional crisis he still couldn't manage sharing his feelings with someone else. It was so long since he'd done it that he'd forgotten how.

It wasn't any less depressing back in the office where, in his absence, nothing much had happened. Fiske was still technically overseeing things but his mind was, understandably, preoccupied with other matters. The team itself seemed to have lost all coherence, too. Mariner recognised that he was still in a state of shock. Tony Knox seemed lower than ever, and recent past history had generated an awkwardness between himself and Millie, all of which was nicely exacerbated by the fact that beyond the initial expression of condolences, suddenly no one quite knew what to say to him.

There had been no progress, either forensic or otherwise, to pin down Shaun Pryce. The grass and soil traces on the blanket in his car were a match with the reservoir, but then Pryce had never denied that he went there. There was a feeling all round that both investigations were beginning to lose momentum as demands on resources continued to be made from elsewhere, and there were mutterings about calling in the murder review team. That and the ominous presence of the PCA was doing little to inspire confidence.

Partly to get out of the building, Mariner went to visit the Akrams, who unusually were both at home. 'You've closed the school?'

'We had to. It was impossible to keep going. We hope to reopen in a few days, but we're in limbo. Until we know who did this to Yasmin we can't get on with our lives. It's like unfinished business.'

'I'm sorry: there's no news, but we're still doing everything we can.'

'Thank you.'

Another uncompromisingly sunny day dawned for Mariner's mother's funeral. He put on one of his lighter suits and perused his collection of dreary ties. Had he been Fiske, he'd have had a whole array of jolly cartoon characters at his disposal, but he wasn't, so in the end he chose a sky/navy stripe.

'Very smart.'

Coming down the stairs, he looked up to see Anna standing in the hallway. She'd let herself in and was waiting by the front door, wearing an elegant floral dress and a wide-brimmed hat.

'I thought you could use some support,' she said. 'After all, I've had some experience at this stuff.' Over the last few years, death had been a loyal companion, as she'd seen both her parents and her older brother killed. It was Eddie's murder that had brought them together in the first place.

'Thanks, I appreciate it,' said Mariner, truthfully.

She saw him appraising her outfit. 'Would she have approved?'

'She'd have approved whatever you were wearing.'

They spoke little on the drive over to Leamington and he was grateful for that, too. His nerves jangled in anticipation. Not because of the funeral: that he could cope with. But in the days after his mother died, he had placed announcements in both local and national press. At the very least he was hoping to meet someone who would be able to tell him who his father was. And then there was the possibility he hardly dared consider: that his father might turn up in person.

In her will his mother had planned out the ceremony to the last detail: a simple cremation with a couple of pieces of music; 'Ave Maria' and the 'Intermezzo' from Sibelius's Karelia Suite. It had been on the programme of the 1958 Promenade Concert he'd found in the loft and, hearing it now, he couldn't help wondering if the piece had a deeper significance. It was all she'd wanted. Mariner introduced Anna to Harry, who sat beside them at the front of the church, along with Mrs Masud. Turning to look, Mariner saw that the chapel was a respectable two thirds full, a congregation disproportionately made up of women, attributable possibly to his mother's lifelong commitment to the feminist cause. He could tell those who'd known her well: they were the ones dressed for a picnic in the park.

'Anyone else you recognise?' Anna asked him.

267

'Not a soul.'

There was to be no wake back at the house. His mother had made no stipulation about it in her will, and to Mariner it seemed pointless to invite a group of total strangers to join him in mourning a woman he hardly knew. But he did formally greet people as they left the chapel.

Most of the mourners turned out to be friends of his mother's from Leamington, but then came the encounter that he'd been praying for: a large woman dressed in flowing pink and turquoise, her grey unruly hair loosely pinned back. She smiled. 'You've changed a bit since we last met,' she said. 'I'm Maggie Devlin. I used to sit for you when you were a baby.'

Mariner's heart thumped against his rib cage. 'We're going for a drink,' he said, with astonishing calm. 'Would you like to join us?'

He was in for a disappointment. Maggie had indeed known his mother from her London days, but was as mystified as he was about who his father might be. 'She kept that one close to her chest,' she told him over a gin and tonic in the garden of a nearby pub. 'Rose was a popular girl and nobody was really sure if she knew who the father of her baby was, though I was certain she was seeing someone for quite a while after you were born.'

'But she didn't give any clue about who it might be?'

'None. She was good at secrets, your mother. There was just the one day—'

'What?'

'It might be nothing at all.'

'Please.'

'When you were born, Rose was living in a flat in Holborn. I came to see you just after you came home from the hospital, and as I arrived, there was a black car pulling away from the kerb. It caught my attention because it was a big car, especially for round there, like a limousine. It was only afterwards though that I began to wonder if it had anything to do with—'

'Did you get the licence plate?' asked Mariner automatically, before laughing with Maggie at his own stupidity. 'Of course not. Why would you?'

'And I doubt that it would be much help after all these years.'

'No.'

'I'm truly sorry that I can't tell you more. But if I should learn of anything that might help—'

'Thanks.' Mariner gave her his card.

The sun blasting in through the window woke Tony Knox. He had a throbbing headache and a raging thirst again, even though he thought he'd been pretty moderate with the booze last night. He glanced over at the clock. Bugger! Twenty past eleven. He should have been at work hours ago. For a moment he debated whether to pull a sickie, but remembered where Mariner had gone today. It would be good to have something for the boss when he got back. Knox made himself get out of bed and into the shower.

Everyone at Granville Lane was either out or preoccupied, so no one noticed his late arrival. Now he was here he couldn't think of anything purposeful to do. While he considered that, unable to resist the urge, he tucked himself away in a corner of the office and logged on to the old friends website again. But before clicking on to Stephen Lamb's name he checked himself. He'd spent hours staring at that message. It wasn't going to change anything. Before he clicked his way out of the website, a further thought occurred: would Shaun Pryce go for something like this? Of course he would, the self-serving little git. If Pryce was keen to publicise himself, one group he'd really want to know would be old schoolfriends, particularly as he'd enjoyed some modest success. He was bound to want to capitalise on that. And what else might he give away? His exploits with middle-aged housewives? There might be something to learn from Pryce's former classmates, too. He'd not a clue which schools Pryce had attended, of course, but it couldn't be that difficult to find out. His web page had indicated that he was a local lad.

All Knox had to do was systematically work through the secondary schools in the area. Right now, he couldn't think of a better way to keep himself occupied and Fiske off his back for the day. He'd start with Kingsmead and work his way out. Pryce would have left the school either in '87 or '89. For a moment, Knox was tempted to pick up the phone and make his life easier by asking Shaun Pryce the direct question. He wouldn't need to know what it was about. But then he caught sight of the Complaints officer in the far side of the office, poring over Ricky Skeet's file and decided that he couldn't risk any more aggro. With a weary sigh, he began opening up the message envelopes beside each of the names. The computer was on a 'go slow' so it took for ever.

A pattern amongst the messages quickly emerged. The people who bothered to leave them all had one thing in common: like Stephen Lamb, they all had shiny, successful lives. Invariably, the message started off with career details: *working as a stockbroker/lawyer/managing director for . . .* There was a distinct dearth of window cleaners, bin men and unemployed. This was always followed by a description of family life: *married with four children/wife Cordelia, children Dominic (10) and Pandora (8) etc.* Occasionally, someone was bold enough to admit to a second marriage, but even that came across as twice the achievement. Generally speaking, life's failures didn't draw attention to themselves. It was all sickeningly up-beat and did nothing to lift Knox's own blackening mood.

For a little light relief, Knox switched to reading the notice boards where former pupils could post their opinions on anything from their former schooldays. Usually it was the teachers who'd become the subject of perceived injustices and occasional downright victimisation, prompting outpourings of resentment and angst. This was more like it, Knox thought: bitterness to match his own. He was busy

270

marvelling at the human capacity for blame when he almost overlooked a name he'd seen before, more than once, in recent days. Bucking the trend, the attached messages indicated relative popularity. One described in great detail an elaborate April Fools' joke that had been admirably taken. But it was followed by a more cryptic note, posted by someone calling himself 'Stewey': *Goody Goodway: did he jump or was he pushed?* There was one response from a Derrick Farmer: *One of life's eternal mysteries. Gone but sadly missed.*

Knox stared at the screen trying to work out what, if anything, it could mean. The school was another local comprehensive where Goodway must have worked prior to teaching at Kingsmead. Running a search, he found Stewart 'Stewey' Blake on the list of leavers from ten years ago.

For the sake of having achieved something this afternoon, Knox e-mailed him, leaving his mobile number, hoping that 'Stewey' was in the habit of checking his in-box regularly. He waited a few minutes in case there was an instant e-mail reply, but then, unlike Knox, Blake would have better things to do on a sunny Saturday afternoon than spend it hunched over his computer. And it would probably turn out to be nothing. Sensationalism knitted out of a few shreds of circumstantial information: perfect Internet fodder. He looked around the office. Millie was at the Akrams', Charlie Glover out on a call; no one to enjoy a round of speculation with. He needed a drink. There was also no one to see him leave early, so he picked up his jacket and went.

On the way home, of its own volition, Knox's brain began composing his own message for the reunion website: 'Wife has left me because of my womanising, I'm an embarrassment to my kids. Could have made DS or even DI, if I hadn't screwed a senior officer's wife.' What an epitaph.

Slamming shut his front door, the noise reverberated around the emptiness for seconds afterwards. He tried to imagine hearing that same sound every day for the next thirty years, destined to spend the rest of his life alone. He hurled his keys on to the hall table in frustration. What was the point? What was the fucking point?

After a couple of hours, the handful of people who'd come back with them for a drink had drifted away, leaving Mariner and Anna alone at the Coach and Horses. The guest beer was a very pleasing Adnams, and the garden was bathed in early evening sunshine, but Mariner couldn't shake off the gloom that had descended.

'Maybe you just have to accept this as one you can't solve,' said Anna, ever the pragmatist.

'I'll add it to all the others waiting for me back at the station.'

'It's not your fault,' Anna said.

'I can't believe that I'll never know.'

'Does it matter?'

'Right now, it feels like the only important thing, but I suppose that will pass.'

'It has before,' she reminded him. 'And, who knows, when you clear the house you may come across something that you've overlooked.'

Mariner shook his head. 'She was too careful.'

'Why do you think she kept it from you for so long?'

'Who knows? To begin with, I thought it was because of who he was. She liked to give the impression he was somebody important: someone whose reputation might have suffered if it was known that he'd fathered an illegitimate child. In the late 50s a child out of wedlock was still a big deal. But, later, I used to think that maybe she played on that because thought it would make me feel better to know that he was someone special.'

'So it could have just been a bloke down the street.'

'It might help to explain why we moved away from London in such a hurry.'

'It's a hell of a secret to keep, isn't it? There's no one

272

else you can think of who would know?'

'As Maggie said, Rose deliberately severed links with a lot of her friends when we moved from London. There may be somebody somewhere, but I wouldn't begin to know how to find out.'

'So maybe it's time to start looking forward instead of back.'

Mariner studied his pint for a moment. He had something to say. He just wasn't sure if now was the right time to say it. 'I regret what happened with Millie,' he said at last. 'Really regret it.'

She placed a hand over his. 'I know. And I'm not sure what gave me the right to be so annoyed about it. We've never had that kind of relationship.'

Mariner could almost feel Tony Knox sitting on his shoulder, urging him on. 'I wish we did,' he blurted out.

She wrinkled her nose, as if trying to make sense of her own feelings. 'Yeah, me too.'

A horde of small children raced by behind them, shrieking with ear-piercing intensity. Mariner swallowed the rest of his pint. 'Let's go home.'

'Your place or mine?'

'Yours. Nobody can reach me there.'

Back at Mariner's house, the phone rang on, unanswered.

When Mariner woke the next morning, Anna was already up. He could hear her moving around and eventually she walked past the bedroom door, already dressed and laden with what looked like an entire jumble sale. It was ten past eight. Mariner propped himself on an elbow and picked up the mug of tea she'd left for him. Anna saw him. 'You all right?' she asked.

'Fine. You?' When she nodded he said: 'Come back to bed.'

She was unsure.

'Half an hour, that's all.'

273

'And then you'll help me?'

'Yes.'

'It's a deal.'

Standing in the shower a little later, Mariner had a strange feeling. It puzzled him until suddenly he recognised it as contentment. Weird.

'Shall I come with you?' he asked when they'd loaded up her car.

'It's up to you. I'll have to man the stall for a couple of hours,' she warned him. 'I can't do anything about that.'

'I wouldn't want you to.'

Bournville Festival was an anachronistic affair dating back to 1902, at a time long before the 'village' had been greedily swallowed up by the suburbs of the spreading city. Although the surroundings had changed, it remained a real village-style event, held on the vast green playing fields fronting the chocolate factory that were for the rest of the year given over to cricket, football or bowls, depending on the season. Alongside the small funfair, exhibition tents, stalls and games had been erected around a small arena, the centre of which was dominated by a traditional maypole wrapped in bright red and yellow ribbons. At the far end of the grounds, an area had been cordoned off for the pyrotechnic display that would end the celebrations late in the evening.

It took several journeys to transfer everything from Anna's car to where the stall was being set up. Here, inevitably, Mariner came face to face with Simon. If he'd expected to be let off lightly with a caricature of a mincing queen he was going to be unlucky. Simon was bronzed, muscular and macho, and Mariner found it hard to believe that what Anna had said was true. He saw her watching him.

'It's not always the ones you expect,' she said.

'No.'

Anna was going to be busy arranging prizes until the festival opened and there were already enough volunteers on

274

hand who seemed to know what they were doing. Mariner felt like a spare part, so he wandered off to see what else was on offer. There were stalls affiliated to every local organisation imaginable. Even the conservation group was represented, he noticed, seeing Eric Dwyer lurking behind a table of soft toys, wooden carved artefacts and the ubiquitous mugs, trying to encourage new recruits to the project.

Even though the festival wouldn't be officially open for another half hour, people were pouring in. At one end of the field was the West Midlands police trailer. Recognising Keith Watson from the OCU, Mariner made for the home security van. In among the advice posters on home security was a display with photographs of Ricky and Yasmin, appealing again for any information anyone might have. Now that the heat was going out of the investigations it was essential to take any opportunities to maintain the profile of the cases and keep the publicity going, but at the same time, even to Mariner, it felt gruesome and out of keeping with the atmosphere of the rest of the event. Unsurprisingly, few people were giving the display much attention. Mariner spent several minutes chatting to Watson before heading towards the exhibitions tent.

Inside the marquee it was bright and oppressive, with the smell of warm canvas on grass that took Mariner back to those childhood camping expeditions. Long trestle tables were covered with pristine white cloths and a series of displays that reflected every creative pastime open to man: everything from home-made cakes, flower arrangements and jam, to prize-winning pumpkins and marrows. There were art competitions for children and adults for which certificates would be awarded later that afternoon for different categories and age groups. The adults' theme was 'Reflections of Birmingham' and the one that most appealed to Mariner's taste was literally that: an impressive pen-and-ink sketch of a bank of trees at sunset, mirrored on to what Mariner guessed was somewhere along one of the city's canals. The view was familiar, not dissimilar to the one

275

from his back door.

'Inspector, I didn't know you lived locally.' It was the artist himself who approached Mariner.

'My partner does,' said Mariner, thinking that it was the first time he'd ever referred to Anna that way. 'And I had no idea that you were so gifted. Congratulations, Mr Goodway, it's a superb drawing.'

'Thank you. I'm a bit rusty these days, but suddenly I find myself with some empty evenings to fill. Art can be very therapeutic. Helps to take my mind off things.'

'Of course.' An unwelcome reminder to Mariner that there was still unfinished business. 'Good luck with the competition.'

'Thank you.'

An announcement over the PA system heralded the opening ceremony, and Mariner moved outside again in time for the arrival of the festival queen, attended by her flower girls, all of whom were selected from children born on the Cadbury estate. Mariner was swept along with the crowds towards the main arena where the maypole dancing would begin. Judging by the number of video cameras trained on the dancing, each child had a minimum of two sets of proud parents and grandparents there. Scanning the crowd, Mariner spotted another familiar face. It took him a moment or two to place Andy Pritchard, especially as today his Ranger's uniform had been replaced by jeans and T-shirt.

He was reaching up to position a digital camera and Mariner wondered if he had a daughter among the dancers, though he seemed to remember Pritchard as a single man. Perhaps a niece then, or goddaughter. At that moment, Pritchard glanced up and saw Mariner watching him. Mariner smiled and nodded, but Pritchard didn't reciprocate. Instead, lowering the camera, he turned and began walking away from Mariner, into the crowd. Purely from curiosity, Mariner followed, just to see what he would do, and was interested to note that Pritchard quickened his

276

pace. There were a number of possible explanations. The simplest was that the recognition hadn't been mutual, or perhaps he just didn't feel like talking. Being a policeman could sometimes have that effect on people. Mariner gave it up.

Tired of the crowds, he sought refreshment in the beer tent, but after standing in a motionless queue for ten minutes he abandoned that idea and decided to go and find a pub. Being on the Bournville trust, Quaker and dry, the nearest was going to be a drive away. The incident with Andy Pritchard was niggling at him, too. The more he thought about it, the more he thought Pritchard's behaviour odd. He glanced over to where the Manor Park stall was. Anna was in her element, hidden somewhere behind a heaving mass of people. She wouldn't miss him for an hour or so.

Chapter Nineteen

Mariner's first stop was Granville Lane. 'Tony Knox in today?' Mariner asked the duty sergeant.

'He was here earlier, but the miserable sod's done us all a favour and gone home,' was the terse reply.

Up in CID, it didn't take Mariner long to find what he was looking for, though: the information Knox had followed up on the indecent exposures. After plotting the incidents on a map, Knox had rightly identified the pattern as being access to railway stations, but when he looked closely, Mariner found another, more subtle pattern. Each of the attacks had also occurred close to a council park or open space: not on it, but close by. Andy Pritchard used his bike to get around, and what better way of covering bigger distances across the city with a bike than on the train?

Mariner switched on his computer. While he was waiting for it to boot up, he sorted through the phone messages in his in-tray. One was an urgent phone message to contact the forensic service. Mariner called back. Most of the scientists were off for the weekend, but the technician on duty was expecting Mariner's call.

'The gaffer thought you might want to know that we've identified the type of wire that was used to strangle Yasmin Akram. It's a kind of annealed wire, coated with a chemical rust inhibitor.'

'Would it have a plastic coating?'

'Wouldn't need it.'

'So not an electrical wire,' said Mariner, disappointed.

'Electrical wire isn't normally exposed like that,' the technician told him. 'It's a fairly soft wire, easily pliable but strong enough to withstand a powerful force.' He sounded as if he was reading from notes.

'Any idea what it would be used for?'

'The clue to that may be in the other substance we found at the joint where the wire had been twisted. In the crook there was a tiny residue of claydium.'

'Which is what?'

'A type of nylon-reinforced clay. Specifically used for modelling. Add that to the wire and I'd say you were looking for someone who's a modelling enthusiast.'

Mariner thought about Pritchard. He could imagine him with his Airfix planes or battalions of model soldiers. Ringing off, he ran a check on Andy Pritchard, but no criminal record appeared and he had no details on the database. Mariner thought about the man. How would he fare with women? Probably not that well. He wasn't particularly good looking, the skin problem had seen to that. Helen Greenwood had mentioned the flasher's complexion. Sunburnt, she'd said. Or could it have been acne? The way he'd looked at Yasmin's partly clothed body had seemed a little off-kilter too. And why had he taken so long to phone it in? What had he been doing in the forty minutes after he found Yasmin's body?

Suddenly, Mariner remembered Croghan's remark about Yasmin's missing underwear. Had it been removed at the time Yasmin was killed or afterwards? Because Pritchard had discovered the body long after Yasmin disappeared, and had no apparent connection with the disappearance, they hadn't thought about checking his alibi. Yasmin's body was discovered in an obscure area of the park. What had prompted Pritchard to even look there? And, most importantly, where had Andy Pritchard been on the afternoon of Tuesday July the third? Mariner wondered what Tony Knox was up to today. He couldn't imagine that it was anything much. Drinking himself into a stupor, probably. The man needed saving from himself.

Mariner rang the doorbell at Knox's house several times and then hammered on the door a couple of times. There was no response. He peered in the window. The place was still a tip. Christ, Knox was hopeless on his own. He went round to the back of the house. The garden was empty and, despite the growing heat, the house still shut up. He peered in through the patio doors and a chill ran through him.

Tony Knox was slumped lifelessly in an armchair. Mariner could see the bottle of spirits on the floor beside him and lying on the sofa within arm's reach, another small, brown bottle. For several moments Mariner's mind raced back over Knox's behaviour during the past few weeks: the mood swings and the pent-up anger, with that unprecedented reluctance to talk about anything, until his recent shame-faced revelation. Putting it all together with the scene before him, it came to one unspeakable conclusion. He banged on the window again. Nothing. Being a policeman the house was like Fort Knox. How appropriate was that? The back door was the flimsiest and, in the end, Mariner smashed the glass to get in. He rushed in on Knox who hadn't moved a muscle. This wasn't good.

'Tony!' Mariner shook him, slapping his cheek with more force than he'd intended. Knox jolted back to life with a start.

'What? What the fuck's going on?' He slurred.

Mariner sat back on his heels, weak with relief. 'Nothing, I thought— Nothing. It doesn't matter.' He'd explain the kitchen window later. His gaze skimmed the brown, stubby beer bottle on the sofa and after a split-second delay, Knox's face cracked into a smile.

'You thought I'd topped myself, didn't you?'

Mariner said nothing.

'I didn't know you cared, boss.'

280

'Piss off,' said Mariner.

'Listen, if I take that way out it won't be quietly in my own living room. It will be off the roof of the Hyatt with the TV cameras rolling. And you'll be among the first to know. Anyway, where the hell have you been? I've been trying to contact you.'

'I was at Anna's last night.'

Knox raised an eyebrow. 'You talked?'

'We talked.'

'About fucking time. Anyway, I think I've found something.'

'Me, too.'

'Really?' Knox looked disappointed, but he listened patiently while Mariner ran through what he'd got. 'Pritchard sounds like he could be our flasher, but did he kill Yasmin?' he said, when Mariner had finished.

'He had every reason to be in the area. The park is just across the road from the reservoir. And he's definitely a bit odd.'

'It doesn't make him a killer.'

He was right. 'OK, so what have you got?'

'Come and have a look.' Knox took him back up to the little office and on to the "old friends" website.

'Is this to do with Theresa?'

'Not exactly.' He logged back on to the website to show Mariner the original message. Mariner was doubtful. 'It's not much.'

'No. But then I started thinking: what would make a good teacher resign or get the sack?'

'Stealing? Embezzling the school fund?'

'Or having the wrong kind of relationship with the students.'

'Goodway doesn't fit the usual profile. He's got three kids of his own. Happily married man.'

'How happy, though? Barbara Kincaid was pretty scathing to Shaun Pryce about her love life, which might indicate that her husband has other preferences.'

281

Mariner thought back to his visit to Brian Goodway's home. 'He made some comment about how young and glamorous Barbara *had been* when he met her. I thought then it seemed an odd way of putting it.'

'Maybe "young" is the operative. And if he went off her as she got older, it might have left both of them looking elsewhere for gratification. He gets his from ogling the kids at school—'

'—and along comes Shaun Pryce, for her.'

'He could easily have been lying about his relationship with her. Which makes me wonder about what really happened to Barbara Kincaid?'

'We've no reason to believe she was murdered,' Mariner pointed out.

'It was a sudden, unexplained death.'

'The suicide verdict is unlikely to be challenged. She was taking powerful anti-depressant medication, and her GP at the time has confirmed that she was under a lot of strain.'

'Great cover for Goodway if he's found out that she's having an affair and decided to off her.'

'You've been watching too much crappy TV. Where would Yasmin come into all this?'

'She could have seen Pryce with Barbara Kincaid and grassed on them to Goodway.'

'But it must have all erupted months ago, so why leave it until now to do anything about Yasmin?'

Knox couldn't provide the answer, but luckily for him his phone trilled, temporarily letting him off the hook. He put it to his ear. 'Great. Thanks for getting back to me. Blake,' he hissed, over his hand, before embarking on a series of monosyllabic responses that left Mariner frustratingly in the dark about what they were discussing. Ending the call, Knox was smug and self-satisfied.

'We're on the right track all right,' he said. 'Goodway's departure from St Martin's was sudden and unexpected. No official explanation was given, but rumour had it that he'd invited a sixth former to model privately for him, very

282

privately. One thing led to another, until the kid blew the whistle on him. It didn't go down too well with the parents.'

'Christ.'

'Perhaps, with his wife safely out of the way, Goodway offered Yasmin the same opportunity.'

'And she threatened to tell someone. We need to ask Brian Goodway a few more questions.'

'Let's hope he's at home.'

'He isn't. He's at the Bournville Festival. He may be up for a prize. He's— Christ, the picture.'

'What picture?'

But Mariner shook his head. 'Goodway will be occupied all afternoon. Let's take advantage of that and pay a visit to his house. I just need to do something else first.'

'What about Andy Pritchard?' said Knox.

'I agree with you. Pritchard is small fry. He's up to something, but he can wait.'

Knox waited in the car at Granville Lane while Mariner went in and picked up a Polaroid camera. After that, their first stop was the reservoir, Knox following like an obedient hound at the heels of its master. They walked round to the patch of crushed-down grass that Shaun Pryce frequented and Mariner looked out across the water. It was as he'd thought. Moving in an arc of 180 degrees, he began taking snaps.

'SOCO have already got all this,' said Knox. 'Now might not be the right time to supplement your photo album.'

'Call it a comparative study,' was all that Mariner would say.

From there they went to Brian Goodway's house. The door was answered by a white-haired, elderly lady; Goodway's mother, and as Mariner had hoped, it seemed she was alone in the house.

'Do you think we could come in, Mrs Goodway?' Mariner asked, walking past her before she had time to protest.

283

'Is this about Barbara?'

'There are just a couple of things we wanted to look at again. We won't take up much of your time,' he assured her.

'Can I make you a cup of tea?'

'That would be lovely,' said Mariner. And keep her out of their hair for a few minutes. The house was three floors of outsized rooms. This might take a while. 'We're looking for the wire and the modelling clay and anything else that might help,' he reminded Knox.

Mrs Goodway was back sooner than he expected, brandishing the same mug he'd been given before: a well-worn version of those on Eric Dwyer's stall.

'Does your son belong to the conservation group?' Mariner asked, wondering if she'd even know.

'He used to, but I don't think he's been for a long time.'

Climbing the stairs, Mariner brushed past pictures hanging on the wall. One in particular stood out. It was almost identical to the one he'd seen this morning in the festival exhibition. At a different time of year, with no leaves on the trees and more rain in the lake, it was an exact copy of the view in Goodway's picture.

'Tony.'

Knox came and peered over his shoulder. 'What have you got?'

'This drawing is almost exactly the same as the pen-and-ink Brian Goodway has entered for the festival competition.'

'So? It's a view.'

Mariner took the Polaroid snaps out of his pocket and held one of them beside the sketch. 'See any similarities?'

'Christ.'

'Strip the trees of their leaves and they're exactly the same. When I came to talk to Goodway after his wife's body was found, he denied even knowing about the reservoir's existence.'

'Maybe he sketched it from a photograph.'

284

'So who took the photograph? His wife, Shaun Pryce or him? I think Brian Goodway is very familiar with the reservoir. He was probably spying on his wife. Not that it proves anything, naturally.'

Knox shrugged. 'So we keep looking.'

They went from room to room: opening drawers, scrutinising cupboards, searching under furniture, but found nothing.

'Maybe he does all his art work at school,' said Knox.

'There must be something. He told me this afternoon that he paints in his spare time. Where does he do it?' Goodway's mother was hovering in the doorway.

'Does your son have a studio or a workshop where he does his art work?'

'Yes, it's up in the roof. You have to open the hatch and pull down the ladder—'

Mariner and Knox were already vaulting the stairs. 'He doesn't really like anyone going up there!' she called after them uncertainly.

'I'll bet he doesn't.'

Though basic, the loft had indeed been converted into a fully equipped artist's studio. Two skylights provided the required natural light. The down side was the lack of evidence that any sculpting went on here: there were only easels and drawing and painting materials; everything strictly two-dimensional. They were not going to find what was used to strangle Yasmin here.

A pile of larger drawings were stacked on end in one corner. Absently, Mariner began to sort through them, unsure of what he was looking for. Until he found it. 'Look at this.'

Knox came and looked over his shoulder. 'Jesus Christ.'

'Actually, Shaun Pryce,' Mariner corrected him. 'This looks like some pretty close-range spying.' The pictures of Pryce were full-length pencil sketches, this time revealing his face, and beautifully drawn. He was also completely naked and in a considerable state of arousal. 'So that's why

285

women throw themselves at him,' remarked Knox.

'And not just women,' added Mariner, as the final piece fell into place. 'We've been barking up the wrong tree altogether.'

A strident female voice rang out from below. 'Who is it, Gran? What's going on?' Chloe Goodway was home for the weekend.

'It's the police,' they heard Mrs Goodway say.

'What are they doing here?'

'I'd better go and explain,' said Mariner, starting down the ladder.

But Chloe wasn't in the mood to wait for explanations. 'You shouldn't have let them in, Gran. They can't just come barging—'

'But they're policemen, darling. I expect they're going to help us find out what happened to Mummy.'

'They know what happened to Mum,' Mariner heard as he descended the last flight of stairs. 'I'm going to call Dad.'

'Miss Goodway, if you could just wait!' Mariner took the last stairs two at a time, but he wasn't fast enough.

'Dad? It's Chloe. The police are here. They're up in your studio. What's going on?'

Too late, Mariner snatched the phone from her. 'I really wish you hadn't done that.'

The girl was unrepentant. 'What are you doing here? We haven't seen a search warrant. You have no right—' But Knox was hard on Mariner's heels, and leaving the girl ranting behind them, they ran out to the car and jumped in. As Knox drove at breakneck speed, Mariner called for an area car to come and keep an eye on Goodway's house, then called ahead to Watson to detain Goodway in the exhibition tent at the festival. They arrived, breathless, to find Watson waiting helplessly.

'I missed him. He'd already gone. One of the stewards saw him leave about ten minutes ago.'

'Let's get out a description of him and his car.'

The car was easy. As it turned out, it was still sitting less than five hundred yards from where they stood, left where Brian Goodway had parked it that morning, in front of the row of shops. One of the shop assistants had a girl at the school and had seen Goodway come back to his car and retrieve something from the boot.

'He knows we'd be able to trace the car,' said Mariner. 'But if he's gone on public transport we don't stand a chance.' He looked across at the steady stream of traffic on the ring road. The festival grounds were at the centre of a network served by the railway station at the back of the factory works and a major bus route to the front and sides.

Knox was more optimistic. 'He won't get far. It may take a while, but somebody, somewhere will recognise him.' All they could do was wait, but waiting wasn't Mariner's forte.

'We never found that wire,' said Knox, suddenly. 'Is it worth checking his classroom?'

The school seemed a desolate place without the noisy bustle of hundreds of students. Today, even the caretaker's family had abandoned their house on the site to go to the festival. Parking outside the locked reception area, they walked round to the side of the building and found the door to Brian Goodway's classroom swinging open.

'He must have his own key,' said Knox, but any hope they might have felt was short-lived. The classroom and those around it were completely devoid of life. If he had been here, Goodway had long since gone. The classroom was as much a mess as it had been last time Mariner was here, the forms of half-finished sculptures dotted about.

'He's left us plenty of modelling clay and wire,' said Knox, bagging up samples. 'So why was he here?'

'There's Lily's tan-coloured suit,' said Mariner, seeing the pristine brown overalls hanging on the back of the door. 'Or, at least, the next generation of clean replacements.' It was then that the smell drifted in on the air: the faint, slightly acrid smell of burning. 'Christ. That's what he's here for.'

Following the smell, they ran round to the rear of the building where they found Goodway standing beside the giant pig bins, black smoke billowing from the nearest.

'What are you doing, Brian?'

Goodway reeled round, shocked to see them. 'It's all right, you don't need to tell me,' Mariner continued calmly. 'I know what you're burning, and I know why. Burning won't get rid of all the evidence. Even if the fabric is charred we can still get DNA. We'll still find Ricky Skeet's blood on those overalls, won't we?'

'And you've given us plenty of circumstantial evidence,' added Knox, 'the pictures of Shaun Pryce and the reservoir; the wire you used to strangle Yasmin.' Goodway's eyes widened.

'There might be a way out of this mess, Brian,' Mariner soothed. 'Why don't you tell us all about it?'

Goodway turned away, wringing his hands. 'I've nothing to say to you.'

'Why don't we start with St Martin's,' Mariner said, ignoring him.

Goodway couldn't help himself. 'Nothing happened at St Martin's,' he said.

'So why did you leave in such a hurry? There were rumours. No smoke without fire, eh, Brian. What was the boy's name?'

'Boy?' Knox was totally lost now.

'We were only partly on the right track,' Mariner told him. 'When Stewey Blake said Brian here had approached a sixth former, we both assumed it was a girl, because Brian here is a red-blooded, heterosexual family man. But that's not true, is it, Brian? It wasn't your wife who was having an affair with Shaun Pryce, it was you.'

Brian Goodway sank to the ground, burying his head in his hands. For several minutes he said nothing, then just as Mariner began to approach him, he spoke, his voice hoarse and trembling. 'I realised I was gay years ago,' he said. 'My whole marriage was a sham. I concealed it for years, satisfying myself with the occasional one-night stand. But it got more and more difficult, always feeling that I was living a lie and never being able to just be myself. I knew that eventually I'd have to give in to temptation.'

'Is that why you went to work at the girls school, so that there couldn't be a repeat of St Martin's?'

'Nothing happened at St Martin's.'

'Only because the kid ratted on you.'

'I'd done nothing improper,' Goodway insisted. 'It was a conversation, a careless gesture, that's all. But I thought working at Kingsmead would be easier. It was. For a while everything was fine, under control. Then when I met Shaun that evening at our house, it was love at first sight. I couldn't get him out of my mind. Inviting him to model at school was just a way of seeing him again. I never dreamed that anything would come of it, especially when I saw him flirting so outra-geously with the girls.'

'Afterwards, I took him out for a drink as a kind of thank you and that's when I discovered that he wasn't averse to male company, either. I couldn't believe my good fortune.'

'Pryce is gay?' Knox was incredulous.

'He's still in the closet,' said Mariner. 'Coming out would ruin his chances of being a leading man. You had an affair?' he asked Goodway.

'This time, I thought it was a proper relationship and I knew I'd have to tell Barbara. She'd been suffering from depression for a long time, partly because of the state of our marriage. I thought we'd be able to work out something civilised between us. But when I told her, she was devas-tated, starting talking about suicide. Then, suddenly, she announced that she was going to tell the children. I couldn't let her do that. Not yet. I wasn't ready. So one night when she went out I followed her. She went down to the reservoir. It was somewhere we used to go together, years ago. I would sketch and she would enjoy the peace and quiet.'

'Not that night, though.'

'I caught up with her on the wooden bridge. I tried to reason with her, but she wouldn't listen. She said that I'd humiliated her and ruined her life and that now she would ruin me. In some strange way I even think she was jealous.'

'She'd made a pass at Pryce. Did you know that?'

Goodway snorted. 'No.'

'So you tipped her into the river.'

'It was an accident. I had her by the shoulders, I was begging her not to tell the children. She just laughed at me. I pushed her—' he frowned '—harder than I thought, the railings gave way and she fell. I went down to help her but knew straight away that she was dead. I was going to drag her out on to the bank and go for help, but then I thought about how it would look. Then I realised that the easiest thing was the drainage tunnel. We'd had a lot of rain and it just carried her down. It was as if it was meant to be.'

'And Yasmin?'

'She was a lovely girl, truly talented. She flirted a little with Shaun but I knew it was harmless.'

'So what, then?'

'She saw us together. Shaun and me. While the weather has been so warm Shaun persuaded me to meet him at the reservoir. I'd introduced him to it when he'd said he needed somewhere private to sunbathe. He talked me into going with him after school. It was exciting.'

'So you were there on that Monday when Yasmin walked past.'

'She'd been to see that boy, Everett, and was taking a shortcut through the reservoir back to the station. The next morning she came to tell me. She said, "You're a queer, aren't you? I saw you with Shaun. It's disgusting." Actually, I think she was quite shocked and upset herself, but she'd come to find out what I'd do to stop her telling anyone. But then I guessed that she was meeting Everett and we came to a tit for tat arrangement: I'd say nothing about Lewis if she would forget Shaun.'

290

'Cosy,' said Knox.

'I knew it wouldn't last, though. Everett was bound to let her down and then I'd never be able to trust the little bitch to keep her mouth shut. If she let it out I'd be ruined.'

This was what Mariner didn't understand. 'What you and Pryce were doing is hardly illegal. You're both consenting adults.'

'There was my reputation though, the reputation of the school. I'd been lucky at St Martin's. It was the word of a young, impressionable boy against that of, as you put it, a heterosexual family man; the interpretation of a conversation. The head believed me and I was able to resign with dignity and take up another post, my record unblemished. If my sexuality became public knowledge now, all that was bound to be dragged up again. Besides, I have my children and my mother to think of. What would it do to them? I couldn't bear it.'

'So what did you do?'

'I started checking Yasmin's phone during lessons. I don't know what I hoped to find, I suppose knowing she was seeing Everett against her parents' wishes I thought there might be something more incriminating that I could use to buy her silence. When I saw the message from Everett cancelling their meeting at the reservoir, I knew that was my chance.'

'Chance to do what?'

'Talk to her. During the lesson I took her travel pass, and before I left I dropped it on the classroom floor, knowing that she'd have to come back for it and giving me time to get there ahead of her.'

'And what happened?'

'When she got there I was waiting on the bridge. I just wanted to talk to her, but she told me there was nothing to say. Before I knew it she was lying at my feet, dead.'

'Do you always carry sculpting wire around with you?'

'I had it . . . just in case.'

'In case of what?'

291

'I don't know.'

'And the brown overalls?'

He had no answer.

'And what about Ricky Skeet?'

'I dragged Yasmin down to the drainage tunnel. The water hadn't released but I knew it would within a matter of an hour or so—'

'And take Yasmin down with your wife.'

'But when I climbed back on to the bridge, this boy just rushed at me from nowhere, shouting and screaming that he'd seen what I'd done. He started hitting me with this chunk of brick, but it slipped out of his hand, so I grabbed it and hit him over the head. He fell, but I had to be sure so I hit him again and then I found that I couldn't stop. I kept hitting him over and over.'

'Why didn't you dispose of Ricky's body in the same way as the others?'

'I was going to, but there was so much blood. The stream flows down into the park: I thought someone might see it. And also there would be two bodies in the tunnel already, a third may have caused some kind of blockage that would have drawn attention. I needed to think.'

'So you just dragged him into the long grass and left him?'

'Something made me look up. I thought I saw someone in the window of the nursing home. I needed to get away. I was going to come back later, after dark to move it, but when I came back he had gone. I looked around a bit but there was no sign of him, so then I thought perhaps I hadn't killed him after all.'

'Weren't you worried that he might turn up somewhere and report what he'd seen?'

'Of course I was. I even phoned round the hospitals to ask if an injured boy had been brought in. There hadn't, so there was nothing else I could do.'

Mariner remembered how strung out Goodway had seemed on that first meeting. He must have been beside

292

himself. 'And you didn't know that Yasmin had dropped her phone.'

'No.'

'It must have been a shock when that turned up. If it hadn't been for that, our search would never have switched to the reservoir.'

While they'd been talking, the light had faded fast. In the gloom Mariner moved towards Goodway. 'Come on,' he said. 'Let's get all this down on paper.' But as he moved forward he saw the glint of something in Goodway's hand, the razor thin blade of a craft knife. 'Don't do anything—' he began, but before either of them could stop him Goodway drew back the knife and slashed violently at his wrist. Blood sprayed out in a wide, crimson arc as over their heads the first dazzling scatter burst of fireworks lit up the sky.

'Call an ambulance.' Mariner sprang forward and seized the knife, just as Goodway collapsed to the ground, groaning in pain.

Epilogue

DCI Jack Coleman stood surveying the building work going on two hundred feet below him when there was a knock on the door. 'Come.' It was DI Mariner. 'Tom.' Coleman moved forward and the men shook hands.

'Good to see you again, sir,' said Mariner.

'Seems you've done rather well without me these last few weeks: a high profile killer and a potential sex attacker arrested within twenty-four hours of each other.' —

'We nearly lost Goodway.'

'But you didn't.'

'No. A dozen stitches and some pretty comprehensive dressings did the job, although I understand they've got him on twenty-four hour suicide watch at Winson Green while he's on remand.'

'And Andy Pritchard?'

'We found dozens of photographs at his place that he must have taken over years, students and young girls around parks in south Birmingham, and we can place him on or near the university campus at the time of each indecent exposure, along with a couple more in other parts of the city.'

'DCI Fiske seems to have left me with a lot to live up to.'

'With all due respect, sir, I'm not sure that Mr Fiske had much to do with either.'

'You got him off the hook with Complaints though, didn't you?'

'I'm sure he's enjoying his refresher course on Risk Assessment. It'll give him lots of opportunity to practise his vocabulary.'

'And Colleen Skeet's happy with that?'

'She's satisfied that we caught Ricky's killer, but I doubt Colleen will ever be happy again.'

'No. I'm sorry about your mother, too, Tom.'

'Yes, sir. Welcome back.'